English G 21

D5

Erweiterte Ausgabe
für differenzierende
Schulformen

Cornelsen

English G 21 • Band D 5 • Erweiterte Ausgabe

Im Auftrag des Verlages herausgegeben von
Prof. Hellmut Schwarz, Mannheim
Wolfgang Biederstädt, Köln

Erarbeitet von
Susan Abbey, Nenagh, Irland
Claire Lamsdale, Llangybi, Wales
Barbara Derkow Disselbeck, Köln
Laurence Harger, Wellington, Neuseeland
Allen J. Woppert, Berlin

unter Mitarbeit von
Wolfgang Biederstädt, Köln
Joachim Blombach, Herford
David Christie, Banbury, England
Helmut Dengler, Limbach
Martina Schroeder, Stedtlingen
Jennifer Seidl, München
Udo Wagner, Voerde
Herbert Willms, Herford
sowie Uwe Chormann, Einselthum

in Zusammenarbeit mit der Englischredaktion
Dr. Christiane Kallenbach (Projektleitung);
Dr. Eva Grabowski (verantwortliche Redakteurin);
Susanne Bennetreu (Bildredaktion); Stefanie Bayer;
Britta Bensmann; Dr. Philip Devlin; Cornelia Frisse;
Bonnie S. Glänzer; Renata Jakovac; Anne Linder;
Michaela Schmidt; Nathalie Schwering;
Kathrin Spiegelberg; Uwe Tröger; Klaus G. Unger;
Bastian Wiesemann *sowie* Olivia Gruver

Beratende Mitwirkung
Walter Droste, Spenge; Manuela Feierabend-Vonhausen, Rossfeld; Birgit Heinemann, Neu Wulmstorf; Bernd Jost, Salzbergen; Heike Jurenz, Neukirch/Lausitz; Heike Meisner, Bad Klosterlausnitz; Gabriele Rotter, Wiesbaden; Karl Starkebaum, Diekholzen

Illustrationen
Silke Bachmann, Hamburg; Roland Beier, Berlin; Carlos Borrell, Berlin; Dylan Gibson, Pitlochry; Christian Görke, Berlin; Graham-Cameron Illustration, UK: Eoin Coveney; Alfred Schüssler, Frankfurt/Main

Für die freundliche Unterstützung bei der Foto-Story Unit 4 „Berlin: City survival kit" danken wir GLS Sprachenzentrum Berlin; „Kauf Dich Glücklich", Berlin; „Berliner Imbiss", Leipziger Straße, Berlin.

Layoutkonzept
Aksinia Raphael; Korinna Wilkes

Technische Umsetzung
Aksinia Raphael; Korinna Wilkes;
Stephan Hilleckenbach; Rainer Bachmaier

Umschlaggestaltung
Klein & Halm Grafikdesign, Berlin

www.cornelsen.de
www.EnglishG.de

1. Auflage, 6. Druck 2016

Alle Drucke dieser Auflage sind inhaltlich unverändert und können im Unterricht nebeneinander verwendet werden.

Druck: Firmengruppe APPL, aprinta Druck, Wemding

ISBN 978-3-06-031323-5 – broschiert
ISBN 978-3-06-031370-9 – gebunden

PEFC zertifiziert
Dieses Produkt stammt aus nachhaltig bewirtschafteten Wäldern und kontrollierten Quellen.
www.pefc.de

Dein Englischbuch enthält folgende Teile:

Units 1 2 3 4	die vier Kapitel des Buches
Getting ready for a test	Hier kannst du dich gezielt auf einen Test vorbereiten.
EXTRA: Text File	viele interessante Texte zum Lesen (passend zu den Units)
Skills File (SF)	Beschreibung wichtiger Lern- und Arbeitstechniken
Grammar File (GF)	Zusammenfassung der Grammatik der Units; Übersichten über die Zeitformen (*present, past, future*)
Vocabulary	Wörterverzeichnis zum Lernen der neuen Wörter jeder Unit
Dictionary	alphabetisches englisch-deutsches Wörterverzeichnis

Die Units bestehen aus diesen Teilen:

Lead-in	Einstieg in das neue Thema
Part A, B, C, D	neuer Lernstoff mit vielen Aktivitäten
Practice	Übungen
How am I doing?	Hier kannst du dein Wissen und Können überprüfen.

In den Units findest du diese Überschriften und Symbole:

Exploring language	Hier lernst du anhand von Beispielen, neue sprachliche Strukturen zu verstehen und richtig anzuwenden.
STUDY SKILLS	Einführung in Lern- und Arbeitstechniken
Dossier	Schöne und wichtige Arbeiten kannst du in einer Mappe sammeln.
SPEAKING COURSE	Sprechkurs in vier Kapiteln
EVERYDAY ENGLISH	Übungen zum Bewältigen wichtiger Alltagssituationen
ENGLISH FOR JOBS	Übungen zur Vorbereitung auf typische berufliche Situationen
MEDIATION	Hier vermittelst du zwischen zwei Sprachen.
VIEWING	Aufgaben zu Filmausschnitten
Now you	Hier sprichst und schreibst du über dich selbst.
REVISION	Übungen zur Wiederholung
WORDS	Übungen zu Wortfeldern und Wortverbindungen
Extra	zusätzliche Aktivitäten und Übungen
[Partner-Symbol] [Gruppen-Symbol]	Partnerarbeit / Gruppenarbeit
[CD-Symbol] [CD-Symbol]	nur auf CD / auf CD und im Schülerbuch
[DVD-Symbol]	Filmausschnitte auf DVD
[Textaufgaben-Symbol]	Textaufgaben
○ ●	leichtere Übungen / schwierigere Übungen
// ○ // ●	parallele Übungen auf zwei Niveaus
more help	Hier findest du zusätzliche Hilfen für das Lösen einer Aufgabe.

Inhalt

Australia	The world of work	Teen world	Exploring cities

6 Unit 1 Australia

Lead-in Blog from Oz
Part A Australia – yesterday and today
Part B Two Australian teenagers
Part C The Aboriginal people of Australia
Part D TEXT: In the outback

Grammatische Strukturen
- Indirect speech I (statements)
- REVISION Simple present
- REVISION Simple past

Wortfelder
- weather
- animals
- sports
- teenage life
- travelling
- small talk
- film review

STUDY SKILLS
Talking about charts
Reading stories
SPEAKING COURSE (1)
Having a conversation
EVERYDAY ENGLISH
WRITING Our lives (Writing an e-mail)
MEDIATION At the police station
READING Signs
VIEWING
Rabbit-proof fence (scene from a film)

26 Revision – Getting ready for a test 1

32 Unit 2 The world of work

Lead-in Top jobs
Part A Personality quiz
Part B Applying for a job
Part C A reality TV show
Part D TEXT: How to be a teenage millionaire

Grammatische Strukturen
- Indirect speech II (commands, requests, questions)
- REVISION Indirect speech

Wortfelder
- jobs, job profiles
- personal qualities
- qualifications, education
- hobbies, interests
- work experience

STUDY SKILLS
Writing a CV
Writing formal letters
SPEAKING COURSE (2)
Taking part in a job interview
EVERYDAY ENGLISH
MEDIATION Summer jobs in Britain
WRITING Filling in a job application form
ENGLISH FOR JOBS
Calling about an interview
VIEWING
The interviews (scenes from a reality TV show)

48 Unit 3 Teen world

Lead-in Pick of the day
Part A Mobile teens
Part B Teens in trouble
Part C Get involved
Part D TEXT: The caller

Grammatische Strukturen
- Understanding participle clauses
- Passive (present perfect, will-future, modals)
- REVISION Passive (simple present, simple past)

Wortfelder
- you and your mobile
- adjectives
- problem teenagers, anti-social behaviour
- volunteer work
- feelings

STUDY SKILLS
A written discussion
SPEAKING COURSE (3)
Having a discussion
EVERYDAY ENGLISH
SPEAKING Say what you think – giving your opinion
WRITING A letter to the editor
ENGLISH FOR JOBS
Useful phrases
VIEWING
High school boot camp (scenes from a documentary)

66 Revision – Getting ready for a test 2

74 Unit 4 Exploring cities

Lead-in Comparing cities
Part A Mumbai
Part B Johannesburg
Part C Berlin: City survival kit

Grammatische Strukturen
- Additional information: conditional sentences type 3

Wortfelder
- city and city life
- describing pictures
- health problems, at the doctor's
- word building: adjectives
- visiting a foreign city

STUDY SKILLS
Using visual materials with a presentation
SPEAKING COURSE (4)
Giving a presentation
EVERYDAY ENGLISH
SPEAKING I'm not feeling great
MEDIATION Sore throat lozenges
ENGLISH FOR JOBS
At reception
VIEWING
Transport in Mumbai (promotional video)

90 Partner B
94 Differentiation

108 Extra Text File Zusätzliche optionale Lesetexte zur Vertiefung und Binnendifferenzierung
109 **TF 1** Australian signs (zu Unit 1)
110 **TF 2 Bilingual module** Ecosystems in Australia (zu Unit 1)
112 **TF 3** Project: What's so special about Australia? (zu Unit 1)
114 **TF 4** Diary of a teenage job hunter (zu Unit 2)
117 **TF 5** Song: Nine to five (zu Unit 2)
118 **TF 6 Bilingual module** A different sort of justice (zu Unit 3)
121 **TF 7** Famous (zu Unit 3)
128 **TF 8** India (zu Unit 4)
130 **TF 9** South Africa (zu Unit 4)
133 **TF 10** Project: An English-speaking city (zu Unit 4)

134 Skills File
158 Grammar File
168 Grammatical terms
169 Lösungen zu den Grammar-File-Aufgaben
170 Vocabulary
192 Dictionary (English – German)
227 English sounds / The English alphabet
228 List of names
229 Countries and continents
230 Lösungen für *How am I doing?*
234 Quellenverzeichnis
236 Irregular verbs
238 Classroom English

Blog from Oz

About me

Name: Judith
Age: 15
From: Born and grew up in Cologne, Germany
Location: (since July) Melbourne, Victoria
Nationality: half German, half Aussie! (Mum's German, Dad's an Aussie)
Languages: English and German

- More about me
- Read comments
- Post comments

Click on my
- photo gallery

for more photos of kangaroos, koalas, the outback, Christmas holidays etc.

Click on my
- sound file

to hear more about the photos.

19th July
Just arrived – too excited to sleep! As we flew across Australia I looked out of the window and saw red earth – just red earth for miles. Australia is huge! I felt very, very small and a bit scared. When I got off the plane in Melbourne it was really cold! I left Cologne on a hot July day, but Down Under things are different of course.

22nd July
Melbourne is very beautiful and very big. Three million people live here. My first view of the city was awesome – the Yarra River, the skyscrapers, the sea. There are parks everywhere and everybody seems to have a house with a garden.

1

24th July
School has started! There are four terms a year in Australia and the third has just started. Here the school day begins at 8.30 – quite nice, but then you have to stay until 3.15 pm! After 3.15 students have lots of extracurricular activities like sport, music or debates. And when that's all over, there's homework.

30th September
It's spring holiday time and I've just come back from a really exciting trip with my class – a 5-day hike in the bush. It was amazing, but a bit scary too. One evening I was getting into bed when one of the girls shouted 'Stop!' There was a snake inside my sleeping bag! The girl saved my life!

14th October
I'm learning to surf – it's fantastic. Here, all the kids know how to surf.

19th November
It's getting hot! Just back from a 'barbie' (barbecue!) at a friend's house. I've got lots of friends here now. We often have parties at someone's place. When you're under 18 in Australia you can't go to clubs, pubs or bars without an adult. (And of course you're not allowed to drink or smoke either.)

Judith´s photo gallery

2

3

4

5

6

1 What's special about Australia?

a) *What does Judith tell us about life in Australia in her blog? Take notes. Compare notes with a partner.*

b) *Listen to Judith's sound file. Write down one interesting thing about each photo.*

► SF Listening (p. 141)

2 Now you

a) *Would you like to go to Australia? Discuss what you would like/wouldn't like about life there.*

b) **Extra** *Write a comment to Judith.*

► Text File 1 (p. 109) • SF Taking notes (p. 142) • WB 1–2 (p. 2)

AUSTRALIA – YESTERDAY AND TODAY

1 READING Group puzzle (part 1)

Divide the class into four groups (A, B, C, D). Group A studies ***A****, Group B studies* ***B****, etc. Look at the tasks and take notes so that you can pass on the information. In your group compare your notes.*

A Down Under: Quick facts

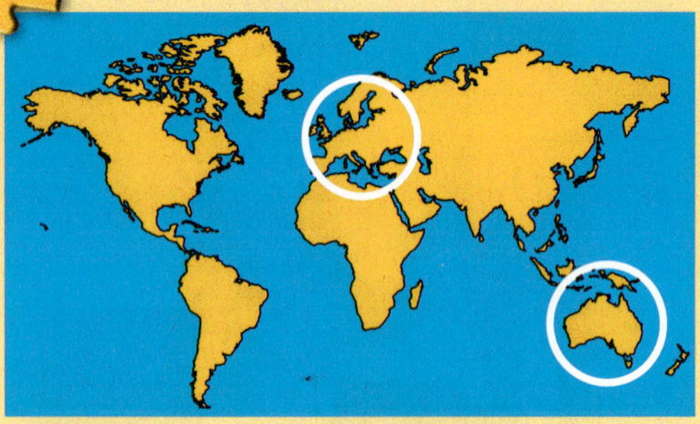

> *1 Why is Australia called Down Under?*
2 Look at the map on the front inside cover and collect interesting facts about Australia:
- parts of Australia (states and territories)
- the five largest cities
- the names of important rivers, deserts, ...
- other interesting facts

Quick facts

Area: 7,686,850 sq km
Population: 21.2 million
Capital: Canberra (348,000)

The Australian flag

The big star at the bottom represents the Australian states and territories. The five stars on the right are in the shape of the Southern Cross. That's a group of stars you can see in Australia, but not in Europe. The British flag on the left shows Australia's historical links with Britain.

> *3 What is special about the stars on the Australian flag?*

B A short history of Australia

When the first European ships came to Australia in the 16th century, between 300,000 and one million Aborigines already lived there. Many Aborigines were killed by the Europeans or died of diseases the Europeans brought with them. At the beginning of the 20th century, there were only about 150,000 Aborigines in Australia. Today there are about 455,000.

In 1770 Captain James Cook claimed the island for Britain. In 1788 the British started a colony for prisoners in Port Jackson (now Sydney).

Between 1788 and 1868 Britain sent more than 160,000 prisoners to Australia.
Soon other immigrants came and started colonies in different parts of the island. In 1901 the Commonwealth of Australia was founded and became independent.

In the 20th century Australia kept its links to Britain. The King or Queen of the UK is still the King or Queen of Australia. But since the 1970s Australia has done more and more business with Asia, and large numbers of Asian immigrants now come to Australia.

> *Find at least four important facts about Australian history. Make a timeline.*

C Australia and the sun

Australians love to spend their time outdoors, but the sun Down Under is dangerous because of the hole in the ozone layer just south of Australia. This means more dangerous ultraviolet (UV) rays get through and burn people. The result is that more people get skin cancer in Australia than in any other country in the world. You should avoid the sun when the UV levels are highest – usually between 10 am and 2 pm.

You can find the UV level in the newspaper every day. When the levels are medium or higher, it's time to 'Slip! Slop! Slap!'

1 Why is it so important to 'get sunsmart'?
2 What are the most important things to remember if you want to spend time outdoors?

D Australia's natural sights

Tourists come to Australia to see its natural sights: deserts, mountains, rainforests, and the Great Barrier Reef. The reef is more than 2,000 km long and about 1,500 kinds of fish live there. Dolphins, whales, sea snakes and salt-water crocodiles can also be seen there. But the reef is in danger. Corals die if the water temperature changes by more than a degree or two. And the oceans around Australia are getting warmer, as they are in the rest of the world.

Australia has some strange animals, which are only found there. Examples are the kangaroo, the koala, the emu and the duck-billed platypus. When people bring animals from other parts of the world to Australia, this can cause problems. A recent example is the cane toad. These toads kill many Australian animals but no animals kill them.

Great Barrier Reef

Duck-billed platypus

Cane toad

Emu

Find the important facts about Australia's natural sights your classmates should know.

2 Group puzzle (part 2)

a) *Each person in your group gets a number (1, 2, 3, 4). Now make new groups (A1, B1, C1, D1; A2, B2, ...). Tell your new group what you found out about Australia. Take notes on the other information.*

▸ *SF Taking notes (p. 142)*

b) *Go back to your first group (A, B, C, D) and compare your information. Did you all understand the same things? If not, read the texts to check your information.*

▸ **Text File 2** *(pp. 110–111)* • *WB 3 (p. 3)*

3 Facts and figures

STUDY SKILLS Talking about charts

The **title** of a chart tells you what it is about. Make sure that you understand what the **figures** on the chart mean.

Bar charts are often used to compare the number or size of two or more things.
Use these phrases to talk about a bar chart:
- The bar chart is about ...
- It compares the size/number/... of a country/...
- ... has the largest/second largest/...
- ... is twice/three times/... as big as ...

Pie charts help you to compare percentages in a whole 'pie'.
Use these phrases to talk about a pie chart.
- The pie chart shows the different ... in ...
- It is divided into ... parts (which show ...)
- A huge majority/small minority/... per cent is ...
- There are more than/nearly twice as many ...

Finish with a conclusion.
- So we can say that .../it must be ...

▸ SF Talking about charts (p. 140)

a) *Explain one of the bar charts below to a partner.*
The first chart compares the ... in four ...

1 Population in millions

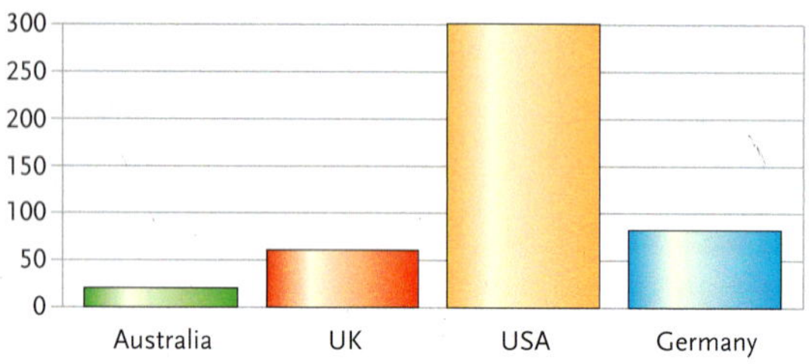

2 Land area in million sq km

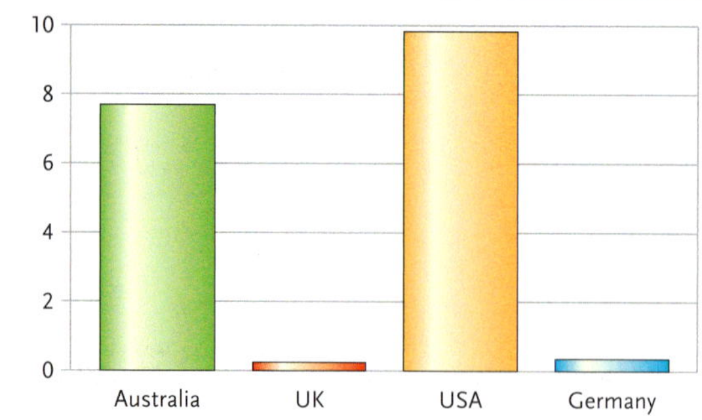

more help ▸ D p. 94

b) *What do the two charts together tell you?*
... is very big, but the ... is very small. So it must be quite ... (crowded/empty) there.

c) *Write about the pie chart below:*
– Say what the chart shows.
– Give details.
– Finish with a conclusion.

The pie chart shows the different ...
It is divided into ...
The largest group is the ... They're about ... of the whole population.
The next largest ...
So we can say ...

3 Ethnic groups in Australia

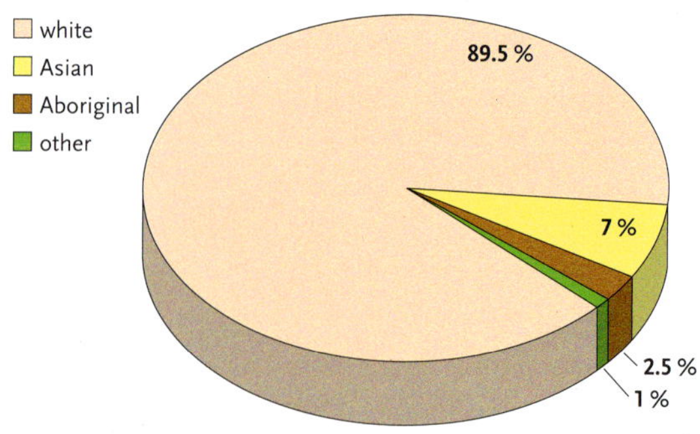

d) **Extra** *Why do you think Asians are the biggest minority in Australia?*

P1 REVISION Facts about Australian animals (Tenses: simple present)

a) *Partner B: Look at p. 90.*
Partner A: Write a text about kangaroos. Use the correct forms of the ***simple present****.*

There ... (be) 43 different kinds of kangaroos. They usually ... (live) in groups. They ... (eat) grass and leaves, but they ... (need) much water. Kangaroos ... (be) more active at night than during the day. And if it's a very hot day, they just ... (sit) under trees and bushes and ... (move). The biggest kangaroo ... (be) the Red Kangaroo. It ... (jump) two metres and ... (move) at about 20–25 km/h.

b) **Extra** *Add to your text. Use the key words below.*

- kangaroo mothers have pouch – kind of bag
- when kangaroo baby born – live in mother's pouch – ten months
- babies fed by mother – until 18 months old – then feed themselves
- kangaroos not get old – live 4–6 years

c) *Read your text to your partner. Then listen to his/her text. Pick out one interesting thing about the animal.*

▸ *GF 1: Talking about the present (p. 159)*

P2 REVISION A trip to Australia (Tenses: simple past)

Lea, from Germany, met Ben on the last day of her trip to Australia. Complete the dialogue.

Ben So when *did you arrive* (you, arrive) in Australia?
Lea I *arrived* (arrive) in Melbourne six weeks ago.
Ben How long ... (you, stay) in Melbourne?
Lea I ... (stay) long. Only about three days.
Ben And where ... (you, go) after that?
Lea I ... (go) to Brisbane.
Ben Wow, that's one of my favourite places. How ... (you, travel)?
Lea I ... (fly). I ... (get) a very cheap flight.
Ben ... (you, learn) to surf there?
Lea I ... (go) to the beach, but I ... (go) surfing.
Ben ... (you, see) any Australian animals?
Lea Well, I ... (see) any koalas, but on our trip to the outback I ... (see) lots of kangaroos. They ... (be) amazing.
Ben What ... (be) your favourite place?
Lea Uluru, of course. It ... (be) awesome.
Ben ... (you, climb) the rock?
Lea No, I ... (climb) it, but some other tourists did.

▸ *GF 2: Talking about the past (pp. 160–161)*

P3 Extra STUDY SKILLS Talking about charts

Write a short text about the chart on the right.
Explain:
– what the chart is about
– what it compares.

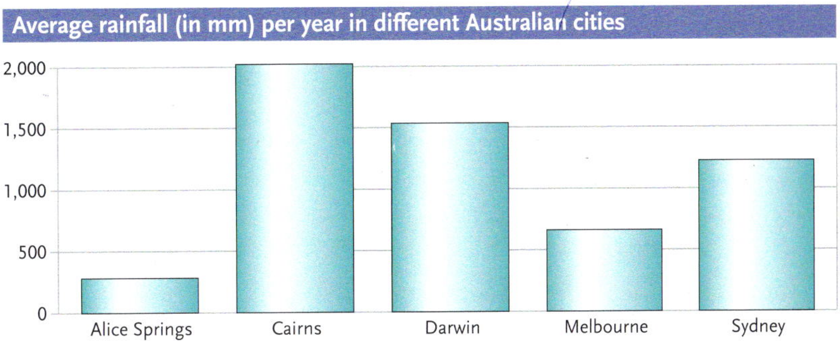

▸ *WB 4–6 (pp. 3–4)*

TWO AUSTRALIAN TEENAGERS

1 Jeannie – in the middle of nowhere

Hi Cath

It was great to get your e-mail. Yes, I'd love to be your online friend, but I don't think my life in Queensland is as interesting as your life in Hong Kong.

My dad works here on a sheep station, so we live in the middle of nowhere. There are only twenty other people on the station but thousands and thousands of sheep. The nearest town is about 500 km away, so we don't have a local cinema, a doctor or even a school. But of course I have school. My school is the Alice Springs School of the Air. It's cool. It comes to me through my computer. That means I don't have to sit in a classroom all day. (I can even take my laptop outside and do my work under a tree!) But I can talk to the teacher and class every day. Alice Springs is 1,000 km away, but my teachers are in a studio so I can see them and talk to them. A lot of our class have webcams, so we can see each other too. We only meet about three times a year at one week courses, but we're good friends.

You talk about all your sports and hobbies – dragon boat racing and tennis and clubs. Well, mine are a bit different. There are no kids here my age, so I do things on my own a lot. I ride every day. I have my own horse, Sally. And because we live in the middle of nowhere, I'm allowed to ride a motorbike – that's really good fun.

I'm attaching some photos. Please mail again soon.

Your new online friend
Jeannie

Describe what you see in the photos. Write a caption for each. You can find words and phrases in the e-mail.

► *SF Describing pictures (p. 135)*

2 Now you

Think: *What might be the advantages and disadvantages of the School of the Air if you compare it to your school? Make notes.*
Pair: *Compare with a partner.*
Share: *Discuss with another pair.*

– It would be much nicer/more fun/...
– I would miss/hate/...
– I think I could learn better because ...

3 Extra Royal Flying Doctor Service

Lonely sheep stations in the outback don't have local doctors, but people can call the Royal Flying Doctor Service (RFDS). Find out more about it (internet, books, ...). How does it work?
Write about 80–100 words. Add photos or maps if you like.
You can put your text in your DOSSIER.

► *SF Research (p. 138)*

4 Rob – sports-mad in Sydney

a) *These are popular sports in Australia. Which one do you think looks interesting? Why?*

start profile friends mail

Rob Mackintosh Hi, and welcome to Australia!

pinboard info photos +

1 2 3 4 5

Skydiving

Surfing

Cricket

Aussie Rules football

b) *Now listen to Rob. Make a list of the sports he talks about. Which ones are not shown on this page?*

c) *Listen again. What are Rob's three favourite sports? Take notes so you can give reasons for your opinion.* ▸ *SF Listening (p. 141)*

d) *Talk about the role of sport in your life.*

- Are you as mad about sport as Rob? Or do you like other activities? (Which ones?)
- Do you do sport for fun/to keep fit/ ... ?
- Are you a couch potato?
- Would you like to try Rob's sports?

5 Extra Guess the sport

Make two teams. Think of a sport. Describe it for the other team (location, equipment, clothes), but don't say what it is. One point for a correct guess.

Team A: You play on a court, you need a racket and you wear white shorts and a shirt.

Team B: Tennis! ▸ *SF Paraphasing (p. 148)*

6 Now you

Think of differences between Jeannie's life and Rob's life. If you could visit one of them for a week, who would you choose? Why?

EVERYDAY ENGLISH

P1 WRITING Our lives (Writing an e-mail)

Look at pages 12 and 13 again. Write an e-mail to Jeannie or Rob.

- *Tell them what you find interesting or surprising about their lives.* → I think it's great/surprising/... that you can ... I was really jealous when I read that you ...
- *What else would you like to know about their lives? Ask some questions.* → I have some questions for you. Where/When/How often do you ...?
- *Tell them something about your life, e.g. your school day, your favourite subject, the sports/ activities you enjoy, ...* → My life in Germany is (not very) different to yours. For example, ...

more help ▸ D p. 94

▸ SF Writing informal letters or e-mails (p. 153)

P2 MEDIATION At the police station

You meet a German tourist at Bondi Beach in Sydney. Someone has stolen his surfboard. He wants to report the theft at the police station. You go with him because his English isn't good.

a) *Read the dialogue. Think about what you could say.*

Tourist Also wir ... also mein ... Sag du ihr, dass mein Surfbrett gestohlen wurde.
You ...
Officer I see. Well, when and where did it happen?
You ...
Tourist Vor 20 Minuten. Drüben am Strand, in der Nähe der *Lifeguard Station*.
You ...
Officer Are there any witnesses?
Tourist Was meint sie?
You Vermutlich will sie wissen, ob es Zeugen gibt. – Excuse me, what does *witness* mean?
Officer Someone who saw something. Did anybody see the thief? Did anyone see anything?

▸ SF Mediation (p. 155)

b) *Listen to the whole dialogue. Help the tourist.*

P3 READING Signs

Look at the signs and answer the questions.

1 Where might you find this sign? What advice does it give?

1

2 Where can you swim safely? What are you not allowed to do at the beach?

2

▸ WB 7–10 (pp. 5–6)

P4 SPEAKING Nice to meet you (Having a conversation)

► SF p. 146

a) Listen to the dialogue between Rob and Anna.
- Where are they?
- What do they talk about at the beginning?
- Is Anna from Australia or is she a tourist?
- What does she want to rent and why?
- How does Rob help Anna?

b) When you meet someone for the first time, you usually talk like this:

Start the conversation	Hi • How are you doing? • Great weather today. • That's a great ... you've got there. • Excuse me, is that seat free? • ...
Introduce yourself	I'm ... by the way. • My name's ... • Nice to meet you. • ...
Make small talk	Where are you from? • So have you been here before? • Have you tried ...? • Do you like ...? • What about you? • ...
Ask for or give help	Do you know where ...? • Can you tell me ...? • Can I borrow ...? • Sure, no problem. • Why don't you ...? • ...
End the conversation	Bye • See you later • Have a good day! • ...

c) Listen to Rob and Anna again. What phrases do they use for the different parts of the conversation?

d) ROLE PLAY With your partner prepare and act out one of the role plays below (1 or 2). Use the phrases from b) to help you.

Role play 1

Partner A:
You're at a youth hostel in a big city. You see another guest who has a good map. Maybe he will let you borrow it?

Partner B:
You're looking at your map. You are going to go out and explore the city. It would be nice to go with someone.

Role play 2

Partner A:
You're at a café. You want to sit down. At last you see one free seat at a table. You like films, especially action and science fiction films.

Partner B:
You're looking at cinema tips in a magazine. There's a James Bond film on in an hour or a Batman film in half an hour.

e) ► D p. 95

► WB 11 (p. 7)

THE ABORIGINAL PEOPLE OF AUSTRALIA

1 Uluru-Kata Tjuta National Park: An imaginary journey

a) *Look closely at the photos for two minutes. Then close your eyes and listen.*

Uluru rises from the flat desert

Cave at Uluru

An Aboriginal man is playing the didgeridoo

Cave painting

The landscape after rain

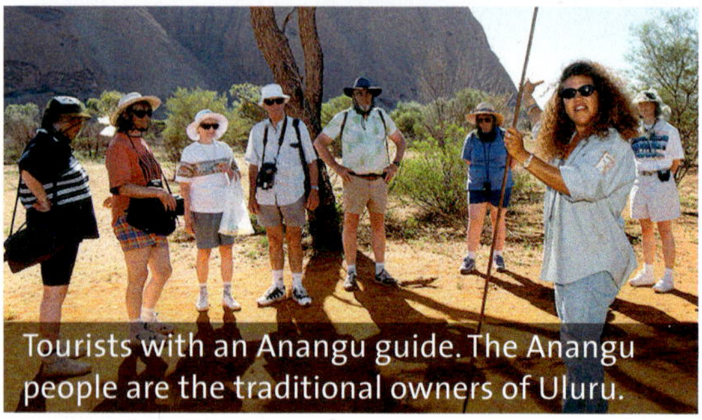
Tourists with an Anangu guide. The Anangu people are the traditional owners of Uluru.

b) *What was your strongest impression from your visit to Uluru? What did you see, hear, smell or feel? Tell your group about it.*

c) **Extra** *Listen again. Give examples from the imaginary journey that show how Aborigines respect nature.* ▸ SF Listening (p. 141)

2 Dreamtime

The Aborigines had lived in Australia for over 40,000 years when the British started to settle there. There were 500 different groups of Aborigines with more than 200 languages, but they shared many traditions and beliefs. Aborigines believe, for example, that the ancestors of everybody and everything once lived below the earth. In the 'Dreamtime' these ancestors came out and made the mountains, valleys, rivers etc., and gave life to animals and people. Aborigines believe that the land, plants and animals are just as important as people. That's why people need to respect the land and everything that grows and lives on it.

Do you think that the land, plants and animals are as important as people? Why (not)?

3 The 'stolen generations'

From 1910 to 1970 the Australian government took thousands of Aboriginal children away from their families. They were called 'the stolen generations'.

The Guardian — 11th February 2008

Children were stolen for a racist policy. Now a nation says sorry.

Barbara McMahon in Alice Springs

Zita Wallace still remembers the day she was stolen from her Aboriginal family and taken to a home for orphans. She was seven years old.

Wallace was with four other girls when she was taken. Some nuns said the girls could go shopping with them. 'They said we would be back that evening. They put us in the back of a truck. We never went near a shop. They took us to a home hundreds of miles away.'

At her house in Worita, Wallace spoke about her first night with the nuns. 'There were lots of children in one big room. We had to sleep on mattresses on the floor. I was terrified.'

She told us that she had seen terrible things. She said she would never forget those first hours. 'There was a 4-year old girl who just cried and cried. I put my head under my blanket and cried too.'

Wallace is one of the 'stolen generations', the thousands of mixed-race children in Australia who were taken from their families. The government wanted them to grow up like white people and forget their language and traditions. 'They hit us if we spoke our language,' Wallace told us.

The policy ended after 60 years in 1970. In 1997 a government report said it was time to apologize to the 'stolen generations'. Now, eleven years later, Australia is saying sorry at last.

Wallace said that she didn't care about getting money from the government. 'But I can't wait to hear that word tomorrow: sorry.'

Zita Wallace with her mother's sister Aggie

How was Zita Wallace stolen? Describe what happened. When was the article written? What important event took place in that year?

▸ SF Reading course (pp. 144–145) • Text File 3 (pp. 112–113)

4 VIEWING Rabbit-proof fence

Rabbit-proof fence tells the true story of three Aboriginal girls who are stolen. They escape and walk back 1,900 kilometres through the outback to get home.

a) *Watch a scene from the film and answer the questions:*

1. Do the girls know about the fence?
2. Does the mother know why the man in the car has come?
3. Does the worker help the children?

b) *Watch again. Talk about the film and how you feel when you watch the film:*

- At the beginning everything is calm. The music is ... The people are ...
- When the music gets louder you feel ...
- When you see the hands on the car, you feel ...
- At the end, the women are ... You feel ...

▸ WB 12 (p. 8) more help ▸ D p. 95

P1 Exploring language | Indirect speech

a) The writer of the newspaper article reports what Zita Wallace said in the interview (p. 17).

She told us that she had seen terrible things. She said she would never forget those first hours.

Study the chart below to learn how we ***report what someone said in the past****.*

Direct speech	Indirect speech
'I don't care about getting money from the government.'	Wallace said that she didn't care about getting money from the government.
'I saw terrible things.'	She told us that she had seen terrible things.
'I'll never forget those first hours.'	She said she would never forget those first hours.
'You can go shopping with us.'	The nuns said the girls could go shopping with them.

b) Look again at the sentences in a). How do the verbs change?

Direct speech	Indirect speech
simple present	simple past
simple past	...
will-future	... + infinitive
can	...

▸ *GF 4: Indirect speech I (p. 163)*

c) Report these statements from another conversation with Zita Wallace.

1 'A lot of Aborigines have no families.' → Wallace said a lot of Aborigines ... no families.
2 'I can't understand why the apology took so long.' → She told the reporter that she ... understand why the apology ... so long.
3 'I found my mother later, but we never were close again.' → She went on to say she ... her mother later, but they ... never ... close again.
4 'I'll be much happier after the apology.' → She said that she ... much happier after the apology.

P2 II O Samantha Harris, Aboriginal model (Indirect speech) ▸ *D p. 95*

1 I'm 17 years old and 1.80 metres tall.
2 I live near Tweed Heads, New South Wales.
3 'My dad is from Germany.'
4 'I have four brothers and one sister.'
5 'My friends call me Sam.'
6 'I like hip hop and reggae.'
7 'I can't imagine leaving home.'
8 'I don't earn a lot of money.'
9 'I want to be the first big Aboriginal model.'

Look at these answers from an interview with Aboriginal model Samantha Harris in 2008. Report what Samantha said.

1 Samantha said in 2008 that she was ...
2 She told the reporter that she ...
3 She added that her dad ...
4 Samantha said that she ...
5 She also said that her friends ... her ...
6 Samantha said she ...
7 She told the reporter that she ...
8 She said that she ...
9 Finally Samantha told the reporter that ...

P3 Tourists at Uluru (Indirect speech)

Report what the tourists said.

1
Lots of people climb Uluru.
My friend climbed it.
I'm sure I'll climb it really quickly.

2
I want to climb Uluru too.
It looks quite dangerous.
I hope I can do it.

1) The woman told the reporter that lots of people ...
She said that ... She was sure that she ...

2) The boy said ... He thought it ... He hoped that he ...

3
I can't climb Uluru.
It's too hot.
I hope it will get cooler later.

4
I read a book of Aboriginal stories.
I won't climb Uluru out of respect for the Aboriginal culture.
The tour with the local guide will be great.

P4 He said, she said ... (Indirect speech)

a) *Write four sentences about yourself. You can use phrases from the box:*

I (don't) like/go/play/eat/want ... • I have/don't have ... • I want to ... • I have to/don't have to ... • I can/can't ... • ...

b) *Make appointments with two partners. Meet each partner and tell him/her about yourself. Then write down what he/she says.*

c) *Meet each partner again. Tell him/her what the others told you.*

P5 WRITING A film review

a) *Complete this review with words from the box.*

ending • interesting • main • director • true story • about • stars • takes place

Rabbit-proof fence is a ... The ... of the film is Phillip Noyce and the ... are Everlyn Sampi, Tianna Sansbury, and Laura Monaghan. They are fantastic! The film ... in Australia in 1931. It's ... three Aboriginal girls who are taken away from their mothers. The ... characters are Molly, Daisy and Gracie. The film is sometimes a bit slow. But I liked it because it was ... I learned a lot about Aboriginal people. I liked the soundtrack too. The ... is happy in one way. But it's also very sad. It's a great film! I'd recommend it to everyone.

b) *Use these questions to make short notes about a film that you've seen recently.*

What's the title?
What kind of film is it?
What's the film about?
Who's the director? Who are the stars?
Where and when does it take place?
Who are the main characters?
What's good/bad/special about the film?
What's the ending like?
Would you recommend it to other people?

more help ► D p. 96

c) *Use your notes and the example in a) to write a review of your film.*

► WB 13–14 (pp. 8–9)

In the outback

adapted from the novel *A prayer for Blue Delaney* by Kirsty Murray

STUDY SKILLS Reading stories

When you read a story, don't read it in the same way you would read a short text – you'll never finish! Read quickly! Don't worry about words you don't understand. The important thing is to follow the plot.

If you really can't follow the plot because you don't understand a word, remember the techniques to work out the meaning of words: look at the **pictures**, use the **context**, think of **words that you already know** – in German or English that look like the new word. If that doesn't help, use a dictionary.

Stop now and then, and think about what you have just read. Summarize it in your head. Then go on reading.

► *SF Reading stories (p. 143)* •
SF Working out the meaning of words (p. 144)

The story so far

In the 1950s the population of Australia was very small. The government wanted more people, so orphans were sent from the United Kingdom to children's homes in Australia. Colm is one of these orphans. He runs away from the children's home because the people are very cruel. In Western Australia he meets an old man, Bill, and his dog, Rusty. Bill wants to work on the Dog Fence in South Australia. When the police start to look for Colm, he decides to go with Bill and Rusty in Tin Annie – Bill's old car, a 'ute'.

As they drove out of Ceduna, Bill said, 'I heard from an old mate that there's work on the Dog Fence. Thought I might take it. No one will follow us in that lonely country.'

The Victoria Desert lay in front of them as they left town. They drove north to the Dog Fence, through a wide, open landscape of earth and sky.

It was slow and hot travelling along the Dog Fence. As they drove inland, the air became hotter until Colm felt he was breathing fire.

He and Rusty put their heads out of the window, but it was worse outside. The sandy air hurt Colm's skin and eyes. He pulled his head back inside. There was nothing to see except bushes and tough little grasses in the rock and sand, and the fence that looked like a thin grey scar across the landscape.

'What if we have problems with the truck?' asked Colm.

'Don't you worry about that. Tin Annie here, she's part camel part jeep, so she'll be fine.'

'But what if we would lose our way?'

Bill smiled. 'We'll follow the fence, mate. It's more than three thousand miles long. We can't lose it.'

Emu

Bill stopped next to the fence where an emu had crashed into it. They both climbed out of the ute.

Bill shook his head. 'She's hit the fence very fast, this one. Looks like she broke her neck.'

Another emu was running across the desert.

'See, they get faster and faster. They run 30 miles an hour but they don't see the fence till they've hit it.'

Colm helped Bill as he looked for the tools he would need for the job and then climbed back into Tin Annie to wait while Bill repaired the fence. Later they stopped to fill in a hole made by a wombat.

Wombat

The day dragged on. They drove so slowly that Colm got tired looking at the fence. When he closed his eyes he still saw the fence. Colm fell asleep. When he woke up, Bill was repairing the fence.

Colm's shirt was wet with sweat. He went round to the back of the ute and drank from the billycan. The water was as warm as tea, but it was good to wet his throat. There were flies around his face and they wouldn't go away. Colm felt as if he was inside a strange and terrifying dream.

The days dragged on, long and boring. Colm's neck hurt from always turning his head one way to watch the fence. After a few days Colm started to fill the wombat holes while Bill repaired the other holes in the fence. They got water in the billycans at every dam or tank, and ate tinned beef and tinned vegetables until Colm felt he couldn't eat them any more. The nearest town was hundreds of miles away.

One morning, Rusty wasn't in camp when they woke up. Colm helped Bill pack the breakfast things. All the time he scanned the scrub and looked for a sign of movement.

'Where is that damn dog?' said Bill. He put two fingers in his mouth and whistled. Nothing moved.

'I'll find her,' said Colm. He walked out into the bushes and then stood very still. If he closed his eyes, he should be able to feel Rusty wherever she was. He was sure she was quite close.

When he opened his eyes he saw a movement.

'Bill,' called Colm. 'Bill, here, I've found her! But something's wrong! Hurry!' Rusty was under a bush: she was shaking terribly.

'What is it?' asked Colm.

'Snakebite, maybe. Or maybe not.'

Rusty started shaking even more. Colm was cold with fear.

'What's wrong?' he asked.

'I think she's eaten dingo bait. Poison. It might be better for her to put her down.'

Colm walked beside Bill as he took Rusty over to the ute and put her on her blanket in the back. Bill picked up the knife he used to kill rabbits.

'No! What are you doing!' Colm grabbed Bill's hand. 'We have to save her.'

'For chrissake, get out of my way,' said Bill. He pushed Colm away and held Rusty's head.

Quickly he made cuts on the side of Rusty's ears. Blood poured down.

'Now go and get some water in the billycan.' Bill pushed it at Colm and then looked for something in the food bag.

When Colm came back, Bill threw lots of salt into the water. He took Rusty in his arms. 'Now I'll keep her mouth open. I want you to pour the salty water down her throat.'

The salt water made Rusty throw up. When Bill put her down, she threw up again and again. As soon as they could, they poured more water down her throat. When she'd finished, Bill laid her on her old blanket under a bush.

'Here, you need a break,' said Bill. 'Go get yourself a drink and sit in the car. I'll call you if I need you.'

'What are you going to do? You can't shoot her, Bill. You can't.'

'I'm hoping it won't come to that.'

Colm walked back to Tin Annie. He tried not to cry.

The morning grew hotter. Colm fell asleep and then, when he woke, he prayed. He was still praying when he heard the sound of Rusty's bark – a weak bark, but a bark. He ran across to where she was.

'I prayed for her,' said Colm. 'Maybe it helped.'

'Maybe it did,' said Bill. 'Between your prayers and my hard work, she'll be better quite soon.'

****

After some more adventures Bill finds work and a place to stay with an old friend at Tara Downs cattle station.

'C'mon. I've got a job to do. Can't sit around all day. A wild boar's been making trouble just south a bit. Get in the ute and you can help.'

They drove out into the landscape where the old trees looked like burnt bones. Rusty put her head out the open window. The fine red sand flew up around the sides of the ute.

'This is the place. We'll go after the bugger on foot from here. You stay close by me.'

Colm followed Bill through the bushes. A hot, foul smell was in the air. As the smell grew stronger, Rusty put her head down and walked in front of them, as if she was following something. She led them to a dead steer. A cloud of flies flew up in the air.

Bill looked at the animal. 'He's not long dead,' he said.

They climbed up a nearby hill and scanned the countryside. They could see nothing.

'Damn, he's heard us. '

Bill turned to walk back to the steer. There was a noise in the bushes and the black boar was on them.

Colm jumped behind a rock as the boar hit Bill. It ran at the old man with its tusks, cutting open his leg. Bill let out a cry of pain.

Boar

Blood poured from Bill's leg as the boar attacked again. Rusty sank her teeth into the boar's leg, but it turned and cut her with its tusks. Rusty yelped and fell.

Colm jumped out from behind the rock. He had to do something.

Bill was afraid. 'Run, Colm, get out of here,' he shouted. 'Get help!'

Colm turned and ran down the path. He had nearly got to Tin Annie when he heard a terrible scream, more animal than human. He stopped and turned. What if Bill was killed before he could get help? What should he do? Run to Tara Downs cattle station? Try to save Bill alone? Suddenly he knew there was only one answer and there was no time to lose.

He ran back to Bill. On the way he picked up a stick. As he came over the hill, he ran at the boar, hitting it again and again. It turned towards Colm. There was a lot of blood on its tusks.

Bill tried to pull himself away, leaving a trail of blood behind him. Colm raised the stick high and hit the boar's head. The boar didn't run at Colm. It turned back to Bill.

Colm threw the stick down and grabbed Bill's gun. He was shaking as he raised the gun to his shoulder. Colm knew that if he hit the animal in the back, it would only make it wild. He let out a scream, a long loud scream. The boar turned round. For a moment it looked at him. Then it put down its head and ran towards him. Colm aimed straight between the eyes.

The kickback from the gun made Colm fall backwards. He fell on the ground next to Rusty.

'Colm, my mate,' said Bill. He held out one bloody hand and smiled. Then he lay back in the red sand and passed out.

Suddenly, everything was quiet. There was a dark circle of blood around Bill. Colm could see the bones of his leg. He would have to stop the blood or Bill would bleed to death. Colm ran back to the ute and grabbed an old shirt to put on the wound on Bill's leg. Then he took off his own shirt and used that for Bill's hands. When he was finished, he sat back and tried to think. He had to get help, but how? There were flies everywhere. He would have to get Bill into the car.

Colm took Bill's arms and put one over each of his shoulders and then tried to pull the old man up. It was almost impossible. He'd never be able to move him like this. He laid Bill down again and ran to Tin Annie. Colm took a deep breath and turned the key. Tin Annie started. He had no idea how to drive back-wards so he moved forward, carefully, bringing the car as close to Bill as he could. Somehow he pulled Bill back on his shoulders and put him into the car. Then he ran and picked Rusty up. He could just hear the dog's heart beat and it gave him hope.

The red sand flew up around the car as Colm drove fast along the track. Every time they hit a stone Bill groaned, but at least that meant he was still alive.

Then Tin Annie stopped. Colm tried to start her up again. He pushed his foot to the floor. But it was a mistake. The old ute died completely.

They were just at the top of the hill and he could see Tara Downs cattle station, but there was still at least a mile to go. He tried to start the car again and again, but nothing happened. He would have to go on foot and leave Bill and Rusty in the car.

He looked at Bill and wished the old man was conscious and could tell him what to do next. Then he began the long run to Tara Downs.

Colm's heart beat hard and his head hurt, but he ran fast. He took the steps up to the house two at a time.

'It's Bill. An accident. He's bleeding, real bad. A boar got him.'

Then Colm sank down on his knees. People appeared from nowhere. They ran, a car started up and strong arms helped Colm to his feet and took him into a bedroom. Colm didn't want to go. 'I have to be with Bill,' he said.

'It's all right.'

'Bill needs me,' said Colm.

'They're getting the Flying Doctor out here. We don't know if the old man will make it if we have to drive him down to the hospital in Katherine. Best to fly him to Darwin.'

Colm felt the blood drain from his face. 'He will make it. He has to make it.'

Working with the text

1 The story

a) *Tell the story in a few sentences. The flow chart can help you.*

Bill and Colm drive into the Victoria Desert ... ▶ repair the Dog Fence where an emu ... ▶ fill holes made by ... ▶ Rusty is gone, something is wrong with the dog ... ▼ A black boar attacks Bill and Colm ... ◀ ... is badly hurt, ... has to help him ◀ ... shoots the boar, takes Bill to the nearest cattle station ◀ The Flying Doctor has to come to help ...

b) *Which part of the story do you like best? Why?*

▸ *GF 1: Talking about the present (p. 159)*

2 The characters

a) *Choose at least three adjectives from the box to describe one of the characters: Bill or Colm. Think of reasons for your choice.*

brave • clever • difficult • easy-going • friendly • hard-working • helpful • honest • kind • lucky • nervous • old • stupid • violent • young

b) *Listen to your partner's description. Do you agree with it? Give reasons. Then describe your character to your partner.*

c) *What do you think Bill and Colm were thinking in these situations?*

1 'Tin Annie here, she's part camel, part jeep, so she'll be fine.' (p. 20, ll. 40–41)
2 Bill picked up the knife he used to kill rabbits. (p. 21, ll. 114–115)
3 Colm aimed straight between the eyes. (p. 23, ll. 218–219)

3 Extra In the outback

In the story you come across a lot of typical Australian animals. Make a list and find more information about them.

or

Find more information about the Dog Fence.

▸ *SF Research (p. 138) • WB 15 (p. 9)*

4 Extra The end of the story

a) *What do you think happened to Colm after Bill's accident? Did he go out into the bush alone? Or was he sent back to the children's home? Write your ending.*

Remember

1 Brainstorm your ideas. Make notes.
2 Write your text. Use **linking words**, **adjectives** and **adverbs** to make it more interesting.
3 Correct your text.

more help ▸ *D p. 97*

b) *Make groups of 4–5. Read your texts to each other. Present the one you like best to the class. You can add pictures to your own text and put it in your DOSSIER.*

▸ *SF Brainstorming (p. 148) • SF Writing course (pp. 150–151)*

How am I doing?

▸ *SF Check yourself (p. 136)*

a) *Find or choose the correct answers.*

Facts about Australia

1 Name three important Australian cities.
2 Name three typical Australian animals.
3 Name two things Australians do to protect themselves from the dangerous UV rays.
4 Name three sports Australians like to do.
5 When it's spring in Germany, it's ... in Australia.
  A spring B summer C autumn D winter
6 What other word do Australians use to talk about the bush?
  A hinterland B outback C desert D Dreamland
7 The largest ethnic group in Australia are ...
  A the Asians.
  B the African Australians.
  C the Aborigines. D the Whites.
8 Aborigines of the 'stolen generations' ...
  A were thieves.
  B were taken away by Whites.
  C lived before 1600.
  D built the Dog Fence.

Grammar

9 What did they say? Put these sentences in indirect speech.
  a) Kim: 'I'll have a great time Down Under.'
  b) Jess: 'I just love kangaroos.'
  c) Tom: 'Frank visited Sydney last year.'
  d) Lara: 'We can go again next year.'

Words

10 Because of the dangerous UV rays you should ... the sun.
  A divide B advise C avoid D miss

You would like to read your friend's new book so you ask him/her:
  A 'Can you borrow it?'
  B 'Can I borrow it?' C 'Can I lend it?'

11 When something doesn't work you can sometimes ... it yourself.
  A revise B release C receive D repair
12 If you want to send somebody a photo, you can ... it to an e-mail.
  A glue B attach C enter D put

Talking about charts

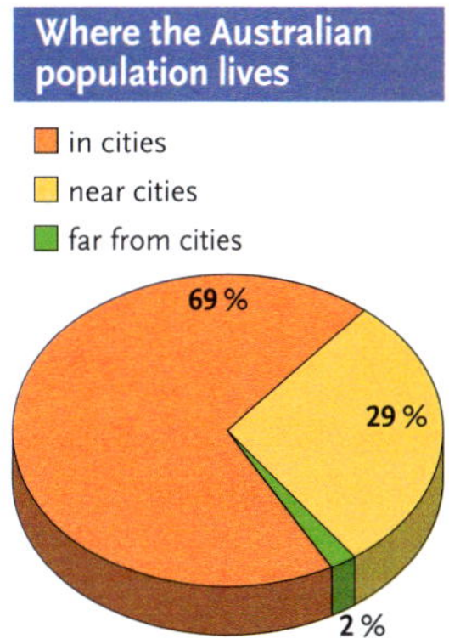

The chart on the right is a ... chart. It shows what ... of the Australian population lives where. It is ... into three parts. The ... group (69%) lives in cities. The next largest group lives ... cities and the ... group lives far from cities. So we can say that ...% of the population don't live in cities.

b) *Check your answers on p. 230 and add up your points.*

c) *If you had 24 or more points, well done! Maybe you can help students who had fewer points. If you had 23 points or fewer, it's a good idea to do some more work before you go on to the next unit. Where did you make mistakes? The chart below will tell you what you can do to improve your English.*

No.	Areas	Find out more	Exercises
1– 8	Australian facts	Unit 1 (pp. 6–10, 13, 17)	WB 1–3 (pp. 2–3)
9	Indirect speech I	GF 4 (p. 163)	P 1–4 (pp. 18–19), WB 13 (p. 8)
10–13	Words	Vocabulary (pp. 171–176)	WB 2, 12 (pp. 2, 8)
14	Talking about charts	Part A (p. 10), SF (p. 140)	P 3 (p. 11), WB 6 (p. 4)

▸ **Skills check 1** *WB (pp. 10–15)*

1 WORDS Travelling

Fill in the right words to complete the sentences. Use the words in the box on the right.

breakfast • (to) change planes • city centre • departure gate • key card • (to) land • meal • single ticket • suitcases • taxi • ticket machines

You're flying to Australia for your dream holiday. At the airport, you first 1 *check in*. Then you go to the 2 ... For your flight it's gate D21.

Now you're on the plane. The flight to Australia is very long and on the way you need to eat and drink. The flight attendant offers you a drink and a hot 3 ... There are lots of nice things on the menu today.

After you 4 ... at Singapore Airport, you finally 5 ... in Sydney. Of course, you hope that your 6 ... arrive too! If not, you'll have to go to the lost luggage office.

So how do you travel from the airport into the 7 ...? Well, the quickest and easiest way is to take a 8 ..., but it's also the most expensive one: it costs about 50 Australian dollars. So you decide to take a train. The 9 ... are easy to use and a 10 ... to the city is only 15 Australian dollars.

Now – tired but happy – you're at your hotel. The receptionist gives you the 11 ... to your room and tells you about the hotel – for example, the times when you can have 12 ... in the mornings.

2 Judy's job (Simple present and present progressive)

a) *Judy is the flight attendant who you can see in the photo above. Finish these sentences about her job. Use the* ***simple present*** *or the* ***present progressive****.*

1 Judy's job is exciting. She often ... (travel) to different countries.
2 Right now, she ... (fly) to Australia.
3 A typical day for Judy starts early. She usually ... (get up) at 5 o'clock. Then she ... (have) her breakfast and ... (drive) to the airport.
4 It's 10 o'clock now and Judy ... (work). She ... (bring) coffee and tea to the passengers on her plane.
5 Now it's 10 o'clock the next morning. Judy ... (arrive) at her hotel.
6 Judy always ... (stay) at a hotel when she is in another country. She ... (sleep) at the hotel – then the next day she ... (fly) home again.

b) *Write sentences about things that you often do and some things that you're doing right now.*

I often surf the internet. Right now, I'm chatting with my friends.

▸ GF 1: Talking about the present (p. 159)

3 Australia's most dangerous animals (Simple past and past progressive)

Read the text about Australia's most dangerous animals on the right, then complete the two stories below. Use the simple past or past progressive of the verbs in brackets.

There's a crocodile in our tent!

In January 2005, two young Australians went camping near the Pentecost River in the north of Australia. At about 2 o'clock in the morning, they (1) *were sleeping* (sleep) when suddenly a crocodile (2) ... (come) into their tent. They (3) ... (run) to their car and (4) ... (climb) onto it. The next morning at 11 o'clock, they (5) ...

(still/sit) on their car when some hunters (6) ... (arrive) and (7) ... (save) their lives.

AUSTRALIA is home to some of the world's most dangerous animals. There are snakes, spiders and sometimes sharks. The most dangerous of all, however, are crocodiles. Two or three people die every year in crocodile attacks.

Smile please!

In 2008, a tourist in Queensland was stupid – but lucky. He (8) ... (sit) in a boat on a river when a crocodile (9) ... (swim) towards the boat. The man's friend (10) ... (stand) on land. 'Put your hand in the water and play with the crocodile!' he (11) ... (shout). 'I'm going to take a photo.' Seconds later, the crocodile (12) ... (try) to bite the man's hand. 'It was a scary moment!', he (13) ... (say) afterwards.

▸ GF 2: Talking about the past (p. 160)

4 WORDS It was scary! (Words that describe experiences)

a) *Look at the box with adjectives. Find five pairs of adjectives that mean (almost) the same: good – ...*

b) *Find at least eight pairs of adjectives that mean the opposite: cool – boring; sad – ...*

c) *Write six sentences using adjectives from the box:*

1) *Yesterday I played table tennis against my younger brother and lost 11–2. It was depressing!*
2) ...

amazing • awesome • awful • bad • boring • cool • crazy • dangerous • depressing • different • difficult • easy • excellent • exciting • fantastic • fine • funny • good • great • horrible • interesting • laughable • mad • nice • OK • sad • scary • silly • strange • surprising • terrible • unbelievable

5 WRITING One day last year ...

a) *Below is a very short story! Can you make it more interesting? Write the story again.*

Jake was riding his bike in the mountains. He fell off and broke his leg. He called for help with his mobile phone. Some people saved him. He went to hospital. He met Anne, a doctor. They fell in love. They got married.

When?	one day last year, last May, first, then, next, after that, in the end, ...
Who?	the man/woman/people who ...
How?	quickly, slowly, suddenly, ... (really) amazing/awful; (feel) happy/sad, ...
Linking words	because, but, so (that), although, when, while, ...

b) *Compare your story with a partner's.*

▸ SF Writing course (pp. 150–151)

1 LISTENING Travelling to Australia

You are flying to Australia with your family. Your are going to hear five announcements or short conversations that you hear on your journey.
- *Look at the questions below. You have 30 seconds.*
- *You will hear all the recordings **once**.*
- *Listen and note down the right answer – A, B or C.*

1 On your way to Australia you have to change planes at Heathrow Airport in London. There you hear this announcement: 'The Qantas flight 201 to Sydney is now boarding at ...'

A GATE 201 B GATE 17 C GATE 70

2 On the plane from London to Sydney, the flight attendant is offering you ...

A an omelette or pasta.

B chicken with a salad or pork chops.

C chicken with a salad or pasta.

3 At Sydney Airport one of your suitcases is missing! The lost luggage office is ...

A just over here.

B opposite the big door.

C next to the passport office.

4 A taxi from the airport into the city costs ...

A AU $ 50 B AU $ 52.50 C AU $ 55.50

5 Now you are at your hotel. Tomorrow breakfast is from ...

A 06:30–9:30 B 07:00–10:00 C 07:00–10:30

2 LISTENING Shark attack!

You are going to hear a radio news programme about how Jon Kerry, a young Australian, was attacked by a great white shark.
– Look at the questions below for 30 seconds.
– You will hear the news programme ***twice****.*
– Now listen and do the tasks.

a) *Which is right? Note down* A, B, C *or* D.

1 Jon was attacked near a beach in ...
A Queensland.
B South Australia.
C New South Wales.
D Western Australia.

2 When he was attacked, Jon was ...
A surfing.
B swimming.
C sunbathing.
D canoeing.

3 The shark bit into Jon's ...
A arm.
B foot.
C stomach.
D leg.

4 It held him for around ...
A 3.5 seconds.
B 5 seconds.
C 40 seconds.
D 5 minutes.

5 After the attack ...
A a boat saved Jon.
B the shark pulled Jon to the beach.
C Jon swam back to the beach.
D a big wave carried Jon to the beach.

6 Jon thought this was the ... part.
A most exciting
B easiest
C scariest
D most painful

b) *Finish the sentences.*

1 Jon's friends probably saved his life when they ... a rope[1] round his ... and stopped the bleeding.
2 Jon is lucky. He will always have a big scar[2] but he ...
3 Experts say that sharks don't normally ...
4 The experts also say that more people die in road accidents in Australia ... than from shark attacks ...
5 You should always swim ... so your friends can help you. And never swim ... or ... because that's when sharks usually feed.

[1] rope [rəʊp] *Seil* [2] scar [skɑːr] *Narbe*

3 LISTENING Young Australians and the internet

Young Australians are among the world's biggest users of the internet. Six Australian students are discussing what they do online.
- *Look at the statements below for 30 seconds.*
- *You will hear the recordings only **once**.*
- *Now listen and do the task.*

True or false? Note down 'T' or 'F'.

1. This student thinks that she spends too much time online.
2. This student never does just one thing at a time when he uses a computer.
3. This student thinks her parents don't care about what she does online.
4. This student thinks that young people know how to be safe online.
5. This student tells a story about something that happened to her.
6. This student thinks the internet isn't good for teenagers.

4 WRITING An online magazine for young Europeans

You often read an online magazine for young Europeans. This week, the magazine wants readers' ideas about the internet and it has a story competition.
Write about one of the two topics below. Write a text of about 120 words.

Topic 1: The internet and me
- When and where do you usually use the internet?
- What do you do online?
- What things do you do most often online?
- What do you do to be safe online?

Topic 2: A scary moment!
Finish this story in your own words.

It was a Saturday afternoon in September. I was bored, so I decided to …

How am I doing?

Check your answers to tasks 1–3 (Listening) on page 230.

About the test

This test gave you the chance to try some of the kinds of tasks that you have to do one day in your exam (*Abschlussprüfung*). If you found some tasks difficult, don't worry. You've got lots of time to practise. Remember: 'Practice makes perfect!'

Listening

The first three tasks in the test were listening tasks. The following questions will help you to think about how you did. Read the questions – which answer right for you?

1 How hard or easy was each task?

	easy	OK	quite hard	very hard
Task 1				
Task 2				
Task 3				

2 What was difficult in the tasks?

a) People spoke too quickly.
b) I found the accents difficult.
c) There was a lot of information. I couldn't find the exact answers.
d) I didn't have time to finish all the tasks.
e) There were words and phrases that I just couldn't understand.

3 How did you do the tasks?

a) I read the tasks carefully first so I knew exactly what I had to listen for.
b) I looked quickly at the tasks first but only read them carefully while I was listening.
c) I wrote as many answers as I could the first time I heard the text and checked them (or filled in gaps) the second time.
d) There were lots of things I couldn't understand and I panicked.

► *SF Listening (p. 141)* • *SF How to do well in a test (pp. 156–157)*

Writing

Task 4 in your test was a writing task. Work with a partner. Swap the texts you've written and read your partner's text.
Copy and fill in the assessment sheet[1] below. Remember: the idea is to help your partner with your feedback!

Assessment sheet	☹		😐		☺	
Name of partner ...	1	2	3	4	5	Comments
Did your partner ...						
1 ... write an interesting text/story?						
2 ... use correct grammar (tenses, plural forms, etc.)?						
3 ... use interesting vocabulary?						
4 ... write longer sentences with linking words?						
5 ... write a text that is clear and easy to understand?						

► *SF Writing course (pp. 150–151)*

[1] assessment sheet *Beurteilungsbogen*

top jobs

Job information for young people

Welcome to the top jobs website.

Are you thinking about the future? Maybe you're not sure if you should leave school or not. Do you need ideas about jobs or training? Do you want to find out about qualifications? Are you thinking about an apprenticeship? Then this is the website for you.

Binita, a police officer in an airport

Amy, a fitness instructor in a sports centre

Zach, a make-up artist for a film company

Ethan, a childcare assistant in a kindergarten

Abby, a chef on a ship

It's just the first step!

Your first job is an important decision for you but it doesn't have to be your job for life! Today some people change their jobs many times in their lives. You will learn important skills in every job you do – even in Saturday jobs or if you work as a volunteer. It's all good experience.

Akeem, a mechanic in a garage

Alfie, a shop assistant in a sports shop

Poppy, a customer adviser in a bank

1 Top jobs?

a) *Choose your favourite and your least favourite job from the website. Make notes about*
- *what you like/don't like about the job*
- *why you would/wouldn't be good at it.*

b) *Make appointments with three partners. Talk about the jobs on the website. Swap roles.*

A: What's your (least) favourite job? Why?

B: I would/wouldn't like a job as a ... because ...

... it looks interesting/difficult/exciting/...

... you have to ...
- work in a team/with ...
- work long hours/weekends/shifts.
- talk to/serve customers.
- meet/look after/advise people.

... I'm (not) good at repairing things/...
... I'm (not) sporty/artistic/organized/calm/easy-going/hard-working/...

... I (don't) know a lot about cars/...
... I (don't) think the pay is good.

c) **Extra** *What are the most popular jobs in your class? And the least popular?*

2 What's the job really like?

a) *Listen to four of the people from the website.*
- *Who is speaking?*
- *Do they like their job?*
- *Do they want to change jobs soon?*

b) *Listen again. Take notes.*
- *Write down two good things and one bad thing that each person says about his or her job.*
- *What plans for the future do they have?*

► SF Listening (p. 141)

3 Now you

Talk about your plans for the future.
- *When do you think you'll leave school?*
- *What kind of job do you want to do?*
- *Do you want to do an apprenticeship?*

more help ► D p. 97

► GF 3: Talking about the future (p. 162) • WB 1 (p. 16)

PERSONALITY QUIZ

What's the right job for you?

Find out your personality type. Our quiz is just for fun, but it might give you some ideas for jobs.

1 You want to print your homework, but your dad says the printer isn't working. You say:

- A 'Stupid printer! I hate it!'
- B 'Don't worry, Dad. It's not important.'
- C 'I can see the problem. I know what to do.'
- D 'OK, I'll print it at school. And I'll phone a friend who can repair the printer.'

2 When you are asked to do jobs at home, ...

- A you disappear!
- B you say OK. You don't mind helping. It's normal that everyone in the family helps.
- C you try to think of better ways to do the jobs.
- D you do the jobs quickly so you can do more interesting things.

3 For a science project at school your group is designing a 'green' house. You say ...

- A 'I'll give the presentation to the class.'
- B 'I'll choose the colours for the model and paint it with Sam. Is that OK?'
- C 'I'll do the internet research.'
- D 'OK, I've made the model. What's next?'

4 How would your teachers describe you?

- A 'Always late!'
- B 'A dreamer.'
- C 'A techie.'
- D 'An organized and reliable student.'

5 You're happy when ...

- A you're with a big group of friends.
- B you make someone smile.
- C you solve a difficult problem.
- D you finish everything on your to-do list.

6 Which is your dream holiday?

7 If you were a fruit, what would you be?

- A A banana.
- B A soft summer fruit, like a strawberry.
- C A tomato. (Did you know they're a fruit, not a vegetable?)
- D I'm not a fruit! I hate silly questions like this!

Count how many As, Bs, Cs and Ds you have.

▸ WB 2 (p. 16)

THE RESULTS

Mostly A

Your personal qualities:

- **You're a confident, energetic and likeable person.**

You're artistic and you enjoy making things. But you get bored easily and you hate rules. You're good at starting things, but not so good at finishing them. You love adventure. You want life to be fun and exciting.

Have you thought of a job as an actor or a fitness instructor? Other ideas: a racing car driver, a waiter, a chef, …

Mostly B

Your personal qualities:

- **You're a calm, friendly, helpful and polite person.**

You're more interested in people than things. You love helping people and you're good at talking to them. You always try to do your best and you're good at working in a team. You want to change the world.

You might be interested in a job as a teacher or police officer. Other ideas: a vet's assistant, a dentist's assistant, …

Mostly C

Your personal qualities:

- **You're a hard-working and logical person.**

You're interested in everything around you – plants, animals, technology – and you want to understand how things work. You love information and you spend a lot of time on the internet. You're good at solving problems. You're more interested in ideas than people.

You could be a builder or a computer technician. Other ideas: a private detective, a truck driver, …

Mostly D

Your personal qualities:

- **You're a reliable, organized and punctual person.**

You're good at making decisions. You always finish what you've started. While everyone else is talking about it, you've done it! You like clear instructions and you think rules are important.

Lots of different jobs might be good for you. What about working in a bank or as a gardener? Other ideas: an office worker, a footballer, …

1 The quiz

a) *Do the quiz and read your results.*

b) *Talk about your results. Do you agree with the description of your personality type?*

– It says here that I'm/you're …
– I (don't) think that's true.
– I think I'm/you're a … person.

c) *What do you think of the jobs that the quiz suggests for you? What does your partner think?*

– I'd like/love/hate a job as a … because …
– … would be a good job for me/you because …
– Maybe you're right. / You're joking!

d) **Extra** *Suggest one more job for each personality type. Explain your choice to your partner.*

2 Personal qualities

a) ***Think:*** *Find adjectives and phrases on this page that match these jobs. Make lists.*

firefighter • make-up artist • mechanic • nurse

b) ***Pair:*** *With a partner agree on the four most important personal qualities for each job.*

c) ***Share:*** *Form a group with another pair. Compare your lists. Explain your choices.*

d) **Extra** *List the personal qualities that are needed for your favourite job.*

P1 WORDS Jobs

a) *Collect as many jobs as you can.*

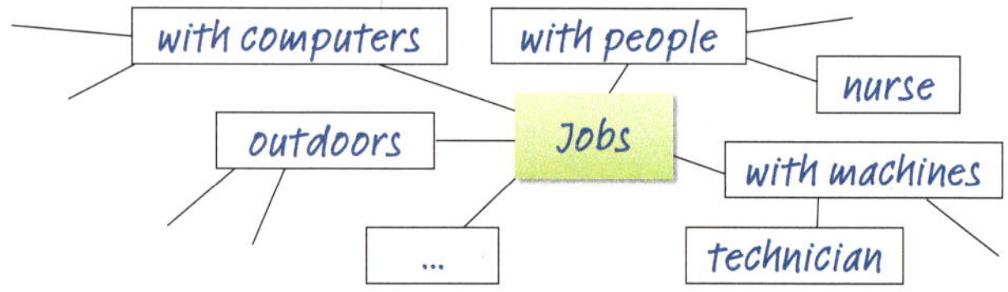

b) *Think of a job. Describe it to a partner. Don't say the name! Can he/she guess the job?*

In this job you ...
- sell things/work with .../repair ...
- have to be careful/energetic/calm/...

It's a job where you ...
- work in a garage/shop/factory/...

Tip

If you can't find an exact English word for a job, you have to paraphrase!

▸ *SF Paraphrasing (p. 148)*

P2 WORDS Job profiles

a) *Read the job profile below. Match it to one of the jobs in the photos.*

In this job you have to be very calm and confident. An important part of the job is checking equipment so you must be very careful. You have to like working in a team too. This is a great job because it's exciting and you can save people's lives. This isn't a good job if you don't like blood. Working shifts might be a problem for some people too.

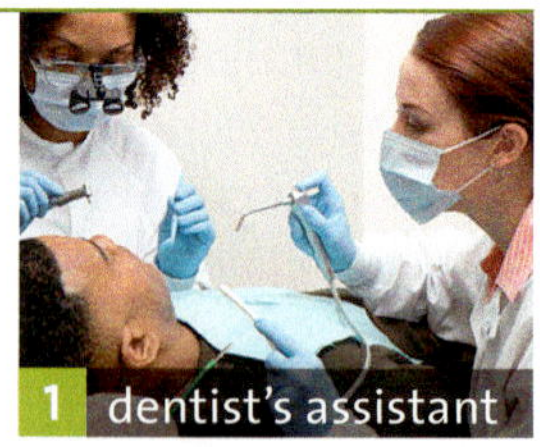
1 dentist's assistant

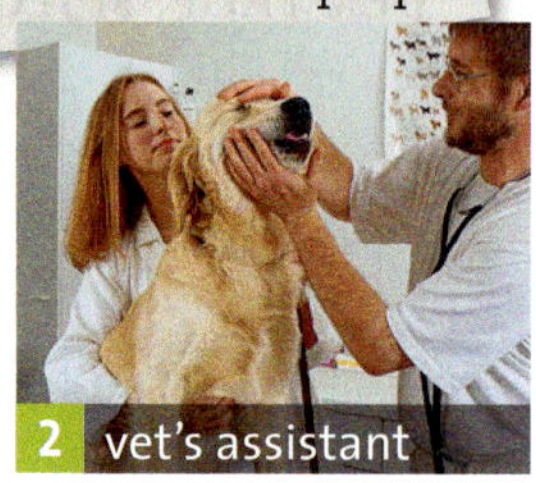
2 vet's assistant

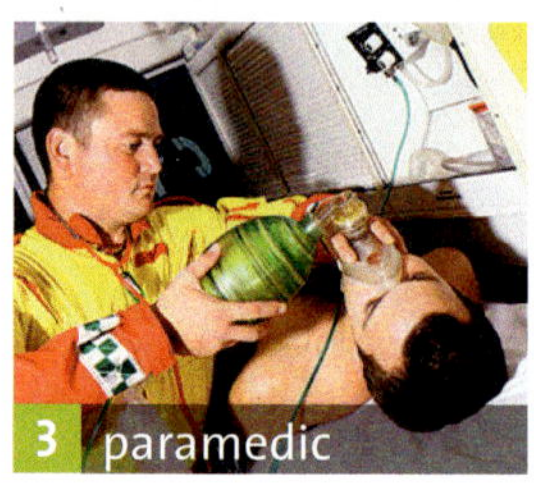
3 paramedic

▸ *SF Giving a presentation (p. 139)*

b) *Write another job profile. Find out about:*
- what personal qualities you need and why
- what you have to do in the job
- what's good/difficult about the job.

c) **Extra** *Prepare a presentation about your job. You can make a poster, use a computer, etc.*

P3 WORDS Your profile

a) *Make a chart for yourself like this. Use words and phrases from p. 35.*

Personal qualities	Interests	Possible jobs
– confident	– computers	– ...
– good at solving problems	– designing things	
– ...	– enjoy ...	

more help ▸ *D p. 98*

b) *Use your chart to write a personal profile. You can put your profile in your DOSSIER.*

Personal qualities: I'm a confident person, but I can be shy when I meet new people. I like working in a group, but I can work alone too. I ...
Interests: I have a lot of interests. I enjoy sport, for example ... And I'm interested in ...
Possible jobs: I'm not sure what job I want to do. Maybe I'll be a ... That might be a good job for me because ... I'm also thinking about becoming a ...

▸ *WB 3–5 (pp. 17–18)*

P4 MEDIATION Summer jobs in Britain

Partner B: Go to p. 90.

a) *Partner A: You and your partner are looking for summer jobs in Britain next year. Tell your partner in German about the job. Say:*

- what you have to do in the job
- what sounds good/bad about the job.

b) *Your partner will tell you about a job that he/she has found. Listen carefully and take notes.*

c) *Which job do you like best? Why?*

BJ'S BURGERS

BJ'S BURGER RESTAURANT

Summer work for energetic people!

We are looking for good people to join our team. You will be the face of BJ's, so you need to be friendly, polite and good at smiling. You also need to be quick and helpful. **We need people to serve customers, prepare and cook food and to clean the restaurant.** Experience useful, but full training will be given.

Download an application form here and send it to us, or bring it to our restaurant.

▸ *SF Mediation (p. 155)*

P5 WRITING Filling in a job application form

a) *Fill in a copy of the form for yourself.*

b) *Check your partner's application form. Use the checklist below:*

- Did your partner fill in the correct information?
- Did your partner write clearly and use black ink?
- Does the form look neat?
- Are there any spelling mistakes?

▸ *WB 6–7 (pp. 18–19)*

Job application form for BJ'S BURGERS

Personal details (Please write clearly and use black ink.)

First name(s) Jade Louise   Surname Hunter

Address 3 Oakwood Close, Cambridge CB1 7LY

Tel no (home) 01223 456238   Tel no (mobile) 07938 575593

Email address jlhunter@mvmail.com

Your work experience

Company	From	To	What did you do?
Sugar'n' Spice Café	July 2008	Sept 2008	Prepared food, served customers, cleaned the kitchen in a busy café

Your education

School	From	To	Subjects
Cambridge High School	2005	to date	GCSEs in Maths, English, French, Art, Design and Technology

More about you

Look at these pairs of statements. Which statement describes you best? For each pair of statements, choose A or B. Example:

	A		B	
	I like working in a team.	X	I like working on my own.	
1	I am organized.	X	I work quickly.	
2	I do what I am asked to do.		I volunteer for work.	X
3	I work best on my own.		I work best with others.	X
4	I think the customer is always right.	X	I think the customer is often wrong.	
5	I like to be part of a group.	X	I like to do my own thing.	

APPLYING FOR A JOB

1 Writing a CV

a) *Jamie wants to apply for this job. Would you like this job? Why (not)?*

b) *Look at the CV. Which of these things are on it?*

address • age • date of birth • nationality • postcode • sex • surname • telephone number

c) **Extra** *What things are usually on a German CV? What is different on this CV?*

► *SF Writing a CV (p. 152)*

Jamie Williams
12 Bluebell Court, Old Hall Green, Hertfordshire SG11 1DS
Telephone: 01920 462233 Email: jwilliams29@aol.com

Personal statement	I am a hard-working, reliable student. I like working in a team. I am looking forward to getting more experience in the workplace.
Education	
2006 to date	The Chauncy School, Ware (secondary school)
1999–2006	Little Hadham school (primary school)
Qualifications	
Studying for GCSEs in:	English, Maths, Geography, Science, Music, French, History, Art
Other skills	First-aid certificate, moped licence, computer skills
Work experience	Two weeks in a hotel; babysitting job at weekends
Hobbies and interests	I play table tennis and basketball in after-school clubs. I am a member of the school camera club and Ware Youth Club.
References	Mrs K Smith, Manager, Hertford House Hotel ksmith@herthousehotel.co.uk

12 Bluebell Court
Old Hall Green
Hertfordshire SG11 1DS

The Coffee Pot
High St
Hertford SG14 3SY

30 November 2010

Dear Sir or Madam

I am writing about your … in the Weekly Gazette of 28th November for a job as a … in your … I would like to … for the job. My … is enclosed.

I am a friendly, … person and I enjoy meeting new people. As you can see from my CV, I have done work experience in a … – I worked in the kitchen and at the reception. I also served … in the restaurant.
The hotel manager will be happy to give me a … Her contact details are in my CV.

I look forward to hearing from you.
Yours faithfully

Jamie Williams
Jamie Williams

2 A letter of application

Complete the letter with words from the box. (Look at the advert and the CV in 1.)

advertisement • apply • café • customers • CV • hotel • reference • reliable • waiter

Tip

In a formal letter like this
– do not use short forms: write 'I am' (not 'I'm'), write 'advertisement' (not 'ad' or 'advert'), etc.
– If you start a formal letter with **Dear Sir or Madam**, you usually end it with **Yours faithfully**.
– If you start with **Dear Ms Smith**, you usually end with **Yours sincerely**.

► *SF Writing formal letters (p. 153)*

P1 STUDY SKILLS Looking at CVs

a) *Look at the job advert below.*
What kind of person are they looking for?
What do you have to do in the job? Take notes.
You must be reliable, ...
You have to help on ...

Meadows Home Farm

We are looking for a **reliable person with lots of energy** to help us this summer on the farm and in our farm shop. **Great job for foreign students who want to practise their English.**

If you like the countryside and you don't mind working at weekends, send CV & letter of application to Jane Hall, The Home Farm Shop, Harston, Cambridge CB22 4BE, Great Britain or jh@homefarm.co.uk

b) *Partner B: Go to p. 91.*
Partner A: Tell your partner about this candidate.
– I've got the CV of someone called ...
– She's got these qualifications: ...
– She did some work experience in ...
– She's interested in ...
Then listen to your partner. He/She will tell you about another candidate.

CURRICULUM VITAE

Lena Dickhaus
Rosenstrasse 12, 42857 Remscheid, Germany
Telephone: 00 49 202 33484
E-mail: ledickhaus@email-rs.de

Education
2004–2010 Sophie-Scholl-Gesamtschule (secondary school), Remscheid, Germany

2000–2004 Eisernstein Primary School, Remscheid, Germany

Qualifications
Studying for *Fachoberschulreife* (similar to GCSEs)
Languages: English (8 years), French (4 years)
European Computer Driving Licence (ECDL)

Work experience
Work experience in a zoo shop (3 weeks)

Hobbies and interests
My hobbies are cycling and badminton. I am very interested in nature and animals.

References
Mrs Schwede (manager of zoo shop),
Zoo Wuppertal, Hubertusallee 30,
42117 Wuppertal, Germany

c) *Look back at your notes from a). Which candidate should get the job? Why? Discuss.*

P2 STUDY SKILLS Writing a letter of application

a) //O ► *D p. 98*
Improve this letter. Rewrite the underlined parts with words and phrases from the box.
(They don't all fit.)

address • advertisement • application • apply for • customers • I am • I do not • I enclose • I look forward to hearing from you • I will • letter • qualification • similar to • team • the experience • three • will be happy to

b) **Extra** *Write your own letter of application to* Home Farm Shop. *Enclose your CV.*

c) ● ► *D p. 99*

d) ● ► *D p. 99*

► **Text File 4** *(pp. 114–116)* • *WB 8–9 (p. 20)*

Dear Ms Hall

I am writing about your ad in the Cambridge News and I would like to have the job. Here is my CV. I'm 17 years old and I'll leave school at the end of June with the *Fachoberschulreife*, which is a bit like GCSEs in Britain.

I am a friendly, helpful person and I enjoy working in a group of people. I am very reliable and I don't mind working at weekends. I have studied English for six years and my level is quite good. This year I worked in a zoo for 3 weeks. I did office work and served people in the zoo shop. I really enjoyed what I did there. The manager can give me a reference.

Write back soon.

Yours sincerely

Lena Dickhaus

Lena Dickhaus

A REALITY TV SHOW

1 Top tips for interviews

Saturday 6.30 pm

THE BUSINESS

The BUSINESS is a reality show for teenagers. On this week's show the big boss is Rita McQueen from the fashion company RMQ. The prize is two weeks' work experience as Rita's assistant. The candidates, Lucy and Mani, have to impress Rita in an interview. They got some tips from their coach, Simon Gubbins.

'Big boss' Rita McQueen. Who will she choose?

Relax! Before an interview listen to music or do yoga.

Listen carefully to the questions!

Dress suitably. Don't wear bright colours or too much make-up.

Show your interest in the company.

Prepare answers to interview questions like 'Tell me about yourself' or 'What are your strengths and weaknesses?'

Smile in the interview!

Don't talk too quickly.

Don't talk too much. But don't give one-word answers either.

▶ *Which three tips do you think are the most important?*

2 VIEWING The interviews

a) Watch the interviews. Give points to Mani and Lucy on copies of the chart.

b) Which candidate should win?

c) Watch the results. What do you think of Rita's decision?

Assessment sheet	☹		😐		☺	
The candidate	**1**	**2**	**3**	**4**	**5**	**Comments**
1 was relaxed and friendly				✓		*smiled a lot*
2 dressed suitably						
3 listened carefully						
4 talked well (not too much/too little)						
5 was well prepared						

3 Internet forum ▶ TV talk ▶ Did you see THE BUSINESS last night?

Max1234 (2 days ago) Did you see the show last night? I loved the part when Mani told Rita that he was the best. The look on Rita's face!! What was your favourite 'Mani moment'?

Flipper (2 days ago) For me, the best part was when they went shopping. Simon told Mani and Lucy to look for clothes for the interview. Simon asked Mani to choose a tie. I laughed so much when I saw the tie that Mani bought!

AliceW (1 day ago) Yeah! That tie was crazy! The coach told them not to be shy – not a problem for Mani!

EJ (1 day ago) He was so cheeky in the interview! Rita asked him what he knew about her business. And he clearly didn't know much. Then Rita asked him if he had any weaknesses. And Mani said no! And then he asked her when he could start!! Rita chose the wrong one!

▶ *Which parts of the show did these people like best? Describe the part you liked best to a partner.*

P1 SPEAKING How would you describe yourself? (Taking part in a job interview) ► SF p. 146

a) *Read this interview for a weekend job in a computer shop. Decide how you would answer the interviewer's questions.*

(1) *Interviewer* Hello, I'm Jack Bond.
You A Hi. B Hello, nice to meet you.

(2) *Interviewer* Did you have a good trip here?
You A It was fine, thanks. B No, but I'm here now.

(3) *Interviewer* Good. Thanks for your application. Can I ask why you want to work for us?
You A Well, my mum saw your advert and she told me to apply.
B Well, I'm really interested in the products that you sell and I know I'd be good at this kind of work.

(4) *Interviewer* How would you describe yourself?
You A I'm hard-working and reliable. I'm also interested in new technology.
B I have a lot of friends and I'm interested in computer games and music.

(5) *Interviewer* Have you got any experience?
You A No, not really. We did work experience at school. I worked in a hotel but that wasn't real work. And it was really boring.
B Yes. I did three weeks' work experience in a hotel. It was very interesting. For example, I learned how to talk to customers.

(6) *Interviewer* What are your weaknesses?
You A I'm not great at Maths.
B My marks in Maths weren't great last year, but my marks are better this year.

(7) *Interviewer* Now, do you have any questions about the job?
You A Yes. Could you tell me what hours I'd have to work?
B Yes. Could you tell me how long the breaks are?

(8) *Interviewer* You have to work from 8.30 to 3 o'clock and you get two 20-minute breaks. – OK? Well, that's it for today. We'll make our decision and will let you know soon.
You A OK. Thanks very much. B Can't you tell me right now? Oh well, goodbye.

(9) *Interviewer* Thanks for coming. Goodbye.
You A Goodbye and thank you very much. B See you later.

b) *Practise the interview with a partner.*

c) *You're going to take part in an interview. **Partner A** is the candidate. **Partner B** will ask the questions. **Partner C** will assess the candidate.*
Partner B: Go to p. 91.
Partner C: Go to p. 92.
Partner A: Read the role card on the right.

ROLE CARD **Partner A:**
You're going to an interview for this job:

Local football club is looking for **friendly students** to work in club shop on match days.
You will get necessary training.
Candidates should live near the stadium. **Apply now!**

HORNBY F.C.

Be ready to tell the interviewer about:
– your personal qualities
– your interests
– why you're interested in the job.
Prepare some questions:
about the pay, what you have to do, etc.

d) *Discuss the assessment. Then swap roles.* ► WB 10 (p. 21)

P2 //O REVISION Talking to the careers teacher (Indirect speech) ▸ D p. 99

Steve had an interview. Complete the text about the interview. Use the simple past.

(1) Steve told his teacher that *he was* a friendly, confident person. (2) He said that ... work in a team. (3) He added that ... lots of ideas. (4) He also said that ... working with children (5) and that ... sometimes ... babysitting. (6) He told the teacher that ... to be a childcare assistant. (7) He also said that ... favourite subjects ... Art and Maths.

(1) I'm a friendly, confident person.
(2) I can work in a team.
(3) I have lots of ideas.
(4) I like working with children.
(5) I sometimes do babysitting.
(6) I want to be a childcare assistant.
(7) My favourite subjects are Art and Maths.

P3 Exploring language Indirect speech: commands and requests • questions

a) *In the internet forum (p. 40) people report what Simon told Mani and Lucy to do. Compare what the coach said (in the speech bubbles on the left) with the sentences on the right.*

Look for clothes for the interview.
Mani, please choose a new tie.
Don't be shy!

– Simon told Mani and Lucy **to** look for clothes for the interview.
– Simon asked Mani **to** choose a new tie.
– The coach told them **not to** be shy.

b) *Report these sentences.*

1 Listen carefully to the questions, Mani. → Simon told Mani to ...
2 Lucy, please talk more. → Simon asked Lucy to ...
3 Mani, don't talk too much. → He told Mani ...
4 Say thank you at the end. → He told them both ...

c) *Now compare the questions in the speech bubbles with the indirect questions on the right. What's the same? What's different? What does 'if' mean here?*

What do you know about **my** business? — Rita asked him **what he knew** about **her** business.

Do you have any weaknesses? — Rita asked him **if he had** any weaknesses.

▸ GF 5: Indirect speech II (p. 164)

P4 Before the interview (Indirect speech: commands and requests)

Grace is going to her first job interview. Her dad has some tips for her. Write down what he said.

1 'Clean your teeth before the interview.'
Grace's dad told her to ...
2 'Don't wear too much make-up.'
He told her not to ...
3 'Please wear your other jacket.'
He asked her to ...
4 'Be polite and friendly.'
5 'Don't talk too quickly.'
6 'Smile!'
7 'Don't be nervous.'
8 'Please send me a text message after the interview.'

▸ WB 11–12 (pp. 21–22)

P5 At the travel agent's (Indirect speech: questions with question words)

a) ▸ D p. 100

Adam applied for a job at a travel agent's. He had an interview with the owner, Mrs Tay. Later Adam's friend Katy wants to know what questions Mrs Tay asked. What does Adam tell Katy? Change the tense.

1 What kind of person are you, Adam?
2 What are your favourite subjects?
3 How many languages can you speak?
4 What do you do in your free time?
5 What qualifications do you have?
6 What do you know about America?
7 What work experience do you have?
8 Why do you want to work at a travel agent's?

1 Mrs Tay asked me what kind of person I was.
2 She wanted to know what my favourite …
3 She asked me … languages I …
4 She wanted to know what I …
5 She also asked what … I …
6 She asked what I …
7 She asked what … I
8 And she asked why I …

b) ▸ D p. 100

P6 I asked her if I could get a cheap holiday (Indirect speech: yes/no questions)

Adam also told Katy about the questions he asked Mrs Tay. What did he tell her? Change the tense.

1 'Can I get a cheap holiday?'
I asked her if I could …
2 'Can I wear jeans to work?'
3 'Do you close for lunch?'
4 'Do I have to work on Saturdays?'
5 'Is the office busy on Saturdays?'
6 'Will you give me some training?'
7 'Will I get the job?'

P7 ENGLISH FOR JOBS Calling about an interview

a) Listen to the phone call. Complete the message.

Phone Message
For: *Mr White*
From: *… … called*
Message: *He wanted to check …*
tomorrow …
His phone no. is 07786 …

b) Listen to the next call. Complete Jemma's notes.

Interview time: – …
Place – … Street …
big … building
Ask for … at the … desk

▸ WB 13–16 (pp. 22–24)

HOME NEWS MUSIC SPORT SCIENCE BUSINESS

BUSINESS

How to be a teenage millionaire

September 2007

> *Before you read the article, talk about these questions:*
> – How do teenagers usually earn money?
> – Do you know anybody who has their own business?

She hasn't got a rich family. She hasn't won the lottery. But at 17, Ashley Qualls, a computer geek from Detroit, has bought a house for $250,000. So where did she get all that money? Well, this amazing teenager from Detroit has her own business and she is already a millionaire.

Ashley's idea was very simple. Her website, whateverlife.com, offers free designs that teenagers can use for their websites.

Ashley, who is known as "AshBo" to her friends, has been working with websites since she was about nine years old. While other children were watching TV or playing outside, she was teaching herself HTML[1]. She loved working with colours and web designs.

In 2004, she borrowed $8 from her mother to buy the web address: whateverlife.com. She didn't want to start a business. She just wanted a website to show her designs to her friends.

More and more people started to visit the website and download Ashley's designs. After a few weeks, she had 100 visitors. Then 5,000. Now her website has over 3,000 designs and gets over seven million visitors a month. "I used to be excited when there were two people on the site and one was me!" says Ashley.

Advertisers started to get interested in advertising on her site and in September 2005 Ashley got her first cheque from the big

[1] *HTML is a programming language that is used for websites*

Ashley with some of her friends

advertising company, Value Click Media. It was for $2,700. "It was more than I made in a month," her mother says. That was just the start. The next cheque was for $5,000, the third was for $10,000.

When the first money arrived, her mother couldn't believe it. She wasn't sure if it was really possible to make money from a website. But Ashley was confident from the start. She told her mother, "I'm really sure about this. I think it's really going to happen."

Ashley was an excellent student at her high school, but as the business got bigger, it was difficult to find time for the business and school. In January 2006, six months before her 16th birthday, she left school. She decided to continue studying from home. It was a big decision, so how did people react? "Everybody was shocked," she says. "They asked, 'Are you sure you know what you're doing?' But I had this crazy chance to do something different."

Most websites for teenagers are designed by adults. When you go to Ashley's site, it is clear that it was designed by a teenager. Ashley has a big advantage because she understands what teenagers want. "They look at me and think, 'She's my age, she must know what I like.' "

The business now brings in about $70,000 a month. (The designs are still free. The money comes from advertising.) Ashley is learning how to be the 'big boss'. Her mother now works for her as a manager and she has a business adviser who helps her too. She also pays some of her friends to work for her after school and at weekends.

It's not easy to be someone's boss and their friend. Last year one of Ashley's friends was helping her, but Ashley thought she wasn't working hard enough. Ashley says that things were difficult between them for a while, but now they are friends again and she has strict rules for everyone who works for her. "I tell them I need a minimum of 25 layouts a week to get paid," Ashley says. "It's just business."

Ashley had the right idea at the right time, and some people would say she was just lucky. But she is ambitious and determined, and she works hard. "You have to believe in yourself and believe in what you're doing," says Ashley. "These have been the best few years of my life, and also the most stressful … If people think running *WhateverLife* has always been easy, they are wrong," she adds.

Sometimes Ashley misses the normal life of a teenager. More than once she has returned to her old school, Lincoln Park High School, just for the day. Her friends will finish high school soon. "I miss the fact that I won't graduate with my friends. They're all getting excited and it's sad to know I won't be a part of that exact moment."

And the future? Ashley hasn't got any definite plans. She wants to go to college, and she's thinking of going to design school in New York, which she calls her "dream city".

Working with the text

1 The story

a) *Match the sentence halves about Ashley.*

1 Ashley Qualls is only 17 years old, but ...
2 Teenagers can download Ashley's designs ...
3 When she was nine, Ashley began to ...
4 Ashley's website became popular very quickly and ...
5 Ashley started to earn money when ...
6 Ashley's website is popular with teenagers because ...
7 Ashley's relationship with some of her friends is special because ...
8 Ashley is not sure about her future,

a advertising companies got interested in her website.
b from her website.
c it now gets over seven million visitors a month.
d but she would like to go to design school in New York City.
e she's already got her own internet company.
f she knows what they like.
g she's their boss.
h teach herself HTML.

b) *All of these sentences are true. But which sums up the article best?*

1 Ashley is the big boss and her friends and family work for her.
2 People were surprised when Ashley left school at 15 because she was a good student.
3 Ashley's business started as a hobby, but she worked hard and now she's very successful.
4 Ashley's website is popular because her designs are free.

2 The person

a) *How would you describe Ashley? Use at least three words from the box. Find examples in the text to support your answer.*

ambitious • artistic • determined • easy-going • energetic • greedy • hard-working • organized

I think she is hard-working because in the text it says that she started when she was nine years old.
...

b) *Find at least four facts that show the positive and negative side of Ashley's success. Take notes.*

+ Ashley's success	–
she is rich	...
...	

c) *Would you like Ashley's life? Tell a partner what you think.*

I'd like to... / But I wouldn't want to...
– study at home / earn lots of money
– pay my friends to work for me / be the boss
– work so hard / have no time to relax / ...
To sum up I would/wouldn't like Ashley's life.

3 Extra Your comment

Write a comment about Ashley Qualls' story for this internet forum.

Today at 13:32 Chris wrote:
Ashley's story is very interesting. She's a role model for young people.

By Lea at 14:01: I don't agree. I don't think she's a role model. She's just a lucky person. We only read about her because she has lots of money. There are lots of young people who are much better role models. I'd like to read about young people who are trying to help other people.

By Maria at 14:24: I disagree with Lea. It wasn't luck. Ashley is successful because she is determined and she works hard. Well done, Ashley! You're a role model for me.

By ...: ...

► Text File 5 (p. 117) • WB 17 (p. 24)

How am I doing?

► SF Check yourself (p. 136)

a) *Find or choose the correct answers.*

Describing personal qualities

1 Use an adjective from the box for the underlined words. There are more adjectives in the box than you need.

ambitious • calm • cheeky • energetic • greedy • logical • punctual • reliable

a) She's very active.
b) She's a person who does what she promises.
c) He's a little bit rude, but in a funny way.
d) I'm someone who wants to be successful.
e) They're never late for anything.

2 Complete the sentences with the two adjectives that are best for a hotel job.
a) I'd say that I'm a ... and ... person.
A calm B cheeky C organized
b) In this job you have to be ... and ...
A informal B punctual C reliable
c) He's successful because he's ... and ...
A energetic B technical C confident

Grammar

3 Ms Hall phoned Lena Dickhaus. Report what she said in indirect speech.
a) 'Come for an interview next week.'
– Ms Hall asked Lena ...
b) 'Don't worry if next week isn't possible.'
– Ms Hall told Lena ...
c) 'Can you come in two weeks?'
– Ms Hall asked if Lena ...
d) 'Do you need directions for getting to the office building?'
– Ms Hall asked if Lena ...

Words

4 What's the English word for ...?
a) Krankenpfleger/in, Krankenschwester
b) Mechaniker/in
c) Reisebürokaufmann/–frau
d) Kindergärtner/in
e) Kundenbetreuer/in, –berater/in
f) Fitnesstrainer/in

CVs

5 Name four headings you can use in a CV.

Letters of application

6 Start a letter of application with **Dear Sir or Madam** when ...
A you know B you don't know the name of the person you're writing to.

7 Say where you found out about the job ...
A at the beginning of the letter.
B at the end of the letter.

8 When you're writing, use ...
A short verb forms (I'm, I don't, etc.).
B long verb forms (I am, I do not, etc.).

9 Saying something about your personal qualities is ...
A usually a good idea.
B something you should never do.

10 Always enclose your ...
A CV. B photo and one of your family.

11 When you know the name of the person you're writing to, end the letter with ...
A Yours faithfully ...
B Yours sincerely ...

b) *Check your answers on p. 231 and add up your points.*

c) *If you had 22 or more points, well done! Maybe you can help students who had fewer points. If you had 21 points or fewer, it's a good idea to do some more work before you go on to the next unit. Where did you make mistakes? The chart below will tell you what you can do to improve your English.*

No.	Areas	Find out more	Exercises
1– 2	Personal qualities	Unit 2 (pp. 32–35)	P 3 (p. 36), WB 3–4, p. 17
3	Indirect speech II	Exploring language (p. 42), GF 5 (p. 164)	P 4–6 (pp. 42–43), WB 12–14, pp. 22–23
4	Words	Vocabulary (pp. 176–179)	P 1–2 (p. 36), WB 15, p. 23
5–11	CV, letter of application	Part B (p. 38), SF (pp. 152–153)	P 1–2 (p. 39), WB 8–9, p. 20

► Self-evaluation 1–2 WB (p. 25) • **Skills check 2** WB (pp. 26–31)

Pick of the day

OUR LIVES | **2.00 pm** | **W3FM Radio**

In this new series, teenagers from all over the world answer questions about their lives. This week we hear from Keira, Connor and Lina.

Radio MONDAY

Keira (left), **15**,
lives in Kent, England

Tell us about your family life.
I'm an only child. I get on OK with my parents. They're quite relaxed.

What are your hobbies?
I love shopping. I buy lots of shoes. At the moment I'm mad about boots. I've got blue boots, black boots ... My favourite boots are white. They look great! – No really, it's true. They look really cool!

What do you like most in your life and what would you change?
My friends are very important to me. Keisha and Emma are my two best friends. If I have a problem – like with a boy – I talk to my friends. I text them all the time. I'm just sending Emma a text now while I'm talking to you! – What would I change? I'd like more pocket money!

Tell us about school.
School's OK. It's a bit boring sometimes.

What's your ideal job?
Mum says I should get a job where I have to talk on the phone a lot!

Connor, 16,
lives in Galway, Ireland

Tell us about your family life.
My parents are very annoying! They want me to work hard at school and get lots of qualifications. All they talk about is school.

What are your hobbies?
I'm crazy about computer games and music. I'm in a band with some friends from school. I play the guitar and sing.

What do you like most in your life and what would you change?
The best thing is hanging out with my mates. What would I change? I'd like to organize my time better so I have more time to do the things I want to do. And I'd like my parents to be less strict.

What about school?
Some of the lessons are OK. I like Art and English.

What's your ideal job?
I want to be a rock star! If I can't do that, I'd like to be a computer games designer.

Lina, 17,
is from Ife, Nigeria

Tell us about your family life.
I have four sisters and two brothers. My father is a mechanic. My mother is a businesswoman who sells bags at the market.

What are your hobbies?
I like reading and listening to music, but I don't get much time for hobbies. When I finish school I help Mum at the market, then I go home to study.

What do you like most in your life and what would you change?
I love my school. I've got lots of friends there. My favourite subjects are Science and Maths. There aren't enough books for every student at our school. It would be nice to have more books and computers.

Tell us more about school.
On school days I get up at 5 am. It takes me an hour to walk to school. School starts at 7.45 and ends at 2 pm but I do extra classes after school until 5 pm. Our teachers are excellent and they help me a lot.

What's your ideal job?
I'd like to be a teacher.

In the next programme in the series, we hear from three more teenagers: Drew, Elin and Adnan.

Drew, 17,
from Eugene, Oregon in the US

Elin, 16,
from the small town of Eno in Finland

Adnan, 17,
was born in Bosnia, but now lives in Cardiff, Wales

1 Teen lives

a) *Read about Keira, Connor or Lina. Choose one of them and take notes on a copy of this chart.*

	Keira	
Family	parents relaxed	
Interests	shopping, friends	
Problems	...	
School		
Future plans		

b) *Work in a group of three and tell the others about Keira, Connor or Lina.*

2 Drew, Elin and Adnan

a) *Listen to the next programme of the radio series 'Our lives'. Who is most likely to say the following things?*

1 Traditions are very important.
2 I got into trouble when I was younger, but I've changed.
3 I don't argue a lot with my parents now.
4 I miss my father.
5 My parents aren't very happy with me.
6 I want to change a lot in my life.

b) *Work in a group of five. Give each member of the group a heading from the chart in* **1** *(Family, Interests, ...). Listen again and take notes on your heading for Drew, Elin and Adnan. At the end put your notes together.*

3 Now you

a) *Talk about the six teenagers. Who did you find the most interesting and why?*

b) *You want to write to one of the six teenagers. Before you start, make notes about yourself. Use a chart or a mind map for your notes.*

more help ► D p. 100

c) *Use your notes to write an e-mail or a letter to one of the teenagers. Explain how your life is similar or different to theirs.*
You can put your text in your DOSSIER.

► SF Writing informal letters (p. 153) • WB 1 (p. 32)

MOBILE TEENS

1

Can you live without your mobile phone?

by Lily Brown

> *Before you read the article: What do you use your mobile phone for? Make a list.*

MY MOBILE is my best friend! I use it to communicate with all my mates, to find out what's happening and generally to organize my life.

I cried when my last phone died. (I was cycling on the road and it fell under a car.) And if I leave home without my mobile phone in my pocket, I just don't feel right. With it, I feel safe and I don't get bored. Without it, I feel lost.

So, could I live without my mobile phone? New research has shown that 13 million people in Britain have got 'nomophobia' (the fear of having no mobile phone). Am I one of them? To find out, I gave up my mobile for a day. This is what happened.

LATE FOR SCHOOL

Arrghhh! My mobile is also my alarm clock. I wake up half an hour AFTER the bus leaves. Not a good start.

I CAN'T COMMUNICATE

I run out of the house. My friend always waits for me at the bus stop. I'll just call to tell her I'll be ... oh no, I can't.

I FORGOT!

Today is my big sister's birthday. As usual I forgot to send her a card. I'll text her and ... no phone! Sorry big sis!

WAITING FOR MY BOYFRIEND

I wait for my boyfriend to meet me outside the school. Where is he? He isn't usually late. But after nearly half an hour he doesn't arrive. I give up and go home. It's SO annoying when you don't know what's happening!

HOT NEWS!

Wow! I just saw Alex and Emily near the park ... together ... hand in hand!! Isn't she going out with Jamie? Hmm, this is very interesting. I must tell someone!
I can't use my mobile, so I find a phone box (not easy) and then find some money (also not easy). Next problem, I don't know anyone's phone number! The hot news will have to wait.

BACK HOME

I'm back at home and feeling bored. The phone rings. 'Where are you?' It's my boyfriend. He's at the shopping centre with some of our mates. He sent me a text this afternoon ... I'm not happy. Not happy at all!

So, have I got nomophobia? I think I have! I can't live without my mobile phone, not even for one day!

> *What does the writer use her mobile for? Does she use it for the same things as you?*
>
> ▸ *SF Reading course (pp. 144–145)*

Are you addicted to your mobile?

	yes	no
1 Is it OK to send a text message while you are talking to somebody?	☐	☐
2 Is it OK to talk on a mobile in a café or restaurant?	☐	☐
3 Would you read or write text messages if you were at a wedding or a funeral?	☐	☐
4 Is it OK to film someone or take a photo of them secretly with your mobile?	☐	☐
5 Do you feel safer if you have your mobile with you when you are out late?	☐	☐
6 Would you feel unwanted if a whole day went by and your mobile phone did not ring?	☐	☐
7 Is it OK to write or read a text message during lessons at school?	☐	☐
8 Have you ever made or received calls that you don't want your parents to know about?	☐	☐
9 Have you ever asked someone out by text message?	☐	☐
10 Have you ever dumped your girlfriend/boyfriend by text message?	☐	☐

Have you answered **YES** to all these questions? Then perhaps you are addicted!

2 Now you

a) *Answer the questions in the questionnaire.*

b) *How many times did you answer YES? Do you think you're addicted to your mobile phone? Why (not)?*

c) *Compare your answers in a group.*

– I answered ... to question 1/2/...
  What did you answer?
– Oh, I had the same answer as you.
  My answer was different. I ...
– I (don't) think it's OK to ... because ...
  What about you?
– I agree/don't agree ... because ...
– I've never read/written/sent/...
  What about you?
– I've done it once/a couple of times/lots.
– ...

d) *Put together the results for your group or your class. How many people in your group/class are addicted to their mobile phones?*

3 Extra You and your phone

Give up your phone for a day. Then write a short article about what happens.

or

Write a short text about why you could/couldn't give up your phone for the day. You can put your text in your DOSSIER.

► SF Writing course (pp. 150–151)

"YES JASON, YOU MAY GO TO THE LAVATORY, BUT NEXT TIME JUST RAISE YOUR HAND."

lavatory = toilet

► WB 2 (p. 32)

EVERYDAY ENGLISH

P1 SPEAKING Say what you think

a) *Read this letter to the editor about the article* **Can you live without your mobile phone?** *on p. 50. Do you agree with the writer or not? Why (not)?*

33 Garden St
Bristol
BS1 6NJ

Bristol Evening Post
Bristol BF99 7HD

25 March 2011

Dear Sir or Madam

I am writing in reply to the article 'Can you live without your mobile phone?' in yesterday's paper. I have to say that the article made me laugh, but it also made me cross. In my opinion it is true that many people are addicted to their mobiles.

I think we all use mobiles too much. When you sit on the train or bus, nobody chats to each other. Everybody is too busy pressing buttons on their mobile. If people chat, they don't do it face to face. They do it on the phone! I get really annoyed if I am sitting next to someone on the bus and I have to listen to their conversation.

I'm fed up with other people and their mobiles. I think mobiles should be banned from buses, trains and all public places!

Yours faithfully

Jonathan Whitbred

Jonathan Whitbred

b) *Prepare to tell a partner what you think of the letter. Make notes. You can use these phrases:*

- I don't agree with the writer at all. First/Second ...
- I agree with the writer of the letter completely, for example ...
- I think it's correct/stupid to say that ... because ...
- When I read the letter about banning mobiles, I felt angry/I had to laugh/... because ...
- In my opinion it's (not) true that ... – I read an article that said ...
- I can/can't understand why the writer gets annoyed when ...
- I think it's a good/ridiculous idea to ban mobiles from public places because ...

c) *Sit in a double circle. Tell two or three different partners what you think about the letter. React to your partners' opinions.*

P2 WRITING A letter to the editor

Read the article **Can you live without your mobile phone?** *on p. 50 again. Write a letter to the editor of the newspaper. In your letter:*

- *Say what you think of the article (interesting/boring/...). Give reasons.*
- *Describe what you and your friends use your phones for.*
- *Do you think it's possible to be addicted to your phone? Give your opinion.*

Tip

This is a formal letter, so follow the rules for formal letter writing, for example:
- Use the correct phrases for the beginning and ending of the letter.
- Don't forget your name and address, or the paper won't print your letter!

▸ *SF Writing formal letters (p. 153) • SF Correcting your text (p. 151) • WB 3–4 (p. 33)*

P3 WORDS You and your mobile

a) *Complete the dialogue with the correct form of the phrases from the box.*

(to) call (2×) • (to) check the time • (to) check sb.'s mailbox • contacts • (to) download • +(to) miss a call • ringtone • +(to) save sb.'s phone number • (to) text • text (message)

A: That ... sounds great. Where did you get it?
B: I ... it from this cool website.
A: Have you got the website address?
B: No, not here. I've got it at home.
A: ... me the address when you get home. Anyway, so who is the ... from?
B: Oh, hang on, it's from Chloe. Oh, no, she's waiting at the wrong place.
A: Well, ... her and tell her to come here.
B: I can't. I haven't got any money on my phone.
A: Let's see if I've ... in my ... – Yes, here it is. I'll ... her right now. Oh, wait, it says here that I've ... – I'll just ... to see who it was.
B: Who was it?
A: My mum. I'll phone her back later. OK, so I'll tell Chloe to meet us here. I'll just ... – It's 5:30 now. So let's meet at 6 o'clock, OK?
B: Yeah, that's OK.

b) ▸ D p. 101

P4 ENGLISH FOR JOBS Useful phrases

a) *Listen to dialogues 1–3. Match them to the photos below.*

A A shop assistant in a mobile shop

B A customer adviser in a bank

C A waiter in a restaurant

b) *Listen again. Who uses these phrases? – Which phrases could you use in any of these jobs?*

- **A** The exchange rate is ... to the pound.
- **B** How do you want to pay – cash or credit card?
- **C** What would you like to drink?
- **D** How do you want your money? Is a 20 euro note OK?
- **E** Of course you can – if the phone isn't blocked.
- **F** Would you like anything else?
- **G** Can you enter your PIN, please.
- **H** Are you ready to order?
- **I** How can I help you?
- **J** That's 15 euros, please.
- **K** There's your receipt.
- **L** What can I do for you?

c) *Choose one of the situations below and prepare a dialogue. Then present it to your group or class.*

A: You're a shop assistant in a mobile shop.
B: You want to buy a cheap mobile phone.

A: You're a customer adviser in a bank.
B: You want to change some Australian dollars (2 AUS dollar = 1 euro) into euros.

A: You're the waiter.
B: You want to order two pieces of apple cake and two hot chocolates in a café.

▸ WB 5–6 (pp. 33–34)

more help ▸ D p. 101

TEENS IN TROUBLE

1

ASBO boy

By Jeremy Armstrong

When SHANE Preston from Darlington (in the North-East of England) was 14, he was a bored troublemaker.

He kicked footballs against his neighbours' houses and cars. He caused trouble at school. He rode motorbikes on the pavement and got into fights with other teenagers.

ASBO

Things got so bad that Shane was given a four-year antisocial behaviour order (ASBO) as a punishment. He was banned from some areas of his town. He was not allowed to leave home between 9 pm and 7 am and the police sent his photo to hundreds of houses in the area.
His mum says: 'It was difficult for him. He saw other kids having fun outside, and he had to stay indoors and watch TV with me. When he saw the posters with his name and photo stuck up in town, it was really bad.'

'When he saw posters with his photo stuck up in town, it was really bad.'
Mum, Paula

Three years later

Some people think that ASBOs are a bad idea, but the surprising thing is that it worked for Shane.
Now, three years later, Shane is 17 and reliable and hard-working. He has volunteered with the YMCA and helped to build a children's play area. He has trained as a builder and he's looking for his first job. 'I've grown up,' Shane says. 'The ASBO has helped me because it has kept me out of trouble. I used to be one of those kids hanging around in front of shops. But that's over and I've got new friends now.'

Who gets ASBOs?

ASBOs are given to people who:

- spray or write graffiti
- say racist things
- make too much noise late at night
- steal or shoplift
- drink in the street
- bully or threaten other people
- drive without a licence
- break windows, vandalize cars, gardens or parks
- fight or attack other people.

What is an ASBO?

ASBOs are given by the courts.
They are lists of rules for troublemakers.
Sometimes there are rules about who they can and can't meet. Often there are places where they can't go.
Some people aren't allowed to meet with more than one person at a time.
Sometimes their name and photo is put on posters in the area or is sent to the neighbours.
If someone breaks the rules, they can go to prison.

1 *What did Shane do wrong? How was he punished?*
2 *What was the worst thing about the punishment for him? What do* ***you*** *think was the worst thing?*
3 *How has Shane's life changed since he got the ASBO?*
4 *Do you think ASBOs would be a good idea in Germany? Give reasons. Discuss in class.*

► *SF Reading course (pp. 144–145)* • **Text File 6** *(pp. 118–120)* • *WB 7 (p. 34)*

2 Extra Your opinion: Gallery walk

a) *Make six groups. Each group gets a statement from the list. Write it on a piece of paper. Discuss the statement, write a short comment on it and put the piece of paper on the classroom wall.*

We think this is a good / bad idea because …
We can / can't understand how it can stop antisocial behaviour. This means that …

b) *Move to the other statements with your group. Discuss them and add your ideas.*

We agree / disagree with this comment because …
Yes, but what about …?

c) *Return to your own statement and discuss the other groups' comments on your statement.*

1. *Local papers should print photos of teenagers who cause trouble.*
2. *Teenagers shouldn't be allowed to meet in groups on the street or outside shops.*
3. *Teenagers aren't as bad as some adults think they are.*
4. *All 16-year olds should be at home before 9 pm.*
5. *People under 21 years old should not be allowed to drink alcohol.*
6. *The reason that teenagers cause problems is that there isn't enough for them to do.*

3 VIEWING High school boot camp

High school boot camp is a film about the Eagle Academy, a military-style school in Florida. Teenagers in trouble volunteer to go there for six months – no one makes them go. Here is what one of them said before he went to the boot camp:

> Dave Murray:
> Right now I'm screwing up, erm, not listening to no one. What I expect to get out of this camp is to get bigger, stronger and straighten up my life.

a) *What do you think might happen at a boot camp? Brainstorm ideas in a group.*

► *SF Brainstorming (p. 148)*

b) *Watch **part 1** of the DVD about the boys' first day at the camp. How do you feel about what goes on there? Say as much as you can about the boys, the drill instructors and the camp. The words in the box might help you.*

> awful • crazy • funny • loud • nervous • quiet • scared • scary • shocked • shocking • stupid • terrified • unfriendly • …

What was the most shocking bit for you?

c) *Watch **part 1** again. In your group make a list of what happens. Then choose one interesting thing about the boot camp from your list. Explain why you think it happens there.*

d) *Watch **part 2** about the boys' last day at the camp. Do they feel good or bad about their time there? List as many of their reasons as you can.*

e) *Look back at what Dave Murray said at the beginning. Do you think boot camps really help people like him to 'straighten up' their lives? Why (not)? Here are some ideas:*

> learn discipline • learn to follow rules • learn something/nothing for their life • discipline is important if you want to do well • can/can't change a person • get really fit • forget everything after they leave • following orders is a good thing • don't think for themselves • stay out of trouble • …

SPEAKING COURSE Part 3

P1 SPEAKING That's a good point! (Having a discussion)

▸ SF p. 147

a) *Collect arguments for and against boot camps. Look back at p. 55 if you need ideas.*

FOR	AGAINST
– boot camps help people to stay out of trouble	– kids forget about boot camps and get in trouble again
– ...	– ...

b) *Match the phrases in the box to the steps in the discussion process.*

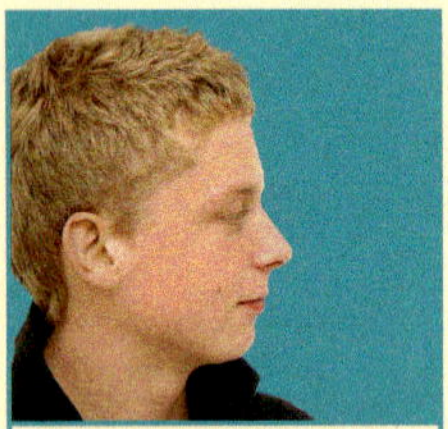

1 Expressing an opinion
2 Giving reasons and examples
3 Asking for clarification
4 Agreeing
5 Disagreeing

... because ... • Could you say that again? • Don't forget that ... • First .../Second .../And finally ... • For example ... • I agree (with you). • I don't think you can say ... • I see what you mean but ... • I think/I feel ... • In my opinion ... • Just think of/remember ... • Let me explain ... • No, that's not right. • Sorry, I don't agree with you. • Sorry, but I don't understand what you mean. • That's a good point! • That's true • That's why ... • Yes, but ... • You're right.

c) *Listen to a classroom discussion at an American high school. Which of the phrases from b) can you hear in the discussion?*

d) *Use your arguments from a) and the phrases from b) to continue the discussion you've just heard. One of you should argue FOR, one AGAINST. Talk for about four minutes.*

e) *Assess your performance in the discussion. Give yourself points out of 5. If you haven't given yourself many points, think about how you could improve.*

Assessment sheet	☹		😐		☺
	1	2	3	4	5
I talked enough in the discussion.					
I used some discussion phrases.					
I asked my partner what he/she thought.					
I listened to my partner carefully.					
If I didn't understand, I asked for clarification.					

f) Extra *Try a fishbowl discussion.*
Put five chairs in a circle. Four people should sit down, leaving one chair empty. They should start a discussion about boot camps.
Other people should watch the discussion and join in when they can. The empty chair is for them.
At the end of the discussion the class should assess how the discussion went.

g) ▸ D p. 102

▸ WB 8 (p. 35)

P2 I/O WORDS A worrying time

► D p. 102

Complete the text with the correct adjectives.

Kelly was a clever girl who was (bored/boring) at school, so it wasn't (surprised/surprising) that she often got into trouble there. When she was 16 she decided she didn't want to go to 'that (bored/boring) old school' any more. Kelly tried to find an (interested/interesting) job, but it was difficult. Companies weren't (interested/interesting) in her because she didn't have qualifications or experience. Kelly found a job in the end, but her mother wasn't (surprised/surprising) when she gave that up. It was a very (worrying/worried) time for Kelly's mother. She didn't know how to help Kelly. Then a new club for teenagers started in the area. When Kelly came back from the first meeting she was very (excited/exciting). The leaders had really (excited/exciting) plans for the youth group. Kelly's mother was happier.

P3 Additional information Boy writing graffiti (Understanding participle clauses)

Look at these two examples from p. 54 (sentences in red). The blue sentences mean the same.

He saw other kids having fun outside. = He saw other kids who were having fun outside.
He saw the posters stuck up in town. = He saw the posters that were stuck up in town.

What do the sentences 1–5 mean? Choose A or B. Explain your answer.

1 I saw a boy writing graffiti on the wall.
A I was writing graffiti.
B The boy was writing graffiti.

2 The graffiti written by the boy was very ugly.
A The graffiti was ugly.
B The boy was ugly.

3 Then I saw a woman talking to the boy.
A I was talking to a woman.
B The woman was talking to the boy.

4 The woman talking to the boy was a police officer.
A The woman was a police officer.
B The police officer was talking to the woman.

5 The graffiti written on the wall was cleaned the next day.
A The graffiti was written the next day.
B The graffiti was cleaned the next day.

► GF 6: Participle clauses (p. 165)

P4 WORDS Problem teenagers

a) *Partner B: Go to p. 92.*
Partner A: Read the definitions to your partner. He/She should say which phrase – A, B or C – is the closest in meaning. Say if you agree with your partner's answer. (Check the answers on p. 103.)

1 When you threaten someone who is not as strong as you ...
A you bully them. B you attack them.
C you get into a fight.

2 When you do something illegal ...
A you follow the rules.
B you break the law.
C you stay out of trouble.

3 If you are in a gang ...
A you belong to a group.
B you get an ASBO. C you go to prison.

4 Antisocial behaviour means ...
A you help people. B you make trouble.
C you don't like to meet people.

5 When you stand in the street and do nothing much ...
A you stay out of trouble.
B you hang around. C you cause trouble.

b) *Listen to your partner. Talk like this:*
– Can you read the possible answers again?
– I don't think B is right. That means ...
– I think A is closest.

► WB 9–10 (p. 36)

GET INVOLVED

1 Volunteering in the US

Volunteering is great for the community, and it's good for you too. You learn new skills, meet new people, get work experience, work in a team, and feel good about yourself. You can also have a lot of fun, as these two online reports from young volunteers show.

http://www.volunteermanatee.org/manateens.html

Volunteer Manatee

ABOUT US | PRODUCTS & SERVICES | PARTNERS | NEWS

PROGRAMS

ManaTEEN Projects

The ManaTEEN Club in Florida is one of the nation's largest teen volunteer programs with over 10,000 teen members. They do more than 1.7 million hours of volunteer work.

Springs Clean-up

Together with some of my ManaTEEN friends, I recently went to the ManaTEEN SOS project at Weeki Wachee Springs. What an experience it was!
We snorkeled through the crystal clear water and collected trash, like bottles, glass, and plastic. So much trash is thrown into the springs. It's such a shame! I pulled up a huge piece of clear glass. It was hard to see and it could have easily cut someone's foot badly! We had a competition to see who could pick up the most trash. I was beaten by my best friend, but that was OK. After a pizza break, we all jumped back in the water and continued our work. Of course trash isn't the only thing that is found at Weeki Wachee Springs. There are lots of beautiful fish and I even saw a turtle. This was my favorite ManaTEEN Club project! – Patrick

hickoryrecord.com

Powered by: Hickory Daily Record — FOR YOU. ABOUT YOU. EVERY DAY. 24 HOURS A DAY.

Hickory Soup Kitchen

This summer, we have been raising money for the Hickory Soup Kitchen, so others can have something to eat. We both like helping and wanted to get more involved.
To raise money we have mainly been to two churches. Lots of people have given money. During vacation Bible school, we held a competition to see who could bring in the most money, so a lot of coins and dollar bills have been collected. All together we've raised $427.
We decided to spend half our money on meat, because the kitchen doesn't get a lot of meat – it costs so much. And we got ketchup and canned vegetables because the soup kitchen is running low on those things. When we heard that, we thought something must be done. We've taken all the food to one of the churches where it can be stored overnight. It will be given to the Hickory Soup Kitchen tomorrow. – Alex & Andrew

1. *Describe the community service that the American students do.*
2. *What reasons do they give for doing community service?*
3. *What do you think they have learned from their experience?*
4. *What kind of community service can young people do in your town or area?*

P1 STUDY SKILLS From outline to written discussion

a) *Collect arguments*

Collect arguments for (or against) the statement below. You can brainstorm your ideas in a group.

German school students should have to do ten hours of community service every year.

FOR	AGAINST
• students can learn new skills • they can meet new people • …	• students don't have time • there are no projects in this area • …

▸ *SF Brainstorming (p. 148)*

STUDY SKILLS A written discussion

In a written discussion you present arguments for or against a statement and draw conclusions. Before you start writing, you should write an **outline**. It helps you to organize the ideas for the discussion in your text. Here is an example for an outline:

1 Introduction
2 Arguments FOR or AGAINST
2.1 First argument
2.2 Second argument
2.3 …
3 Conclusion

▸ *SF From outline to written discussion (p. 154)*

b) *Use an outline to organize your arguments.*

Decide if you personally are for or against the statement. Then write a three-part outline using the arguments you collected in a).

c) *Write a text*

1 **Introduction**

First introduce the problem you are going to write about. Start with a personal experience or a general statement or a question.

People often say that young people don't do anything for the community. Well, I decided to change that. I work as a volunteer in …
In my experience …

When I read articles about community service in America, it sounds quite interesting. But is it a good idea for teenagers in Germany? – I think …

2 **Presenting your arguments**

Present different arguments in a logical order. For each argument keep the following three steps in mind:
– Give your argument
– Give reasons for your argument
– Give examples to support your argument.

First … / Second … / Another argument for / against … is … / Finally …
… because … / So … / That's why …
For example, … / A good example of … is …

3 **Conclusion**

In your conclusion you usually present your own opinion. Don't give new arguments.

To sum up I think that German students should have to do community service. In my opinion they should do more than ten hours …

To sum up, there are a number of arguments against the idea that … – I think …

d) Extra ● *Find arguments for or against one of these statements. Write an outline. Then write your text.*
– German students should wear school uniforms.
– Teenagers shouldn't have a TV in their room.

▸ *SF Correcting your text (p. 151)* • *WB 11 (p. 37)*

P 2 Exploring language | The passive

a) The passive is used when what happens to something or to someone is important. Often we don't know who caused the action or it's not important (like in sentence 1).

1 So much trash is thrown into the springs. 2 I was beaten by my best friend.

b) Look at the passive sentences from p. 58.

1 A lot of coins and dollar bills	have been collected.	
2 ... we thought something	must be done.	
3 The food	can be stored	there overnight.
4 It	will be given	to the Hickory Soup Kitchen tomorrow.

Complete the rules:

1 The passive in the **present perfect** is formed with: have + ... + past participle.

2 The passive with **must**, **can** and **will** is formed with ..., ... or ... + ... + ...

▸ GF 7: Passive (p. 166)

P 3 //O REVISION Lots of good work is done (Passive: simple present/simple past)

▸ D p. 102

Complete the sentences. Use the passive.

1 In America young people ... (expect) to work as volunteers.
In America young people are ...
2 Beautiful fish and turtles ... (find) at Weeki Wachee Springs in Florida.
3 Unfortunately bottles, glass and plastic ... (throw) in the water too.
4 At the last Springs Clean-up lots of trash ... (collect) by the volunteers.
At the last Springs Clean-up lots of trash was ...
5 Lots of pizzas ... (eat) by the volunteers in their break.
6 Alex and Andrew heard that money ... (need) to buy food for the Hickory Soup Kitchen.
7 Half of Alex and Andrew's money ... (spend) on meat.
8 The rest of the money ... (use) to buy vegetables and ketchup.

P 4 Discos will be held ... at the youth centre (Passive: will future/modals)

The youth centre has a lot of information and rules for visitors. Make sentences in the passive.

1 Discos ... (will – hold) once a month.
2 Table tennis ... (can – play) in the garden.
3 DVDs ... (can – watch) in the TV room.
4 The toilets ... (must – clean) every day.
5 Rubbish ... (must – throw) in rubbish bins.
6 The games room ... (should – tidy) daily.
7 The age of all visitors ... (will – check).
8 This year's rock concert ... (will – hold) in July.
9 A film night ... (will – organize) next Friday.
10 Alcohol ... (must – not bring) into the centre.

▸ WB 12–13 (pp. 37–38)

P5 Today's police report (Passive: present perfect)

a) Complete the policeman's report.

1 a statue • (steal) • from the museum
A statue has been stolen from the museum.
2 two shop windows • (break) • in High Street
3 the station wall • (spray) • with graffiti
4 a student • (attack) • on the way to school
5 four mobiles • (steal) • at Oldham School
6 two telephone boxes • (vandalize) • in Bond Street
7 lots of rubbish • (throw) • into the river
8 three handbags • (steal) • at the railway the station

b) *Write a short report on antisocial behaviour at your school (at least five sentences). You could start like the example on the right.*

So far this year there's been a lot / hasn't been much antisocial behaviour at ...
Quite a few / No bikes have been ...

P6 MEDIATION Volunteering in Germany

You're thinking of doing a Freiwilliges Soziales Jahr. You've found an online brochure and want to tell an American e-mail friend about it.

- Give some examples of the jobs you can do.
- Say where you can do community service.
- Explain how it will help you in the future.

Ein Beitrag für sich und die Gesellschaft

Aus freien Stücken anderen helfen. Behinderte Menschen im Alltag unterstützen. Im Naturschutzpark Nistkästen anbringen und Fußwege sauberhalten. Im Jugendklub eine Disco organisieren oder einen Musik-Workshop vorbereiten. Mit alten Menschen mal einen Spaziergang unternehmen. In Russland in einem Kinderheim arbeiten. Im Sportverein Kids das Dribbeln beibringen. Sportspiele im Schulhort organisieren. Oder auf der Open-Air-Bühne mit Kindern Griffe auf der Rockgitarre üben – das und vieles mehr ist möglich im Freiwilligen Sozialen Jahr (FSJ) – oder im Freiwilligen Ökologischen Jahr (FÖJ). Dem freiwilligen Engagement sind keine Grenzen gesetzt und auch im Ausland gibt es zahlreiche Möglichkeiten.
Wer sich dafür entscheidet, zwischen Schule und Ausbildung einen Freiwilligendienst zu absolvieren, bekommt oft mehr als nur eine berufliche Orientierung. Erste Fachkenntnisse und die erworbenen sozialen Kompetenzen machen junge Menschen fit für den Berufseinstieg und erhöhen ihre Beschäftigungschancen. Zugleich tut es gut, sich für andere einzusetzen und Verantwortung zu übernehmen. Manch einer sammelt dabei die ersten Auslandserfahrungen. Von dem einjährigen Engagement profitieren also beide Seiten: die jungen Freiwilligen und die Gesellschaft.

Quelle: Bundesministerium für Familie, Senioren, Frauen und Jugend

▸ SF Mediation (p. 155) • SF Paraphrasing (p. 148) • WB 14–15 (pp. 38–39)

The caller by Robert D. San Souci (adapted)

Look at the pictures. What do you think the story is about? What kind of story do you think this is?

▸ *SF Reading stories (p. 143)*

It was hot at Aunt Margaret's funeral. Lindsay was uncomfortable in her black dress.

She was angry because she *should* be with her best friend, Missy, getting ready for a party.

Lindsay's father's cellphone rang. Everyone looked. He went red and turned it off.

At the end of the funeral, Lindsay went behind a tree, and called Missy's number. It was busy. Lindsay was not happy. Her friend was probably making plans for the party with Noelle or Candice.

She went back to her mother, who wanted her to talk to some boring old ladies. She had to nod and look sad as they talked about her aunt. Her father was talking on his phone. When he finished, Lindsay asked, "Can we go now?"

"I just have to make one more call," her father said.

Lindsay said to her mother, "Please, please make Daddy get off the phone so we can go!"

"Stop complaining," her mother said. But she told Lindsay and her brothers, Darren and David, to go to the car. Then she went over to her husband. He ended his call. "All right, all right, let's go," he said.

Some people came to Lindsay's house and talked about how nice Aunt Margaret had been.

"But she could get angry," said Lindsay's father, laughing. "She could be terrible if she thought someone was rude or unkind or if she thought someone was lying."

When the people left, Lindsay ran to her room to change her clothes for the party. She took out Aunt Margaret's gold ring with real diamonds. She had always loved it, and Aunt Margaret had promised it to her before she died. Her mother had told her to only wear the ring at special times. Well, showing the ring off to Missy, Noelle and Candice was special!

Her cellphone rang.

A tired, old voice said, "Lindsay, dear, this is Aunt Margaret."

"Right! Nice try, Missy! Guys, I'll see you in a few minutes." Lindsay hung up and put her phone into her party bag. She put her ring in her pocket so her parents wouldn't see and ran down the stairs.

"Where's Dad? He said he would drive me to Missy's."

"He's looking for his phone in the car," her mother said. "It fell out of his pocket."

Lindsay went out and helped her father, but they couldn't find the phone.

At Missy's party, all the girls were jealous of the real diamonds shining on Lindsay's finger. She forgot about the phone joke.

Her cellphone rang.

She heard the same, old voice saying, "Lindsay, this is Aunt Margaret. I must talk to you."

OK, so it wasn't her friends. She whispered to them, "It's my horrible brothers. They want

me to think it's my aunt's ghost ... Is it *really* you, Aunt Margaret?" asked Lindsay. She tried to sound scared.

"Yes. I just wanted to hear your voice again. You were my favorite. You loved me best."

Lindsay looked at the ring as she talked. "Well, it was really your ring I loved. I hated going to see you in that old people's home. I only came because I wanted your ring. Goodbye, Aunt Margaret!" Lindsay ended the call.

She checked the phone. Her brothers were calling from her father's cellphone. They must have found it in the car.

Lindsay was spending the night at Missy's. After the party, the two girls went upstairs. They lay on Missy's bed and chatted. Missy's parents were visiting neighbors – they would be back soon.

Lindsay's phone rang.

"Lindsay, I am very disappointed in you." The same voice. "I don't think you deserve my ring. I'm coming to get it back."

"Get real!" Lindsay ended the call. It had come from her father's cellphone. She called the number but there was no answer. She called home. Her mother answered.

"Mom," she said, "Darren and David are so stupid. They're calling me on Dad's phone."

"That's not possible," said her mother. "They're watching TV. And your father is sure he dropped his phone at the funeral this afternoon. Maybe someone ..."

There was a loud noise. The phone died and the lights in the house went out.

"This is cool," said Missy. "We can tell ghost stories."

"I don't want to," said Lindsay. She wanted to be at home, not in a dark house.

There was a knock downstairs at the front door. *Thump. Thump. Thump.*

Missy got up to look who was at the door.

"Don't!" cried Lindsay. She couldn't say why, but she was scared. "Please, don't go."

"Don't be stupid," said Missy. "Stay here if you're so scared. What a baby!" She left.

Lindsay closed the bedroom door and locked it. She heard the front door open and close a moment later. She thought she heard a sound. Then quiet.

Her cellphone rang.

"Lindsay, I've come for my ring, you unhappy child. I'm at the bottom of the stairs right now. Let's play that game we played when you were a little girl. You loved it, didn't you – you loved being scared."

"Missy? This isn't funny."

But Missy's phone was on the bed.

"One step, two – I'm coming for you," said the voice on the phone.

Thump, thump on the stairs.

"Three steps, four – better lock the door. Five steps, six – say your prayers quick."

Lindsay hung up and called home.

"Seven steps, eight – not long to wait," said her mother's voice.

She hung up and dialed 911.

"Nine steps, ten – we're near the end," said a man's voice.

She threw the phone onto the bed.

"Eleven, twelve, and one step more – too late for you, I'm at the door!" It was Aunt Margaret's angry voice.

Someone knocked loudly. *THUMP! THUMP! THUMP!*

"Go away! Leave me alone! I didn't mean what I said!" Lindsay started to cry.

"Ha ha!" cried Missy through the door. "You're crying! This is better than telling ghost stories! I'm going to tell everyone you cried. You and that stupid ring you think is so cool."

Lindsay opened the door. "I never want to talk to you again!" she shouted.

But it wasn't Missy with Lindsay's father's phone in a muddy hand as the lights came on.

Working with the text

1 The story

a) *Whose 'muddy hand' do you think it is at the end of the story?*

b) *When you have read the story, finish these sentences:*

1 Lindsay gets a diamond ring from ...
2 After Lindsay has got dressed for the party, she gets a call from someone who says ...
3 She thinks the next two calls are from ...
4 While Lindsay is speaking to her mother there's a loud noise and ...
5 When there is a knock at the door of Missy's house, Missy ... but Lindsay ...
6 When Lindsay hears footsteps behind the bedroom door ...
7 While the bedroom door is still closed ...
8 Lindsay opens the bedroom door but ...

2 A thrilling story?

a) *In line 42 on p. 62, the author starts to create suspense: 'Lindsay, dear, this is Aunt Margaret'. Find more places in the story where the suspense rises or falls. Make notes like this:*

Event	Line	What happens
1	42	First phone call
2	45	Lindsay thinks it's Missy
3	62	Second phone call
4	68	...
5	95	...
6	...	...

b) *Look at the list of events and decide when the suspense is highest. Give this event 10 points. Give all the other events a mark between 1 and 10.*

c) **Extra** *Draw a 'suspense graph' for the story.*

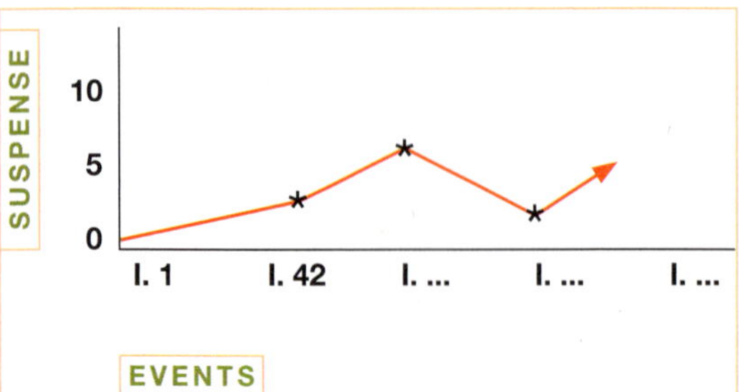

3 Lindsay's feelings

a) *Read these sentences from the story and say how Lindsay might be feeling at that moment.*

afraid • angry • annoyed • bored • cross • disappointed • excited • happy • impressed • nervous • sad • ...

1 She had to nod and look sad as they talked about her aunt. (ll. 13–15)
2 Get real! (l. 99)
3 She heard the front door open and close a moment later. (ll. 123–124)
4 But it wasn't Missy with Lindsay's father's phone in a muddy hand ... (ll. 164–165)

b) *Read lines 8–11, 40–41 and 56–60 again. What do they tell you about Lindsay's character? Describe what's important to her in her relationship with Missy and the other girls.*

c) *How does Lindsay feel about her aunt? Find a sentence from the story that shows this best.*

d) *Compare your idea with a partner's. Who has the better sentence?*

e) **Extra** *Choose a moral for the story from those below, or write your own:*

– If you do and say bad things, bad things will happen to you.
– Be nice – don't be rude or unkind.
– Respect other people.

4 Extra Beyond the story

a) *Do you like scary stories or scary films like* ***The caller****? Give reasons for your answer.*

b) *Write a script for a three minute film based on this story.*

► Text File 7 (pp. 121–127) • WB 16 (p. 39)

How am I doing?

a) *Find or choose the correct answers.*

Teen world

1 UK teenagers can get ASBOs for ...
A good school work. B bad school work. C antisocial behaviour. D success at sport.

2 Which one is NOT an example of antisocial behaviour?
A bullying B shoplifting C spraying graffiti D cleaning up trash

3 The ManaTEEN club is for teenagers who ...
A like cleaning. B want to volunteer. C have got ASBOs. D like water sports.

Words and phrases

4 Can I change a ten-pound ... into two fives?
A cash B money C note D receipt

5 I'll just save your phone number in my ...
A mailbox. B contacts. C text. D ringtone.

6 For the underlined words put in one of these words or phrases: communicate, dump someone, enter, store.
a) keep it in the fridge
b) end a relationship
c) talk with someone
d) put in your PIN

7 Complete the sentences with these verbs: ask someone out, hang on, knock, set.
a) Don't forget to ... your alarm clock.
b) If you like her, you should ... her ...
c) ... , I'll be with you in a minute.
d) ... on the door before you enter the room.

8 Complete the sentences with these words: at all, completely, as usual.
a) Well, he's my friend, but yesterday I didn't like his behaviour ...
b) He was late for school ...
c) You're right, I agree with you ...

9 Choose the correct word:
a) I hate (bored/boring) lessons.
b) Jo found an (interested/interesting) job.
c) I was (surprised/surprising) when she phoned yesterday.

Grammar

10 The girl helping the old lady was a volunteer. Which is correct A, B or C?
A The old lady was a volunteer.
B The girl was helping a volunteer.
C The girl was helping an old lady.

11 Complete the sentences. Use the passive.
a) A boy who vandalized a park yesterday ... (take) to the police station.
b) His name ... (can – not print) in the newspapers because he is under 16.
c) He ... (take) to court tomorrow.
d) I think he (must – punish).

Study skills

12 Write one phrase you learned in Unit 3 ...
a) to express an opinion.
b) to agree with an opinion.
c) to disagree with an opinion.
d) to ask for clarification.

13 What's the order in an outline?
A conclusion **B** introduction
C your arguments for or against

b) *Check your answers on p. 232 and add up your points.*

c) *If you had 26 or more points, well done! Maybe you can help students who had fewer points. If you had 25 points or fewer, it's a good idea to do some more work before you go on to the next unit. Where did you make mistakes? The chart below will tell you what you can do to improve your English.*

No.	Areas	Find out more	Exercises
1– 3	Teen world	Unit 1 (pp. 54, 58)	WB 3 (p. 33)
4– 9	Words	Vocabulary (pp. 182–186)	P 3–4 (p. 53), P 2, 4 (p. 57), WB 2 (p. 32), 5–9 (pp. 33–36)
10–11	Grammar	GF 6–7 (pp. 165–166)	P 3 (p. 57), P 2–5 (pp. 60–61), WB 10 (p. 36), 12–14 (pp. 37–38)
12–13	Study skills	SF (pp. 147, 154)	P 1 (p. 56), P 1 (p. 59), WB 11 (p. 37)

1 WORDS Free-time activities

a) *Work with a partner. How many free-time activities can you add to the list below?*

horse riding • drawing and painting • listening to music • playing a musical instrument • watching TV or DVDs • playing basketball • playing football • cycling • using a computer • reading books or magazines • relaxing • meeting friends • ...

b) *Look at your list and put the activities into groups.*

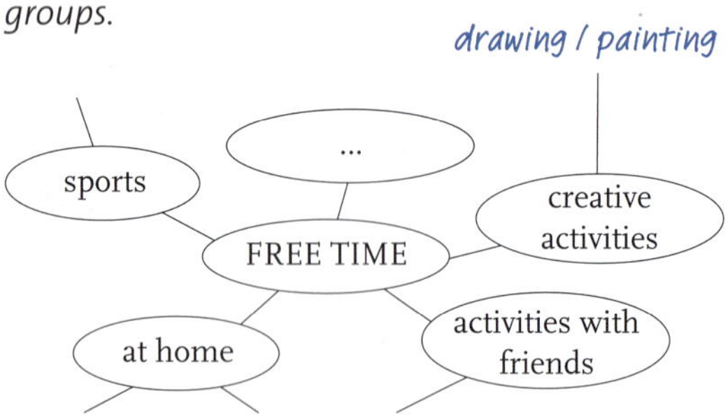

c) *Talk about the free-time activities from b). Tell each other why you like/don't like doing them.*

A: I often go horse riding. I love horses and I think it's great to be with them every day.

B: Well, maybe, but it sounds like a lot of work. I enjoy listening to music ...

2 WORDS Talking about films

You see this film review on a movie website. Put in the correct form of the words and phrases in the box to complete the text.

(to) act • actor • famous • main character • star • (to) take part in • talents • (to) tell the story • true

Take the Lead *****

Ballroom dancing meets New York's gangs

The 1 *drama* *Take the Lead* 2 ... of Pierre Dulaine, a ballroom dance teacher, who goes to work in one of New York's most difficult city schools full of problem kids. *Take the Lead* is actually a 3 ... story, and Pierre Dulaine is a real person. He still works with American teenagers around the USA and has become quite 4 ... since the film came out.

The 5 ... of the film is the Spanish American 6 ... Antonio Banderas. He plays the 7 ... Pierre Dulaine. When Dulaine first arrives in the school, the kids all think he is crazy. They are into hip hop, not classical dance. But after Dulaine shows them a tango with another professional dancer, the kids start to get interested. The film ends when they all 8 ... a national ballroom competition.

The kids are all 'normal' American teenagers and had never 9 ... before. But they are all great natural acting 10 ... and some of them are amazing hip hop dancers.

In 2006, *Take the Lead* won an award for 'Best Teen Movie.'

3 I'd love to be a movie star (Conditional sentences type 2)

Finish these sentences about being a movie star. All the sentences are conditional sentences type 2.

1 If a famous director *chose* (choose) me for one of his films, I*'d / would be* (be) famous too.
2 I ... (go) to Hollywood if I ... (become) a famous actor.
3 I ... (live) here if I ... (be) rich.
4 If I ... (act) in a movie, all my friends ... (come) to see me.
5 If I ... (have) lots of money, I ... (buy) a yacht.
6 If I ... (play) a part in a movie, I ... (meet) famous actors every day on the film set.
7 But the problem is, if I ... (be) a movie star, I ... (see) my family very often.
8 Perhaps I ... (be) so happy if I ... (be) a film star!

► GF 4: Conditional sentences (2) (p. 167)

4 SPEAKING Having a conversation ► SF p. 146

Talk to your partner for about two minutes about something that interests you – films, magazines, music, what you did last weekend, the town where you live, ... The phrases below will help you.

Starting a conversation	Hello. / Hi. / My name's ... / What's your name? / ...
Likes and dislikes	I like / don't like ... / What about you? / And you? / ...
Showing interest	Really? / Oh, that's interesting! / Sounds great! / Wow! / ...
Agreeing and disagreeing	Yes, me too. / That's right! / Oh, I don't. / Sorry, I don't agree. / ...
Asking questions	So when did you ...? / Why ...? / How long ...? / Where ...? / Sorry, can you say that again, please? / Sorry, what's that? / ...
Ending the conversation	See you soon. / Bye!

5 WORDS Jim and Kate (Words that describe feelings)

a) *Complete these sentences with words or phrases from the box on the right.*

angry • be afraid • be mad about sb./sth. • bored • cool • cross • depressed • different • disappointed • embarrassed • excited • great • happy • impressed • independent • jealous • lonely • (to) look forward to sth. • nervous • proud • relaxed • sad • safe • scared • silly • strange • surprised • terrible • tired • shy

1 Jim and Kate have been together for a month now and they ... still ... each other.
2 Kate was ... when Jim asked her if she'd like to go out with him. She thought he liked Laura.
3 Jim wasn't nervous on their first date. He is usually very ...
4 But when Kate left his MP3 player on the bus last week, he was very ... with her.
5 Sometimes Kate is ... when Jim tries to be funny – his jokes are very strange!
6 At first she didn't want to meet Jim's parents because she always feels a bit ... with new people.
7 When Kate met her old boyfriend Pete at a party, Jim was a bit ... at first – until he saw that she wasn't interested in Pete any more.
8 They're ... the summer holidays this year: they're going to Canada for three weeks!

b) *Write six more sentences about Jim and Kate with words you haven't used in a).*

1 READING Choosing a book

These American high school students are in their English literature class. They have to choose a book to read. To help them, their English teacher has written short summaries of some books.

Read the profiles of the five students and the seven book summaries below. Choose the best book for each student.

Answer: Student A – Book ...

Student A : Conrad

Conrad doesn't really enjoy reading short stories or novels, but he reads magazines. He loves sport and is also interested in music and skateboarding.

Student B : Brittany

Brittany has her own blog where she writes her thoughts. She is fascinated by young people, their loves and fears, their relationships, and their problems.

Student C : Jeanette

Jeanette loves reading stories. For her, a 'good book' is one where the characters have lots of real life adventures. She doesn't like fantasy, crime or horror stories.

Student D : John Paul

John Paul is interested in football but the thing he likes best is computer games. He particularly loves fantasy games where 'anything is possible'.

Student E : Ricki

Ricki's family came to the US from Puerto Rico. Now, as a teenager, he is interested in politics and wants to help people from ethnic minorities.

BOOK SUMMARIES

Fiction

1 **Dark Universe** Three teenage friends fall through a 'time hole' and find themselves in a parallel world where amazing and fantastic things happen. Can they survive – and will they ever return to their old lives?

2 **Something** Something is 'out there'. Waiting. Watching. Looking for you! VERY scary!

3 **Lola and the Detective Agency** When Lola and her friends find out about a crime, nobody believes them. They have to set up their own detective agency to catch the criminals. Lots of action right up to the last page!

Non-fiction

4 **Voices from the fields** Fascinating interviews with migrant workers from Mexico who talk about their lives in California where they work on huge farms.

5 **Strategies for teens** Being a teenager is not always easy but this book is full of great advice about families, boy/girlfriends and many other aspects of teen life.

6 **The Journey West** The book uses diaries, letters and old photos to tell the fascinating story of the long journeys to the West in America's history.

7 **Babe** Babe Ruth was probably the greatest baseball player who has ever lived. This biography tells the true story of his life. Wonderful descriptions of exciting games!

2 MEDIATION A note to your friend

Your American friend is staying with you in Germany at the moment. Your friend would like to know about some interesting things to do.

Read the brochure below and write a short note in English to your friend. Give the main points about the tour:
- how many people
- what is the tour about
- when/where does it start
- how long is it
- how much is it

Use the example below to help you.

> Hi!
> Hope you slept well. You wanted to know about some interesting things to do while I'm at school. I found out about some guided cycle tours that sound great. Here are the main points:
> –
> –

Erleben Sie die Stadt per Rad

Fahrrad-Stadtrundfahrten

Fahrrad-Rundfahrten durch die Stadt – für Gruppen von 10–15 Personen – begleitet von erfahrenen Stadtführern.

Sehen Sie unsere Stadt und ihre Attraktionen vom Fahrrad aus. Wir machen Halt an interessanten Punkten. Dort werden Sie Informationen über die Geschichte der Stadt und touristische Highlights erhalten.

Dauer
Unsere abwechslungsreiche Tour führt durchs Stadtzentrum und verschiedene Stadtteile und dauert ca. 120 Minuten, in denen wir etwa 12 km zurücklegen.

Abfahrt
März – September
täglich 10:00 und 14:00 Uhr.

Treffpunkt ist vor dem Informationszentrum neben der Liebfrauenkirche im Stadtzentrum (bei schlechtem Wetter im Informationszentrum).

Preise
€ 29,– pro Person inkl. Fahrradmiete
(Bei angemeldeten Gruppen mit mehr als 25 Teilnehmern € 22,50 pro Person.)

3 READING Dev Patel

This text is from an online British movie magazine. Read the whole article through first, then do the two tasks on p. 71.

Meet Dev Patel, teenage movie star

The hit movie *Slumdog Millionaire* tells the story of 17-year-old Jamal, one of the millions of extremely poor people (the 'slumdogs') who live in the slums of India's largest city, Mumbai. Jamal goes on the Indian TV gameshow *Who Wants to Be a Millionaire?*, answers all the questions correctly, wins the top prize – and finds the girl he loves. The movie won eight Oscars. Its star was the young English actor Dev Patel …

When Dev Patel arrived in Mumbai to film *Slumdog Millionaire*, it was only his second visit to India. In fact, learning the Mumbai accent was, he says, one of the hardest things he had to do. He wasn't a famous actor, either. He had liked drama very much at school in England, and he had played a small part in a British TV series, but that was all. So how did he become Jamal and what was it like when he was suddenly an international movie star?

Dev was born near London in 1993. His parents are Indians who had moved to England when they were young. His dad is a computer technician, his mum a carer[1].

Dev went to a 'typical' English secondary school. His first hobby was martial arts – karate then tae-kwon-do. He was excellent at both and even took part in the Youth Olympics. But after a role in a school play, Dev found that what he really loved was acting.

His mum wanted to encourage him, and when Dev was 14, she showed him a small advertisement in a newspaper. A TV company wanted people for a series called *Skins*, about a group of teenage friends. Dev wrote a reply – and got a part.

Three years later – Dev was now 17 – the successful British film director Danny Boyle was looking for someone to play Jamal in *Slumdog Millionaire*. Mumbai is the home of the huge Indian movie industry. People sometimes call it Bollywood: Bombay (the old name for Mumbai) plus Hollywood. The problem was that young, male Bollywood actors are all very strong and handsome. Boyle wanted a young man who looked more like a 'slumdog'. It was Boyle's daughter who told her dad about Dev – she often watched *Skins*. Dev had five auditions[2] ('I was crying at the end because I didn't think I'd get the part', he says) but then he was Jamal.

For Dev, the next five months were like a dream. He was in Mumbai and on a movie set. With him were a world-famous director, some of the best known older Bollywood stars, real kids from the slums of Mumbai, and the beautiful young actress who is his girlfriend in the movie. 'I grew up five years in those five months,' Dev says.

What did the real people from Mumbai's slums think? Dev was amazed by them. They were so proud that they were in the movie. 'Don't tell people we're poor,' they said to Dev and Boyle. 'Tell them we're happy. We aren't poor because we're happy.'

---

[1] carer ['keərə] *(Alten-)Pfleger/in* [2] audition [ɔː'dɪʃn] *Sprechprobe*

Questions on the text

a) *Choose the correct answer* A, B, C *or* D.

1 What do you learn most about in this article?
- A The Indian movie industry.
- B The film *Slumdog Millionaire.*
- C The young English actor Dev Patel.
- D The life of the poor people in the slums of Mumbai.

2 The article says it was ... that Dev Patel got the role in *Slumdog Millionaire.*
- A because he was at school with Boyle's daughter
- B because of his good looks
- C quite surprising
- D decided very quickly

3 In the movie, Dev plays the role of a young Indian man who ...
- A wins an Oscar.
- B becomes a millionaire.
- C moves to Mumbai.
- D tells a story.

4 Before he acted in the film *Slumdog Millionaire,* Dev ...
- A was already a famous actor.
- B had lived for a long time in Mumbai.
- C had only played a small role in a TV series.
- D could speak with a Mumbai accent.

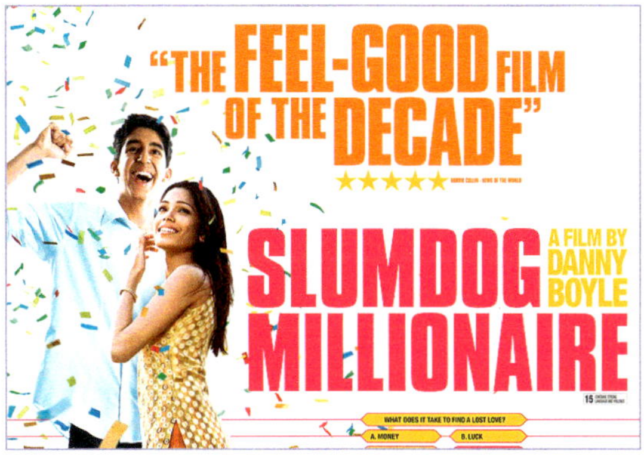

5 Dev ...
- A has Indian parents but grew up in England.
- B has English parents and grew up in England.
- C has Indian parents and moved to England when he was small.
- D has English parents but grew up in India.

6 Which activity interested Dev most when he was at school?
- A Tae-kwon-do.
- B Acting.
- C The Youth Olympics.
- D Karate.

7 How did Dev get the part in *Skins*?
- A His dad helped him.
- B A TV company wrote to him.
- C He often watched it on TV.
- D He replied to a newspaper advertisement.

b) *Finish the sentences with information from the text.*

8 Danny Boyle, the director of *Slumdog Millionaire,* chose Dev for the part of Jamal and not a young, male Bollywood actor because Dev ...

9 Mr Boyle found out about Dev from ...

10 At the end of his auditions, Dev was crying because ...

11 Filming *Slumdog Millionaire* in Mumbai changed Dev a lot. He describes this change when he tells us that ...

12 Dev expected the people who lived in the slums of Mumbai to be really sad. In fact, he found that although they are poor, ...

4 SPEAKING Talking about a picture

Partner A

Describe to your partner what you can see in the photo on the right.
(Partner B: just listen).
Speak for around one minute.

- Who are the people in the photo? Where are they?
- What are they doing?
- Describe their feelings.
- Would you like to be one of the people in the photo? Why (not)?

Partner B

Now it's your turn. Describe to your partner what you can see in the photo on the right.
(Partner A: just listen).
Speak for around one minute.

- Who are the people in the photo? Where are they?
- What are they doing?
- Describe their feelings.
- Would you like to be one of the people in the photo? Why (not)?

5 SPEAKING Hobbies and interests

Have a conversation with your partner. Tell each other about your hobbies and interests.
Talk together for about three minutes. Here are some ideas:

- What do you like doing in your free time? Why?
- Where, when and how often do you do those things?
- Do you do them alone, with your family or with friends?
- Describe the last time you did one of the activities.
- Is there one thing you hate doing?

How am I doing?

Check your answers to tasks 1 and 3 (Reading) on p. 233.

About the test

This second test gave you another chance to try some of the kinds of tasks that you will do one day in your exam (*Abschlussprüfung*). This time, the tasks tested your reading, mediation and speaking skills. If you found some tasks difficult, don't worry. You've got lots of time to practise. Remember: 'Practice makes perfect!'

Reading

Task 1 and task 3 in the test were reading tasks. The following three questions will help you to think about how you did. Read the questions – which answer is right for you?

1 How hard or easy was each task?

	easy	OK	quite hard	very hard
Task 1				
Task 3				

▸ *SF Reading course (pp. 144–145)*

2 What was difficult in the tasks?

a) The texts were quite long and complicated.
b) There were words and phrases that I just couldn't understand.
c) There was a lot of information.I couldn't find the exact answers.
d) The tasks weren't like the tasks that we do in class.

3 How did you do the tasks?

a) I read each task carefully so that I knew what to look for in the texts.
b) I tried to understand the main ideas of the text first. That helped me to guess words that I wasn't sure about.
c) If there was a task that I wasn't sure about, I left it out and came back to it later.
d) I scanned the text when I looked for a special piece of information.
e) I checked my answers at the end to make sure I hadn't made a 'silly' mistake.

▸ *SF How to do well in a test (pp. 156–157)*

Speaking

1 Task 4: Talking about a picture

Copy and fill in the assessment sheet below about your partner's description in the fourth task.

Assessment sheet	☹		😐		☺	
Name of partner ...	1	2	3	4	5	Comments
Did your partner ...						
1 ... speak clearly and loudly enough?						
2 ... say enough?						
3 ... answer all the questions?						
4 ... use interesting vocabulary?						
5 ... explain his/her ideas well?						

2 Task 5: Hobbies and interests

Look at the checklist on the right and talk about how well you did in the dialogue about your hobbies and interests.

a) We listened to each other.
b) Our answers were long enough.
c) We showed interest in what our partner said.
d) There was a good flow in our dialogue.[1]

▸ *SF Speaking course (pp. 146–147)*

[1] There was a good flow in our dialogue. *Unser Gespräch verlief flüssig.*

Unit 4 Exploring cities

Mumbai

A A traffic jam in Mumbai

B Juhu beach in Mumbai

City fact file

Country: India • **Continent:** Asia

Other names: Bombay, City of Dreams, City of Gold, Maximum City

Population: 13.9 million • **Size:** about 440 sq km

Languages: Marathi is the official language. Other languages spoken are Hindi, Gujarati and English. Many schools teach in English and English is the main language spoken by office workers.

What's good? Going to the beach, sightseeing, exciting street markets, delicious food

What's bad? Traffic, overcrowding, pollution, the big contrast between rich and poor people

Other facts: Mumbai (then Bombay) became British in the 1660s and was an important port for the British until 1947 when India became independent.
Today Mumbai is India's most important port, its financial centre and home to Bollywood – one of the largest film industries in the world. A third of the population live in slums in poor quality homes and many live on the streets.

C The Gateway of India in Mumbai

1 Comparing cities

Look at the photos and the fact files. How are the two cities different? How are they similar?

2 City visits

a) Listen to Karen, Rohan and Amy talk about the cities that they visited. Take notes about:

- where they are from
- what city they travelled to
- how long they stayed
- why they went there
- what they liked about the city

b) Listen again. What aspects of city life does each person talk about? Take short notes in a copy of the chart on the right.

D Johannesburg city centre

JOHANNESBURG

F A shopping street in Johannesburg

City fact file

Country: South Africa • **Continent:** Africa

Other names: Joburg, Jozi, Egoli, City of Gold

Population: 3.9 million • **Size:** over 1,600 sq km

Languages: Most people speak Afrikaans, Zulu, Sesotho or English, all of them are official languages in South Africa.

What's good? Shopping in the malls, perfect weather, exciting art and music scenes, more than six million trees, international sports events

What's bad? Crime, AIDS, unemployment, the contrast between rich and poor people

Other facts: The city was founded in 1886 when gold was discovered in the area. Today it is South Africa's most important financial centre. Banks and other big companies have their offices there. Many people are rich, but a lot are poor – 20 % of the people live in townships with no electricity or water. The suburb of Sandton is called the richest square kilometre in Africa.

E Children in a township in Joburg

	Karen	Rohan
– the difference between rich and poor people	✔ big contrast ...	...
– public transport	✗	
– crowded streets		
– pollution		
– sightseeing		
– crime		
– weather		
– speaking English		

3 Now you

a) *Name some other big cities. Which city would you like to visit? Why?*

b) **Extra** *Write a city fact file for Berlin or another city you know. Put it in your DOSSIER.*

▸ WB 1 (p. 40)

MUMBAI

1

The real Mumbai?

Hi! I'm going to Mumbai next month (I'm from the US). What's it like? I would like to know about the 'real' Mumbai (not the tourist Mumbai). What's good and what's bad?

Best answer

Hi! I live in Mumbai and I will try to answer your questions. I came here from a small village in India when I was seven. My parents wanted to find a better life. They knew that in the city there are good schools, modern hospitals and more jobs.
When I first came to Mumbai I hated it. It was so different from my village. I hated the dirt and the pollution. I hated the crowded streets, buses and trains. The difference between rich and poor made me sad. There are so many poor and homeless people in Mumbai. I think most people feel like I did when they first arrive. They are shocked. Mumbai is a crazy, crowded, fast, noisy, dirty place.
Now I'm older, I see different things. I love the friendly people – they are really positive and helpful. And I love the energy of the city. Life here is never boring – every day there is something new and exciting. To see some of my photos of Mumbai click here.

Other answers

I think Deepa's story is typical of the 'real' Mumbai. Every day more people come here from India's villages. They hope that they will find work and a better life. There are lots of rich people here, but a lot of very poor people too. I recently read in a newspaper that six million people live on less than 1 US dollar a day.

I ❤ MUMBAI!!! It's the best city in the world! It has great public transport (OK the trains and buses are crowded in the rush hour, but at other times they're great). You can shop in big modern shopping malls or colourful street markets. You can hang out where all the rich and famous people go. You might even see a Bollywood film star!

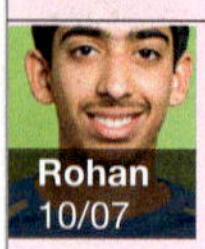

Hi Balu! I've just been to Mumbai – it's an amazing place! Here are some tips:
1. Be prepared for a big culture shock when you arrive!
2. Do a tour of the city with a local tour guide.
3. Eat at Swati Snacks. (Like most tourists, I was nervous about Indian food because I didn't want to get sick, but this place is very clean and the food is delicious.)

1 *Why did Deepa's family move to Mumbai? How did she feel about Mumbai at first? And now?*
2 *Pick out the good and bad things about Mumbai and write them down in two lists.*
3 *Would you like to visit Mumbai? Why (not)?*

▸ *SF Reading course (pp. 144–145)*

2 Mumbai rush hour adapted from *Mumbai* by Suketu Mehta

Read the introduction to the text. What does the word 'adjust' mean?

'Adjust' is a favourite word in Mumbai. If there is a problem, Mumbaikar 'adjust', and find a way to go on. Mumbai trains are unbelievably crowded in the rush hour. Here, the writer describes how people adjust and help each other on the trains.

Anyone who travels on an Indian train is familiar with this word: adjust.
If you are late for work in the morning in Mumbai, and get to the station just as the train is leaving the platform, you can run up to the crowded train and you will find that many hands will pull you on board. As you run along next to the train you will be picked up and some tiny space will be made for your feet in the open door. The rest is up to you; you will probably have to hold on to the door frame with your fingers and be careful not to lean out too far. But just think about what has happened: the other passengers are already packed tighter than cattle, their shirts wet with sweat. They have stood like this for hours, but they can still feel with you, know that your boss might shout at you or cut your pay if you miss this train. They make space where there is no space to take one more person with them.
At the moment of contact, they do not know if the hand belongs to a Hindu or Muslim or Christian or if you were born in this city or arrived only this morning or if you're from Mumbai or New York. All they know is that you're trying to get to the city of gold, and that's enough. Come on board, they say. We'll adjust.

1 Are you surprised that passengers help others to get on the crowded train? Why (not)?
2 If people arrive late for work, what can happen to them?
3 Are differences between people important on the train? What examples does the writer give?

3 A big city: a good or a bad place to live?

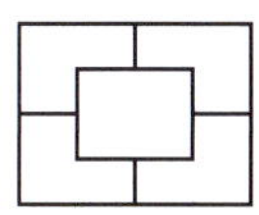

a) *Form groups of four. Each student should think about the question: Is a big city a good place or a bad place to live? Why? Write your ideas into a placemat.*

b) *Discuss your ideas in your group and agree on three important points.*
- I think there are good things and bad things about life in a big city. For example ...
- I think a big city is a great place to live because ...
- I think so too. / I (don't) agree.
- What about ...? / Let's choose ...
- Who's for (against) ...?

c) *Decide who will report your ideas to the class.*
- We all think that ... because ...
- In our opinion ...

d) **Extra** *Fishbowl*
Each group sends one person into the fishbowl to speak for them. Discuss your ideas with the people from other groups.

► *SF Having a discussion (p. 147)* • **Text File 8** *(pp. 128–129)*

P1 WORDS Cities and city life

a) *Look at the* ***nouns*** *in the orange box below. Find more words about cities and city life. Look at pp. 76–77 for ideas.*

b) *Match the nouns from the orange box to suitable* ***adjectives*** *from the blue box on the right to make phrases. Here are some ideas:*
a modern airport, wide streets, ...

c) *Find* ***verbs*** *from the green box that go with the phrases you have made. Here are some ideas:*
– meet fashionable people
– go to a huge mall, ...

d) *Write a short text about a big city. Use as many words from this exercise as you can.*

Nouns
- airport, traffic jam, rush hour, ...
- concerts, jobs, business, shopping, education, ...
- suburbs, areas, mall, parks, streets, ...
- museum, zoo, factories, skyscrapers, ...
- +poverty, +homelessness, graffiti, pollution, vandalism, ...
- tourists, business people, ...

Adjectives
ambitious • dangerous • excellent • expensive • +fascinating • +fashionable • +glamorous • huge • modern • polluted • trendy • ...

Verbs
find • go • learn • live • meet • relax • see • travel • visit • work • ...

P2 VIEWING Transport in Mumbai

a) *This film looks at the main types of transport that tourists in Mumbai can use. What do you think they are? Write a list. Then watch the film and check your answers.*

b) *Watch again and answer these questions in a few words:*
1. Give one advantage and one disadvantage of buses and trains in Mumbai.
2. Which is the best type of transport for tourists in the city centre?
3. Which type of transport is good for short journeys, especially outside the city centre?
4. What can be a problem for tourists who walk through Mumbai?

c) **Extra** *Complete these tips:*
1. I suggest that you travel with a local person the first time you go on ...
2. It's best to take a prepaid taxi from ...
3. Remember to allow ..., even for short journeys, because of traffic jams.
4. Most people in Mumbai will be happy to help you with ...

Auto-rickshaws in a Mumbai street

d) *Choose A or B and answer the questions.*

A If you were in Mumbai, what kind of transport would/wouldn't you use there? Why?

B What tips would you give tourists to your area? What types of transport are there? When should tourists use them and why?
- In my town there are ...
- For short journeys it's a good idea to go by ...
- ... is/are cheap/expensive/comfortable/fast ...

e) **Extra** *Watch another video clip about Mumbai. What is similar to a big city in Germany? What's different? Find examples.*

► WB 2–3 (p. 41)

P3 SPEAKING I'm not feeling great

It's not nice to get ill when you're travelling. But if it happens, you sometimes need to see a doctor.

a) *Do you know these words? Add more words if you can.*

a cold • +the flu • a headache • +a pain in my arm/knee/... • a sore throat • +a virus • a stomach ache • a temperature • ...

feel cold/hot/ill/weak/... • be sick • my head/stomach/... hurts

+cream • +medicine • +pills • +prescription

b) *Complete this dialogue with words from the boxes in a). Then check with your partner.*

Doctor So what seems to be the problem?
Patient I feel ..., Doctor.
Doctor Does anything ... ?
Patient Yes, I have a pain in my ... and I ...
Doctor Mmm, when did it start?
Patient Last night. And I ... too.
Doctor I'm sure you've got a ...
I don't think it's serious. Take this ...
You'll feel better soon.
Patient Thank you.

c) *Choose from one of the situations in the box below or think of one yourself. Write a dialogue. Practise your dialogue, taking it in turns to be the patient. Then act it out in class.*

1 You've had an accident in the street. You were walking and someone on a bike hit you. A paramedic arrives to help you.
2 You wake up with terrible earache and a sore throat. You go to the doctor.
3 You have been sick for two days with a stomach ache. Ask a chemist what he/she recommends.

more help ► D p. 103

P4 MEDIATION Sore throat lozenges

Imagine you're in Mumbai on holiday. You wake up with a sore throat. You don't think it's serious. It's probably the air conditioning. But you'd like to get something for it.

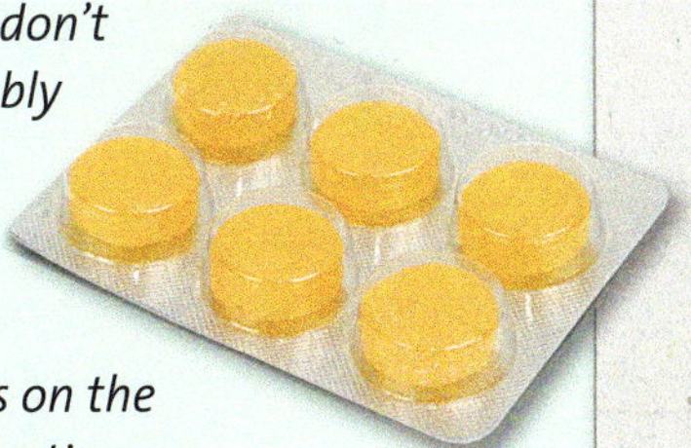

a) *Look at the instructions on the right and answer these questions.*
– Wogegen ist das Medikament?
– Wie muss man es einnehmen?
– Wann sollte man das Medikament nicht nehmen?
– Wann sollte man einen Arzt aufsuchen? (Nenne zwei Dinge.)

b) *Do you think the lozenges are suitable for your problem?*

Drug facts

Uses: In case of minor irritation, pain, sore throat and sore mouth.

Directions: One lozenge every two hours.

Warnings: Do not use this product if you have a history of allergies.
A severe sore throat or sore mouth that occurs with a high temperature, a headache and vomiting may be serious. Ask doctor right away.
When using this product do not use more than directed. Stop use and ask doctor if:
– symptoms do not improve in 7 days
– irritation, pain or redness worsens
– swelling or a high temperature develops
– difficulty in breathing occurs.

► SF Mediation (p. 155) • WB 4–5 (p. 42)

JOHANNESBURG

1 In the township: Karen's blog

Karen, from Ireland, has come to Johannesburg for two weeks to work as a volunteer. She is helping to build houses in a township. In her blog she writes about her experience.

▪ **Sunday** Arrived in Joburg today. It's a big, big city. Saw very impressive modern buildings and huge shopping malls from the bus. Some people here have a lot of money! Our hotel is in a rich area called Sandton. You see lots of people (black and white) out in restaurants and going to nightclubs etc. We start work tomorrow. Feeling a bit nervous! I've read lots of stories on the internet about problems in Johannesburg (crime, AIDS, pollution etc). The hotel and all the houses near here have guards with big dogs because of problems with crime.

▪ **Monday** We went to the township today. What a contrast to the area where our hotel is! The people in the township are mainly black. They have no running water in the houses. Their houses are very small, they are just shacks really and are made of bits of wood, metal, anything the people can find. The houses I saw were reeeally tidy. I feel bad that I have a big (very untidy!!) hotel room and my own bathroom. People in the township don't even have an indoor toilet. I talked to a girl today who said she's too scared to go outside to the toilet at night because it isn't safe. I was shocked.

▪ **Tuesday** It was very hot today. I painted all day. There are always kids around when we're working. They don't speak much English but they're very funny. I love the way they're always laughing and joking.

▪ **Thursday** Talked to a teacher from the township. She talked a bit about the old days under apartheid. She told me that townships were the only places where black people were allowed to live when she was young. From 1948 until the early 1990s South Africa had a white racist government. White people and black people had to live and work in different areas and black people had no rights although they were 70 % of the population. It's hard to believe that really happened. Her hero is Nelson Mandela, the first black president. He was elected in 1994 after the end of apartheid. She also told me that some of the kids in the group that hangs around with me probably have AIDS. It's so sad.

▪ **Friday** Our two weeks are over. I'll be back in Ireland in three days time. This has been an unforgettable experience. We've built more than 200 houses. I'm proud of our work, but so much more is needed. I'll never forget the people. Especially the kids. They gave me more than I gave them.

> *Where did Karen stay? Where did she work? How were the two parts of the city different? Do you think Karen had a good time? Why (not)? Find phrases which show Karen's feelings.*

▸ **Text File 9** *(pp. 130–132)*

2 We've come a long, long way

In South Africa, nearly half the population is under 21 and kwaito music – the music of South Africa's Y generation – is everywhere. The writer of this text used to live in Johannesburg, but he moved away in 1994. Years later, he came back and found a city that was hard to recognize. For him, the music that came in with the end of apartheid tells us a lot about the new freedom and confidence of young people in Johannesburg today.

It's lunchtime at The Zone, an American-style shopping mall in the Rosebank area of Johannesburg. There was a time when only whites could come here. Today, black teenagers, cell phones to ears, walk along the mall, wearing baggy jeans and trainers, the hip-hop uniform of American kids. But they're wearing it in an African style with floppy hats that they pull over their eyes so that they look like local gangsters, and T-shirts by trendy local fashion designers. Some of the shirts have political slogans from South Africa's apartheid past.

A popular place in the mall is outside the YShoppe and YFM Studio. YFM is the Joburg youth music radio station that first brought kwaito to the people. Kwaito is South Africa's hip-hop, a mix of slowed-down Western dance tracks and lyrics in the street language of the townships. It became popular soon after the election of Mandela in 1994. Its songs are less about race or politics and more about the life and confidence of the young black people.

Today YFM's audience is almost two million and Joburg's youth are known as the Y generation. Kwaito's biggest stars, who were once poor township kids, are millionaires with their own TV shows, fashion labels and record companies. How far have we come? I'm about to order lunch when a tall black man is stopped by two white kids in baseball caps. They want his autograph. Who's this, I wonder. Later I find out it's Oscar waRona, a superstar DJ at YFM. You can tell: we've come a long, long way.

Adapted from Johannesburg Travel and Leisure, Go2SouthAfrica

What is kwaito? What's it like? Why is the story about Oscar waRona important?

3 Finding out more

a) *Work in a group. Half the group works on text 1 on p. 80, the other half works on text 2 on p. 81. Scan your text for information about how Johannesburg has changed since the end of apartheid. Make notes. Compare notes with people who read the same text.*

b) *Now share your information with the people in your group who read the other text.*

4 Extra Now you

Choose one of the following writing tasks. Write about 100 words.

Do you think you would like to go to Johannesburg? Why (not)?

or

Write a short email to Karen about her blog. Say what you think of her trip to Johannesburg and ask her some questions about her trip.

▸ *SF Writing course (pp. 150–151)*

P1 SPEAKING Describing photos

a) ○ *Listen to the description. Which photo is it? Describe the other photo in a similar way.*

A

B

b) *Find a picture in this unit and prepare to describe it to a partner.*
more help ▸ D p. 104

c) *Your partner should listen carefully to the description. Can he/she find the picture?*

d) **Extra** *Describe the photo on the right. What do the shacks look like? The street? What do you think the young people's lives might be like?*

e) ● ▸ D p. 105

▸ SF Describing pictures (p. 135)

P2 WORDS Word building (Adjectives)

a) ○ *Look at the adjectives in the orange box. You know the nouns or verbs they come from. Say what you think the adjectives mean. Check your ideas in the Dictionary if you aren't sure.*

bloody • careless • colourful • fruity • hairy • icy • impressive • juicy • oily • thoughtful • unforgettable • unforgivable

A: I think 'bloody' comes from blood, so it probably means *blutig*.
B: I agree. My turn. We know the word 'careful'. That means ... So 'careless' probably means ...

b) //○ ▸ D p. 105
Think of a noun to go with each adjective in the orange box. There are some ideas in the box below, e.g. a bloody nose, ...

bird • building • drink • experience • hands • legs • mistake • moment • nose • present • road • rubbish • strawberries • ...

c) *Complete the sentences with suitable adjectives.*

1 Seeing elephants in the safari park was a/an ... experience.
2 This is one of the most ... skyscrapers in Johannesburg.
3 I also loved the ... street markets in the city.
4 These oranges are really sweet and ...
5 I'm so sorry! Forgetting your birthday was a/an ... mistake.

▸ WB 6–7 (p. 43)

P 3 Apartheid in South Africa

a) *Partner B: Go to p. 93.*
Partner A: Read the text below and find answers to the questions.

1 What advantages did white people have in South Africa during apartheid?
2 What disadvantages did black schools have?
3 Why did black students protest in 1976?
4 How has the school system changed since the end of apartheid?

b) *Ask partner B about the following:*

– into which ethnic groups the government of South Africa divided the people during apartheid
– why South African football is a good example of the apartheid system
– why South Africa was thrown out of FIFA
– what happened when apartheid ended
– what happened in 2010.

c) *Now answer partner B's questions.*

d) **Extra** *Write a short text about apartheid. You can put it in your DOSSIER.*

Apartheid and schools

Under South Africa's apartheid system, the white minority (less than 20 % of the population) had big advantages over other ethnic groups. About 87 % of the land was in white hands. And only whites could be in the government.

From the 1950s South Africa had separate education systems for the different 'races'. Much more money was spent on the schools for whites. From an early age, blacks were victims of discrimination. Black students had less equipment in their schools, fewer classrooms and fewer school books. The government did not want blacks to have a good education, because it knew that they would then want more rights.

When the government tried to force black schools to teach in Afrikaans, the language of the majority of white people, black students protested in Soweto (the biggest township in Johannesburg) on 16 June, 1976. The protests became violent ('Soweto Uprising'), and hundreds of young black people were killed – although the government spoke only of 23 dead people.

Apartheid ended in the early 1990s. Today there is one state school system with no segregation. Every year on 16 June, South Africa remembers the Soweto Uprising and honours the students who were killed in 1976.

▸ WB 8 (p. 44)

Berlin: City survival kit

When you go to a foreign city for the first time, things are not always as you expect them to be – as these young visitors to Berlin discovered …

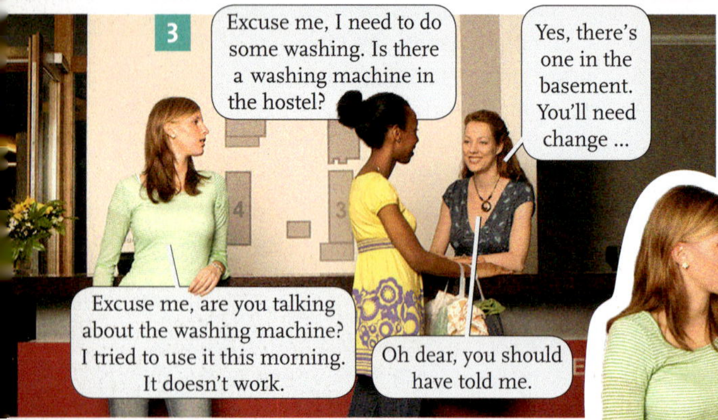

1 *The foreign visitors find some things different in Germany. Find the four examples in the text.*

2 *Talk about the must-see sights of Berlin with a partner. Have you been there? When? Which sights would you recommend to visitors? Why?*

▸ WB 9 (p. 44)

P1 ENGLISH FOR JOBS At reception

Hotel receptionists all over the world have to be very polite. And they have to manage lots of situations with very different guests.

a) *Which of these phrases are used by receptionists?*

... your full name and address, please.

Would you please fill in this form?

Certainly, sir/madam. | Is there a message for me? | I'm (very) sorry. | We'll take it.

You're welcome. | Can I have a wake-up call, please? | Can I have my key, please?

What can I do for you? | Have a pleasant stay. | I'm afraid we're nearly fully booked.

b) // ► D p. 105
Listen to three dialogues. What do the guests want? Look at the box on the right.
In dialogue 1/2/... the guest ...

has a problem with the TV • is waiting for an important message • wants a wake-up call • wants breakfast in the room • wants to book a room • wants to check in

c) *Choose one of the situations below and prepare a dialogue. The phrases in a) can help you. Present your dialogue to your group or class.*

A
– A new guest has arrived. He/She has to fill in the form before he/she gets the key for room 253.

B
– A guest is asking for a single room with a bathroom.
– He/She needs an internet connection in the room too.

C
– A guest comes back in the evening and asks for his/her keys.
– He/She would like to have a snack in his/her room.

D
– A guest phones the reception to say that the shower is broken.
– Somebody will come and repair it at once.

d) **Extra** ► D p. 107

more help ► D pp. 106–107

P2 LISTENING Can I leave a message?

a) *Listen to three telephone messages. Look at the notes below. Then listen and write down the complete messages.*

b) **Extra** *Your partner is the receptionist. You call to leave a message for a friend. Check the message when you've finished. Swap roles.*

Telephone message
For: *Lilly Good, Room ...*
From: ...
Message: *Please phone ...*
She said ...
...

Telephone message
For: *Ben Smith*
From: ...
Message: *Meet at the ...*
Text ...
Mobile number: ...

Telephone message
For: ...
From: ...
Message: ...

► WB 10–11 (p. 45)

P3 Exploring language | Additional information | Conditional sentences type 3

a) *Look at the pictures and answer the questions.*

Can they catch the bus?

Why didn't they catch the bus?

b) *Choose the right ending for the sentences.*

1 If we had bought a better map, ...
A we would have found the way quickly.
B we wouldn't have found the way.

2 If the music had been better, ...
A I would have stayed longer.
B I would have left early.

c) **Extra** *Look at the conditional sentences in b) carefully.*

1 What verb form follows 'if' here? A simple present B simple past C past perfect
2 The verb form in the main clause is new. How is it formed?

► *GF 8.2: Conditional sentences (3) (p. 167)*

P4 I would have taken the bus

What would you have done differently?
Make short dialogues like the one in the photo.

1 *A:* Tom was late for our meeting, so I went home.
B: (wait for him) *I would have ...*
2 *A:* I wore jeans to my job interview.
B: (wear a dress/suit) *I would have ...*
3 *A:* I stayed in a hotel in London.
B: Hotels are expensive. I ... (Bed & Breakfast)

Now change roles.

4 *B:* A man climbed through our neigbour's window yesterday, but I didn't do anything.
A: I would have ... (phone the police)
5 *B:* I bought a pink T-shirt last Saturday.
A: (buy a blue one) I *would have ...*
6 *B:* I watched football on TV yesterday.
A: Football's boring. I ... (a film)

► *WB 12–13 (p. 46)*

P5 SPEAKING A talk about Berlin (Giving a presentation)

▸ SF p. 147

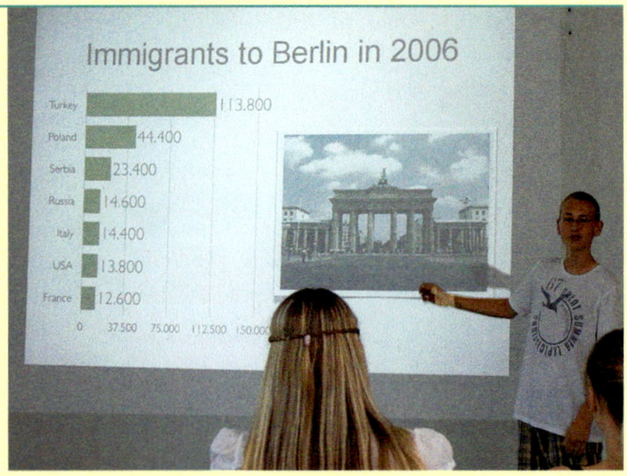

a) *A talk needs a structure. Put these steps in the right order.*

A Make clear when you are starting a new section of your talk.
B Summarize your main points and make clear that you've finished.
C Give an outline of your talk.
D Introduce your topic.
E Invite questions and/or discussion.
F Explain visual materials as you use them.

b) *Listen to the talk on Berlin and complete the sentences below. The phrases in the box can help you.*

> +basic • +draw your attention to • divide • +feel free • First • have a look • look at • present • pie chart • sections • +slide • sum up • topic

1 The ... of my talk today is 'Berlin: yesterday, today, tomorrow'.
2 I'm going to ... this talk into four ...
3 ..., I'll give you some general facts about the city of Berlin.
4 Next I'll ... the history of Berlin.
5 Finally I'll ... some interesting highlights of Berlin's culture.
6 Now please ... at the population of Berlin.
7 On the next ... you'll see a ... of the ethnic groups in the city.
8 Those were the ... facts. Now I'd like to ... the history of Berlin.
9 To ... my talk, I think we have seen that Berlin is a pretty exciting place to visit.
10 Please ... to ask questions or comment on anything I've said.

Tip

Here are some English phrases for your talk about Berlin. Do you know what they are?

> the Brandenburg Gate • the fall of the Wall • the reunification of Germany

Collect other useful phrases that you find in your research.

c) *Match the phrases in b) to the steps for a talk from a).*

d) *Work in a group of three or four. Collect information for your own talk about Berlin or another city. Possible topics are:* the sights of the city, the history of the city, the city for young people, ...
Use the internet, encyclopedias, history books, brochures, etc.

▸ SF Research (p. 138)

e) *In your group agree on the main topics for your talk. Divide your talk into clear parts. Decide if you want to use a poster, transparencies or a computer.*

f) *Make notes for your talk (only key words) and practise it. Speak freely – don't read from your notes.*

STUDY SKILLS Using visual materials

Visual materials (pictures, maps, timelines, posters, transparencies, charts, etc.) make your presentation more interesting and easier to understand.
They will also help you while you are talking. When you talk about the pictures, charts etc. use phrases like:

- In this photo/chart/... you can see ...
- The next picture/slide/... shows ...
- On the left there's a ...
- As you can see in this chart ...

▸ SF Using visual materials (p. 139) • **Text File 10** (p. 133) • WB 14–17 (pp. 47–48)

How am I doing?

a) *Find or choose the correct answers.*

City facts

1 Mumbai became British in the ....
A 1660s. B 1820s. C 1950s.

2 Mumbai's famous film industry is called ...
A Indywood. B Jollywood.
C Bollywood.

3 Johannesburg was founded in 1886 when ... was dicovered in the area.
A gold B oil C silver

4 Most of the poor people in Johannesburg live in ...
A the city centre. B townships.
C Sandton.

5 South Africa had ... football teams during apartheid.
A two B three C four

6 During rush hour trains in Mumbai are ...
A empty. B expensive. C crowded.

Grammar

7 In which of these sentences is Tom talking about a situation in the past?
A If you had come early, you would have met Pam.
B If you come early, you'll meet Pam.
C If you came early, you would meet Pam.

8 Choose the right ending for this sentence: If I had scored one more goal, ...
A we would win the match.
B we'll win the match.
C we would have won the match.

Giving a presentation

9 What is the best order for these steps in a presentation?
A Sum up your main points.
B Introduce your topic.
C Invite questions and comments.
D Give an outline of your talk.

Words

Find words that mean nearly the same:
a) trendy: f_____
b) very small: t_____
c) difference: c_____

10 Complete the sentences with these prepositions: **at**, **on**, **out**, **with**.
a) Are you familiar ... this area?
b) Lots of people in the world live ... less than 1 US dollar a day.
c) Don't lean ... of the window – it's dangerous.
d) I need your help. Can you come ... once?

11 Complete the sentences with these words: **dormitory**, **double room**, **fully booked**, **queue**.
a) Mia and Zoe want a ... in the hotel.
b) They can't get a room there because it's ...
c) Not far away is a hostel where they can stay but only in a ...
d) There are lots of people waiting outside the museum so Pia and Linn have to ...

12 For each group of nouns choose one which can form an adjective ending with **-ful**.
a) cloud – culture – colour – danger
b) health – hope – fruit – race
c) office – storm – success – rain

b) *Check your answers on p. 233 and add up your points.*

c) *If you had 18 or more points, well done! Maybe you can help students who had fewer points. If you had 17 points or fewer, it's a good idea to do some more work. The chart below will tell you what you can do to improve your English.*

No.	Areas	Find out more	Exercises
1– 6	City facts	Lead-in, Parts A–B (pp. 74–83)	
7– 8	if-clauses	P 3 (p. 87), GF 8 (p. 167)	P 3–4 (p. 87), WB 12 (p. 46)
9	Giving a presentation	SF (p. 147)	P 5 (p. 88), WB 14 (p. 47)
10–13	Words	Vocabulary (pp. 187–191)	P 1 (p. 78), P 3 (p. 79), P 2 (p. 82), WB 2 (p. 41), 7 (p. 43), 13 (p. 46), 16 (p. 48)

▸ *Self-evaluation 3–4 WB (p. 49)*

Unit 1 **Part A**

P1 REVISION Facts about Australian animals (Tenses: simple present)

▸ Unit 1, Part A (p. 11)

a) *Write a text about koalas. Use the correct forms of the* ***simple present****.*

Koalas ... (be found) only in parts of Australia. They ... (look) like bears, but they ... (~~belong~~) to the bear family. They only ... (eat) the leaves of one kind of tree (eucalyptus tree). There ... (be) so much water in the leaves of that tree that the koalas ... (~~have~~ to) drink. Koalas ... (~~sleep~~) at night. That's when they ... (move) around.

b) **Extra** *Add to your text. Use the key words below.*

- when baby koala born – move into its mother's pouch – kind of bag
- live in pouch – fed by mother – about ten months
- when baby too big for pouch – ride on mother – until one year old
- live 10–12 years

c) *Listen to your partner's text. Pick out one interesting thing about the animal. Then read your text to your partner.*

▸ *GF 1: Talking about the present (p. 159)*

Unit 2 **Part A**

EVERYDAY ENGLISH

P4 MEDIATION Summer jobs in Britain

▸ Unit 2, Part A (p. 37)

a) *You and your partner are looking for summer jobs in Britain next year. Your partner will tell you about a job. Listen carefully and take notes.*

b) *Tell your partner in German about the job on the right. Say:*
– what you have to do in the job
– what sounds good/bad about the job.

c) *Which job do you like best? Why?*

Sales assistant for Gino's ice cream vans

Spend your summer in the park! You must be able to speak good English and be good at maths. You will sell ice creams, cold drinks and snacks. Great job for students looking for summer work! Jobs for 6 people.

Please contact Maria on **07978-569-0897**

Unit 2 **Part B**

P1 STUDY SKILLS Looking at CVs

▸ *Unit 2, Part B (p. 39)*

b) *Listen to your partner. He/She will tell you about a candidate for the job. Then tell your partner about this candidate.*

I've got the CV of someone called ...
He's got these qualifications: ...
He did some work experience in ...
He's interested in ...

c) *Look back at your notes from a). Which candidate should get the job? Why? Discuss.*

Arda Demir
Kantstrasse 65, 24943 Flensburg, Germany
Telephone: 0049 122 39 09 090
E-mail: arda.demir@flensmail.de

Personal statement
I am a hard-working person. I am good at working as part of a team, or on my own. I am interested in solving technical problems and working with machines.

Education
2008 to date Eckener-Schule-Flensburg (technical college)
2002–2008 Kurt-Tucholsky-Schule (secondary school), Flensburg
1998–2002 Eickum Primary School

Qualifications
2008 *Fachoberschulreife* (GCSEs)
Driving licences: tractor licence since 2008, car licence since 2010

Languages
English (8 years), Danish (3 years)

Work experience
Apprenticeship as mechanic

Hobbies and interests
Computers, repairing cars and motorbikes, football, helping on uncle's farm

References
Mr Altermann (manager, engineering company), Boge GmbH, Lister Rund 12, 24943 Flensburg, Germany.

Unit 2 **Part C**

P1 SPEAKING How would you describe yourself? (Taking part in a job interview)

c) Partner B*: You have to interview partner A for a job. Read the role card to prepare for the interview.*

▸ *Unit 2, Part C (p. 41)*

Partner B: Role card
You're going to interview a candidate for this job ▸

- Welcome the candidate. Say who you are. Be friendly!
- Ask the candidate
  - about his/her personal qualities
  - about his/her interests
  - why they're interested in the job.
- At the end ask the candidate if he/she has any questions.

  Here's some extra information about the job:
  - Workers have to sell soft drinks, ice cream and fast food, clean the shop, work for about 5 hours.
  - Pay: £5.52 per hour
  - Workers can watch the matches!
- Thank the candidate and say goodbye.

HORNBY F.C.

Local football club is looking for **friendly students** to work in club shop on match days. You will get necessary training. Candidates should live near the stadium. **Apply now!**

Unit 2 **Part C**

Part 2 SPEAKING COURSE

P1 SPEAKING How would you describe yourself? (Taking part in a job interview)

▸ *Unit 2, Part C (p. 41)*

***c) Partner C**: Partner B will interview Partner A for this job. You have to watch the interview and assess the candidate.*
Read the advert. Then copy the assessment sheet below to prepare for the interview.

Local football club is looking for **friendly students** to work in club shop on match days.
You will get necessary training. Candidates should live near the stadium. **Apply now!**

HORNBY F.C.

ASSESSMENT SHEET

Name of candidate ....

The candidate:	Points	Comments
1 was relaxed and friendly	...	...
2 dressed suitably		
3 listened carefully		
4 talked well (not too much / too little)		
5 was well prepared		

Points	
1	poor
2	below average
3	average
4	good
5	very good

When the interview is finished, tell the candidate how he/ she did in the interview.
- You were very relaxed/nervous/...
- That was good. I gave you 5/4/... points for that.
- You didn't talk very much. / ...
- That wasn't so good. I gave you 2/1/... points for tha
- You have ... points all together.

Unit 3 **Part B**

P4 WORDS Problem teenagers

▸ *Unit 3, Part B (p. 57)*

***a)** Partner B: Listen to the definitions that your partner reads out. Say which phrase – A, B or C you think is the closest in meaning. Talk like this:*

- Can you read the possible answers again?
- I don't think B is right. That means ...
- I think A is closest.

***b)** Read these definitions to your partner. Listen to his/her answers. Say if you agree with them. (Check the answers on p. 107.)*

6 When you vandalize something ...
- A you break or destroy it.
- B you steal something.
- C you say racist things.

7 When you shoplift ...
- A you steal something from a supermarket.
- B you take something from someone else's bag.
- C you threaten someone.

8 If you are a troublemaker ...
- A you follow the rules.
- B you break the rules.
- C you do what the police, your teachers, and your parents tell you.

9 If you stop someone from causing problems ...
- A you have problems with them.
- B you feel bad about them.
- C you help them to stay out of trouble.

10 If you are violent towards someone ...
- A you attack them.
- B you help them.
- C you annoy them.

Unit 4 **Part B**

P3 Apartheid in South Africa ▸ *Unit 4, Part B (p. 83)*

a) *Read the text below and find answers to the questions.*

1 How did apartheid laws divide people up in South Africa?
2 Why was South African football an example of the apartheid system?
3 During apartheid, was the South African football team successful in international competitions? Why (not)?
4 What happened when apartheid ended?
5 What happened in 2010?

Apartheid and football

South Africa's apartheid laws (1949–1991) divided people into four 'races': whites, Bantu (black Africans), coloured (mixed race) and Asian (Indian or Pakistani).

Like everything in South Africa, football was divided by race. There were four football associations, one for each 'race'. The white association, FASA, chose the players for South Africa's all-white national team.

FASA had difficult relations with FIFA, the international football organization, which was against racism.

In 1976, when government security forces killed hundreds of young black protesters in the township of Soweto, FASA was banned from FIFA. From then on South Africa was not allowed to take part in the World Cup. In other sports too, the country was banned from international competitions.

When apartheid ended in the early 1990s, South Africa's four football associations came together and from then on there was only one organization for South Africans of every colour: the South African Football Association (SAFA). In 1992, SAFA became a member of FIFA.

In 2010 the FIFA World Cup took place in South Africa. The first and the last matches were played in Johannesburg. It was the first time that the World Cup was held in an African country.

SOUTH AFRICAN FOOTBALL ASSOCIATION (OVERSEAS TEAM, 1924).

b) *Answer partner A's questions.*

c) *Now ask about the following:*

– what advantages the white people had in South Africa during apartheid
– who had disadvantages in education, what these disadvantages were
– why black students in Soweto protested in 1976
– how the education system has changed since the end of apartheid

d) **Extra** *Write a short text about apartheid. You can put it in your DOSSIER.*

Unit 1 **Part A**

3 Facts and figures

a) more help ▸ *Unit 1, Part A (p. 10)*

Complete the sentences about the charts.

The first chart compares the ... in four countries: Australia, the UK, the USA and Germany.
The USA has the biggest population – 300 ... people.
The populations of the other countries are much ...
... has the next biggest population.
The population of Germany and ... are nearly the same.
Australia has the ... population.

The second chart compares the ... of the same four countries.
... is the biggest country.
... is the next biggest ...
... and ... are nearly the same size. They are much smaller than ...

1 Population in millions

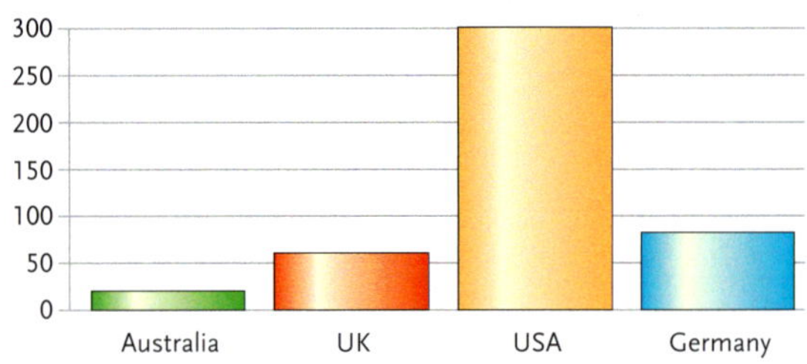

2 Land area in million sq km

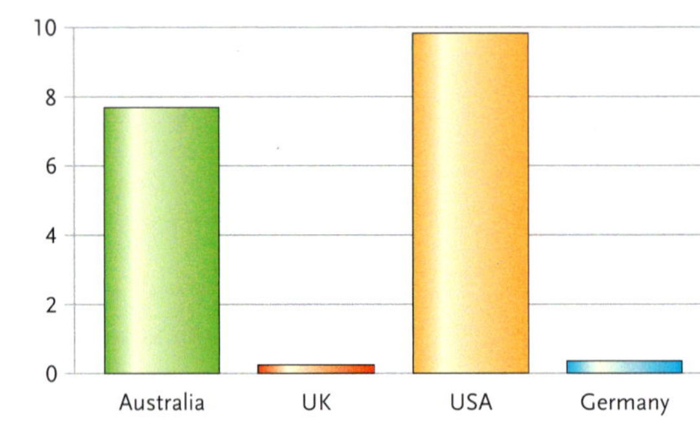

Unit 1 **Part A**

EVERYDAY ENGLISH

P1 more help WRITING Our lives (Writing an e-mail) ▸ *Unit 1, Part B (p. 14)*

Look at pages 12 and 13 again. Write an e-mail to Jeannie or Rob.

- *Tell them what you find interesting or surprising about their lives.* →
- *What else would you like to know about their lives? Ask some questions.* →
- *Tell them something about your life, e.g. your school day, your favourite subject, the sports/activities you enjoy, ...* →

Dear ...

My name is ... and I live in ... in Germany. I think it's very interesting to learn about your life in Australia.

I was really interested to read that .../to hear about ...
I think it's great that you can .../have ...
I was really jealous when I read that you ...

I have some questions for you.
What's your favourite ...?
Where/When/How often do you ...?
Are you allowed to ...?

My life in Germany is (a bit/very) different to yours.
For example, ...

Best wishes / Hope to hear from you soon ...

▸ *SF Writing informal letters or e-mails (p. 153)*

Unit 1 Part B

P 4 SPEAKING Nice to meet you (Having a conversation) ▸ Unit 1, Part B (p. 15)

e)

In a group of three, prepare and act out this situation:

The three of you meet on a bush walk. **A** is German, **B** is Australian and **C** is American. Talk to each other about your holidays so far.

Unit 1 Part C

4 VIEWING Rabbit-proof fence ▸ Unit 1, Part C (p. 17)

b) more help

Watch again. Talk about the film and how you feel when you watch the film. Some of the words in the box might help you.

– At the beginning everything is calm. The music is ... The people are ...
– When the music gets louder you feel ...
– When you see the hands on the car, you feel ...
– At the end, the women are ... You feel ...

angry • awful • bad • calm • cross • depressed • fine • happy • horrible • loud • nervous • noisy • puzzled • quiet • relaxed • scared • sad • shocked • strange • terrified • unhappy • upset • worried • ...

Unit 1 Part C

P 2 // Samantha Harris, Aboriginal model (Indirect speech) ▸ Unit 1, Part C (p. 18)

You find an interesting interview with Samantha from March 2008.

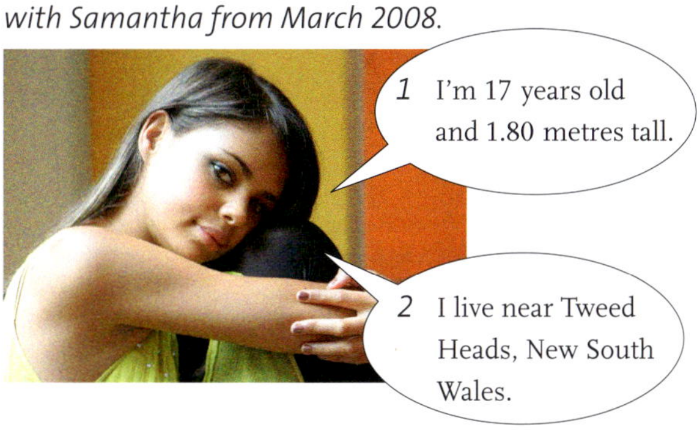

3 'My dad is from Germany.'
4 'I have four brothers and one sister.'
5 'My friends call me Sam.'
6 'I like hip hop and reggae.'
7 'I can't imagine leaving home.'
8 'I don't earn a lot of money.'
9 'I want to be the first big Aboriginal model.'

Report what Samantha Harris said about herself.

1 Samantha said in 2008 that she was ...
2 She told the reporter that she ...
3 ...

Unit 1 **Part C**

P5 WRITING A film review

▸ *Unit 1, Part C (p. 19)*

b) more help

Use these questions to make short notes about a film that you've seen recently. The words in the boxes might help you.

What's the title? (The title of the film is ...)

What kind of film is it? (It's a/an ...)

What's the film about? (It's about ...)

Who's the director? Who are the stars? (The director is .../The stars are ...)

Where and when does it take place? (It takes place in ...)

Who are the main characters? (The main characters are ... He/She is a ...)

What's good/bad/special about the film? (The film is exciting/... The special effects/... are great/boring/...)

What's the ending like? (The ending is (a bit/very) strange/silly/...)

Would you recommend it to other people? (People who like action films/... should see this film.)

Kinds of films

action film • adventure film • cartoon • comedy • detective film • documentary • drama • historical film • love story • musical • science fiction film • true story • ...

What's special about it?

actors • landscape • soundtrack • story • music • songs/singers • dance scenes • ...

the whole film/the ending

amazing • annoying • awful • boring • brilliant • clever • crazy • cruel • exciting • fantastic • funny • great • happy • horrible • interesting • perfect • sad • scary • silly • strange • stupid • surprising • terrible • violent • ...

Unit 1 **Part D**

In the outback Working with the text

4 Extra The end of the story

a) more help ▸ *Unit 1, Part D (p. 24)*
Choose one of these endings. Use the notes and write your ending.

Ending 1

The next day – two policemen – come
Colm – opens door – ask the boy – for name
tell him – has to come with them – take him – children's home
Colm – says: 'can't come with you – have to stay with – Rusty.'
help Bill – when back from hospital
The two policemen ... (leave Colm there/take him to .../...)
...

Ending 2

Three weeks later – in the outback – with Bill and Rusty
this time – Colm – drives – car
Bill – problems with his legs – watches Colm
Colm – repairs – fence – does good job
Bill – happy with Colm's work
Colm – stay with Bill – as long as – wants to stay
...

Unit 2 **Lead-in**

3 more help Now you ▸ *Unit 2 (p. 33)*

Before you start the discussion, think about what you want to say. These phrases might be helpful:

– When do you think you'll leave school?
I think/I'm sure/... I'll leave school (this year/next year/in 2 years/...)
I think I'll stay at school and study for ...

– What kind of job do you want to do?
I want to do a job in/on/as a ...
I would like to do this job because I like.../I'm good at ...

– Do you want to do an apprenticeship?
I want to start an apprenticeship with .../as a ...
I don't know what I want to do. / I haven't got any plans.

Unit 2 Part A

P3 WORDS Your profile ▸ Unit 2, Part A (p. 36)

a) more help *Make a chart for yourself like this.*

Write down words and phrases that describe you: sporty, fit, energetic, artistic, calm, polite, organised, serious, hard-working, ...

Personal qualities	*Interests*	*Possible jobs*
– confident,	*– computers*	*– ...*
– good at solving problems	*– designing things*	
– ...	*– enjoy*	

Write down jobs that you might be interested in.

Write down phrases that describe what you are good at:
- talking to people
- helping/looking after people
- working in a team/in a group/alone/...
- working with children/old people/...
- working with machines/computers/...
- following instructions
- solving problems
- ...

Write down what you like or are interested in: cars, sport, films, travel, computers, making things, repairing things, designing things, cooking, doing people's hair, ...

Unit 2 Part B

P2 STUDY SKILLS Writing a letter of application ▸ Unit 2, Part B (p. 39)

a) // ● *Improve this letter. Rewrite the underlined parts.*

Tip

If you need some help, look at the letter on p. 38.

Dear Ms Hall

I am writing about your ad in the Cambridge News and I would like to have the job. Here is my CV. I'm 17 years old and I'll leave school at the end of June with the the *Fachoberschulreife*, which is a bit like GCSEs in Britain.

I am a friendly, helpful person and I enjoy working in a group of people. I am very reliable and I don't mind working at weekends. I have studied English for six years and my level is quite good. This year I worked in a zoo for 3 weeks. I did office work and served people in the zoo shop. I really enjoyed what I did there. The manager can give me a reference.

Write back soon.

Yours sincerely

Lena Dickhaus

Lena Dickhaus

Unit 2 Part B

P2 STUDY SKILLS Writing a letter of application ▸ Unit 2, Part B (p. 39)

c) ● *Imagine you want a summer job in Britain. Choose one of the jobs below and write your own CV and letter of application.*

✦ PARKVILLE HOTEL ✦

Are you looking for a summer job?
Hard-working person needed to help in the kitchen of our busy hotel restaurant. Must be happy to do evening and weekend work. Free meals, uniform and use of our gym and sauna.

Interested? E-mail your CV and letter of application to The Personnel Manager, Parkville Hotel jobs@parkvillehotel.co.uk

Can you ride?
Do you love horses?

LONG'S RIDING CENTRE CAMBRIDGE

Prize-winning riding centre is looking for people to work in July and August.
It's hard work – we start at 7.30. But if you love **working with horses,** if you're good at working in a team and you don't mind getting your hands dirty, then this is the job for you!
Please send a letter of application and CV to Mr S. Long, Long's Riding Centre, Cambridge CB24 4GG

d) ● *Work with students who applied for the same job. Who should get the job? Why?*

Unit 2 Part C

P2 //● REVISION Talking to the careers teacher (Indirect speech) ▸ Unit 2, Part C (p. 42)

Steve had an interview. Report what Steve said. Change the tense..

1 Steve told his teacher that he was …
2 He said that he …
3 He added that …
4 He also said …
5 …

Unit 2 Part C

P5 At the travel agent's (Indirect speech: questions with question words)

▸ Unit 2, Part C (p. 43)

a) //● *Adam applied for a job at a travel agent's. He had his interview with the owner, Mrs Tay. Later Adam's friend Katy wants to know what questions Mrs Tay asked. What does Adam tell Katy? Change the tense.*

1 What kind of person are you, Adam?
2 What are your favourite subjects?
3 How many languages can you speak?
4 What do you do in your free time?
5 What qualifications do you have?
6 What do you know about America?
7 What work experience do you have?
8 Why do you want to work at a travel agent's?

1 Mrs Tay asked me what kind of person I was.
2 She wanted to know what my favourite ...
3 She asked ...

b) ● *Ask a partner some of the questions in a). Your partner doesn't have to tell the truth! Report to the group what question you asked and your partner's answer. The group has to guess if the answer was true or not.*

A: I asked Paul what his favourite subject was. He said it was Science.
B: I don't believe that.
C: I think it's true.
A: Paul, is it true ...

Unit 3 Lead-in

3 Now you

▸ Unit 3 (p. 49)

b) more help
You want to write to one of the six teenagers. Before you start, make notes about yourself. Use a chart for your notes, for example:

	About me
Family	
Interests	
Problems	
School	
Future plans	

Complete the notes with your own ideas, or choose words/phrases from the box on the right.

do a lot of sport • download music/films • go to parties • play in a band • have a girlfriend/boyfriend • chat online • talk on the phone • help at home • have a job at weekends/in the holidays • help old people • do volunteer work • argue with my parents/sister/... • parents divorced • live in a flat/house • do a lot of homework • favourite subjects • get good/bad grades • do tests • boring town • bullies • get into trouble • not enough pocket money • get an apprenticeship • leave school • train as a ... • travel to ... • ...

Unit 3 **Part B**

P3 WORDS You and your mobile

▸ Unit 3, Part A (p. 53)

b) *What should a good mobile do? Write a short text. Describe your perfect mobile.*

- I'd like a mobile which can ...
- The only thing I can't do with my phone is ...
- I've got a good mobile. I can ... with it.
- If I had enough money, I'd buy a ... because ...

Unit 3 **Part B**

P4 ENGLISH FOR JOBS Useful phrases

▸ Unit 3, Part A (p. 53)

c) more help *Choose one of the situations below. Write the dialogue with a partner, then practise it.*

Partner A: You're a shop assistant in a mobile shop.
Partner B: You want to buy a cheap mobile phone.

A A shop assistant in a mobile shop

Assistant ______ (Say hello to the customer.)
Customer ______ (Say what you're interested in.)
Assistant ______ (Ask which one the customer likes.)
Customer ______ (Ask questions about the phone.)
Assistant ______ (Answer the customer's questions.)
Customer ______ (Say you'll take the phone.)
Assistant ______ (Ask the customer how they want to pay – cash or credit card.)
Customer ______ (Say how you want to pay.)
Assistant ______ (If necessary ask for the PIN. Then give the customer the phone and the receipt.)
Customer ______ (Reply to the assistant. Take the phone and receipt.)

Partner A: You're a customer adviser in a bank.
Partner B: You want to change some Australian dollars into euros (2 AUS dollar = 1 euro).

B A customer adviser in a bank

Adviser ______ (Say hello to the customer.)
Customer ______ (Say what you want to do.)
Adviser ______ (Ask how much he/she wants to change.)
Customer ______ (Say how much you want.)
Adviser ______ (Give the exchange rate.)
Customer ______ (Give the adviser your money.)
Adviser ______ (Give the customer the dollars.)
Customer ______ (Say thank you.)
Adviser ______ (Say thank you and goodbye.)

Partner A: You're the waiter.
Partner B: You want to order two pieces of apple cake and two hot chocolates in a café.

C A waiter in a restaurant

Waiter ______ (Ask the customer if he/she is ready to order.)
Customer ______ (Say what you want to eat.)
Waiter ______ (Ask if the customer wants something to drink.)
Customer ______ (Say what you want to drink.)
Waiter ______ (Ask if there's anything else.)
Customer ______ (Reply.)
Waiter ______ (Finish the conversation.)

Unit 3 **Part B**

SPEAKING COURSE Part 3

P1 SPEAKING That's a good point! (Having a discussion)

▸ Unit 3, Part B (p. 56)

g) Choose one of the statements on the right. Brainstorm arguments for and against it. Then have a short discussion about it in your group or in class.

- We should ban music with violent lyrics.
- Teenagers should be allowed to drive a car at the age of 16.

Unit 3 **Part B**

P2 // WORDS A worrying time

▸ Unit 3, Part B (p. 57)

Complete the text with suitable adjectives from the box.

bored • boring • excited • exciting • interested • interesting • surprised • surprising • worrying

Kelly was a clever girl who was ... at school, so it wasn't ... that she often got into trouble there. When she was 16 she decided she didn't want to go to 'that ... old school' any more. Kelly tried to find an ... job, but it was difficult. Companies weren't ... in her because she didn't have qualifications or experience. Kelly found a job in the end, but her mother wasn't ... when she gave that up. It was a very ... time for Kelly's mother. She didn't know how to help Kelly. Then a new club for teenagers started in the area. When Kelly came back from the first meeting she was very ... . The leaders had really ... plans for the youth group. Kelly's mother was happier.

Unit 3 **Part C**

P3 // REVISION Lots of good work is done (Passive: simple present/simple past)

Complete the sentences with a suitable verb from the box. Use the passive.

▸ Unit 3, Part C (p. 60)

collect • eat • expect • find • need • spend • throw • use

1 In America young people ... to work as volunteers.
In America young people are ...
2 Beautiful fish and turtles ... at Weeki Wachee Springs in Florida.
3 Unfortunately bottles, glass and plastic ... in the water too.
4 At the last Springs Clean-up lots of trash ... by the volunteers.
At the last Springs Clean-up lots of trash was ...
5 Lots of pizzas ... by the volunteers in their break.
6 Alex and Andrew heard that money ... to buy food for the Hickory Soup Kitchen.
7 Half of Alex and Andrew's money ... on meat.
8 The rest of the money ... to buy vegetables and ketchup.

Unit 4 Part A

EVERYDAY ENGLISH

P3 SPEAKING I'm not feeling great

▸ Unit 4, Part A (p. 79)

c) more help *Here are some phrases that might help you when you're writing your dialogue.*

Situation 1 or 2

What the paramedic/doctor might ask or say to the patient:
So what seems to be the problem?
Does anything hurt?
Where does it hurt?
What happened?
When did it start?
Let's see if you have a temperature.
Well, 37.8 degrees, that's a little bit too high but not serious.
I (don't) think it's serious.
I'm sure you have the flu/...
Take this prescription.
The pills/medicine/cream/... should help you soon.
You have to go to hospital.
...

What the patient might answer or ask the paramedic/doctor:
I feel sick/tired/hot/...
I have a cold/the flu/a temparature/ a headache/a sore throat/a pain in my hand/ ...
My arm/leg/knee/... hurts.
Maybe I have a virus.
It started two days ago/last week/...
I fell off my bike/I fell in the shower. /
I hurt my leg when I was playing football. / ...
Do you think it's serious?
What do you think it is?
...

Situation 3

What the patient might ask or say to the chemist:
I feel sick/tired/...
I have a cold/a headache/a sore throat/...
What can I take to feel better?
What can you recommend?
How often do I have to take ...?
How much is it?
...

What the chemist might ask or say to the patient:
What can I do for you?
Have you got a prescription?
Have you been to a doctor?
You could try these pills/...
Take one every two hours/...
I think you should see a doctor.
...

Unit 3 Part B

P4 WORDS Problem teenagers

▸ Unit 3, Part B (p. 57)

***a) Answers** for partner A:*

1 When you threaten someone who is not as strong as you ...
A you bully them.

2 When you do something illegal ...
B you break the law.

3 If you are in a gang ...
A you belong to a group.

4 Antisocial behaviour means ...
B you make trouble.

5 When you stand in the street and do nothing much ...
B you hang around.

Unit 4 **Part B**

P1 SPEAKING Describing photos

▸ *Unit 4, Part B (p. 82)*

b) more help *You have to describe a picture from the unit to your partner. If you need some help, follow these steps.*

Step 1 *Look through all the pictures in Unit 4. Choose a picture that you find interesting.*

Step 2 *Collect as many words and phrases as you can for the people and things in your picture.*

Step 3 *Try to answer these questions. Make some notes.*

What can you see in the picture?
- This is a picture of ...
- I can see ... in the middle (in the background, on the right, on the left, etc.)
- There's a .../There are some ... behind the ...
- I think it's a ...
- Perhaps/Maybe it's a ...
- The people are wearing ...
- ...

What do you think is happening in the picture? If you're not sure, try to guess.
- The people are walking/sitting/...
- I think/Perhaps/Maybe they are going to ...
- The boy/girl/... looks tired/angry/... – I think he/she ...
- ...

Can you say anything more about the picture?
- The picture shows what it's like in a ...
- I (don't) like the picture because ...
- When I look at the picture I feel ... because ...
- I'd like to/I wouldn't like to go to this place because ...
- ...

Step 4 *Practise saying your description.*

▸ *SF Describing pictures (p. 135)*

Unit 4 Part B

P1 SPEAKING Describing photos ▸ Unit 4, Part B (p. 82)

e) *In July 2007 one hundred people in the townships of Johannesburg were given cameras and asked to document their lives. The project was called Shooting Jozi. These are some of the photos they produced. Choose one of the photos. Describe it. What does it tell you about life in the townships? Write at least 100 words.*

A

B

C

D

Unit 4 Part B

P2 WORDS Word building (Adjectives) ▸ Unit 4, Part B (p. 82)

b) // *Think of as many nouns as you can to go with each adjective in the green box, e.g.* *a bloody nose, ...*

bloody • careless • colourful • fruity • hairy • icy • impressive • juicy • oily • thoughtful • unforgettable • unforgiveable

Unit 4 Part C

P1 ENGLISH FOR JOBS At reception

b) // ▸ Unit 4, Part C (p. 86)
Listen to three dialogues. What do the guests want?
In dialogue 1/2/... the guest ...

Unit 4 **Part C**

P1 ENGLISH FOR JOBS At reception

► *Unit 4, Part C (p. 86)*

c) more help

You have to make a dialogue. There are lots of different things you can say. Here are some ideas.

A A new guest has arrived. He/She has to fill in the form before he/she gets the key for room 253.

Receptionist — Begrüße den Gast. Frag, was du für sie/ihn tun kannst.
Guest — Nenne deinen Namen. Sag, dass du ein Zimmer reserviert hast.
Receptionist — Du findest die Reservierung. Der Gast muss nur ein Formular ausfüllen.
Guest — Frag, was du ausfüllen musst.
Receptionist — Sag, dass du eine Adresse brauchst. Zeige, wo er/sie die Adresse eintragen muss. Gib dem Gast den Schlüssel und nenne die Zimmernummer 253.
Guest — Bedanke dich.
Receptionist — Verabschiede dich höflich.

Wenn ihr mehr machen wollt:
- Mehr Auskunft geben: in welchem Stockwerk ist das Zimmer, wo ist der Aufzug, ...
- Vielleicht hat der Gast mehr Fragen, z. B. wo ist das Restaurant, wann gibt es Frühstück oder vielleicht möchte der Gast im Zimmer frühstücken, ...

B A guest is asking for a single room with a bathroom. He/She needs an internet connection in the room too.

Receptionist — Begrüße den Gast. Frage, was du für sie/ihn tun kannst.
Guest — Sag, was für ein Zimmer du möchtest.
Receptionist — Du hast so ein Zimmer. Der Gast muss nur ein Formular ausfüllen.
Guest — Frag, was du ausfüllen musst.
Receptionist — Sag, dass du einen Namen und eine Adresse brauchst.
Guest — Buchstabiere, wenn etwas kompliziert ist.
Receptionist — Zeig, wo er/sie unterschreiben muss. Gib dem Gast den Schlüssel, nenne die Zimmernummer.
Guest — Sag, dass du einen Internetanschluss brauchst.
Receptionist — Sag, dass alle Zimmer einen Internetanschluss haben.
Guest — Bedanke dich.
Receptionist — Verabschiede dich höflich.

Wenn ihr mehr machen wollt:
- Was ist, wenn das Hotel kein Zimmer mit Internetanschluss hat? Gibt es andere Möglichkeiten (Internetcafé in der Nähe, ...) oder sucht der Gast nach einem anderen Hotel?

C A guest comes back in the evening and asks for his/her key. He/She would like to have a snack in his/her room.

Guest ___ Nenne deine Zimmernummer.
Receptionist ___ Wiederhole die Nummer, überreiche den Schlüssel.
Guest ___ Frag, ob du noch etwas im Hotelrestaurant essen kannst.
Receptionist ___ Sag, dass es dir Leid tut, die Küche hat schon geschlossen.
Guest ___ Bedanke dich und verabschiede dich.

Wenn ihr mehr machen wollt:
– Sag dem Gast, wo er/sie in der Nähe noch etwas zu essen bekommen kann.

D A guest phones the reception to say that the shower is broken. Somebody will come and repair it at once

Receptionist ___ Melde dich.
Guest ___ Nenne deinen Namen und deine Zimmernummer. Sag, dass die Dusche in deinem Zimmer kaputt ist.
Receptionist ___ Entschuldige dich. Sag, dass sofort jemand kommen wird.
Guest ___ Bedanke dich.

Wenn ihr mehr machen wollt:
– Vielleicht möchte der Gast jetzt gleich duschen, weil er/sie gleich losgehen muss. Was könnte man da machen?

Unit 4 Part C

P1 ENGLISH FOR JOBS At reception

▸ *Unit 4, Part C (p. 86)*

d) **Extra** *With a partner think of one other situation at the reception, e.g. a guest needs a taxi, wants to buy a map or tickets. Write a dialogue. Then act it out in your group or in class.*

Unit 3 Part B

P4 WORDS Problem teenagers

▸ *Unit 3, Part B (p. 57 and 92)*

***a) Answers** for partner B:*

6 When you vandalize something ...
A you break or destroy it.

7 When you shoplift ...
A you steal something from a supermarket.

8 If you are a troublemaker ...
B you break the rules.

9 If you stop someone from causing problems ...
C you help them to stay out of trouble.

10 If you are violent towards someone ...
A you attack them.

Extra	TF 1–10	Inhalt	Seite	
Unit 1	TF 1	Australian signs	109	
Unit 1	TF 2	*Bilingual module – Biology* Ecosystems in Australia	110–111	
Unit 1	TF 3	*Project:* What's so special about Australia?	112–113	
Unit 2	TF 4	Diary of a teenage job hunter	114–116	
Unit 2	TF 5	*Song:* Nine to five	117	
Unit 3	TF 6	*Bilingual module – Social studies* A different sort of justice	118–120	
Unit 3	TF 7	*Short play:* Famous	121–127	
Unit 4	TF 8	India	128–129	
Unit 4	TF 9	South Africa	130–132	
Unit 4	TF 10	*Project:* An English-speaking city	133	

TF 1 Australian signs

1 Signs talk

a) Make groups of five. Each person describes one of the signs 1–5. You can use a dictionary.

– On sign ... you can see ...
– It says that there might be ...

b) Discuss in your group. What do you think each sign means? Where would you find the signs?

– I think sign ... means that you have to be careful because ... /it's dangerous to ...
– You'd probably find this sign by the road/...

c) What have you learned from the signs about Australia? Make notes and report to the class.

2 Role play

You and your partner want to go swimming, but you see sign 3 or 4.
Partner A: You still want to swim.
Partner B: You don't want to go into the water because of the sign.
Start your dialogue like this:

A: Let's go swimming/surfing.
B: Are you sure? It might be dangerous/ ...
A: ...

3 Funny signs

a) What do you think the signs on the right mean?

b) Draw a sign of your own – it can be serious or funny.

c) What does your partner think your sign means?

TF 2 Ecosystems[1] in Australia

1 Food chains[2]

Plants and animals need energy, which they get from food. Plants can make their own food, so they are called **producers**. Animals must get their food by eating plants or other animals, so they are called **consumers**.

a) *Is a tree a producer or a consumer? Why?*

b) *Complete the food chain in diagram A. Use the words in the box.*

insects • crocodiles • plants • frogs

Diagram A: A food chain

Producers ⟶	Primary consumers ⟶	Secondary consumers ⟶	Tertiary consumers[3]
... are eaten by	... are eaten by	... are eaten by	...

2 Food webs

A food web is a lot of food chains put together, like these food chains from the food web below:
grass ▸ kangaroos ▸ dingos
grass ▸ grasshoppers ▸ frogs ▸ kookaburras

a) *Find four more food chains in the food web in diagram B and describe them.*

b) *How many different kinds of food do snakes eat?*

Diagram B: A food web

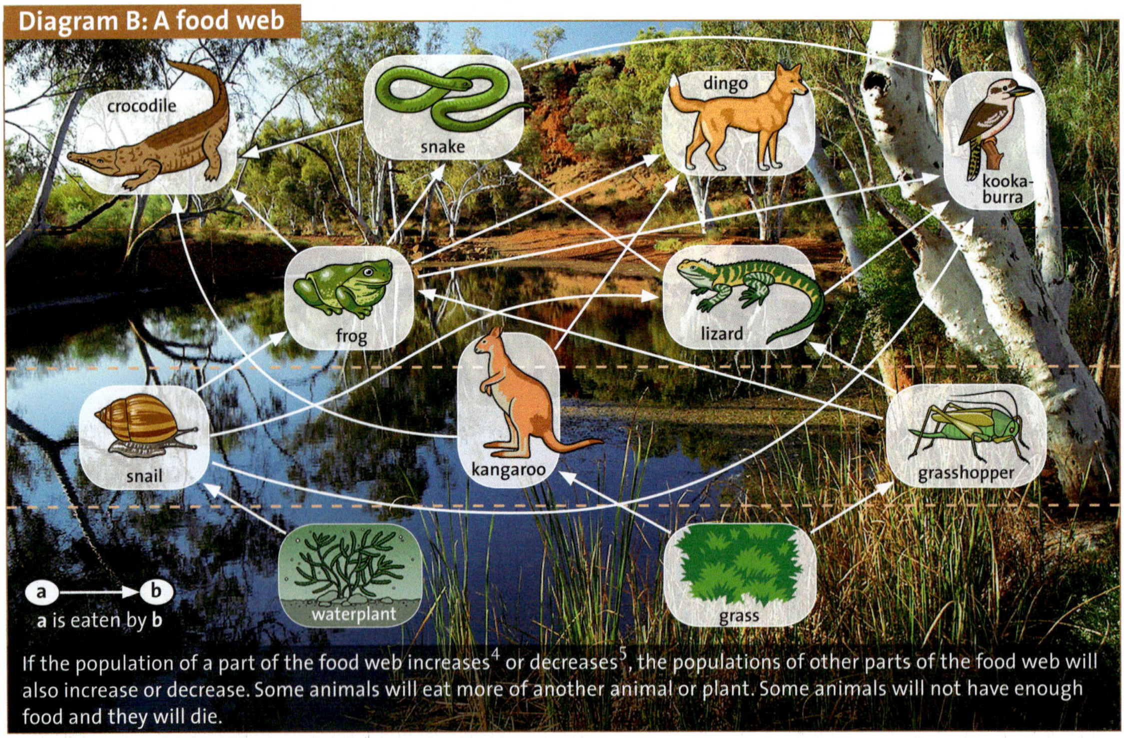

If the population of a part of the food web increases[4] or decreases[5], the populations of other parts of the food web will also increase or decrease. Some animals will eat more of another animal or plant. Some animals will not have enough food and they will die.

c) *What will happen if the population of an animal in the food web increases or decreases? Talk about what will happen to the populations of the other animals in the web.*

If the population of	snakes frogs dingoes ...	increases/ decreases,	then the population of	snakes frogs dingoes ...	will increase/ decrease.

[1] ecosystem ['iːkəʊsɪstəm] *Ökosystem* [2] food chain ['fuːd tʃeɪn] *Nahrungskette* [3] primary/secondary/tertiary consumer ['praɪməri kən,sjuːmə, 'sekəndri, 'tɜːʃəri] *Primär-/Sekundär-/Tertiärkonsument* [4] (to) increase [ɪn'kriːs] *zunehmen* [5] (to) decrease [dɪ'kriːs] *zurückgehen, abnehmen*

3 An ecosystem in disorder[1]

TOADZILLA!

27 March 2007

A cane toad as big as a small dog was found in Australia this week. The cane toad was 20 cm long – twice as big as most toads.

In 1935, farmers in Queensland brought 102 cane toads to Australia because they had problems with insects in their fields. They wanted the cane toads to eat the insects.

Unfortunately that was a really bad idea! Today there are about 200 million cane toads and native[2] Australian animals are in danger.

The government is now asking people to hunt cane toads and kill them. So, why is the situation so bad for the native animals of Australia?

The main reason is the fact that cane toads are poisonous. Animals (like crocodiles, snakes, lizards and birds) that try to eat the cane toad, or its eggs, die from the poison.

Another problem is that cane toads eat almost anything that moves, like native snakes, frogs, lizards and birds.

Now scientists are searching for a way to control the cane toad population in Australia ... before it's too late.

Fast facts: Cane toads

From: South America

Scientific name: Bufo marinus

Size: About 10 to 15 cm long.

What do they eat? Almost anything: insects, lizards, frogs and small snakes, even cat and dog food.

What are they eaten by? Snakes, lizards, crocodiles, birds (But most of them die from the toad's poison!)

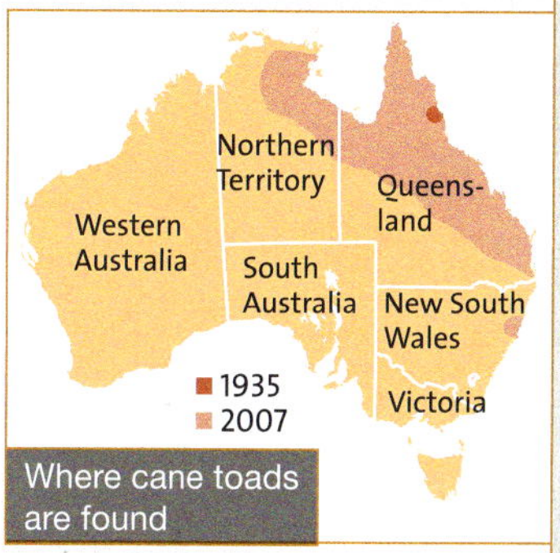

Where cane toads are found

Reproduction: Cane toads have about 8,000 to 35,000 eggs twice a year.

a) *Answer the questions about the article.*

1 How did cane toads arrive in Australia?
2 What does the Australian government want people to do about cane toads?
3 Why are cane toads a problem for native animals? Give two reasons.

b) *Look at the photos, the map and the fast facts box. Describe what they show.*

c) *Look at the food web on p. 110 again. What will happen if the cane toad arrives in this place?*

Activate your English

- The photo/map/fast facts box shows/gives information about ...
- It says that ... / It shows ...
- This is a photo/map of ...
- In 1935 cane toads were found in ... In 2007 they were found in ...

d) *Do you think that it would be a good idea to bring a new animal to Australia that could eat the cane toad? Why (not)?*
I think it might make the situation better/worse because the new animal might ...

4 Rabbits in Australia

Find out how rabbits arrived in Australia and write a short text. Where did they come from and when were they brought to Australia? Include[3] a fast facts box, a map and/or a diagram. You can put your text in your DOSSIER.

[1] in disorder [dɪs'ɔ:də] *in Unordnung; (funktions)gestört* [2] native ['neɪtɪv] *einheimisch* [3] (to) include [ɪn'klu:d] *aufnehmen, einschließen*

TF 3 PROJECT: What's so special about Australia?

Divide the class into groups. Each group chooses a topic about Australia. Do the project in your group. Then present your project to the class.

Project work

1 **Organize your group work**
In your group, brainstorm and decide: What topic will you do? Who will do what? When can you meet again to discuss the project?
It's important that you listen to the ideas of everyone in your group.

2 **Research and take notes**
Collect information on your topic. Choose the best information and take notes.

3 **Decide how to present the information**
Do you want to make a poster, a booklet, or do a video or a slide show? Collect suitable materials like photos, film clips, etc.

4 **Agree on the next steps**
Who will do what? By when?

5 **Prepare your presentation**
Structure the notes and materials you have collected. Write short notes and practise the presentation with the other members of your group.

▸ *SF Brainstorming (p. 148)* • *SF Research (p. 138)* • *SF Giving a presentation (p. 139)*

Will the Great Barrier Reef survive?

Here are some ideas for a topic:

Topic 1 The geography of Australia

Australia is a whole continent, so it has lots of different landscapes, from desert to rain forest. What are these places like? Who or what lives there? How do they survive? And what about the island of Tasmania?

Can you find the Daintree Rain Forest on a map?

Where's the Simpson Desert?

Topic 2 The animals of Australia

Everyone has heard of the kangaroo, and everybody loves koalas. But Australia has lots of other fascinating animals. Which ones can only be found in Australia? Which ones are dangerous? Are any of them threatened? And what's the worry about rabbits?

Why do they call it a 'Tasmanian Devil'[1]?

What's unusual about the platypus?

You wouldn't want to meet a 'salty'!

Topic 3 The first people of Australia

What else is there to know about the Aborigines? And who are the Torres Strait Islanders? How do these groups live in modern Australia – are their lives different to those of white Australians? Their beliefs and legends? Their art and music?

What were the origins of Aborigine dot[2] paintings?

Topic 4 The sports of Australia

What sports are Aussies especially good at? Who are their famous sports stars? And what is special about Australian Rules football?

What are the rules of Aussie Rules football?

[1] devil ['devl] *Teufel* [2] dot [dɒt] *Punkt*

TF 4 Diary of a teenage job hunter by Ewan Denham, 17, Swindon, Wiltshire

What would be your dream summer job? Why? How would you find a summer job?

Diary of a teenage job hunter

Day 1

Yay! Summer's nearly here! And summer means money! It's time to start looking for my dream summer job. I've only got one rule for summer work: I will NOT work in a café. I worked in our neighbour's café once. It was OK, but I don't want to spend another summer serving customers who tell me that the tea's too hot, or the ice cream's too cold!

I bet I would be a good receptionist. I'm friendly and I hear it's good money for sitting at a desk all day. Yeah. I could definitely do that. Well, now that I've decided that, I think I've done enough for today. Tomorrow, I'll apply for some jobs.

Day 2

Today I will find my job. I can just feel it. Jobs4u.co.uk has a good selection[1], so I'll start there.

This will be so easy. I put in 'receptionist' as my key word and I choose the 'office work' section. I find 7 great possibilities straightaway. I apply for each of them. In my application I am confident, but not too confident. I say that my CV is attached. It's a very nice CV. It's got a personal statement and it tells you everything you need to know about me. I quickly check the email before I send it. No spelling mistakes, it looks great. I expect I will get the phone calls about the interviews by the end of the week.

Day 3

No one has called yet. The companies have probably had a lot of applications. No problem. Jobs4u has lots of new opportunities[2] today. I sent yesterday's email to 18 new companies.

Mum says why don't I go next-door and ask Sandra if she needs any help in the café. I tell her the perfect job is out there waiting for me. I just need to find it.

Day 4

Hum. Still no calls. Also, I realize that none of the 18 emails I sent yesterday had my CV attached. Oops! That's OK. I sent out another twelve emails today (with CVs). The interviews should start very soon.

Day 7

No replies! Nix, nothing, nada! How is that possible? I have sent out 37 applications! Maybe I need to change my key words. I start looking in the 'tourism' and 'general' sections

[1] selection [sɪ'lekʃn] *Auswahl, Angebot* [2] opportunity [ɒpə'tju:nəti] *Gelegenheit*

of Jobs4u. I also look at giveusajob.co.uk. I'm starting to think that Jobs4u is some kind of joke. Perhaps there aren't any real jobs on there at all. (Maybe I'm getting a bit paranoid?)

Day 12

Yes! I've got an interview! At last! It's a customer service job where I'll earn £600 a week. That's really good money. I don't mind serving customers for £600 a week! But my interview is in less than two hours, so I need to get ready.

Day 12, later

That job seemed just a little bit strange. After the interview, I think I know less about the job than when I went in. This is what happened in the interview:

Interviewer – – Hi, Ewan. I'm Carla. Did you have any problem getting here today?
Me – – No, no problems, thank you.
Interviewer – – Well, we are happy to have you in our team, Ewan.
Me – – Huh. I've got the job?
Interviewer – – (Laughs) I mean if you get the job ... Now, as you know, the money's good. Do you have any questions?
Me – – Um ... What exactly do I have to do in this job?
Interviewer – – You will work with a fantastic product and deliver[1] a great customer experience. Anything else?
Me – – Um, er, no, I don't think so.
Interviewer – – Well, that's great! I think you're perfect for the job.
Me – – I am?
Interviewer – – Come in tomorrow, at 9 am.

Day 13

I arrive at the office at 9 and Carla is there with a small group of people.
Carla – – Hello and welcome everyone! Please sit down.
(I find a chair.)
Carla – – You are all here today because you have been chosen for a very important and exciting job.
(Sounds good)
Carla – – You are hard-working, reliable people who want to be part of a great team.
(That's me!)
Carla – – That's why you have been chosen to be part of this amazing opportunity.
(Great!)
Carla – – For just £200 we can show you the easy way to earn £600 a week. For this small price we will give you everything you need to start ...
(Huh? I have to pay them?)

I'm out of here!

Day 14

Back to the hunt.

Day 15

Mum says why don't I contact some temp agencies[2]. Brilliant! Why didn't I think of that? I need a temporary job. Temp agencies give people temporary jobs. We were made for each other. I contact 6 of them.

---

[1] (to) deliver [dɪˈlɪvə] *liefern; leisten* [2] temp (=temporary) agency [ˈtemp eɪdʒənsi] *Zeitarbeitsfirma*

Day 16

One of the agencies has called me! They don't actually have a job right now, but they want me to come in for an interview. This sounds good.

Day 17

That interview went a lot better than the last one. They haven't got a job for me right now, but they think they'll have a suitable job soon. And I don't have to pay them money first.

Day 21

I give up. I can't do it anymore. I've heard nothing from the temp agency. I don't want to waste any more time looking at Jobs4u. It's time to break the rules!

Day 23

I've done it! I've finally got a job. I will spend my summer working at Sandra's café. It's a great job and the money's OK! It's good to know that dreams can come true, isn't it?

1 Understanding the text

Are these sentences true or false? Explain.

1 In the beginning, Ewan doesn't want to work in a café.
2 He doesn't want to work as a receptionist.
3 He checks his CV for spelling mistakes.
4 On Day 7 Ewan tries another website.
5 At the job interview on Day 12, Ewan finds out all about the customer service job.
6 On Day 13 Ewan leaves because he doesn't want to give Carla £200.
7 Ewan gets a job with a temp agency.
8 In the end, Ewan still doesn't want to work in a café.

2 Tips for job hunters

a) *What did Ewan do right? What did he do wrong?*

b) *Write three tips for people who want a summer job.*

3 Ewan's diary

Write Ewan's diary entry at the end of his first week at Sandra's café.

4 Now you

Write about your own experience of looking for a part-time job.

– What kind of job did you want?
– What did you do to find a job?
– What kind of job did you get?
– What did you have to do?

TF 5 Nine to five by Dolly Parton

Listen to the song. What sort of job do you think the woman does? Does she like her job? Does she like her boss?

Tumble outta bed and I stumble to the kitchen
Pour myself a cup of ambition
Yawnin', stretchin', try to come to life
Jump in the shower and the blood starts pumpin'
Out on the streets the traffic starts jumpin'
And folks like me on the job from nine to five

Chorus:
Workin' nine to five
What a way to make a livin'
Barely[1] gettin' by[2]
It's all takin' and no givin'
They just use your mind
And they never give you credit[3]
It's enough to drive you
Crazy if you let it

Nine to five, for service and devotion
You would think that I
Would deserve[4] a fair promotion[5]
Want to move ahead
But the boss won't seem to let me
I swear sometimes that man is out to get me
Mmmmm ...

(...)

Nine to five, yeah
They got you where they want you
There's a better life
And you think about it, don't you?
It's a rich man's game
No matter what they call it
And you spend your life
Puttin' money in his wallet

1 Understanding the song

What do these phrases from the song mean?

1 'It's all takin' and no givin'' (l. 10)
- A The boss only takes and doesn't give anything back.
- B The worker only takes and doesn't give anything back.

2 'you spend your life / Puttin' money in his wallet' (ll. 28–29)
- A You work hard and your boss gets rich.
- B You give your boss money.

2 Men and women at work

a) *Can you think of any jobs that were traditionally only for men or only for women? Make two lists. What's the situation today?*

b) *What does the chart below tell you about pay for men and women who do the same job?*

Job	Weekly pay in 2007 (US $)	
	Men	Woman
Care assistant	435	350
Nurse	420	383
Waiter/waitress	399	327
Shop assistant	380	313
Cook	356	319

c) *In groups of three to five, write a short comment on each of these statements.*
- There are jobs that only men can do.
- Men and women should earn the same if they do the same job.
- An interesting job is more important than earning lots of money.

[1] barely ['beəli] *kaum* [2] (to) get by *(infml) durchkommen* [3] credit *hier: Anerkennung* [4] (to) deserve [dɪ'zɜːv] *verdienen*
[5] promotion [prə'məʊʃn] *Beförderung*

TF 6 A different sort of justice[1]

1 Crime in England and Wales: some facts and figures

a) *Look at the chart and describe what it shows.*

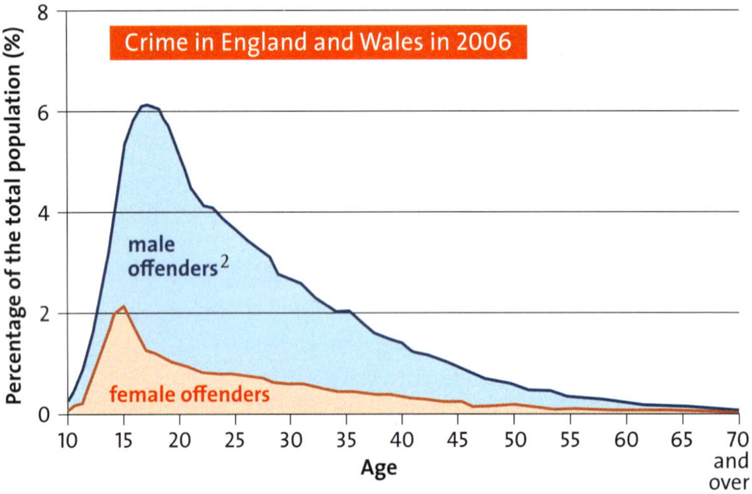

Activate your English

- The chart gives information on ...
- The ... blue/red line shows...
- The percentage of ... is/rises/drops ... between (the age of) ... and ...
- The number of ... is more than/less than/the same as ...

b) *Discuss these other facts and figures with your partner.*

- In **2006**, **1.42 million** offenders were found guilty[3] of crimes or warned in England and Wales.
- In June **2006** there were **10,230** young offenders aged **15–20** in prison.
- **4** out of every **10** young offenders commits another crime in the first year after leaving prison.

2 Bus attack (Part 1)

Read this case study[4] of two young offenders in England.

Over a period of time two boys had been throwing stones at the Number 67 bus as it went past Gateway School. The bus wasn't hit but some passengers were frightened[5].

One day a stone came through the bus window next to the seat of 71-year-old Margaret Wilson. Mrs Wilson was shocked and had a mild heart attack.

The bus driver, Phil Saunders, stopped the bus and called an ambulance. Mrs Wilson was taken to hospital.

Mr Saunders had never experienced anything like this in his fifteen years as a bus driver and was shocked by the attack. His bus company contacted the police.

Sergeant Brian Yates, a police officer who worked with schools, went to Gateway School.

[1] justice ['dʒʌstɪs] *Gerechtigkeit* [2] offender [ə'fendə] *Straftäter/in* [3] (to) find sb. guilty ['gɪlti] *jn. schuldig sprechen, für schuldig befinden*
[4] case study ['keɪs stʌdi] *Fallstudie* [5] frightened ['fraɪtənd] *verängstigt*

He held an assembly[1] in which he told the students about the attack and asked them to put a note in a box if they knew who the stone-throwers were.

The notes in the box named two 15-year-old boys, Luke and Reece. After Sergeant Yates spoke to them, Luke and Reece admitted[2] that they were guilty.

a) *Match the sentence halves correctly.*

1 Two boys sometimes threw stones ...
2 One day a stone ...
3 This shocked ...
4 She had ...
5 She was taken ...
6 A police officer held ...
7 He asked students to write notes ...
8 Two boys, Luke and Reece, ...

a a mild heart attack.
b an assembly at Gateway School.
c an old lady.
d at the number 67 bus.
e if they knew who the stone-throwers were.
f to hospital.
g went through the bus window.
h were named.

b) *Why do you think the boys threw stones at the bus? Collect ideas.*
I think they were fed up (with ...) / were angry about ... / wanted to look big /...

c) *What would happen to them if they were students at your school? Discuss.*
They would have to see the headteacher / say sorry to ... / go to court / ...

3 Bus attack (Part 2)

Sergeant Yates didn't want Luke and Reece to be prosecuted[3] and get a criminal record[4]. He said the boys were still young and they had never been in trouble with the police before. So he suggested a restorative justice conference[5] where the two boys would meet the people they had harmed[6] face to face.

Next, Sergeant Yates visited the boys' families. Luke lived with his grandparents. They were terribly upset by the case, especially by what had happened to the victim, Margaret Wilson.

At first Luke and Reece were not sorry about what they had done – only about getting caught. So Brian Yates and some teachers at the school spent a lot of time with them before the conference.

They wanted to help them understand what harm they had done.

At the conference, Luke and Reece sat face to face with people from the police and the

[1] assembly [ə'sembli] *Versammlung* [2] (to) admit [əd'mɪt] *zugeben* [3] (to) prosecute ['prɒsɪkjuːt] *strafrechtlich verfolgen*
[4] criminal record [ˌkrɪmɪnl 'rekɔːd] *Vorstrafe* [5] restorative justice conference [rɪˌstɔːrətɪv 'dʒʌstɪs ˌkɒnfərəns] *ein außergerichtliches Treffen von Täter/in, Opfer und Vermittler/in mit dem Ziel des Täter-Opfer-Ausgleichs* [6] (to) harm [hɑːm] *schaden, schädigen*

bus company, the bus driver and Mrs Wilson's daughter.

The conference had a very big effect on Luke and Reece.

'I'm sure Mum would be sad to see how upset the boys are,' Mrs Wilson's daughter told the conference. 'And she'll be happy to hear that they've promised to make up for[1] what they've done.'

In the end, Luke and Reece promised to go to the bus company every Saturday for six months to clean the buses. And they did. Their families reported that it had changed their behaviour.

But Luke and Reece still didn't understand why other students had 'grassed' on[2] them. So Sergeant Yates organized another assembly at school. Here, a number of children explained why they had named Luke and Reece. They said it had given Gateway School a bad reputation[3] and that someone could have been badly hurt.

Luke and Reece were respected more at school for cleaning the buses. The other students thought it showed they were sorry. The two boys felt they had made up for what they had done and this made a big difference to them.

a) *Complete this chart to show how this case is 'different'.*

What would happen in a traditional case	What happened in this case
– The boys would go to court. – They wouldn't discuss what had happened with the victims. – A judge[4] would say what they must do. – They might go to prison for young offenders. – They wouldn't try to make up for what they had done.	– *The boys went to …* – …

b) *Why did the other students tell the police who had thrown the stones? Give two reasons.*

4 Discussing the case

Discuss the case in your group. The following questions might help you. Present your ideas to the class.

- Do you think Luke and Reece should have gone to a traditional court? Why (not)?
- Was the restorative justice conference a good idea in their case? Give reasons.
- Do you think the other students were right to name Luke and Reece? Why (not)?
- Do you think the agreement at the conference was fair? Give reasons.

► *SF Having a discussion (p. 147)*

SOCIAL STUDY SKILLS Case study

You usually look at a case from the **outside**. Think about:

- Who was involved in the case and what did they do?
- What happened exactly?
- What are the possible solutions[5] and the consequences[6] (e.g. for the offenders)?
- What can you learn from the case?

You can also try to look at the case from the **inside**. Think about:

- How did the people who were involved feel?
- What would you have done in their position?

[1] (to) make up for sth. *etwas wieder gutmachen* [2] (to) grass on sb. [grɑːs] *(infml) jn. verpfeifen* [3] a bad reputation [ˌrepju'teɪʃn] *ein schlechter Ruf* [4] judge [dʒʌdʒ] *Richter* [5] solution [sə'luːʃn] *Lösung* [6] consequence ['kɒnsɪkwəns] *Folge, Konsequenz*

TF 7 Famous abridged and adapted from *Totally over you* by Mark Ravenhill

Before you read

What makes someone famous? Brainstorm with a partner and write down your ideas.
Now read the play.

CAST (all aged 14 to 16)

Kitty	Jake
Rochelle	Dan
Hannah	Tyson
Sinita	Framji
	Victor

An empty stage.
Kitty and Jake enter. Kitty is carrying a bag.

Kitty Don't laugh, Jake, don't laugh at me.

Jake I'm sorry, Kit. But when you talk about celebrity[1], when you tell me that you and Roche and H and Sin are going to be famous ...

Kitty We are.

Jake – I have to laugh.

Kitty Because ...?

Jake Because ... In six months – six months when I thought we'd told each other all our secrets – six months and you've never told me that –

Kitty And when I do you laugh at me.

Jake I'm sorry, Kit.

Kitty I choose to share my dream with you and you laugh.

Jake I shouldn't but – I just never knew. Tell me. Tell me what you dream about.

Kitty You mustn't laugh.

Jake I won't.

Kitty Even a little laugh and I'll stop.

Jake I promise. I want to understand girls. I want to understand what goes on in their heads. I want to know what you talk about. You and Roche and H and Sin. Tell me. Tell me about your dream.

Kitty OK. We're going to be celebrities. Pretty soon, you're going to see us everywhere. Huge billboards[2] with our faces on. TV screens with us talking, moving, dancing, laughing. The front pages will tell you what we're up to[3] every day. You go to buy a can of coke – they'll have our faces on the side. Lots of Japanese kids are going to dress like us. Your screensaver, your desktop, your mobile's welcome screen – all of them will be me and Roche and H and Sin.

Pause. Then Jake laughs.

Kitty Oh piss off[4], Jake. Just piss off.

Jake I'm sorry, Kit. I just ... You know.

Kitty What?

Jake Look at us. This town, this school. It just seems such a fantasy.

Kitty An ambition. That's the trouble with you, Jake. You don't want anything.

Jake I want ...

Kitty I am so fed up with you.

Jake I'm sorry, I'll ...

Kitty I don't want to see you any more.

Jake What, you're ...?

Kitty I'm ending this relationship. Here. Now. Goodbye.

Jake No. Kit. Wait. You can't just walk away.

Kitty Why not?

Jake Because I love you.

Kitty That's nice.

Jake And you love me.

Kitty Do I? Do I really, Jay? I don't think so. No. I think I used to. But I'm growing up fast. Six months ago I was a kid and now ...

Jake Now you're a celebrity.

---

[1] celebrity [sə'lebrəti] *berühmte Persönlichkeit* [2] billboard ['bɪlbɔːd] *Reklametafel* [3] what we're up to *was wir machen, was wir so treiben*
[4] Piss off. [ˌpɪs‿'ɒf] *(Vorsicht! Slang, vulgär) Hau ab!* [5] relationship [rɪ'leɪʃnʃɪp] *Beziehung*

Kitty — Now I'm ready to be a celebrity. And I don't need you any more.

Jake — Kitty, please.

Kitty — You're a nice guy. You're quite good-looking. You have a sense of humour[1]. Someone else will go out with you.

Jake — No.

Kitty — Goodbye. I'm not your girlfriend any more.

Jake — I've still got the photo of you up beside my bed. The photo I put up the day I asked you out and you said yes.

Kitty — You have to go now. Rochelle's on her way here and we've got a lot to talk about.

Jake — Plans for the future?

Kitty — Sort of.

Jake — So what now? Talk to your stylists? Talk to your PR[2] people? Sort out a few photo-shoots? A few interviews?

Kitty — Piss off, Jake.

Jake — Or maybe you're just going to sit here with your magazines like Heat and Hello ...

Kitty — No, actually, no.

Jake — ... sit here and waste[3] your time with pointless[4], pointless dreams?

Rochelle enters.

Rochelle — Hi, guys.

Jake — What are you going to be?

Kitty — How do you mean?

Jake — In five years, ten years, twenty years. What are you going to be?

Kitty — I told you, Jacob. Celebrities.

Rochelle — That's right.

Jake — Are you going to be in a band?

Kitty — Maybe. I don't know.

Jake — Or act?

Kitty — Yeah. Could do.

Jake — Or model or present on MTV or –?

Kitty — Yeah, yeah, Jake ...

Jake — Well – which one? What's going to make you famous?

Kitty — I don't know. I don't care. It doesn't matter.

Jake — You've got to have a talent.

Kitty — Of course, yeah.

Jake — And I hate to tell you this, girls, but you can't sing, you can't act, you're OK-looking but you're not models ...

Kitty — We'll find a way.

Jake — You're dreaming, the pair of you.

Kitty — OK. You want to know? You want to know what's going to make us famous?

Jake — Yes. I want to know.

Kitty — OK. We're going to date[5] celebrities.

Rochelle — That's right.

Kitty — By the end of the day I'm going to be dating a celeb.

Rochelle — That's right

Jake — That's a promise?

Kitty — That's a promise.

Jake — Ha. Ha. Ha.

Jake exits[6].

Kitty — Loser. We're going to show him.

Rochelle — Maybe he's right, Kit. Maybe we're never going to make it.

Kitty — No. You know what that horoscope said.

Rochelle — I know.

Kitty — 'Finish old relationships and prepare to live your dreams.' And that's exactly what we've got to do. Did you do it?

Rochelle — Yeah. I did it just like you said. Only ...

Kitty — I need you with me, Rochelle. We've got to stick together[7]. Everybody else in this stupid school, this stupid town, is going to laugh at us, but you and me and H and Sin, we've got to be there for each other. OK?

Rochelle — OK. Just ...

Kitty — Yeah?

---

[1] sense of humour [ˌsens‿əv 'hjuːmə] *(Sinn für) Humor* [2] PR (Public Relations) *Öffentlichkeitsarbeit; Werbung* [3] (to) waste [weɪst] *verschwenden* [4] pointless ['pɔɪntləs] *sinnlos* [5] (to) date sb. [deɪt] *mit jm. (aus)gehen* [6] (to) exit ['eksɪt] *hinausgehen; von der Bühne abgehen* [7] (to) stick together *(infml) zusammenhalten*

Rochelle Dan cried. When I said, 'I don't want to be your girlfriend any more,' he started to cry. With great big tears. And I wanted to say, 'Dan, Dan. Stop. I didn't mean it. I still love you.'

Kitty But you didn't.

Rochelle No, Kit. I didn't.

Kitty You had to do it, Roche. Dan's a nice guy –

Rochelle He's a really nice guy.

Kitty – but can you imagine him with David Beckham or Sting or the Queen?

Rochelle No. No, I can't.

Kitty He'd say all the wrong things.

Hannah enters.

Hannah Oh God. I feel like such a bitch[1]. I said, 'Tyson, this is the end.' He just kept on repeating in this really miserable voice: 'Why? Why? Why?' Over and over again. 'Why? Why? Why?' And now he wants back everything he ever gave me: CDs, videos, T-shirts. Everything. I'm going to miss them so much. This better be worth it[2], Kit.

Kitty Worth it? H, what's Tyson when you are going to have your pick of film stars[3], singers, footballers, models? You want Brad Pitt?

Hannah I'd love Brad Pitt but ...

Kitty Then work it, girl. We're going to be so famous he won't resist[4].

Hannah But isn't he with ...?

Kitty You'll be all over the papers for days. Your PR people will have to work so hard. 'I'm sorry about all the hurt I've caused,' you'll say. 'But Brad and I are so happy together.'

Hannah Yes. A quiet wedding. Brad. Our families. And a few friends.

Kitty That's it. And where's Tyson going to be? The supermarket? The call centre?

Hannah Car-park attendant[5] maybe.

Kitty Let him read about it in the papers.

Hannah Brad and I are going to meditate together for an hour every morning.

Sinita enters, crying.

Sinita I hate you, Kitty. Why did you make me do that? I love Framji, I do. And now. I finished with him. *(She cries.)*

Rochelle Come on, babe.

Sinita He says he never wants to see me again. Or walk down the same street as me. Or take the same bus as me. Or use the same search engine as me. Totally – gone. Forever. And what am I going to do without him?

Kitty Do without him? Do without him? You know what you're going to do without him. Same as me without Jay, same as Roche without Dan, same as H without Ty. Be a celebrity.

Sinita And are you sure about that, Kit?

Kitty Yes of course. Totally sure. Aren't you?

Sinita Well ...

Kitty Sin. You can't give up this easily. I know this is hard. But think of the reward[6]. Think of waking up in this totally fantastic house next to your totally fantastic boyfriend.

Rochelle And there's a TV crew already there as you open your eyes. They're making a documentary about you 24/7[7]. There's a whole channel that shows it all totally live.

Hannah And then you exercise with your personal trainer.

Kitty Make some calls to Japan as you eat your breakfast – they're planning this Barbie-type doll of you for markets all around the world.

Rochelle The morning: photo-shoots – a calendar. Some measurements[8] for your wedding dress. Hello is sponsoring your wedding. Only fourteen months to go.

---

[1] bitch [bɪtʃ] *(Vorsicht! Slang, abwertend) Schlampe, Miststück* [2] this better be worth it [wɜːθ] *etwa: Ich kann nur hoffen, dass es das wert ist* [3] you're going to have pick of film stars *du wirst jeden Filmstar haben können, den du willst* [4] (to) resist [rɪ'zɪst] *widerstehen* [5] car-park attendant [ə'tendənt] *Parkplatzwächter/in* [6] reward [rɪ'wɔːd] *Belohnung* [7] 24/7 *rund um die Uhr* [8] measurement ['meʒəmənt] *Maß*

Hannah Lunch with Beyoncé and Madonna. Chatter, chatter. You debate: is hatha yoga now out? Then cameras: flash, flash, flash.

Kitty The afternoon: a massage and a meeting with a team from LA who want to turn you into a cartoon series for TV. You tell them: nice idea but you want to see what happens with the movie rights first.

Rochelle Then off to a gallery. You've done a painting for charity[1]. Just a fun thing. 'I'm no artist,' you tell the reporters. 'But I do care about sick children and I just wanted to do what I could to help.'

Hannah And then up the red carpet at a film première. 'Is it true that they're making you into a musical?' 'No comment.' Then party, party. 'Hi, Nicole! Hi, Ewan! Hallo, Uma!'

Kitty And as you fall into your bed you say: 'I did it. This is me. My dream, my hope, my destiny[2]. Celebrity.' Today was hard. I know that, girls. 'Finish old relationships'; that's hard. But now it's time, time to live your dreams. Are you going to do that, Sin?

Sinita Will I have a stalker[3]?

Kitty Maybe.

Sinita I'd like a stalker. Someone who fills their house with pictures of me. Goes through my bins. Names all their children after me. Who can't get me out of their head.

Kitty Of course you'll have a stalker.

Sinita And says he'll shoot himself if I don't return his calls.

Kitty Yes. Absolutely.

Sinita Oh wow.

Kitty Are we sticking together, girls? Are we sistas?

Rochelle, *Hannah*, *Sinita* *(together)* Yeah.

Kitty Then come on. New OK out today. New Sugar. See what our horoscopes say today.

Kitty takes magazines from her bag and hands them round.

Kitty OK. Horoscope time. Oh my God. Oh my God. Look at this. 'A stranger[4] will show you the way to future happiness today.' What does that mean? Keep your eyes open for a stranger, girls.

Kitty, Rochelle, Hannah and Sinita exit. Jake and Victor enter.

Jake Victor. Will you stop following me? I want to be alone.

Victor But we said we'd go to a movie.

Jake Yeah. Well, I've changed my mind.

Victor There's a sci-fi thing. Which sounds good. Or an action thing. Which sounds OK. Or a comedy. Which sounds really funny. Which do you fancy?

Jake None of them.

Victor I've got some DVDs if you want to ...

Jake No.

Victor Or games. My mum left pizza and some oven chips ...

Jake Vic. I want to be by myself. Please.

Victor But – why?

Jake Kit finished with me.

Victor No way.

Jake Yeah. She chucked[5] me. So ...

Victor I'm sorry.

Jake And I just want to go into my room and be alone.

Victor But surely a movie would ...

Jake No, Vic. I'm sorry.

Victor Or a pizza or just hanging out at Burger King.

Jake Victor. No.

Victor But I'm your friend.

Jake I know and ...

Victor All the things we've done together. Things I've done for you.

---

[1] charity ['tʃærəti] *hier: wohltätige Zwecke* [2] destiny ['destəni] *Schicksal* [3] stalker ['stɔːkə] *jd., der eine andere Person (meist eine/n Prominente/n) verfolgt und belästigt* [4] stranger ['streɪndʒə] *Fremde(r)* [5] (to) chuck sb. [tʃʌk] *mit jm. Schluss machen*

Jake But Vic – you're a dork[1]. You've never been out with a girl.

Victor I'd like to.

Jake And I don't want to talk to someone who doesn't know anything about girls.

Victor You know Letitia?

Jake If you haven't been out with a girl you're a child, Vic.

Victor She did the Nurse in that scene from Romeo and Juliet.

Jake That's the difference between us, Vic.

Victor I like Letitia. I keep on having dreams about her. I want to ask her out.

Jake You're a child and I'm a man.

Dan enters.

Dan I don't believe it. I just don't believe it. Roche finished with me.

Jake She chucked you?

Dan Just sat down and said: 'I don't want to see you any more. We're finished. Over.' She wants to be a celebrity, Jay.

Jake Oh my God.

Tyson enters.

Tyson Bitch. Bitch. Bitch.

Jake What's that, Ty?

Tyson Hannah. What a freaking bitch. Chucked me. I've never been chucked. Never.

Jake Did she say she wanted to be …?

Tyson A celebrity. Can you believe that? I told her: no freaking way, baby. And then she got mad at me and chucked me. I'm just so angry.

Victor Maybe going to a movie would help?

Tyson What's he doing here? What are you doing here?

Victor There's a sci-fi movie …

Tyson Shut up, Victor, shut up.

Framji enters.

Framji Guys. You'll never guess. Sin finished with me.

Jake We know. Same for all of us, Fram. Me and Kit. Dan and Roche. H and Ty. You and Sin. We've all been chucked.

Dan On the same day.

Tyson At the same time.

Framji But – they must have planned this.

Jake That's right.

Framji I don't believe it. What a bitch.

Tyson Yeah. Total bitches. All of them.

Kitty, Rochelle, Hannah and Sinita enter.

Kitty Oh, hi. We didn't know you were here.

Jake Yeah. That's right. We're here.

Hannah We're looking for a stranger. To show the way to future happiness.

Tyson Right.

Rochelle Like it says here. You seen a stranger?

Dan No. Don't think so. No.

Kitty Come on, girls. They're not going to help us.

Kitty, Rochelle, Hannah and Sinita exit.

Framji Did you see that? Didn't even look at me.

Jake We need to show them, guys.

Tyson Yeah. We need to punish them.

Dan We need to hurt them.

Framji To teach them a lesson.

Jake To show them how stupid they are.

Dan But how?

Victor Maybe if I …?

Dan What's the best way to make them suffer[2]?

Victor Can I …? I've got an idea.

Tyson Victor. You don't know anything about girls. You go off to the library and let us figure this thing out[3].

Framji They're coming back. They're coming this way.

Dan Run.

Jake Stay.

Tyson Hide.

Victor Guys. I'm going to show you … Can I show you? Guys.

---

[1] dork [dɔːk] *(infml) Trottel, Langweiler* [2] (to) suffer [ˈsʌfə] *leiden* [3] (to) figure sth. out [ˌfɪɡər_ˈaʊt] *etwas herausfinden*

Jack, Dan, Tyson and Framji hide. Kitty, Rochelle, Hannah and Sinita enter. Victor covers his face.

Victor — The future. The future. I see the future.
Rochelle — Ugh. Look. A loony[1].
Sinita — A loony homeless person.
Hannah — Ugh. Gross. They don't wash. And they really smell.
Sinita — And they get really aggressive if you don't give them money.
Rochelle — Well, I'm not giving him anything.
Kitty — Girls. Listen for a moment. Just listen to what he's saying.
Victor — The mortal[2] man walks backward
His face toward what's gone
The future is a mystery
But still he travels on.
Sinita — It's like mad person's talk.
Kitty — No. It makes sense[3] if you listen.
Victor — But I am not as other men
Who only see what's done
My brain is burnt with future lives
I see the world to come.
The future. The future. I see the future.
Kitty — Who are you?
Hannah — Kit, I think we ought to be going now.
Kitty — No, no. We've got to talk to him. Find out ...
Rochelle — He's really creepy[4], Kit.
Sinita — Yeah. I think he may be dangerous.
Kitty — But girls – if he sees the future ...
Victor — I know you. I know you. I know you. I know you.
Sinita — Oh my God. He's going completely mental[5].
Rochelle — I want another Diet Coke. Let's all go and buy another Diet Coke.
Sinita — Yeah, Roche. Good idea.
Kitty — Girls. We've got to ask him. We've got to make him tell us. What happens to us? How do we get to be celebrities?
Hannah — There's no point asking him. He's a loony.
Kitty — Stick together, girls. We've got to stick together.
Victor — I know you. I know you. I know you. I know you.
Kitty — Me?
Victor — Everybody knows you.
Kitty — In the future.
Victor — You are famous in the future.
Kitty — Oh my God. That's amazing.
Victor — Your picture is everywhere in the future. A hotel in Bangkok, an IMAX in New Mexico, a hologram in Times Square – it's you.
Kitty — I knew it. I knew I was right.
Victor — You are a line of clothes, a cola drink, a fitness video, a salad dressing, a doll, a video game, a mouse pad, a car sticker, a newspaper column, a talkshow, the most hits in a day on AOL, a remix, beauty tips, a diet plan, a chain of restaurants, a sex symbol, role-model superstar. You are live action, animation, computer-generated, holographic, CD ROM, exclusive pictures, pay-to-view. All of them are you and you are all of them. Oh, yes, I know you. In the future I know you. In the future everybody knows you.
Kitty — And Roche and H and Sin as well?
Victor — And Roche and H and Sin as well.
Rochelle — Oh, my God.
Hannah — Oh, my God.
Sinita — Amazing.
Victor — The bedrooms that you live in now will be museums – a place for all your fans to come. Coaches will stop outside your school: 'That's the place. That's where she studied.'
Rochelle — That is so cool.
Victor — Everybody who ever knew you will sell everything you gave them. 'This item personally touched by Kitty.' And everything bought – instantly[6].
Sinita — What will we be famous for?

[1] loony ['lu:ni] *Verrückte(r)* [2] mortal ['mɔ:tl] *sterblich* [3] (to) make sense *(einen) Sinn ergeben* [4] creepy ['kri:pi] *unheimlich* [5] (to) go mental ['mentl] *verrückt werden, durchdrehen* [6] instantly ['ɪnstəntli] *(adv) sofort*

Victor — Do you know the band 'Awesome'?

Sinita — No.

Victor — Four boys. The finest voices, best dance routines. Best songs. The four most famous faces of the future.

Kitty — And we're ...

Victor — You date them. And they bring you fame.

Hannah — And when do we meet them? Where do we meet them?

Victor — You've already met them.

Kitty — We have?

Victor — They are here in your town, your school right now. 'Awesome' are amongst you. The four most famous faces of the future, the biggest celebrities the world has ever known are Jake and Dan and Ty and Framji.

Sinita — But we just ... Oh no ...

Victor — Yes?

Rochelle — We just chucked them.

Victor — You ...? Oh no. Then you must unchuck them fast. You can't meddle with[1] the future. You have to date them or the future's empty: blank[2] videos, blank ads, blank T-shirts, blank covers on the magazines. Without your faces, there is nothing. Quick, quick. Find your friends. Oh God. It's hurting. When time is bent[3] like this it hurts me. Ugh. Ugh. Put the future right. Go out with Jake and Dan and Ty and Fram. Date 'Awesome'! Agh! Agh!

Kitty — Oh my God!

Victor — Before it's too late! Aaaaaaggh!

Kitty, Rochelle, Hannah, Sinita exit.

Working with the text

1 Understanding the play

a) *What is the play about? What is its message? Write down five ideas on five cards.*

b) *Compare your ideas in a group and choose the three best ones. Present your ideas to the class.*

2 Understanding the details

a) *Answer these questions:*

1 What dream does Kitty tell Jake about on p. 121?

2 What reasons does Kitty give for finishing with Jake? Find as many reasons as you can.

3 How do Kitty and her friends plan to become celebrities?

b) *Write five more questions about the play. Collect the ten best questions on the board and try to answer them in class.*

3 Your reactions to the play

Which of the adjectives on the right describe what you think of the play? Explain your reactions.

annoying • boring • clever • funny • interesting • realistic • sad • silly • uninteresting • unrealistic • ...

[1] (to) meddle with ['medl] *herumspielen mit, sich einmischen in* [2] blank [blæŋk] *leer, unbespielt* [3] (to) be bent [bent] *gekrümmt, gebogen, verbogen sein*

TF 8 India

1 India FAQ

Is Mumbai the capital of India?
No. Mumbai is India's biggest city, but it's not the capital. The country's second biggest city, New Delhi, in northern India, became the capital of British India in 1912 and it has been the capital of independent India since 1947.

Does everyone in India speak English?
The main languages in India are Hindi and English, but there are over 20 other languages, like Urdu, Telugu, Punjabi, Marathi, Bengali, Tamil, Kannada, Oriya, and Kashmiri.

Why is English such an important language in India?
India was a British colony for nearly 200 years and so English became the language of government, education and business in India.
India won independence[1] from Britain in 1947, but English is still important, especially in the cities. Many schools teach all school subjects in English and it is the main language spoken by office workers.
In a country with so many different languages, English is often used so that people can understand each other. It is often said in India that if you want to succeed, you have to speak English.

Why is Gandhi such an important person in India?
Mahatma Gandhi, the 'Father of India', was born in India in 1869 and died in 1948 after being shot by a Hindu.
He is famous for non-violent protest and he spent most of his life fighting for India's independence from Britain. In the end, he won freedom[2] for his country without using violence.
Gandhi's ideas about non-violent protest were important to Martin Luther King Jr in the civil rights movement in the US and Nelson Mandela in the fight against apartheid[3] in South Africa.

a) *What do you think is the most interesting thing about India on this page?*
– I think the most interesting thing is that …
– I think it's more interesting that …

b) *What else would you like to know about India? Write a question. In your group vote for the most interesting question. Do some research and write the answer.*

[1] independence [ˌɪndɪˈpendəns] *Unabhängigkeit* [2] freedom [ˈfriːdəm] *Freiheit* [3] apartheid [əˈpɑːtheɪt] *Apartheid (bis 1994 Trennung von Schwarzen und Weißen in Südafrika)*

2 BOLLYWOOD

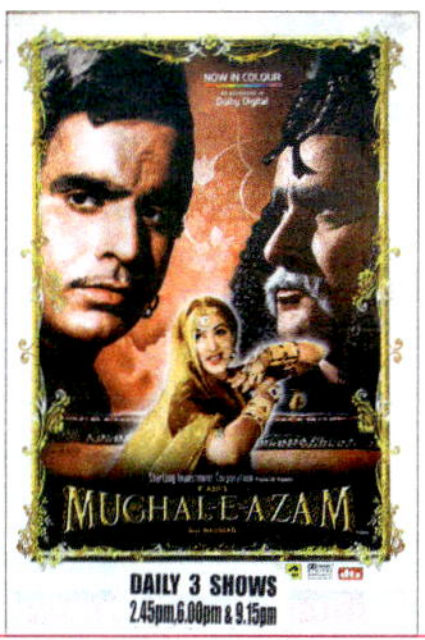

Bollywood, Bombay's Hindi language film industry, is the largest film producer in India and one of the largest in the world.

It seems that everyone in India loves a good film. Indians went to the cinema 3.9 billion times in 2007. In fact, India makes more films than Hollywood. Entertainment Weekly reported that more than 900 films are produced every year. That's more than two films every day.

Bollywood films are popular outside India too, especially in countries with a big Asian population, like Malaysia and Singapore, England, Canada, South Africa, Australia and the US.

A typical Bollywood movie is always spectacular[1] and full of colour and energy.

It always has a good-looking guy and a good-looking girl, singing and dancing, romance and drama. The poor guy always wins against the rich bad guy and there is always a happy ending.

'When people in India go to the cinema they want to forget what is happening in their real lives. They want to escape and enjoy themselves,' says Kishore Lulla, Chief Executive of Bollywood film company Eros International.

a) *Read the text and find important facts about Bollywood.*

b) *With a partner agree on the four most important facts and share them with the class.*

3 VIEWING A shop in Mumbai

a) *Watch the film. Are these sentences right or wrong?*

1 The film clip is about a DVD shop.
2 The owner says it is a business plus hobby.
3 All his customers are from India.

b) *Do you know any of the Bollywood stars?*

c) *How have the posters changed since the early days of Bollywood?*

The older/newer posters ...
- have actors wearing western/traditional clothes.
- are handpainted/more modern/more romantic/...

---

[1] spectacular [spek'tækjələ]

TF 9 South Africa

1 South Africa FAQ

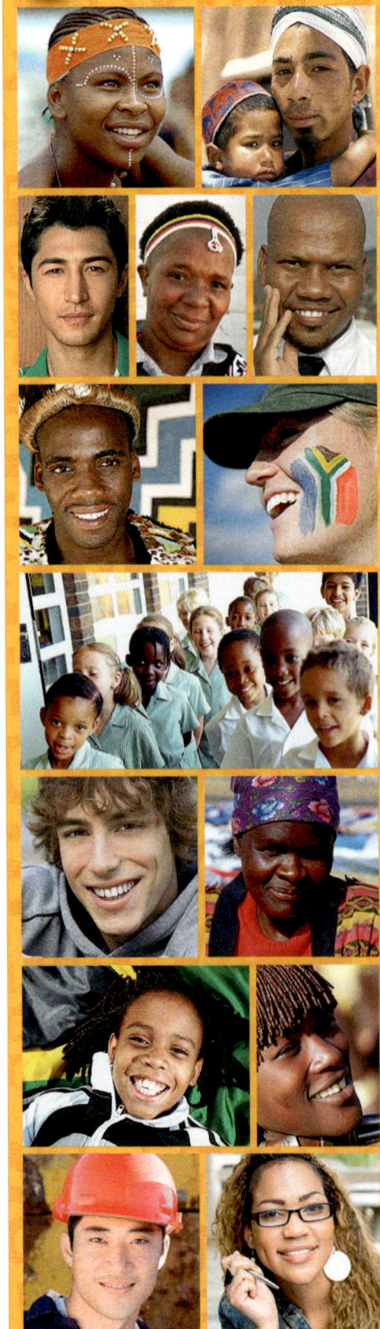

Is Johannesburg the capital of South Africa?
No. Johannesburg is South Africa's biggest city, but it isn't the capital. There are three capitals: Bloemfontein, Cape Town and Pretoria. Why are there three capitals? It goes back to 1910 when different areas came together to make a union[1], but they couldn't agree where the capital should be.

Which ethnic[2] groups make up South Africa's population today?
South Africa is called 'The Rainbow[3] Nation' because there are so many different groups of people. The population of about 49 million is made up of 79.2 % African, 9.2 % White, 8.9 % Coloured[4] and 2.5 % Asian.

How long have there been white people in South Africa?
The ancestors of some of today's white South Africans arrived in the 17th and 18th centuries. They came from the Netherlands, France, Britain and Germany. Many more Europeans arrived after gold was discovered in the 19th century.

Do most people speak English in South Africa?
There are eleven official languages in South Africa: Zulu, Xhosa, Afrikaans, Pedi, English, Tswana, Sotho, Tsonga, Swati, Venda and Ndebele. The number of people whose first language is English is quite small (about 8 % of the population) but a lot of people speak English as a second or third language. Today, English is seen as a very important international language and in South Africa it is the language that is most often used in newspapers, on TV, radio and websites. It is also used in business and politics.

Why is Nelson Mandela such an important person in South Africa?

Nelson Mandela was born in 1918. He spent many years in prison because he fought against apartheid in South Africa. In 1994 he became the country's first black president. A lot of people thought there would be terrible hatred[5] and violence in South Africa when apartheid ended. Nelson Mandela worked hard to bring together all the different groups in the country and to build peace[6] and democracy[7].

Compare the information on this page with the information about India on page 128. Make notes like this:
– India has got one capital. South Africa has got three. – In both countries people speak ...

---

[1] union ['juːniən] *Union, Vereinigung* [2] ethnic ['eθnɪk] *ethnisch, Volks-* [3] rainbow ['reɪnbəʊ] *Regenbogen* [4] Coloured *(in Südafrika) Mensch mit schwarzen und weißen Vorfahren* [5] hatred ['heɪtrɪd] *Hass* [6] peace [piːs] *Frieden* [7] democracy [dɪ'mɒkrəsi]

2 A tour of Soweto adapted from the novel *Many Stones* by Carolyn Coman

This story takes place in South Africa after the end of apartheid. Berry is a high school student in the US. Her older sister Laura was murdered in South Africa when she was working there as a volunteer teacher.

A year later, Berry and her father decide to go to South Africa and visit the school where Laura worked. In this part of the story they have just arrived in Johannesburg and they're on a tour of Soweto.

I have never been surrounded by so many black people in all my life – all black people, because not one white person lives in Soweto. Mr Joseph Otambo, a big black man in a brightly coloured shirt, is driving us around the neighborhoods of Soweto.

Mr Joseph Otambo

He tells us that in the huge hospital we drive past, one third of the babies is born with AIDS.

In a neighborhood of bigger, nicer homes, he stops and points to a house. "This is the home of Desmond Tutu, winner of the Nobel Peace Prize[1]." A little while later he shows us the home where Nelson Mandela once lived. "Also a Nobel Peace Prize winner." Mr Otambo turns and looks at my father and me and holds up two fingers. "The only neighbourhood in the world with two winners!" And he laughs out loud.

Nelson Mandela's house (now a museum)

I don't feel embarrassed any more about being here and doing what we are doing, because Mr Otambo doesn't seem to be. He points to places and tells us things, laughs a lot.

Naledi High School, Soweto

We drive past a small school and he tells us, "The schoolchildren were shot here during the uprising[2] in 1976."

Squatter village

At the first squatter village[3] we come to – miles of tents and shacks that were put together with cardboard[4] and metal and pieces of wood – he points to an outhouse and says, "This is a toilet the people here use." I sit quietly in the car and look at what he has shown us: an outhouse, falling apart.

[1] Nobel Peace Prize [ˌnəʊbel 'piːs praɪz] *Friedensnobelpreis* [2] uprising ['ʌpraɪzɪŋ] *Aufstand* [3] squatter village ['skwɒtə] *illegale Siedlung*
[4] cardboard ['kɑːdbɔːd] *Pappe*

It reminds me of the toilet we had at summer camp, but the one at camp was a lot better.

Outhouse

"Now you can see the inside of the toilet," he says, at another broken outhouse without a door. "There are not enough for all the people who live here."

Mr Otambo invites us to go inside one of the shacks. It is part of the tour. He tells us it's all right with the woman who lives there. People in the village want visitors to see with their own eyes what it is like for some of the people who live here in Soweto.

I don't know if anybody can see I'm scared. My father goes first. We leave the car and enter the shack closest to the road. There is a woman there, she's sitting on a small bed. She says her name is Mary and we all shake hands and then we are silent inside the dark tent. There is a picture from a magazine on the wall, but the wall is a piece of cardboard. A towel hangs and divides the space into rooms, but the whole place is no bigger than the playhouse Laura and I had behind our old home. When my father asks, Mary tells us she has six children.

Six kids, six. In this place where I am standing, crowded together with just her and my father. I wish she hadn't told us. I don't want to know that she's a mom. Suddenly I can't stand it[1] that Mary, this woman, is a mom, just like my mom is a mom. I want her to be different so that the way she lives somehow[2] is OK. But how can it be OK? It can't.

Mary's home

3 Understanding the story

a) *Make a chart like this. What information does Mr Otambo give at each place on the tour?*

Place	Information
hospital:	1/3 of babies born with AIDS
1st house:	...

b) *Why do people in Soweto welcome tourists?*

c) *Why did Berry feel embarrassed at the start and why did she stop feeling embarrassed? How does she feel at the end?*

d) *Do you think it's OK to go as a tourist to visit poor places like Soweto? Say why (not).*

4 Background research

a) *Mr Otambo talks about the following topics. Find out more about one of them.*

- AIDS in South Africa
- Desmond Tutu
- Nelson Mandela
- The 1976 Soweto Uprising

b) *Tell your group what you have learned.*

[1] I can't stand it *ich kann es nicht ertragen* [2] somehow ['sʌmhaʊ] *irgendwie*

TF 10 Project: An English-speaking city

Which city?

During the last five years, your English book has taken you to lots of big cities where English is the main language: Atlanta, Bristol, Johannesburg, London, Los Angeles, Mumbai, San Francisco, Sydney, Toronto. Which of these cities would you like to know more about? Or is there another English-speaking city that you would like to find out about?

Sydney

Los Angeles

Toronto

London

What makes the city special?

- What is there to do and see?
- Are there any songs or poems about the city?
- Are there any special dishes to eat?
- What's the weather like?
- What kind of sports events and teams are there?
- What famous people are connected with the city?

Would you like to ...

... try some delicious food in Singapore?

... go shopping in Hong Kong?

... see the sights of Dublin?

Your city project

1 *Find other students who want to work on the same city as you, or work alone.*
2 *Work on the project, dividing the tasks between you if you're in a group.*
3 *Think of an interesting way to present your information. The boxes on the right may give you some ideas.*
4 *Present your project to the class. You can do a computer presentation, make posters or handouts, ...*
5 *Listen to/Look at the other presentations and assess them.*

Create a booklet
Put together a mix of your own writing, newspaper articles, photos, songs, maps ... For each thing, explain why you chose it.

Design a quiz
Write a good mix of question types (A/B/C or D, true/false, yes/no, who/what/when/where/why, ...) and remember to write an answer key.

Plan a two-day visit to the city
How will you get from the airport to the city centre? Where will you stay? What sights will you visit? What will you eat?

▸ *SF Research; Giving a presentation; Using visual materials with a presentation (p. 138–139)*

Skills File – Inhalt

		Seite
STUDY AND LANGUAGE SKILLS		
REVISION	Learning words	135
REVISION	Describing pictures	135
REVISION	Check yourself	136
REVISION	Using a bilingual dictionary	137
REVISION	Research	138
REVISION	Giving a presentation	139
Using visual materials with a presentation		139
Talking about charts		140
LISTENING AND READING SKILLS		
REVISION	Listening	141
REVISION	Taking notes	142
REVISION	Marking up a text	142
Reading stories		143
REVISION	READING COURSE	144–145
	Working out the meaning of words	144
	Skimming and scanning	144
	Finding the main ideas of a text	145
	Drawing conclusions	145
SPEAKING AND WRITING SKILLS		
SPEAKING COURSE Zusammenfassung		146–147
	Having a conversation	146
	Taking part in a job interview	146
	Having a discussion	147
	Giving a presentation – useful phrases	147
REVISION	Paraphrasing	148
REVISION	Brainstorming	148
REVISION	Summarizing texts	149
REVISION	WRITING COURSE	150–151
	The steps of writing	150
	Writing better sentences	150
	Using paragraphs	150
	Writing a report – collecting and organizing ideas	151
	Correcting your text	151
Writing a CV		152
Writing formal and informal letters		153
From outline to written discussion		154
MEDIATION SKILLS		
REVISION	Mediation	155
EXAM SKILLS		
REVISION	How to do well in a test	156–157

Im **Skills File** findest du Hinweise zu Arbeits- und Lerntechniken. Was du in den Skills-Kästen der Units gelernt hast, wird hier näher erläutert.

Was du bereits aus Band 4 von English G 21 kennst, ist mit **REVISION** gekennzeichnet, z. B.

- **REVISION Describing pictures**, Seite 135
- **REVISION Giving a presentation**, Seite 139.

Viele neue Hinweise helfen dir bei der Arbeit mit Hör- und Lesetexten, beim Sprechen, beim Schreiben von eigenen Texten, bei der Sprachmittlung und beim Lernen von Methoden.

Manchmal gibt es auch Aufgaben dazu.

STUDY AND LANGUAGE SKILLS

SF REVISION Learning words

Worauf solltest du beim Lernen und Wiederholen von Vokabeln achten?

- Lerne immer 7–10 Vokabeln auf einmal.
- Lerne neue und wiederhole alte Vokabeln regelmäßig – am besten jeden Tag 5–10 Minuten.
- Lerne mit jemandem zusammen. Fragt euch gegenseitig ab.
- Schreib die neuen Wörter immer auch auf und überprüfe die Schreibweise mithilfe des *Dictionary* oder *Vocabulary*.

Wie kannst du Wörter besser behalten?

Wörter kannst du besser behalten, wenn du sie in Wortgruppen sammelst und ordnest:

- **Gegensatzpaare** sammeln, z. B. alive ◂▸ dead, majority ◂▸ minority, forget ◂▸ remember
- Wörter mit **gleicher Bedeutung** sammeln, z. B. (to) train – (to) practise
- Wörter in **Wortfamilien** sammeln, z. B. (to) dance, dance, dancer, dancing lessons; friend, boyfriend, girlfriend, friendly, unfriendly, ...
- Wörter in **Wortnetzen** *(networks)* sammeln und ordnen.

SF REVISION Describing pictures

Wie kann ich Bilder beschreiben?

- Um zu sagen, wo genau etwas abgebildet ist, benutze:
  at the top/bottom • in the foreground/background • in the middle • on the left/right
- Diese Präpositionen sind auch hilfreich:
  behind • between • in front of • next to • under
- Um zu beschreiben, was die Personen auf dem Bild tun, benutze das **present progressive**.
  Jeannie is riding her horse.

Wie kann ich beschreiben, was die Personen fühlen?

Oft sollst du dich in eine Person auf einem Foto hineinversetzen und beschreiben, was sie fühlt oder denkt. Schau dir das Foto genau an und nimm dir Zeit, dir die Situation vorzustellen. Beim Formulieren helfen dir *phrases* wie:
Maybe the woman/man in the photo feels ... /is thinking about ... •
I think he/she feels/wants to/...

SF REVISION Check yourself

How am I doing?

Damit du weißt, in welchen Bereichen des Englischen du noch Schwächen hast und welche du schon beherrschst, solltest du dich immer wieder selbst überprüfen. Das kannst du auf unterschiedlichen Wegen tun. Eine Reihe von Tipps kennst du vermutlich schon.
Du kannst dich auch nach jeder Unit mithilfe der *How am I doing*-Seiten selbst überprüfen, die du schon aus Band 3 kennst. Dabei gehst du wie folgt vor:

1. Du machst die einzelnen Aufgaben und überprüfst deine Ergebnisse.
2. Dann schaust du dir die Bereiche, in denen du Fehler gemacht hast, nochmal an. Halte dich dabei an die Hinweise in der Spalte *Find out more*.
3. Nun übst du gezielt diese Bereiche. Dazu schaust du in der Spalte *Exercises* nach, wo du im Englischbuch und *Workbook* Übungen dazu findest.
4. Nach einiger Zeit machst du die Aufgaben in *How am I doing?* noch einmal und vergleichst die Lösungen mit deinen Ergebnissen vom ersten Mal.

Die Arbeit mit einer persönlichen Fehlerliste

Führe eine Liste der Fehler, die du oft machst, und nutze sie beim Schreiben von Texten als persönliche Checkliste. Hefte diese Listen in deinem Englischordner ab oder lege dir dafür ein extra Heft an (z.B. in DIN-A5).
Das Heft kannst du z.B. nach folgenden Schwerpunkten unterteilen:

1. Drittel: *Words* 2. Drittel: *Grammar* 3. Drittel: *Spelling*

Dann untersuchst du deine Klassenarbeiten und andere schriftliche Arbeiten auf deine Fehlerquellen hin. Dein/e Englischlehrer/in zeigt durch Abkürzungen am Rand, was für eine Art Fehler du gemacht hast.

WORDS

Wrong	Correct	REMEMBER
He goes to school ~~with the~~ bus.	He goes to school by bus.	mit dem Bus fahren – go by bus
We've got a ~~strong~~ teacher.	We've got a strict teacher.	Nicht verwechseln! streng – strict / strong – stark
I climbed ~~on~~ a tree.	I climbed a tree.	auf einen Baum klettern – climb a tree

Tipp

- Ergänze das Heft jedes Mal, wenn du eine Klassenarbeit oder einen Text von deinem Lehrer/deiner Lehrerin zurückbekommen oder wenn du eine *How am I doing*-Seite bearbeitet hast.
- Überprüfe, ob du bestimmte Fehler immer wieder machst. Wenn ja, such dafür Übungen in deinem Englischbuch, deinem *Workbook*, deinem *e-Workbook* oder frag deinen Lehrer/deine Lehrerin nach Übungen.
- Schau dir vor jeder Klassenarbeit die Fehler an, die du oft machst.
- Mach dir mithilfe des Grammatikteils die Regeln noch einmal bewusst, die dir besonders schwerfallen.

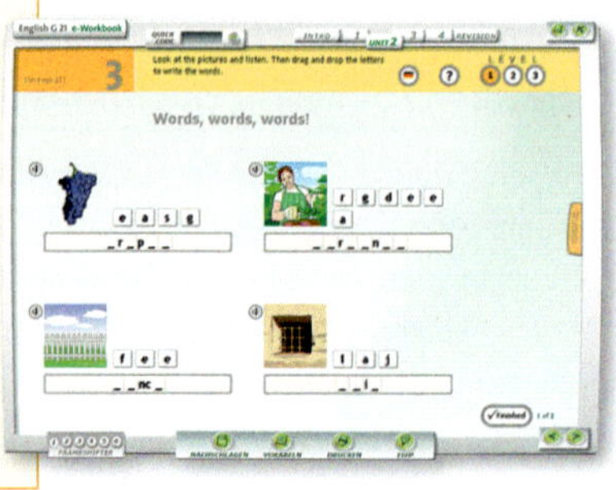

SF REVISION Using a bilingual dictionary

Wann brauche ich ein zweisprachiges Wörterbuch?

Du verstehst einen Text nicht, weil er zu viele Wörter enthält, die dir unbekannt sind, und die Worterschließungstechniken (▸ *SF Working out the meaning of words, p. 144*) helfen dir nicht weiter?
Du sollst einen Text auf Englisch schreiben, und dir fehlt das eine oder andere Wort, um deine Ideen auszudrücken? Du willst z. B. sagen, die Geschichte *In the outback* (S. 20–24) dreht sich um Bill und Colm und Bills Hund Rusty, aber du kennst das englische Wort für „drehen" nicht?
In jedem Fall hilft dir ein zweisprachiges Wörterbuch.

Wie benutze ich ein zweisprachiges Wörterbuch?

- Die **Leitwörter** oben auf der Seite helfen dir, schneller zu finden, was du suchst. Auf der linken Seite steht das erste Stichwort, auf der rechten Seite das letzte Stichwort der Doppelseite.
- Drehen ist das **Stichwort**. Alle Stichwörter sind alphabetisch geordnet: d vor e, da vor de und dre vor dri usw.
- Die **kursiv gedruckten** Hinweise helfen dir, die für deinen Text passende Bedeutung zu finden.
- Die **Ziffern** 1, 2 usw. zeigen, dass ein Stichwort mehrere ganz verschiedene Bedeutungen hat.
- **Beispielsätze** und **Redewendungen** sind dem Stichwort zugeordnet. In den Beispielsätzen und Redewendungen ersetzt eine **Tilde** (~) das Stichwort.
- Im englisch-deutschen Teil der meisten Wörterbücher findest du außerdem Hinweise auf **unregelmäßige Verbformen**, auf die **Steigerungsformen der Adjektive** und Ähnliches.
- Die **Lautschrift** gibt Auskunft darüber, wie das Wort ausgesprochen und betont wird. (→ *English sounds, p. 227*)

Dr.

Dr. (*Abk. für* ***Doktor***) Dr., Doctor
Drache dragon
Drachen *Papierdrachen* kite; *Fluggerät* hang glider

Drehbuch screenplay, script
drehen **1** *Verb mit Obj* turn; *Film* shoot*; *Zigarette* roll **2:** ***sich ~*** turn; *schnell* spin*; ***sich ~ um*** *übertragen* be* about
Drehkreuz turnstile; **Drehorgel** barrel organ ['ɔːgən]; **Drehort** location; **Drehstuhl** swivel chair; **Drehtür** revolving door
Drehung turn; *um eine Achse* rotation
Drehzahl (number of) revolutions *Pl od.* revs *Pl*
Drehzahlmesser rev counter
drei three
Drei three; *Note etwa* C; ***ich habe eine ~ geschrieben*** I got a C
dreidimensional **1** *Adj* three-dimensional **2** *Adv:* ***etwas ~ darstellen*** depict sth. three-dimensionally; **Dreieck** triangle ['traɪæŋgl]; **dreieckig** triangular [traɪ'æŋgjʊlə]

Bei kniffligen Wörtern gibt es in vielen Wörterbüchern **Info-Boxes**, in denen dir mehr Hilfen und Hinweise gegeben werden, hier z. B. für das deutsche Wort „bringen".

bringen

bring (**herbringen; mitbringen**) wird nur verwendet, wenn jemand oder etwas zum Ort des Sprechers oder Hörers gebracht wird:

Schön, dass du zu meiner Party	I'm glad you can come to my party. Can

take (**weg-, hinbringen; mitnehmen**) wird verwendet, wenn jemand oder etwas woanders hingebracht oder mitgenommen wird:

Kannst du morgen deinen Bruder zur Schule bringen?	Can you take your brother to school tomorrow?

Welche englische Entsprechung von **drehen** brauchst du in diesen Sätzen?
1. She's a good dancer, she loves to ... round and round as fast as she can.
2. Lots of Hollywood stars come to Berlin to ... their films here.

Tipp

Nimm nicht einfach die erste Übersetzung, die dir angeboten wird! Lies den Wörterbucheintrag, bis du die richtige Übersetzung gefunden hast.

SF REVISION Research

Wo kann ich Informationen finden?

Find some information about the Flying Doctor Service in Australia – so oder so ähnlich lauten Aufgaben, die dir oft als Hausaufgabe gestellt werden.
Wenn du nach Informationen suchst, solltest du immer **mehrere Quellen** verwenden. Du kannst im Internet, in einem Lexikon, Atlas, Wörterbuch, Schulbuch oder in anderen Quellen suchen. Auch CDs und DVDs sind mögliche Quellen. Benutze auch einige englische Quellen, das kann dir beim Ausformulieren deines englischen Textes helfen.

- Internet/Lexikon: alle Wissensgebiete, wichtige Personen und Ereignisse
- Atlas: geografische und politische Übersichten, Städte, Flüsse
- Wörterbücher: Rechtschreibung und Bedeutung von Wörtern
- Schulbücher: verschiedene Wissensgebiete
- Zeitungen/Zeitschriften: aktuelle Informationen zu allen Themenbereichen

Wie kann ich das Internet zur Recherche nutzen?

Eine wichtige Informationsquelle ist das Internet. Aber manchmal findest du dort so viele Informationen, dass du schnell den Überblick verlierst. Diese Tipps sollen dir helfen, damit du nicht im *world wide web* verloren gehst.

- Fertige eine Liste mit Schlüsselwörtern (**key words**) zu deinem Thema an: *Australia, flying, doctor, service, ...*
- Überlege, welches Schlüsselwort oder welche Kombination von Schlüsselwörtern am besten sein könnten: **„Flying Doctor Service" Australia** oder **Australia+flying+doctor+service**
- Wenn du dir zunächst einen Überblick verschaffen willst, kannst du auch ein Nachschlagewerk im Internet anklicken wie z.B.: www.infoplease.com www.en.wikipedia.org
  Manchmal gibt es dort auch Links, die dir weiterhelfen können.
- Suchmaschinen (wie z.B. *Google*, *Altavista* oder *Yahoo*) helfen dir, Websites zu deinem Thema zu finden. Verwende eine Suchmaschine und gib deine Schlüsselwörter in das Suchfenster ein.
- Wenn die angezeigten Websites dir nicht helfen oder du zu viele Websites angezeigt bekommst, versuch es noch einmal, indem du deine Schlüsselwörter präzisierst.

mit **allen** Wörtern	Australia	10 Ergebnisse
mit der **genauen Wortgruppe**	"Flying Doctor Service"	
mit **irgendeinem** der Wörter		
ohne die Wörter		

Tipp

- Verwende immer mehrere Internet-Quellen, um sicherzugehen, dass die Informationen stimmen.
- Suche Antworten auf die **5 Ws** (**who**, **what**, **where**, **when**, **why**).
- Bei englischen Quellen brauchst du nicht alles zu verstehen. Konzentrier dich auf das Wesentliche.
- Schreib die Quellen nicht wortwörtlich ab, sondern mach dir Notizen in deinen eigenen Worten (▸ *Reading course S. 144*).

SF REVISION Giving a presentation

Wie mache ich eine gute Präsentation?

Vorbereitung

- Schreib die wichtigsten Gedanken in Stichworten auf, z.B. auf nummerierte Karteikarten oder in der Mindmap.
- Übe deine Präsentation zu Hause vor einem Spiegel. Sprich laut, deutlich und langsam und mach Pausen an geeigneten Stellen.

Folien oder Poster

- Overhead-Folien oder Poster sind gut, um
  - zu zeigen, wie dein Vortrag aufgebaut ist
  - Tabellen, Diagramme usw. für alle lesbar zu präsentieren
  - die wichtigsten Punkte zusammenzufassen.
- Schreib groß und für alle gut lesbar.

Durchführung

- Bevor du beginnst, sortiere deine Vortragskarten.
- Häng das Poster auf oder leg deine Folie auf den ausgeschalteten Projektor oder bereite den Beamer vor.
- Warte, bis es ruhig ist. Schau die Zuhörer an.
- Erkläre zu Anfang, worüber du sprechen wirst. Lies nicht von deinen Karten ab, sondern sprich frei.

Schluss

- Beende deinen Präsentation mit einem abschließenden Satz.
- Frag die Zuhörenden, ob sie Fragen haben. Bedanke dich fürs Zuhören.

Ausführlichere sprachliche Hilfen für Präsentationen findest du unter:
▸ *Giving a presentation – useful phrases (p. 147)*

SF Using visual materials with a presentation ▸ *Unit 4, Part C (p. 88)*

Wofür sind visuelle Materialien gut?

Deine Zuhörer/innen werden deinem Vortrag mit mehr Aufmerksamkeit folgen. Sie können sich viel mehr merken, wenn du nicht nur sprichst, sondern ihnen auch etwas zum Anschauen bietest (Visualisierungen). Das können z.B. Fotos, Cartoons, Landkarten, Zeitleisten, Diagramme, Poster oder Filmausschnitte sein.

Was muss ich bei visuellen Materialien beachten?

Vorbereitung

- Das Gerüst deines Vortrags sollte stehen, bevor du anfängst, dir darüber Gedanken zu machen, welche Visualisierungen gut passen könnten.
- Diagramme und Tabellen sind gut, um Zahlen zu verdeutlichen; Zeitleisten sind gut, um eine Entwicklung zu zeigen; Fotos und Cartoons sind gut, wenn man seinen Vortrag auflockern will.

Durchführung

- Bezieh deine visuellen Materialien in deinen Vortrag ein, um etwas zu veranschaulichen, aber lies nicht einfach von der Folie etc. ab.

SF Talking about charts ▸ *Unit 1, Part A (p. 10)*

Welche Informationen kann ich Diagrammen (charts) entnehmen?

Diagramme stellen statistische Vergleiche zwischen mindestens zwei Dingen dar. Es werden entweder absolute Zahlen oder Prozentsätze miteinander verglichen.

Welche unterschiedlichen Formen von Diagrammen gibt es?

- **Bar charts (*Säulendiagramme*)** beschreiben häufig die Anzahl oder Größe von zwei oder mehr Dingen.
- **Pie charts (*Kreis-/Tortendiagramme*)** geben einen schnellen Überblick über die prozentuale Verteilung.
- **Charts (*Tabellen*)** ermöglichen den Vergleich unterschiedlicher Daten anhand von Zahlen und Prozentsätzen.
- **Line graphs (*Kurvendiagramme*)** stellen den Zusammenhang zwischen zwei zu vergleichenden Größen dar.

Wie kann ich beschreiben, was die Diagramme darstellen?

Um ein Diagramm zu beschreiben, solltest du folgende Fragen beantworten:

- **What is the chart/table/graph about?**
  The bar/pie chart is about ... • The line graph deals with ... •
  It is taken from ...
- **What does the chart/table/graph compare or show?**
  The chart/table/graph compares the size/number of ... •
  It shows the different ... • The pie chart is divided into ... slices that show ...
- **What does the chart tell you? What information does it give you?**
  ... has the largest/second largest • ... is twice/three times/... as big as ... •
  There are more than/nearly twice as many ... as there are ... •
  A huge majority/small minority/ ... • ... per cent of ...

Wenn vorhanden, solltest du Aussagen über den Zeitraum der Statistik ergänzen:
The chart is about the years ... • The chart shows the number of immigrants from ...

Tipp

Benutze das **simple past**, wenn du dich auf einen Zeitpunkt in der Vergangenheit beziehst: In 2008 the rainfall in Cairns was 1992 mm.

Benutze das **simple present** bei Aussagen über die Gegenwart oder bei allgemeingültigen Aussagen: The average rainfall in Cairns is 2215 mm per year. Benutze das simple present auch, wenn du deine Schlussfolgerungen wiedergibst. Cairns is a city with lots of rain per year.

Benutze das **present perfect**, wenn du dich auf einen Zeitraum beziehst, der von der Vergangenheit bis heute reicht: Over 400,000 Asians have immigrated to Australia since 2000.

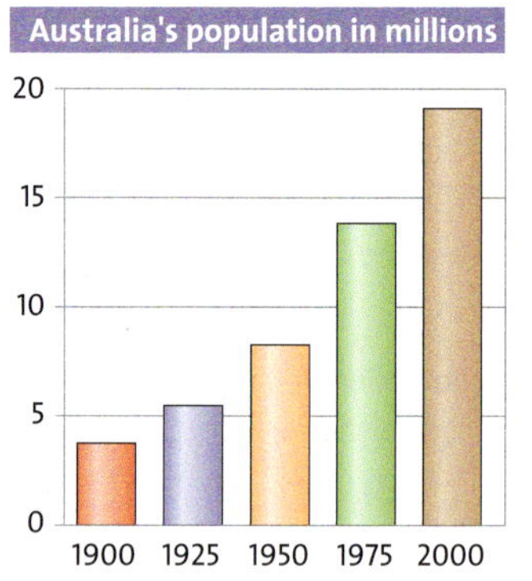

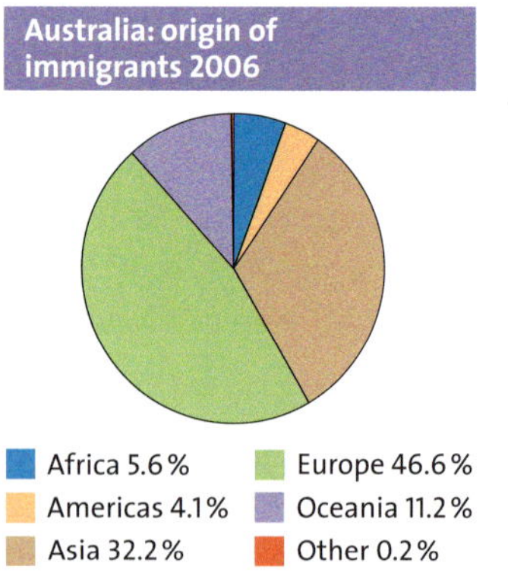

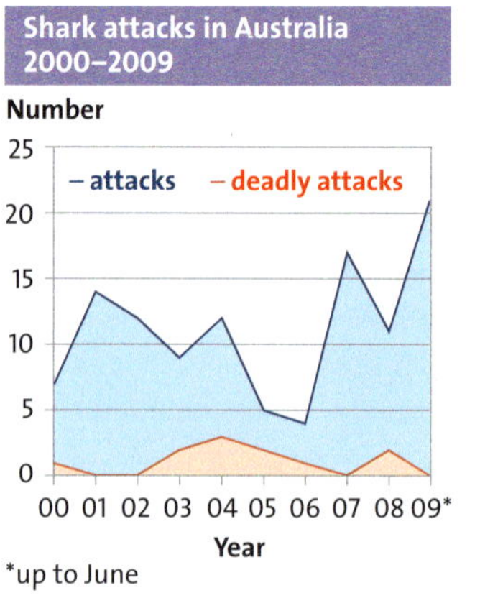

LISTENING AND READING SKILLS

SF REVISION Listening

Was muss ich allgemein beim *Listening* beachten?

Vor dem Hören:

- Überlege, worum es in dem Hörtext gehen wird. Frag dich, was du schon über das Thema weißt.
- Lies die Aufgabe gut durch, damit du weißt, worauf du achten sollst:
  - auf die Hauptgedanken oder
  - auf bestimmte Informationen, wie z.B. Namen, Uhrzeiten, Jahreszahlen.
- Bereite dich darauf vor, Notizen zu machen. Leg z.B. eine Tabelle oder Liste an.

Beim Hören:

- Keine Panik! Du musst nicht alles verstehen. Konzentriere dich auf das Wesentliche. Oft werden wichtige Informationen auch wiederholt.
- Achte auf Geräusche und unterschiedliche Stimmen. Was ein Sprecher/eine Sprecherin besonders betont, das ist wichtig!
- Wenn du gezielt nach Informationen suchst, denk an die Aufgabe und lass dich von anderen Einzelheiten nicht ablenken.
  Aufgepasst! Die Informationen, die du suchst, kommen vielleicht in einer anderen Reihenfolge vor, als du sie erwartest.

- Manche Signalwörter machen es dir leichter, den Hörtext zu verstehen:
  - Aufzählung: **and**, **another**, **too**
  - Gegensatz: **although**, **but**
  - Grund, Folge: **because**, **so**, **so that**
  - Vergleich: **larger/older/... than**, **more**, **most**
  - Reihenfolge: **before**, **after**, **then**, **next**, **later**, **when**, **at last**, **at the same time**
- Mach nur kurze Notizen, z.B. Anfangsbuchstaben, Symbole oder Stichworte, schreib keine ganzen Sätze.
  Unterteile Telefonnummern beim Aufschreiben: 0171 572 42 589.

Nach dem Hören:

- Vervollständige deine Notizen sofort.
- Konzentriere dich beim zweiten Hören auf das, was du zuerst nicht gut verstanden hast.

Worauf sollte ich bei automatischen Telefonansagen achten?

Wenn du eine telefonische Auskunft einholen willst, hörst du manchmal eine automatische Telefonansage.

- Keine Panik! Du kannst eine automatische Telefonansage mehrmals hören.
- Achte besonders auf Zahlen! Meist wirst du aufgefordert, bestimmte Tasten auf deinem Telefon zu drücken, um die gewünschte Information zu erhalten. Oft werden diese Zahlen wiederholt.
- Überlege dir vorher, welche Informationen du suchst und auf welche Schlüsselwörter du dafür achten solltest. Schreib sie auf.
- Höre dann besonders genau zu, wenn deine Schlüsselwörter genannt werden, und mach dir Notizen zu ihnen.

SF REVISION Taking notes

Worum geht es beim Notizenmachen?

Wenn du beim Lesen oder Zuhören Notizen machst, kannst du dich später besser an das Gehörte oder Gelesene erinnern, wenn du etwas vortragen, nacherzählen oder einen Bericht schreiben sollst.

Wie mache ich Notizen?

In Texten oder Gesprächen gibt es immer wichtige und unwichtige Wörter. Die wichtigen Wörter werden Schlüsselwörter (**key words**) genannt und nur die solltest du notieren. Meist sind das Substantive und Verben, manchmal auch Adjektive oder Zahlen.

Tipp

- Verwende Ziffern (z. B. „7" statt „seven").
- Verwende Symbole und Abkürzungen, z. B. ✔ (für „ja") und + (für „und") oder US für United States, C. für Caitlin.
  Du kannst auch eigene Symbole erfinden.
- Verwende not oder ✗ statt „doesn't" oder „don't".

SF REVISION Marking up a text

Wann sollte ich einen Text markieren?

Du hast einen Text mit vielen Fakten vor dir liegen und sollst später über bestimmte Dinge berichten. Dann wird es dir helfen, die für die Aufgabenstellung wichtigen Informationen im Text zu markieren.

Wie gehe ich am besten vor?

Lies den Text und markiere nur die für dein Thema wichtigen Informationen. Nicht jeder Satz enthält für deine Aufgabe wichtige Wörter, und oft reicht es aus, nur ein oder zwei Wörter in einem Satz zu markieren.

- Du kannst wichtige Wörter einkreisen.
- Du kannst sie unterstreichen.
- Du kannst sie mit einem Textmarker hervorheben.

ABER:
Markiere nur auf Fotokopien von Texten oder in Büchern, die dir gehören, oder verwende eine Folie und einen wasserlöslichen Folienstift.

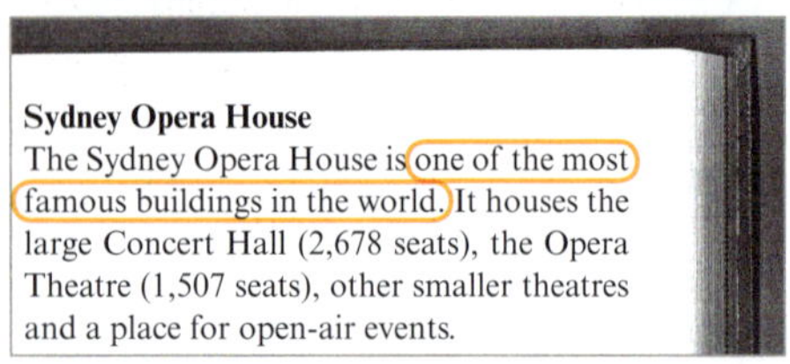

Sydney Opera House
The Sydney Opera House is one of the most famous buildings in the world. It houses the large Concert Hall (2,678 seats), the Opera Theatre (1,507 seats), other smaller theatres and a place for open-air events.

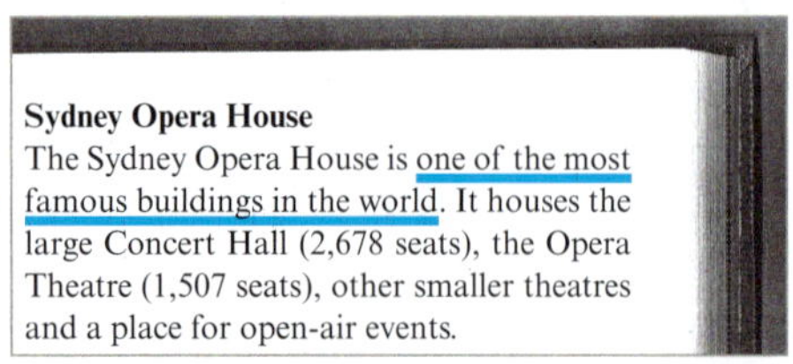

Sydney Opera House
The Sydney Opera House is one of the most famous buildings in the world. It houses the large Concert Hall (2,678 seats), the Opera Theatre (1,507 seats), other smaller theatres and a place for open-air events.

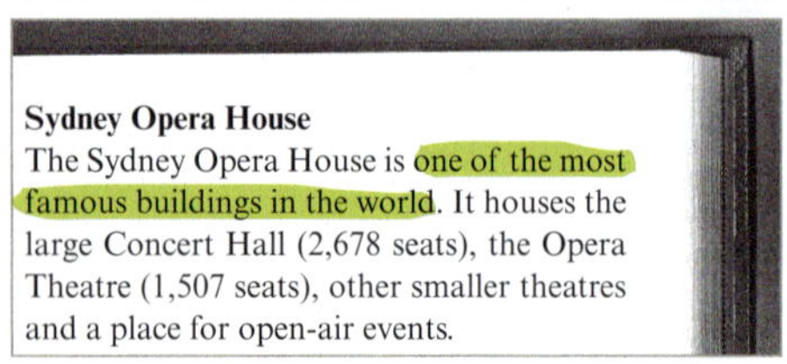

Sydney Opera House
The Sydney Opera House is one of the most famous buildings in the world. It houses the large Concert Hall (2,678 seats), the Opera Theatre (1,507 seats), other smaller theatres and a place for open-air events.

SF Reading stories ▸ *Unit 1, Part A (p. 20)*

Was ist das Besondere beim Lesen von längeren Geschichten auf Englisch?

Geschichten lesen macht Spaß. Du tauchst in eine andere Welt ein, lernst Menschen kennen, die du im wirklichen Leben nie treffen würdest (wie z.B. Colm im Outback Australiens) und erhältst Einblicke in ihr Leben, erfährst, was sie denken, was sie fühlen.
Dabei ist es nicht so wichtig, dass du beim Lesen jedes Wort verstehst. Lass dich einfach von der Handlung durch die Geschichte tragen.

Hier nun ein paar Tipps, die es dir erleichtern, eine längere Geschichte auf Englisch zu lesen.

Vor dem Lesen

1. Lies die **Einführung** und die **Überschrift**(en) und sieh dir die **Bilder** zum Text an. Sie geben dir erste Informationen über das, was dich erwartet. Stell dir vor, worum es in der Geschichte gehen könnte.
2. Bei Lektüren oder Romanen gibt es hinten auf dem Buchumschlag meist einen kurzen **Klappentext** mit einer kleinen Zusammenfassung der Handlung – natürlich ohne, dass das Ende verraten wird.

Während des Lesens

1. Tauche ein in die Geschichte. Lies zügig! Kümmere dich nicht um einzelne Wörter, die du nicht kennst oder nicht verstehst. Lies einfach weiter! Das Wichtigste ist, dass du im Großen und Ganzen die Handlung verstehst.

Wenn du merkst, dass du der Handlung nicht mehr folgen kannst, weil du zu viele Wörter nicht verstehst oder wenn du denkst, dass bestimmte unbekannte Wörter sehr wichtig sind, dann nutze alle dir bekannten Techniken, um die Bedeutung zu erschließen:
- Sieh dir noch einmal die Bilder an.
- Beachte den Textzusammenhang.
- Kennst du ähnliche englische oder deutsche Wörter?
- Vielleicht kennst du Teile der unbekannten Wörter?

(▸ *SF Working out the meaning of words, p. 144*).

2. Wenn das alles nicht hilft und du immer noch das Gefühl hast, dass ein bestimmtes Wort für das Verständnis des Fortgangs der Handlung wichtig ist, schlag es im Wörterbuch nach. (▸ *SF Using a bilingual dictionary, p. 137*).
3. Um der Handlung besser folgen zu können, kann es helfen, wenn du nicht die ganze Geschichte hintereinander liest. Hör ab und zu auf zu lesen, schließ das Buch und denk darüber nach, was du bis dahin gelesen hast. Erzähl jemandem, was bisher geschah und was du noch nicht verstanden hast. Oft klären sich manche Fragen im Gespräch. Dann lies weiter.
4. Mach ruhig auch mal eine Lesepause, das ist bei Lektüren besonders wichtig. Zum Beispiel fünf Minuten Pause nach 20 oder 30 Minuten helfen dir, das Gelesene besser aufzunehmen.

Tipp

Beim Lesen von englischen Lektüren oder Büchern kann dir eine Lesetagebuch (**reading log**), wie du es sicher aus dem Deutschunterricht kennst, das Verstehen und Behalten erleichtern.

REVISION READING COURSE – Zusammenfassung

Working out the meaning of words

Das Nachschlagen unbekannter Wörter im Wörterbuch kostet Zeit und nimmt auf Dauer den Spaß am Lesen. Oft geht es auch ohne Wörterbuch!

Was hilft dir, unbekannte Wörter zu verstehen?

1. **Bilder** zeigen oft die Dinge, die du im Text nicht verstehst. Wenn es Bilder zum Text gibt, dann schau sie dir vor dem Lesen genau an.
2. Oft hilft dir der **Textzusammenhang**, z.B. *When we* ***reached*** *the station, Judy went to the ticket machine to buy our tickets.*
3. Manche englischen Wörter werden **ähnlich wie im Deutschen** geschrieben oder ausgesprochen, z.B. **excellent**, **millionaire**, **nation**, **reality**.
4. Manchmal stecken in unbekannten Wörtern **bekannte Teile**, z.B. **friendliness**, **helpless**, **understandable**, **gardener**, **tea bag**, **waiting room**.

Skimming and Scanning

Skimming: Lesen, um sich einen Überblick zu verschaffen

Beim **Skimming** überfliegst du einen Text schnell, um dir einen ersten **Überblick** zu verschaffen, worum es geht. Du willst herausfinden, ob ein Text, den du im Internet oder in einem Buch gefunden hast, überhaupt nützliche Informationen zu deinem Thema (z.B. für ein Referat) enthält. Achte beim Skimming auf:
- die **Überschrift**
- die **Zwischenüberschriften** und **hervorgehobene** Wörter oder Sätze
- die **Bilder** und **Bildunterschriften**
- den **ersten** und **letzten Satz** jedes Absatzes
- **Grafiken**, **Statistiken** und die **Quelle** des Textes.

Scanning: Lesen, um nach bestimmten Informationen zu suchen

Beim **Scanning** suchst du in einem Text nach **bestimmten Informationen**, die z.B. für ein Referat wichtig sind. Dazu brauchst du nicht den gesamten Text zu lesen, sondern du suchst nach Schlüsselwörtern (**key words**) und liest nur dort genauer, wo du sie findest. Geh dabei so vor:

Schritt 1: Denk an das Schlüsselwort, nach dem du suchst, oder schreib es auf.

Schritt 2: Geh mit den Augen und dem Finger schnell durch den Text, in breiten Schlingen wie bei einem „S“ oder „Z“ oder von oben nach unten wie bei einem „U“. Dabei hast du das Schriftbild oder das Bild des Wortes, nach dem du suchst, vor Augen. Das gesuchte Wort wird dir sofort „ins Auge springen“. Lies nur dort weiter, um Näheres zu erfahren.

Schritt 3: Wenn das Schlüsselwort, nach dem du suchst, im Text nicht vorkommt, überleg dir, welche anderen Wörter mit den benötigten Informationen zu tun haben, und such nach diesen.

Finding the main ideas of a text

Wenn du Texte wie Zeitungsartikel, Berichte oder Kommentare richtig verstehen willst, ist es gut, wenn du ihre Hauptaussagen erkennst und nachvollziehst, wie sie zusammenhängen. Dabei hilft dir ein Blick auf die Struktur dieser Texte.

Wie finde ich die Hauptaussagen eines Textes?

1. Jeder Text dreht sich um ein Thema oder hat eine Hauptaussage, z.B.
   This summer we have been raising money for the Hickery Soup Kitchen.
   Diese Hauptaussage findest du oft im **ersten Absatz**. Lies ihn deshalb besonders gründlich durch (vgl. den Text auf S. 58 unten).
2. Die Hauptaussage wird in der Regel durch weitere Aussagen bzw. Gedanken unterstützt, z.B.
   To raise money we have mainly been to two churches.
   Du findest sie oft im ersten oder letzten Satz der nachfolgenden Absätze.
3. Diese weiteren Aussagen bzw. Gedanken werden meist durch Beispiele und Begründungen ergänzt, z.B.
   Lots of people have given money ... Altogether we've raised $427.

Tipp

Die folgenden Wörter oder Wendungen werden oft im Zusammenhang mit Begründungen oder Beispielen verwendet:
and so • because • e.g. / for example • etc. • for lots of reasons • this shows that • that's why • ...

Drawing conclusions

Wenn du bei einer Arbeit Fragen zu einem Text beantworten sollst oder bei einer Recherche Informationen zu einer bestimmten Frage in einem Text suchst, kann es gut sein, dass du an mehreren Stellen schauen musst oder dass die Antwort nicht 1:1 im Text steht.

Wie funktioniert schlussfolgerndes Lesen?

1. Die einfachste Form des schlussfolgernden Lesens besteht darin, die Informationen aus verschiedenen Textstellen zusammenzuführen. Beim Text auf S. 17 z.B. sollst du beschreiben, wie Zita Wallace gestohlen wurde. Dazu musst du dir mehrere Textstellen ansehen.
2. Manchmal steht die Antwort auf eine Frage nicht direkt im Text. Dann musst du sie dir erschließen. Du fragst dich z.B., ob die Kinder der „stolen generations" lange auf eine Entschuldigung der australischen Regierung warten mussten. Dafür musst du Fakten im Text finden, die etwas mit der Frage zu tun haben:

   FACTS: – the policy (of stealing children) ended after 60 years in 1970
   – Australian government apologized in 2008.
   CONCLUSION: the Australian government apologized 38 years later – that's a very long time

SPEAKING AND WRITING SKILLS

SPEAKING COURSE – Zusammenfassung

Having a conversation

▸ *Unit 1, Part A (p. 15)*

Ein Gespräch beginnen

Es gibt immer mehrere Möglichkeiten:

- **wenn du etwas erfragen willst** *(z.B. den Weg oder die Uhrzeit)*
  Excuse me, do you know ... • Excuse me, can you tell me ...
- **wenn du jemanden begrüßen möchtest oder kennen lernst**
  Hi • Hello oder Good morning • Good evening (bei Erwachsenen) ...
  Oft kann man das Gespräch dann mit einer allgemeinen Bemerkung weiterführen: Great day today! • That's a great ...
- **wenn du jemanden wieder triffst**
  Hi, how are you going? Hi, ..., how are things? • Hi, ... Good to see/meet you.

Tipp

- Oft hört man zur Begrüßung auch How are you? oder How do you do? Das sind einfache Begrüßungsformeln. Es wird nicht erwartet, dass man darauf eine Antwort gibt.
- Am besten sagst du einfach Fine, thanks. How about you?

Ein Gespräch führen

Für den weiteren Verlauf des Gesprächs sind diese Wendungen nützlich:

- **sich vorstellen:** By the way, my name's ... • I'm ... • Nice to meet you.
- **Smalltalk machen:** Have you ... before? • Have you ever ...? • Where are you from? • Do you like ...? • What about you?
- **um Hilfe bitten und anderen helfen:** Do you know where ...? • Can you tell me ...? • Sure, no problem • Why don't you ...?
- **sich verabschieden:** See you tomorrow/next week. • Bye!

Und wenn du etwas nicht verstanden hast, kannst du immer nachfragen:
Sorry, I didn't get that. • Sorry, can you say that again, please?

Taking part in a job interview

▸ *Unit 2, Part C (p. 41)*

Sich vorbereiten

Auf ein Vorstellungsgespräch musst du dich unbedingt vorbereiten. Du solltest Fragen zu den folgenden Bereichen beantworten können:

- deine Eigenschaften (**personal qualities**), Stärken (**strengths**) und Schwächen (**weaknesses**)
- deine Interessen (**interests**) und Arbeitserfahrungen (**work experience**)
- was dich an dem Jobangebot reizt (**why you're interested in the job**).

Überleg dir auch eigene Fragen, zum Beispiel zu deinem Tätigkeitsbereich (**What kind of work would I have to do?**) oder zur Bezahlung (**What is the pay?**).

Im Vorstellungsgespräch

Im Vorstellungsgespräch ist es wichtig, dass du freundlich bist und dich als positiver und interessierter Mensch präsentierst.

- **bei der Begrüßung:** Hello, nice to meet you. • Good morning.
- **warum du dich bewirbst:** I'm really interested in • I'm good at ..., so I think ...
- **wenn es um deine Joberfahrungen geht:** I really enjoyed working with ...
- **bei der Verabschiedung:** Goodbye and thank you very much.

Tipp

- Hör gut zu, wenn du etwas gefragt wirst.
- Sprich nicht zu viel, aber auch nicht zu wenig.
- Sprich nicht zu schnell.

Having a discussion ▸ *Unit 3, Part B (p. 56)*

Seine Meinung zum Ausdruck bringen und erklären

1. **Expressing an opinion:** In einer Diskussion ist es gut, wenn du möglichst klar und deutlich sagst, was du zu einer bestimmten Frage denkst:
   I think … • In my opinion …

2. **Giving reasons and examples:** Genauso wichtig ist es, dass du Beispiele und Argumente nennst, die deine Meinung unterstützen – schließlich willst du deine Gesprächspartner von deinem Standpunkt überzeugen!
   because … • First … / Second … / And finally… • For example … • Let me explain … • That's why …

Auf andere in einer Diskussion reagieren

1. **Asking for clarification:** Manchmal ist es notwendig nachzuhaken, weil man ein Argument nicht verstanden hat:
   Could you say that again? • Sorry, but I don't understand what you mean.

2. **Agreeing with someone:** Wenn du die Meinung eines anderen unterstützen willst, kannst du das so zum Ausdruck bringen:
   I agree (with you/…) • That's a good point. • You're right.

3. **Disagreeing with someone:** Oft widerspricht man nicht direkt, sondern leitet seine Reaktion mit **Sorry, …** oder **I don't think** … ein. Zeig immer Respekt für die Meinung des oder der anderen.
   I don' t think you can say … • I see what you mean, but … •
   Sorry, but that's not right. • Sorry, I don't agree with you • Yes, but …

▸ *Classroom English (pp. 238–239)*

Giving a presentation – useful phrases ▸ *Unit 4, Part C (p. 88)*

Einleitung

Nenne zu Beginn deines Vortrags dein Thema und gib einen kurzen Überblick darüber, worum es in deinem Vortrag geht:
The topic of my talk today is … • I'm going to divide this talk into four sections. • First, I'll give you some general facts about … • Next I'll look at … • Finally I'll …

Während der Präsentation

Mach deutlich, wenn du einen neuen Abschnitt in deinem Vortrag beginnst.
Now please have a look at … • On the next slide … • Now I'd like to draw your attention to … • As you can see in …

Schluss

Am Ende deines Vortrags fass die wichtigsten Punkte zusammen. Frag deine Zuhörer, ob sie etwas nachfragen oder kommentieren möchten.
To sum up my talk I … • Please feel free to ask questions or comment on anything I've said.
Ausführlichere Hinweise zur Vorbereitung und Durchführung einer Präsentation findest du unter: ▸ *Giving a presentation (p. 139)*

SF REVISION Paraphrasing

Worum geht es beim Paraphrasing?

Paraphrasing bedeutet, etwas mit anderen Worten zu erklären. Das ist hilfreich, wenn dir ein bestimmtes Wort nicht einfällt oder wenn dein Gegenüber dich nicht verstanden hat (siehe auch ▸ *SF Mediation, p. 155*).

Wie gehe ich beim Paraphrasing vor?

- Man kann mit einem Wort umschreiben, das dieselbe Bedeutung hat:
  to train is the same as to practise
  Oder man sagt das Gegenteil: **alive is the opposite of dead**
- Manchmal braucht man mehrere Wörter, z.B. wenn man etwas beschreibt oder erklärt. Dabei benutzt man ein allgemeines Wort (**general word**) und nennt weitere Eigenschaften.
  A racing car is a very fast car.
- Oder du umschreibst das Wort mit **... is/are like ...**
  A chef is like a cook, he or she is the main cook in a restaurant.
- Du kannst auch einen Relativsatz (**relative clause**) verwenden:
  A garage is the place where cars are checked and repaired.
  A nurse is a person who looks after people who are ill, usually in a hospital.

SF REVISION Brainstorming

Wofür ist Brainstorming gut?

Bei vielen Aufgaben ist es nützlich, wenn du im ersten Schritt möglichst viele Ideen zum Thema sammelst. Dabei hilft dir das Brainstorming.

Wie gehe ich beim Brainstorming vor?

Schritt 1:
Schreib alle Ideen so auf, wie sie dir einfallen. Es ist zunächst völlig egal, ob sie gut sind oder nicht. Du kannst die Ideen durcheinander auf einen Zettel schreiben oder schon etwas geordnet, z.B. für jede eine neue Zeile.

Schritt 2:
Lies alle deine Ideen durch und wähle die besten aus. Dann sortiere sie und fasse sie sinnvoll zusammen. Dabei kannst du folgende **Techniken** anwenden:

1. Leg eine **Mindmap** an. Schreib das Thema in die Mitte eines Blattes Papier. Überlege, welche Oberbegriffe zu deiner Sammlung von Ideen passen. Verwende unterschiedliche Farben. Ergänze jede Idee, die zu einem Oberbegriff passt, auf einem Nebenast. Nimm dafür nur wichtige Schlüsselwörter. Du kannst statt Wörtern auch Symbole verwenden und Bilder ergänzen.
2. **The 5 Ws**: Schreib die **5** W-Fragen **Who? What? Where? When? Why?** in eine Tabelle. Die Ideen, die dir zu jeder Frage kommen, kannst du darunter schreiben.

SF REVISION Summarizing texts

Wenn du einen Text zusammenfasst, gibst du die wichtigen Informationen oder Ereignisse in kürzerer Form wieder.

Wie gehe ich beim summarizing vor?

1. Lies den Text mindestens einmal genau durch, damit du verstehst, worum es geht. Mach dir noch keine Notizen.
2. Lies den Text erneut, Satz für Satz, durch und mach dir Notizen zu den 5 Ws:

Who?	Who is the text about?
What?	What happens?/What does he/she do?
Where?	Where does it happen?
When?	When does it happen?
Why?	Why does it happen? / Why does he/she do this?

Was auf diese Fragen Antwort gibt, ist wichtig. Auslassen solltest du dagegen Beispiele, Vergleiche, Zitate, direkte Rede, ausschmückende Adjektive und andere Textteile, die der Beschreibung dienen.

3. Leg den Text nun beiseite und schreib mithilfe deiner Notizen eine Zusammenfassung des Texts in deinen eigenen Worten.

– Erklär in den ersten ein oder zwei Sätzen, worum es in dem Text geht.

• Vergleiche diese drei Anfänge einer Zusammenfassung von *In the outback* (S. 20–23). Welcher gibt am besten das Thema der Geschichte wieder?

IN THE OUTBACK is a story about Australia.

IN THE OUTBACK is a story about Bill and Colm.

IN THE OUTBACK is a story about Bill and Colm's journey along the Dog Fence.

Du kannst für deine einleitenden Sätze die folgenden phrases verwenden:
The story is about ... • **The text describes ...** • **The article shows ...** • **In the story we get to know ...**

– Im Hauptteil solltest du die wichtigen Ereignisse (z.B. einer Geschichte) oder die Hauptpunkte eines Textes (z.B. eines Zeitungsartikels) wiedergeben. Bring die Informationen in eine logische Reihenfolge.
  - Verwende dafür deine Notizen zu den **5 Ws**.
  - Schreib den Text nicht ab, sondern benutze deine eigenen Worte.

They're getting the Flying Doctor out here. We don't know if the old man will make it if we have to drive him down to the hospital in Katherine. Best to fly him to Darwin. → *They call the Flying Doctor Service to fly Bill to the hospital in Darwin.*

– Schreib im **simple present**, auch wenn die Geschichte oder der Artikel in der Vergangenheit spielt. Nicht vergessen: im **simple present** wird in der 3. Person Singular **-s** angehängt: **He/She thinks...**

REVISION WRITING COURSE – Zusammenfassung

The steps of writing

1. Brainstorming – Ideen sammeln, dann sortieren (▸ *SF Brainstorming, p. 153*).
2. Schreiben. Dabei achte darauf,
   - deine Sätze zu verbinden und auszubauen (*Writing better sentences*)
   - deinen Text gut zu strukturieren (*Using paragraphs*)
   - bei einem Bericht die 5 Ws abzudecken (*Writing a report*)
3. Deinen Text inhaltlich und sprachlich überprüfen (*Correcting your text*)

Writing better sentences

Linking words

Eine Geschichte klingt interessanter, wenn du die Sätze mit **linking words** miteinander verbindest. Dabei gibt es mehrere Möglichkeiten:

- **Time phrases** wie at 7 o'clock, every morning, a few minutes later, then, next ...
- **Konjunktionen** wie although, because, but, so ... that, that, when, while
- **Relativpronomen** wie that und who

Adjektive und Adverbien

- Mit Adjektiven kannst du Personen, Orte oder Erlebnisse genauer und interessanter beschreiben. Vergleiche: The man looked into the room.
  ▸ The young man looked into the empty room.
- Mit Adverbien kannst du beschreiben, **wie** jemand etwas macht:
  The young man looked nervously into the empty room.

Using paragraphs

Structuring a text

Ein längerer Text ist besser zu verstehen, wenn er in mehrere Absätze unterteilt ist:

- eine Einleitung (**beginning**) – hier schreibst du, worum es geht
- einen Hauptteil (**middle**) – hier schreibst du mehr über dein Thema
- einen Schluss (**end**) – hier bringst du den Text zu einem interessanten Ende.

Topic sentences

Am Anfang eines Absatzes sind kurze, einleitende Sätze (**topic sentences**) gut, weil sie den Lesern sofort sagen, worum es geht, z. B.

1. Orte: My trip to ... was fantastic. / ... is famous for ... / ... is a great place.
2. Personen: ... is great/funny/interesting/clever ...
3. Aktivitäten: ... is great fun. / Lots of people ... every day.

Wie kann ich meine Absätze interessant gestalten?

- Beginne mit einem interessanten Einstiegssatz:
  You'll never guess what happened to me today! / Did I tell you that ...?
- Fang für jeden neuen Aspekt einen neuen Absatz an.
- Beende deinen Text mit einer Zusammenfassung oder etwas Persönlichem.

Writing a report – collecting and organizing ideas

Worauf kommt es bei einem Bericht an?

- Gib dem Leser **eine schnelle Orientierung**, was passiert ist.
- Beginne mit **wichtigen Informationen** und gib erst dann Detailinformationen.
- Ein Bericht gibt immer Antworten auf die **5 Ws**:
  Who? What? When? Where? Why? und manchmal auch auf **How?**
- Verwende das **simple past**.

Correcting your text

Ein Text ist noch nicht „fertig“, wenn du ihn zu Ende geschrieben hast. Du solltest ihn immer mehr als einmal durchlesen:
- einmal, um zu sehen, ob er vollständig und gut verständlich ist
- noch einmal, um ihn auf Fehler zu überprüfen, z.B. Rechtschreibfehler *(spelling mistakes)* oder Grammatikfehler *(grammar mistakes)*.

tomato [tə'mɑːtəʊ], *pl* **tomatoes** Tomate II

wife [waɪf], *pl* **wives** [waɪvz] Ehefrau II

drop (**-pp-**) [drɒp] fallen lassen I

forget (**-tt-**) [fə'get] vergessen I

Spelling mistakes

Lies deinen Text langsam, Wort für Wort, Buchstabe für Buchstabe. Wenn du unsicher bist, hilft dir ein Wörterbuch. Beachte folgende Regeln:

Tipp

- Manche Wörter haben Buchstaben, die man nicht spricht, aber schreibt, z.B. **knife**, **climb**.
- Manchmal ändert sich die Schreibweise, wenn ein Wort eine Endung erhält,
  z.B. **take** → **taking**, **terrible** → **terribly**, **lucky** → **luckily**,
  try → **tries** (**aber stay** → **stays**), **run** → **running**, **drop** → **dropped**.
- Beim Plural tritt manchmal noch ein **-e** zum **-s**, z.B. **church** → **churches**.

Grammar mistakes

Diese Tipps helfen dir, typische Fehler zu vermeiden:

Tipp

- Im **simple present** wird in der 3. Person Singular **-s** angehängt: **she knows**
- **Unregelmäßige Verben:** Manche Verben bilden die Formen des *simple past* und des Partizip Perfekt *(past participle)* unregelmäßig. Die unregelmäßigen Formen musst du lernen. Die Liste steht auf S. 258–259.
  go – went – gone; buy – bought – bought
- **Verneinung bei Vollverben:** Im *simple present* mit ***don't/doesn't***, im *simple past* mit **didn't**, z.B. **He doesn't speak French, he didn't learn it at school**.
- **Satzstellung**: Im Englischen gilt immer (auch im Nebensatz):
  a) subject – verb – object (SVO) **... when I saw my brother.**
  ... als ich meinen Bruder sah.
  b) Orts- vor Zeitangabe **I bought a nice book in the city yesterday.**

SF Writing a CV ▸ *Unit 2, Part B (p. 38)*

Was ist ein CV?

„CV“ bedeutet „Lebenslauf“. Ein CV ist eine Zusammenfassung deiner bisherigen Ausbildung, deiner Fähigkeiten und deiner Interessen. Du brauchst einen CV, wenn du dich um eine berufliche Anstellung bewirbst. Amerikaner benutzen statt „CV“ das Wort „résumé“.

CURRICULUM VITAE
Oliver Schäfer

Tulpenweg 34 32051 Herford, Germany
Telephone: 00 49 5221 978036
Email: oliver.schaefer@email-hf.de

Education
2003-2009 Gutenberg-Realschule (secondary school), Herford, Germany
1999-2003 Regenbogen Grundschule (primary school), Herford, Germany

Qualifications
Studying for Fachoberschulreife (equivalent of GCSEs)
Languages: English (6 years), French (4 years)
Driving licence since 2008

Work experience
Work experience at a garage (3 weeks)

Hobbies and interests
My hobbies are cycling, doing workouts, repairing all kinds of machines. I am very interested in technical things and computers.

References
Available on request

Geburtsdatum und – ort werden in einem britischen CV **oft nicht** genannt.

Gib bei deiner Telefonnummer auch die **internationale Vorwahl** mit an.

Fettgedruckte Überschriften und eine **klare Gliederung** erleichtern das Lesen.

GCSEs gibt es nur in Großbritannien, in den USA entspricht das dem **US highschool diploma**.

An dieser Stelle kann auch eine **konkrete Person** als **Referenz** genannt werden wie im CV auf S. 38. Selbstverständlich musst du ihn oder sie vorher fragen!

Im CV auf S. 38 findest du auch die Abschnitte **Personal statement** und **Other skills** – diese Abschnitte sind möglich, aber nicht zwingend notwendig für einen CV.

Tipp

Bevor du deinen CV losschickst, geh folgende Checkliste durch:
- Habe ich weißes A4-Papier benutzt? Ist das Blatt sauber und ordentlich?
- Habe ich den CV mit einem Computer geschrieben?
- Ist die Seite klar gegliedert und gut lesbar?
- Habe ich alle zentralen Bereiche abgedeckt: meine Erfahrungen, meine Interessen, meine Fähigeiten und persönlichen Eigenschaften?
- Habe ich auch wirklich keine sprachlichen Fehler in meinem Schreiben?.

SF REVISION Writing formal and informal letters

Beim Schreiben von Briefen und E-Mails musst du unterschiedliche Regeln beachten, je nachdem, ob du einen förmlichen Brief (*formal letter*) an unbekannte Personen, Behörden, Zeitschriften usw. schreibst oder einen persönlichen, informellen Brief (*informal letter*) an Freunde oder Verwandte.

Worauf kommt es bei förmlichen Briefen an? (Formal letters)

1. Schreibe deine Adresse (ohne Namen) und das Datum in die rechte obere Ecke. Verwende keine typisch deutschen Buchstaben wie z.B. ß, ä, ö, oder ü.
2. Die Anschrift steht links.
3. Die Anrede lautet *Dear Sir or Madam*. Wenn du den Namen des Adressaten kennst, beginne deinen Brief mit *Dear Mr/Mrs/Ms* ...
4. Verwende Langformen (*I am, I would like* statt *I'm, I'd like* etc.).
5. Nenne zu Beginn den Grund deines Briefes.
6. Bedanke dich bei Bitten und Anfragen im Voraus (*I look forward to hearing from you. Thank you.*).
7. Beende den Brief mit *Yours faithfully*, wenn du den Adressaten nicht kennst. Hast du den Adressaten am Anfang des Briefes mit Namen angeredet, dann schreibe *Yours sincerely*.
8. Unterschreibe den Brief und tippe zusätzlich deinen Namen.

Tipp

Beachte, was du zum Schreiben von Texten gelernt hast:
- Vor dem Schreiben: Ideen sammeln, dann sortieren.
- Während des Schreibens: Sätze verbinden und ausbauen; strukturieren.
- Nach dem Schreiben: Überprüfe deinen Brief inhaltlich und sprachlich. ► *SF Writing course, pp. 150–151*

Example for a letter of application

(1) Schillerstr. 17
37067 Goettingen
Germany

(2) Jane Hall
Meadows Home Farm Shop
Harston
Cambridge CB22 4BE
Great Britain

4 May 2010

(3) Dear Ms Hall

(5) (4) I am writing to you about the advertisement from April 21st in the Cambridge Weekly News. I would love to (4) work for you at Meadows Home Farm this summer.

I am 16 years old and I have a good level of English but would like to improve my speaking skills. I am hard-working, friendly and a fast learner. At home I look after two horses so farm work is not new to me. I have also worked in a sports shop so I have experience in serving people and working in a team. My hobbies are horse riding, playing volleyball and hiking. Please find my CV with this letter.

Thank you for your time. I look forward to hearing (6) from you.

(7) Yours sincerely

(8) *Tamara Wille*
Tamara Wille

Was ist bei persönlichen Briefen anders? (Informal letters)

Hier sind die Regeln nicht ganz so streng. Aber beachte Folgendes:
- Schreibe deine Adresse (ohne Namen) und das Datum in die rechte obere Ecke.
- Verwende keine typisch deutschen Buchstaben wie z.B. ß, ä, ö, oder ü.
- Du benötigst keine Anschrift.
- Du kannst deinen Brief mit *Dear/Hello/Hi* ... beginnen.
- Nenne zu Beginn den Grund deines Briefes, stelle auch Fragen.
- Beende den Brief mit einem freundlichen Gruß/Ausblick/Erwartungen/...
- Schließe deinen Brief mit *Yours/Best wishes/Love/*... ab.

Alles klar? Wohin gehören die Wendungen im blauen Kasten?

	Formal letter	Informal letter
opening	Dear Mr Smith, ...	Dear Pete, ...
closing	...	...

Best wishes • Dear Pete • I look forward to hearing from you • Yours faithfully • Dear Mr Smith • Yours sincerely • Lots of love • I look forward to meeting you. • Love • Dear Sir or Madam • See you soon! • Hello Sarah • Thank you very much. • Happy birthday! I've just heard ...

SF From outline to written discussion

▸ *Unit 3, Part A (p. 59)*

Worum geht es bei einer Gliederung?

Oft sollst du zu strittigen Fragen wie z.B. **German students should have to do ten hours of community service every year** schriftlich Stellung nehmen und deine Position überzeugend darlegen. Dabei sollst du zeigen, dass du dich intensiv mit dem Thema auseinandergesetzt hast. Dafür ist es hilfreich, wenn du erst Argumente sammelst und sie dann **noch vor** dem Schreiben des Textes gliederst, also sortierst und in eine sinnvolle Reihenfolge bringst. Die Gliederung (**outline**) erleichtert dir das anschließende Schreiben.

Wie gehe ich bei einer Gliederung vor?

1. Collecting ideas
Entscheide dich, ob du für oder gegen die geäußerte Meinung Stellung nehmen möchtest. Dann sammle Ideen für deine Argumentation dafür oder dagegen. Es ist sinnvoll, wenn du neben den Argumenten auch konkrete Beispiele notierst, die deine Aussage verdeutlichen.

▸ *SF Brainstorming (p. 148)*

2. Outlining
Mit Hilfe des *Outline* strukturierst du dann deine zuvor gesammelten Ideen. Du bringst damit deine Argumente und Beispiele in eine sinnvolle und logische Reihenfolge (z.B. das wichtigste Argument zum Schluss). Ordne deine Ideen stichwortartig nach dem Schema rechts.

1 Introduction

2 Arguments FOR or AGAINST
  2.1. First argument
  2.2. Second argument
  2.3. …

3 Conclusion

Wie mache ich aus der Gliederung eine Erörterung?

1. Introduction
In der Einleitung stellst du das Thema vor und beschreibst, worum es geht. Dabei kannst du von einer persönlichen Erfahrung oder einem allgemein bekannten Problem ausgehen.
Lots of people think … • It is generally believed that … • I once … • You often hear people say that … • …, so the question is: should … or not?

2. Present your arguments (for or against)
Präsentiere alle deine unterschiedlichen Argumente in einer logischen Reihenfolge. Beachte dabei für jedes Argument die folgenden drei Schritte:
- Nenn das Argument.
- Erläutere es näher und begründe deine Meinung.
- Unterstütze deine Meinung durch Beispiele (z.B. aus deiner eigenen Erfahrung).

First …; second …; • another argument for/against … is … • People think that … because … • For example, … • It might also be argued that … • Lots of people feel … • One could well say that … • Finally … • So … • That's why …

3. Conclusion
Am Ende erläuterst du deine persönliche Schlussfolgerung aus den bereits genannten Argumenten. Nenn keine neuen Argumente mehr.
To sum up, I would say that … • After looking at all the arguments I think …

MEDIATION SKILLS

SF REVISION Mediation

Wann muss ich zwischen zwei Sprachen vermitteln?

Manchmal musst du zwischen zwei Sprachen vermitteln. Das nennt man *mediation*.

1. Du gibst englische Informationen auf Deutsch weiter:
Du fährst z. B. mit deiner Familie in die USA und deine Eltern oder Geschwister wollen wissen, was jemand in einem Café gesagt hat oder was an einer Informationstafel steht.

2. Du gibst deutsche Informationen auf Englisch weiter:
Vielleicht ist bei dir zu Hause eine Austauschschülerin aus den USA oder Dänemark zu Gast, die kein Deutsch spricht und Hilfe braucht.

3. In schriftlichen Prüfungen musst du manchmal in einem englischen Text gezielt nach Informationen suchen und diese auf Deutsch wiedergeben. Oder du sollst Informationen aus einem deutschen Text auf Englisch wiedergeben.

Worauf muss ich bei *mediation* achten?

- Übersetze nicht alles wörtlich.
- Gib nur das Wesentliche weiter, lass Unwichtiges weg.
- Verwende kurze und einfache Sätze.
- Wenn du ein Wort nicht kennst, umschreibe es oder ersetze es durch ein anderes Wort.

Was kann ich tun, wenn ich ein wichtiges Wort nicht kenne?

Vielleicht findest du es manchmal schwer, mündliche Aussagen oder schriftliche Textvorlagen in die andere Sprache zu übertragen, z. B. weil:
- dein Wortschatz nicht ausreicht
- dir bekannte Wörter „im Stress" nicht einfallen
- spezielle Fachbegriffe auftauchen.

Manche Wörter kannst du umschreiben, z. B. mithilfe von Relativsätzen wie:
It's somebody/a person who ...
It's something that you use to ...
It's an animal that ...
It's a place where ...

► *SF Paraphrasing, p. 148*

EXAM SKILLS

SF REVISION How to do well in a test

Countdown zum Testerfolg

Ein Test ist angekündigt? Kein Grund zur Panik. Wichtig ist, dass du weißt, worauf du dich vorbereiten musst. Im Zweifelsfall frag deine Lehrerin oder deinen Lehrer. Der Countdown kann beginnen!

Eine Woche vor dem Test

1. Lies noch einmal die **Texte** der zuletzt durchgenommenen Unit (vor allem *Lead-in*, *A-Section* und *Text*, eventuell auch das *Background File*). Fasse mündlich oder schriftlich zusammen, worum es ging.

2. Wiederhole den **Wortschatz** der Unit mithilfe des *Vocabulary*, des *Wordmaster* oder des *English Coach*. Schreibe dir die Wörter und Wortverbindungen, die du immer wieder vergisst, auf ein Blatt Papier. Eine Mindmap oder ein Wortfeld helfen beim Behalten.

3. Geh noch einmal die neue **Grammatik** durch. Aufgaben zur Selbstüberprüfung und zum Üben findest du im *Practice*-Teil, auf der *How am I doing?*-Seite, im *Grammar File*, in deinem *Workbook* und im e-*Workbook*.
   (▸ *SF Check yourself, p. 136*)

Zwei oder drei Tage vor dem Test

1. Wiederhole den **Wortschatz**. Manche Wörter sitzen noch nicht? Schreibe einen kurzen Text, in dem du sie verwendest.

2. Lies die **Schülerbuch-Texte** ein weiteres Mal.

3. Erkläre einem Freund oder einer Freundin die neue **Grammatik**. Klappt nicht richtig? Dann lies nochmal im *Grammar File* nach.

Am Abend vor dem Test

1. Entspanne dich. Du kannst lesen, dich in die Badewanne legen, Musik hören, fernsehen, ...

2. Geh zur gewohnten Zeit ins Bett.

Am Morgen des Tests

1. Steh rechtzeitig auf, damit du dich nicht hetzen musst.

2. Lies etwas „zum Aufwärmen", aber schau nicht mehr in dein Schülerbuch.

Während des Tests

1. Denk daran: Du hast dich gut vorbereitet. Es gibt keinen Grund, nervös zu sein.

2. Konzentriere dich auf den Test, lass dich nicht ablenken.

3. Lies dir die Aufgaben genau durch. Dann löse zuerst die Aufgaben, die dir einfach scheinen. Wende dich erst danach den schwereren Aufgaben zu.

4. Aufgaben, die du bearbeitet hast, hakst du ab. So siehst du, wie du vorankommst, und behältst den Überblick.

5. Schau ab und zu auf die Uhr. Du solltest dir für den Schluss noch Zeit einplanen, um deine Antworten noch einmal durchzulesen und zu korrigieren.

Good luck!

Aufgabenstellungen verstehen

Bevor du damit anfängst, die Aufgaben zu bearbeiten, stell sicher, dass du genau weißt, was du machen sollst. Lies die Aufgabenstellung Wort für Wort langsam und gründlich und von Anfang bis Ende durch. Du kannst besonders wichtige Dinge der Aufgabenstellung unterstreichen und die Aufgabe, wenn nötig, für dich in einzelne Schritte unterteilen.

Worauf sollte ich bei Multiple-Choice-Aufgaben achten?

- Lies die Frage oder den Satz sehr genau durch.
- Bevor du dir die Lösungsangebote anschaust, deck sie mit Papier ab. Überleg dir, was die richtige Antwort sein könnte. Wenn das dann auch als eine Lösungsmöglichkeit angeboten wird, ist es meistens richtig.
- Lies immer alle vorgegebenen Lösungen, bevor du dich entscheidest.
- Achte darauf, dass du nur **eine** der Antworten ankreuzt – es sei denn, dass in der Aufgabenstellung ausdrücklich gesagt wird, dass mehrere Antworten richtig sein können.
- Mach erst alle Aufgaben so gut du kannst. Lass keine Aufgabe aus, aber geh zum Schluss zu den Fragen zurück, bei denen du unsicher bist.
- Wenn das alles nicht hilft, such nicht mehr nach der richtigen Antwort, sondern nach den falschen Antworten. Weil drei Antwortmöglichkeiten falsch sein müssen, kannst du erschließen, dass die vierte Antwort richtig ist. Hier ist ein Beispiel. Stell dir vor, du hörst folgenden Dialog.

  Boy *Wow, that was great, Dad. Thanks. Can we do it again next weekend?*

  Dad *Sure, Greg – if the weather's nice. But let's find an easier tour then – I'm a bit tired.*

Dazu wird dir die Multiple-Choice-Frage hier unten gestellt.
Greg und sein Vater müssen etwas im Freien gemacht haben, denn Gregs Dad spricht über das Wetter. Also sind die Antworten **B** und **C** falsch. Man schwimmt keine Touren, also ist **A** auch falsch. Daher muss **D** die richtige Antwort sein.

1. Greg and his dad have just
- A been swimming.
- B been to a fitness club.
- C seen a movie.
- D been on a bike ride.

Grammar File – Inhalt

			Seite
Unit 1–4	GF 1	**Talking about the present** Über die Gegenwart sprechen	159
Unit 1–4	GF 2	**Talking about the past** Über die Vergangenheit sprechen	160
Unit 1–4	GF 3	**Talking about the future** Über die Zukunft sprechen	162
Unit 1	GF 4	**Indirect speech (I)** Die indirekte Rede (I)	163
Unit 2	GF 5	**Indirect speech (II) – commands, requests, questions** Die indirekte Rede (II) – Aufforderungen, Bitten, Fragen	164
Unit 3	GF 6	**Participles** Partizipien	165
	GF 7	**The passive** Das Passiv	166
Unit 4	GF 8	**Conditional sentences** Bedingungssätze	167
Grammatical terms (Grammatische Fachbegriffe)			168
Lösungen der Grammar-File-Aufgaben			169

Im **Grammar File** (S. 158–169) wird zusammengefasst, was du in diesem Band **über die englische Sprache** lernst.

In der **linken Spalte** findest du **Beispielsätze** und **Übersichten**.

Indirect speech (reporting verb: simple past) — Zita Wallace said **that** she had seen terrible things. She added **that** she would never forget those first hours.

He said his name was Paul.
Er sagte, dass er Paul heißt.

Veränderungen der Zeitformen bei einleitende

	Direct speech
present ▸ past	'I don't care about money.'

In der **rechten Spalte** stehen **Erklärungen** und nützliche **Hinweise**.

Das **rote Ausrufezeichen** (**!**) macht dich auf besondere Fehlerquellen aufmerksam.

Hinweise wie ▸ *Unit 1, Part C: P 1–3 (pp. 18–19)* geben an, welche Übungen zu einem **Grammar-File**-Abschnitt gehören.

Die **grammatischen Fachbegriffe** (*grammatical terms*) kannst du auf den Seiten 168–169 nachschlagen.

Additional information

So gekennzeichnete Abschnitte enthalten Grammatik, die du nicht selbst zu verwenden brauchst. Du solltest aber verstehen, was dort erklärt wird, damit du keine Schwierigkeiten mit Texten hast, in denen diese Grammatik vorkommt.

Am Ende der Abschnitte stehen wieder kleine Aufgaben zur Selbstkontrolle. Schreib die Lösungen in dein Heft. Überprüfe sie dann auf Seite 169.

GF 1 Talking about the present Über die Gegenwart sprechen

Du möchtest ausdrücken,

– dass etwas **regelmäßig** geschieht ▸ *The simple present: GF 1.1*	→ Hanna **gets up** at 7 o'clock every morning. Hanna steht jeden Morgen um 7 Uhr auf.
– dass etwas **gerade jetzt** geschieht ▸ *The present progressive: GF 1.2*	→ It's 7 o'clock. Hanna **is getting up**. Es ist 7 Uhr. Hanna steht (gerade) auf.

1.1 The simple present

Das ***simple present*** wird verwendet,

Dave Wilson **usually** gets the bus to school.
On Mondays his mother takes him in the car.
He **never** cycles to school because it's too far.

◂ um über Handlungen und Ereignisse zu sprechen, die **wiederholt, regelmäßig, immer** oder **nie** geschehen (oft mit Zeitangaben wie *always, never, usually, sometimes, often, every week, on Mondays* usw.).

Dave and his family live in Manchester.
He plays hockey and collects models of old cars.
His dad works for a building company.

◂ um über **Dauerzustände**, **Hobbys** und **Berufe** zu sprechen.

! ***He, she, it*** **– das „s" muss mit.**

Verneinte Sätze	I don't cycle to school.	Dave doesn't walk to school.
Fragen	Do you go to school by bus? **Where** do the Wilsons live?	Does your mother take you in the car? **When** does Dave's mother take him in the car?

1.2 The present progressive

Das ***present progressive*** wird verwendet,

What's Dave doing? –
Just now he's cleaning his bike.

◂ um über Handlungen und Ereignisse zu sprechen, die **jetzt gerade im Gange** sind (oft mit Angaben wie *at the moment, now, just*).

Dave (on the phone) I can't talk right now, Jack. I'm cleaning my bike.

! Die Handlung, um die es geht, kann für einen Augenblick unterbrochen sein, z.B. durch ein Telefonat. Wichtig ist, dass sie noch nicht abgeschlossen ist.

This week Dave's grandma is staying at the Wilsons' because Dave's mum is ill.

◂ um über **vorübergehende Zustände** zu sprechen (begrenzter Zeitraum: *this week*).

Verneinte Sätze	The Wilsons aren't working.	Dave isn't watching TV.
Fragen	Are you watching TV? **What** are you doing?	Is Dave cleaning his bike? **Who** is Dave talking to?

Dave's dad works for a building company.
Look, he's working at his desk at the moment.

GF 2 Talking about the past Über die Vergangenheit sprechen

Du möchtest ausdrücken,

– dass etwas in der Vergangenheit **geschah**; das Geschehen ist **abgeschlossen** und **vorbei** ▸ *The simple past: GF 2.1*	→	Emma **left** school in 2007. Emma ging im Jahr 2007 von der Schule ab.
– dass etwas in der Vergangenheit **gerade im Gange (noch nicht abgeschlossen) war** ▸ *The past progressive: GF 2.2*	→	We **were leaving** the building when we heard the explosion. Wir waren gerade dabei, das Gebäude zu verlassen, ...
– dass etwas **vor etwas anderem** in der Vergangenheit stattgefunden hatte ▸ *The past perfect: GF 2.3*	→	Connor **had** already **left** when we arrived. Connor war schon gegangen, als wir ankamen.
– dass etwas **irgendwann** geschehen ist, oft mit **Auswirkungen auf die Gegenwart**	→	Jane **has left** her purse at home, so she can't pay for her bus ticket. Jane hat ihre Geldbörse zu Hause gelassen, ...
– dass ein Zustand **in der Vergangenheit begonnen** hat und **noch andauert** ▸ *The present perfect: GF 2.4*	→	We**'ve had** our dog for three years now – since 2007. Wir haben unseren Hund jetzt seit drei Jahren ...

2.1 The simple past

Last Friday Katie's family flew to Spain.
Letzten Freitag ist Katies Familie nach Spanien geflogen / flog Katies Familie nach Spanien.
Two years ago the Websters moved to Bath.
Vor zwei Jahren sind die Websters nach Bath gezogen.

Wenn man über Vergangenes berichtet, benutzt man überwiegend das ***simple past***. Man beschreibt damit Handlungen, Ereignisse und Zustände, die zu einer bestimmten Zeit in der Vergangenheit *(yesterday, last Friday, two years ago, in 2003, between 2005 and 2008, ...)* stattfanden.

! Im Deutschen wird in diesen Fällen oft das Perfekt verwendet, im Englischen jedoch nicht.

Verneinte Sätze	They didn't fly to France.	Katie didn't want to go at first.
Fragen	Did you go on holiday last year? **Where** did you go?	Did Katie like it? **When** did the Websters move to Bath?

2.2 The past progressive

What were you doing yesterday at 3.30? –
I was waiting for my sister at the school doors.
She was still talking to our Maths teacher.

Angela was just crossing the road when she saw her boyfriend.
Angela war gerade dabei, die Straße zu überqueren, ...

Das ***past progressive*** wird verwendet,

◂ um über Handlungen und Ereignisse zu sprechen, die zu einer bestimmten Zeit in der Vergangenheit noch im Gange, also noch nicht abgeschlossen waren.

◂ wenn man beschreiben will, was gerade vor sich ging *(she was just crossing the road)*, als etwas anderes passierte *(she saw her boyfriend)*.

Verneinte Sätze	You weren't listening.	It wasn't snowing when we left the house.
Fragen	Were you watching TV? **What** were they doing?	Was she crossing the road when it happened? **What** was she doing?

2.3

The past perfect

When Emma arrived home, her parents had already eaten.
Als Emma zu Hause eintraf, hatten ihre Eltern bereits gegessen.

Wenn man sagen will, dass etwas noch vor etwas anderem in der Vergangenheit stattgefunden hatte, dann benutzt man das ***past perfect***.

Verneinte Sätze	They hadn't gone to bed.	Emma hadn't eaten anything all day.
Fragen	Had you seen that film before? **What** had they done?	Had Emma eaten when she came home? **Where** had she been all day?

2.4

The present perfect

Will Smith is great. I've seen most of his films.
Luke has **already** done his Maths homework, but he hasn't started his French **yet**.
Have you **ever** been to Paris?
– No, I haven't. But I've **always** wanted to go.

Mel has lost her mobile. Her dad is very angry.

! Das ***present perfect*** hat mit der **Vergangenheit und mit der Gegenwart** zu tun. Es wird verwendet,

◄ wenn man sagen will, **dass** jemand etwas getan hat oder **dass** etwas geschehen ist. Dabei ist nicht wichtig, wann es geschehen ist – ein genauer Zeitpunkt wird nicht genannt. Das *present perfect* steht oft mit Adverbien der unbestimmten Zeit wie *already, just, never, ever, not ... yet*.
Oft hat die Handlung Auswirkungen auf die Gegenwart (Mels Vater ist wütend, weil sie ihr Handy verloren hat).

We've had our new car **since April**.
Wir haben unser neues Auto seit April.

***since* + Zeitpunkt**

We've had our new car **for three months**.
Wir haben unser neues Auto seit drei Monaten.

***for* + Zeitraum**

◄ für **Zustände**, die in der Vergangenheit begonnen haben und jetzt noch andauern (oft mit ***since*** bzw. ***for***).

! Im Deutschen steht in diesen Fällen meist das Präsens, im Englischen muss das *present perfect* stehen.

Verneinte Sätze	I haven't been to Paris yet.	Luke hasn't done his French homework.
Fragen	Have you been to Paris? **What** have you done?	Has Mel found her mobile yet? **Which** of these films have you seen already?

Additional information

2.5

The present perfect progressive

I've **been writing** e-mails all day.
Ich **schreibe** (schon) den ganzen Tag E-Mails.

We've **been learning** French for four years.
Wir **lernen** seit vier Jahren Französisch.

Auch das ***present perfect progressive*** hat mit der Vergangenheit und mit der Gegenwart zu tun. Es wird verwendet für **Vorgänge** und **Handlungen**, die in der Vergangenheit begonnen haben und jetzt noch andauern (oft mit ***since*** bzw. ***for***).

! Auch hier steht im Deutschen meist das Präsens – aber im Englischen das *present perfect progressive*.

GF 3 Talking about the future *Über die Zukunft sprechen*

Du möchtest ausdrücken,

– dass etwas für die Zukunft **geplant** ist ▸ *The going to-future: GF 3.1*	→ I'm **going to watch** the new Bond film tonight. Ich sehe mir heute Abend den neuen Bond-Film an.
– wie etwas in der Zukunft **sein wird** (**Vorhersagen, Vermutungen**) ▸ *The will-future: GF 3.2*	→ It **will be** warm and sunny in Spain. I'm sure you**'ll like** it there. Es wird warm und sonnig sein in Spanien. Ich bin sicher, dass es dir dort gefallen wird.
– dass etwas für die Zukunft **fest verabredet** ist (es steht schon im Kalender) ▸ *The present progressive: GF 3.3*	→ We**'re having** a party on Saturday. Would you like to come? Wir geben nächsten Samstag eine Party. ...

3.1 The *going to*-future

Das **Futur mit *going to*** wird verwendet,

My boyfriend says he's going to be an engineer.
Mein Freund sagt, er will Ingenieur werden.

◂ wenn man über **Vorhaben, Pläne, Absichten** für die Zukunft sprechen will.

Look at those clouds. There's going to be a storm.
... Es wird ein Gewitter geben.

◂ um auszudrücken, dass etwas **wahrscheinlich gleich geschehen wird** – es gibt bereits deutliche **Anzeichen** dafür (*hier:* die Wolken am Himmel).

3.2 The *will*-future

Das **Futur mit *will*** wird verwendet,

It will be cold and windy, and we will get some rain in the afternoon.
I'll be 15 next October.

◂ um **Vorhersagen** über die Zukunft zu äußern. Oft geht es dabei um Dinge, die man nicht beeinflussen kann, z.B. das Wetter.

I expect Ella will be late again as usual.
Ich nehme an, Ella kommt wie üblich wieder zu spät.

◂ um eine **Vermutung** auszudrücken (oft eingeleitet mit *I think, I'm sure, I expect, maybe*).

Just a moment. I'll open the door for you.
Moment. Ich mache Ihnen die Tür auf.
I won't tell anyone what's happened. I promise.
Ich sage niemandem, was passiert ist. ...

◂ wenn man sich **spontan** – also ohne es im Voraus geplant zu haben – zu etwas **entschließt**. Oft geht es dabei um **Hilfsangebote** oder **Versprechen**.

3.3 The present progressive (future meaning)

We're driving to Scotland next Friday to visit my grandparents.
I'm meeting a friend in town tonight.

Das ***present progressive*** wird verwendet, wenn etwas **für die Zukunft fest geplant** oder **fest verabredet** ist (manchmal spricht man vom *diary future*). Durch eine Zeitangabe wie *tonight* oder aus dem Zusammenhang muss klar sein, dass es um etwas Zukünftiges geht.

Additional information

3.4 The simple present (future meaning)

The next train to Bath **goes** in ten minutes.
The next drawing class **starts** on 2 September.

Das ***simple present*** wird verwendet, wenn ein **zukünftiges Geschehen** durch einen **Fahrplan**, ein **Programm** oder Ähnliches festgelegt ist (manchmal spricht man vom *timetable future*). Verben wie *arrive, leave, go, open, close, start, stop* werden häufig so verwendet.

Unit 1

GF 4 Indirect speech (I) Die indirekte Rede (I)

Direct speech	Zita Wallace says, 'I **saw** terrible things. I**'ll** never **forget** those first hours.'	◄ In der **direkten Rede** wird **wörtlich** wiedergegeben, was jemand sagt oder gesagt hat. Direkte Rede steht in Anführungszeichen (deutsch: „...“; englisch: '...').
Indirect speech (reporting verb: simple present)	Zita Wallace says **that** she **saw** terrible things and **that** she **will** never **forget** those first hours.	◄ In der **indirekten Rede** (*indirect* oder *reported speech*) wird berichtet, was jemand sagt oder gesagt hat. Die indirekte Rede wird mit Verben wie *say, tell sb., add, answer, explain, write* eingeleitet.
Indirect speech (reporting verb: simple past)	Zita Wallace said **that** she had seen terrible things. She added **that** she would never forget those first hours.	◄ Wenn das **einleitende Verb im *simple past*** steht (*she said/told us/explained/answered* usw.), dann werden die Zeitformen der direkten Rede meist verändert: Sie werden um eine Zeitstufe in die Vergangenheit „zurückverschoben“ *(backshift of tenses)*.

He said his name was Paul.
Er sagte, dass er Paul heißt.

! Im Englischen steht vor der indirekten Rede kein Komma und das Wort *that* wird oft weggelassen.

Veränderungen der Zeitformen bei einleitendem Verb im *simple past*

	Direct speech	Indirect speech
present ► past	'I don't care about money.' 'I'm waiting for an apology.'	She **said** she didn't care about money. She **said** she was waiting for an apology.
past ► past perfect	'I saw terrible things.'	She **told** us she had seen terrible things.
can* ► *could	'You can go shopping with us.'	The nuns **said** that the girls could go shopping with them.
***will*-future ► *would* + infinitive**	'I'll never forget those days.'	She **said** she would never forget those days.
***going to*-future ► *was/were going to* + infinitive**	'The government is going to apologize.'	They **said** the government was going to apologize.
present perfect ► past perfect	'I haven't forgotten that evening.'	She **added** that she hadn't forgotten that evening.

Verben im *past perfect* bleiben unverändert, da man sie nicht weiter „zurückverschieben“ kann.

► *Unit 1, Part C: P 1–3 (pp. 18–19)*

Berichte, was Ella ihrer Freundin Lucy am Telefon erzählt hat. Schreib die Sätze in indirekter Rede in dein Heft.

1 'My mom is still at work.'	Ella **said** her mom ...
2 'She has to work late.'	She **told** Lucy that her mom ...
3 'Mom won't be home till nine.'	She **added** that her mom ...
4 'Dad will probably want a pizza.'	She also **said** her dad ...
5 'I'll call again later.'	She **told** Lucy she ...

Unit 2

GF 5 Indirect speech (II) Die indirekte Rede (II)

5.1 Commands and requests

Aufforderungen und Bitten

Simon Look for clothes for the interview.
And don't be shy.

Simon told them to look for clothes for the interview. And he told them not to be shy.
Simon sagte ihnen, sie sollten sich nach Kleidung für das Interview umsehen. Und er sagte ihnen, dass sie nicht schüchtern sein sollten.

◀ **Aufforderungen, Anordnungen** und **Ratschläge** werden in der indirekten Rede meist mit ***tell sb. to do sth.*** (bzw. ***tell sb. not to do sth.***) wiedergegeben.

Simon Mani, please choose a new tie.

Simon asked Mani to choose a new tie.
Simon bat Mani, eine neue Krawatte zu wählen.

◀ Eine **Bitte** wird meist mit ***ask sb. to do sth.*** (bzw. ***ask sb. not to do sth.***) wiedergegeben.

▸ *Unit 2, Part C: P 3a–b, P 4 (p. 42)*

Berichte, was die Lehrerin gesagt hat. Verwende told ... *oder* asked ...

1 'Emily, please don't argue with Jacob.' — The teacher asked Emily not to ...
2 'Jacob and Emily, discuss your opinions quietly.' — She told Jacob and Emily ...
3 'Emily, don't use bad language in my classroom.' — She ...
4 'Jacob, please revise your essay.' — She ...

5.2 Questions

Fragen

Auch bei Fragen in der indirekten Rede werden die Zeitformen in die Vergangenheit „zurückverschoben", wenn das einleitende Verb im *simple past* steht.

Direct question (with question word)	What do you know about my business?
Indirect question	Rita asked Mani **what** he knew about her business.

◀ Wenn die direkte **Frage mit einem Fragewort** beginnt (*what, when, where, why, how* usw.), dann wird das Fragewort in der indirekten Frage beibehalten.

Direct question (yes/no question)	Do you have any weaknesses?
Indirect question	Rita asked him **if** he had any weaknesses.

◀ Handelt es sich bei der direkten Frage um eine **Frage ohne Fragewort** *(yes/no question)*, dann wird die indirekte Frage mit ***if*** („ob") eingeleitet.

▸ *Unit 2, Part C: P 3c, P 5–6 (pp. 42–43)*

Olivia war in London. Im Englischunterricht stellen ihre Mitschüler/innen Fragen. Berichte.

1 'Did you go to Camden Lock Market?' — Mike asked if Olivia ...
2 'Where did you stay?' — Sophie asked ...
3 'Are London restaurants expensive?' — Jessie wanted to know ...
4 'Can you buy cheap clothes and CDs in London?' — Antonia wanted to know ...

Unit 3

GF 6 Participles Partizipien

6.1 REVISION Participle forms

Formen des Partizips

Present participle *(-ing)*:

play	→	**playing**	try	→	**trying**
phone	→	**phoning**	plan	→	**planning**

◀ Das **Partizip Präsens** *(present participle)* bildet man durch Anhängen von ***-ing*** an den Infinitiv. Beachte die Besonderheiten bei der Schreibung.

Past participle, regular verbs *(-ed)*:

play	→	**played**	try	→	**tried**
phone	→	**phoned**	plan	→	**planned**

◀ Das **Partizip Perfekt** *(past participle)* eines regelmäßigen Verbs wird durch Anhängen von ***-ed*** an den Infinitiv gebildet. Beachte auch hier die Besonderheiten bei der Schreibung.

Past participle, irregular verbs:

go	→	**gone**	make	→	**made**
take	→	**taken**	write	→	**written**

Bedenke, dass unregelmäßige Verben eigene 3. Formen haben, die man einzeln lernen muss.

► *Unregelmäßige Verben (pp. 236–237)*

Additional information

6.2 Participle clauses instead of relative clauses

Partizipialsätze anstelle von Relativsätzen

1 He saw other kids **having fun outside.**
... andere Jugendliche, die sich draußen amüsierten.

2 Shane is a reliable young man **looking for his first job.**
... junger Mann, der seine erste Anstellung sucht.

3 He saw the posters **stuck up in town.**
... die Poster, die in der Stadt aufgehängt waren.

► *Unit 3, Part B: P 3 (p. 57)*

Partizipialsätze können Relativsätze ersetzen.

◀ Partizipialsätze mit ***present participle*** (Sätze **1** und **2**) entsprechen Relativsätzen im **Aktiv**:

1 ... ***having*** *fun* = ... ***who were having*** *fun*

2 ... ***looking*** *for his first job* = ... ***who is looking*** *for ...*

◀ Partizipialsätze mit ***past participle*** (Satz **3**) entsprechen Relativsätzen im **Passiv**:

3 ... ***stuck*** *up in town* = ... ***that were stuck up*** ...

GF 7 The passive Das Passiv

7.1 REVISION Active and passive

Active: The ManaTEEN friends found bottles and glass in the springs.
Die ManaTEEN-Freunde fanden Flaschen und Glas in den Quellen.

◄ Ein **<u>Aktivsatz</u>** beschreibt, **wer oder was etwas tut**. Der Aktivsatz links handelt von den ManaTEEN-Freunden und ihren Aktivitäten.

Passive: Bottles and glass were found in the springs.
Flaschen und Glas wurden ... gefunden.

◄ Ein **<u>Passivsatz</u>** beschreibt, **mit wem oder womit etwas geschieht**. Der Passivsatz links handelt von dem Müll, der in den Quellen gefunden wurde.

A lot of trash is thrown into the springs. But of course trash is not the only thing that is found at Weeki Wachee Springs.

In **Passivsätzen** steht nicht, wer die Handlung ausführt. Oft ist das unwichtig oder nicht bekannt. Das Passiv wird oft in Nachrichten, in Zeitungsartikeln, in technischen Beschreibungen und auf Schildern verwendet, wenn man den „Täter" oder „Verursacher" nicht nennen kann oder nicht nennen will.

I was beaten by my best friend.
Ich wurde von meinem besten Freund besiegt.

! Wenn in einem Passivsatz der „Täter" oder „Verursacher" doch genannt werden soll, dann verwendet man ***by ...*** .

7.2 Form

Form

Das Passiv bildet man mit einer **Form von *be*** und der 3. Form des Verbs (Partizip Perfekt, *past participle*).

The passive

Simple present: ***am/are/is*** + past participle	So much trash is thrown into the springs. So viel Müll wird in die Quellen geworfen.
Simple past: ***was/were*** + past participle	I was beaten by my best friend. Ich wurde von meinem besten Freund besiegt.
Present perfect: ***have/has been*** + past participle	A lot of coins and bills have been collected. Eine Menge Münzen und Noten sind gesammelt worden.
will*-future:** ***will be + past participle	The food will be given to the Soup Kitchen tomorrow. Morgen werden die Lebensmittel der Suppenküche übergeben (werden).
Modal auxiliaries: ***can/must/should/... be*** + past participle	The food can be stored there overnight. Die Lebensmittel können dort über Nacht gelagert werden. Something must be done / should be done to help people in need. Es muss / sollte etwas getan werden, ...

► *Unit 3, Part C: P 2–5 (pp. 60–61)*

Vervollständige die Passivsätze. Achte auf die richtige Zeitform.

1 Every week bottles and trash ... (throw) into our garden, or graffiti ... (spray) on our wall.
2 Last week three bikes ... (steal) from the school yard.
3 This week so far two mobiles ... (steal) from kids in my class – and it's only Wednesday.
4 I expect a few windows ... (break) in our school before the end of the month.
5 A lot more ... (must / do) to stop thieves, bullies and vandalism.

Unit 4

GF 8 Conditional sentences Bedingungssätze

8.1 REVISION Type 1 and type 2

If you run, you'll catch the bus.
Wenn du rennst, kriegst du den Bus noch.

If you miss the bus, you can take / should take / must take a taxi.
Wenn du den Bus verpasst, kannst/sollst/musst du ein Taxi nehmen.

Typ 1 und Typ 2

◄ **Typ 1** („**Was <u>ist</u>, wenn ...**"-**Sätze**)
Diese Bedingungssätze beziehen sich auf die **Gegenwart** oder die **Zukunft**.
Sie drücken aus, was unter bestimmten Bedingungen **geschieht** oder **geschehen kann/soll** usw.

***if*-Satz (Bedingung)**	**Hauptsatz (Folge)**
If you run,	*you'll catch the bus.*
If you miss the bus,	*you can take a taxi.*
simple present	**– *will-future*** **– *can/should/must* + Infinitiv**

If you ran, you would catch the bus.
Wenn du rennen würdest, würdest du den Bus noch kriegen.

If you caught the bus, you could be home in time for dinner.
Wenn du den Bus kriegen würdest, könntest du rechtzeitig zum Abendessen daheim sein.

◄ **Typ 2** („**Was <u>wäre</u>, wenn ...**"-**Sätze**)
Diese Bedingungssätze beziehen sich auch auf die **Gegenwart** oder die **Zukunft**.
Sie drücken aus, was unter bestimmten Bedingungen **geschehen würde** oder **könnte**.

***if*-Satz (Bedingung)**	**Hauptsatz (Folge)**
If you ran,	*you would catch/could catch the bus.*
simple past	***would/could* + Infinitiv**

Additional information

8.2 Type 3

If you had run, you would have caught the bus.
Wenn du gerannt wärst, hättest du den Bus noch gekriegt.

If you had caught the bus, you could have had dinner with us.
Wenn du den Bus gekriegt hättest, hättest du mit uns Abendbrot essen können.

► *Unit 4, Part C: P 3 (p.87)*

Typ 3

◄ **Typ 3** („**Was <u>wäre gewesen</u>, wenn ...**"-**Sätze**)
Diese Bedingungssätze beziehen sich auf die **Vergangenheit**.
Sie drücken aus, was unter bestimmten Bedingungen **geschehen wäre** oder **hätte geschehen können**.
Der Sprecher stellt sich nur vor, was geschehen wäre, aber in Wirklichkeit nicht geschehen ist:
Wenn du gerannt wärst, hättest du den Bus erwischt – aber da du nicht gerannt bist ...

***if*-Satz (Bedingung)**	**Hauptsatz (Folge)**
If you had run,	*you would have caught/ could have caught the bus.*
past perfect	***would/could* + *have* +** **Partizip Perfekt**

Grammatical terms (Grammatische Fachbegriffe)

active ['æktɪv]	Aktiv	Beckham **scored** the final goal.
adjective ['ædʒɪktɪv]	Adjektiv	good, red, new, boring
adverb ['ædvɜːb]	Adverb	always, badly, here, really, today
adverb of frequency ['friːkwənsi]	Häufigkeitsadverb	always, often, never
adverb of indefinite time [ɪnˌdefɪnət 'taɪm]	Adverb der unbestimmten Zeit	already, ever, just, never
adverb of manner ['mænə]	Adverb der Art und Weise	badly, happily, quietly, well
article ['ɑːtɪkl]	Artikel	the, a/an
auxiliary [ɔːg'zɪliəri]	Hilfsverb	be, have, do; will, can, must
backshift of tenses ['bækʃɪft]	Verschiebung der Zeitformen *(bei der indirekten Rede)*	'I'**m** sorry.' ► Sam said he **was** sorry.
command [kə'mɑːnd]	Befehl, Aufforderungssatz	Open your books. Don't talk.
comparison [kəm'pærɪsn]	Steigerung	old – older – oldest
conditional sentence [kənˌdɪʃənl 'sentəns]	Bedingungssatz	I'd call him if I knew his number.
conjunction [kən'dʒʌŋkʃn]	Konjunktion	and, or, but; because, before
contact clause ['kɒntækt klɔːz]	Relativsatz ohne Relativpronomen	She's the girl **I love**.
countable noun ['kaʊntəbl]	zählbares Nomen	girl – girls, pound – pounds
definite article ['defɪnət]	bestimmter Artikel	the
direct speech [ˌdaɪrekt 'spiːtʃ]	direkte Rede, wörtliche Rede	**'I'm sorry**.'
gerund ['dʒerənd]	Gerundium	I like **dancing**. **Dancing** is fun.
***going to*-future**	Futur mit *going to*	**I'm going to watch** TV tonight.
***if*-clause** ['ɪf klɔːz]	*if*-Satz, Nebensatz mit *if*	**If I see Jack**, I'll tell him.
imperative [ɪm'perətɪv]	Imperativ (Befehlsform)	Open your books. Don't talk.
indirect speech [ˌɪndərekt 'spiːtʃ]	indirekte Rede	Sam said **(that) he was sorry**.
infinitive [ɪn'fɪnətɪv]	Infinitiv (Grundform des Verbs)	(to) open, (to) see, (to) read
irregular verb [ɪˌregjələ 'vɜːb]	unregelmäßiges Verb	(to) go – went – gone
main clause	Hauptsatz	**I like Scruffy** because I like dogs.
modal, modal auxiliary [ˌməʊdl_ɔːg'zɪliəri]	modales Hilfsverb, Modalverb	can, could, may, must
negative statement [ˌnegətɪv 'steɪtmənt]	verneinter Aussagesatz	I don't like bananas.
noun [naʊn]	Nomen, Substantiv	Sophie, girl, brother, time
object ['ɒbdʒɪkt]	Objekt	My sister is writing **a letter**.
object form ['ɒbdʒɪkt fɔːm]	Objektform (der Personalpronomen)	me, you, him, her, it, us, them
participle ['pɑːtɪsɪpl]	Partizip	planning, taking; planned, taken
participle clause [ˌpɑːtɪsɪpl 'klɔːz]	Partizipialsatz	I saw a boy **playing in the street**.
passive ['pæsɪv]	Passiv	The goal **was scored** by Beckham.
past participle [ˌpɑːst 'pɑːtɪsɪpl]	Partizip Perfekt	cleaned, planned, gone, taken
past perfect [ˌpɑːst 'pɜːfɪkt]	Plusquamperfekt, Vorvergangenheit	He cried – he **had hurt** his knee.
past progressive [ˌpɑːst prə'gresɪv]	Verlaufsform der Vergangenheit	At 7.30 I **was having** dinner.
personal pronoun [ˌpɜːsənl 'prəʊnaʊn]	Personalpronomen (persönliches Fürwort)	I, you, he, she, it, we, they; me, you, him, her, it, us, them
plural ['plʊərəl]	Plural, Mehrzahl	
positive statement [ˌpɒzətɪv 'steɪtmənt]	bejahter Aussagesatz	I like oranges.
possessive determiner [pəˌzesɪv dɪ'tɜːmɪnə]	Possessivbegleiter (besitzanzeigender Begleiter)	my, your, his, her, its, our, their
possessive form [pəˌzesɪv fɔːm]	*s*-Genitiv	Jo's brother; my sister's room
possessive pronoun [pəˌzesɪv 'prəʊnaʊn]	Possessivpronomen	mine, yours, his, hers, ours, theirs
preposition [ˌprepə'zɪʃn]	Präposition	after, at, in, next to, under
present participle [ˌpreznt 'pɑːtɪsɪpl]	Partizip Präsens	cleaning, planning, going, taking
present perfect [ˌpreznt 'pɜːfɪkt]	*present perfect*	We**'ve made** a cake for you.
present perfect progressive [ˌpreznt ˌpɜːfɪkt prə'gresɪv]	Verlaufsform des *present perfect*	We**'ve been waiting** for an hour.

present progressive [ˌpreznt prəˈgresɪv]	Verlaufsform der Gegenwart	*The Hansons* ***are having*** *lunch.*
pronoun [ˈprəʊnaʊn]	Pronomen, Fürwort	
quantifier [ˈkwɒntɪfaɪə]	Mengenangabe	*some, a lot of, many, much*
question tag [ˈkwestʃən tæg]	Frageanhängsel	*This place is great,* ***isn't it?***
question word [ˈkwestʃən wɜːd]	Fragewort	*what?, when?, where?, how?*
reflexive pronoun [rɪˌfleksɪv ˈprəʊnaʊn]	Reflexivpronomen	*myself, yourself, themselves*
regular verb [ˌregjələ ˈvɜːb]	regelmäßiges Verb	*(to) help – helped – helped*
relative clause [ˌrelətɪv ˈklɔːz]	Relativsatz	*There's the girl* ***who helped me****.*
relative pronoun [ˌrelətɪv ˈprəʊnaʊn]	Relativpronomen	*who, that, which, whose*
reported speech [rɪˌpɔːtɪd ˈspiːtʃ]	indirekte Rede	*Sam said* ***(that) he was sorry****.*
request [rɪˈkwest]	Bitte	*Can you help me with this?*
short answer [ˌʃɔːt_ˈɑːnsə]	Kurzantwort	*Yes, I am. / No, I don't.*
simple past [ˌsɪmpl ˈpɑːst]	einfache Form der Vergangenheit	*Jo* ***wrote*** *two letters yesterday.*
simple present [ˌsɪmpl ˈpreznt]	einfache Form der Gegenwart	*I always* ***go*** *to school by bike.*
singular [ˈsɪŋgjələ]	Singular, Einzahl	
statement [ˈsteɪtmənt]	Aussagesatz	
subject [ˈsʌbdʒɪkt]	Subjekt	***My sister*** *is writing a letter.*
subject form [ˈsʌbdʒɪkt fɔːm]	Subjektform (der Personalpronomen)	*I, you, he, she, it, we, they*
subordinate clause [səˌbɔːdɪnət ˈklɔːz]	Nebensatz	*I like Scruffy* ***because I like dogs****.*
tense [tens]	Zeitform	
uncountable noun [ʌnˈkaʊntəbl]	nicht zählbares Nomen	*bread, milk, money, news, work*
verb [vɜːb]	Verb	*hear, open, help, go*
will**-future**	Futur mit *will*	*I think it* ***will be*** *cold tonight.*
word order [ˈwɜːd_ˌɔːdə]	Wortstellung	
yes/no question	Entscheidungsfrage	*Are you 13? Do you like comics?*

Lösungen der Grammar-File-Aufgaben

p.163
1 Ella said her mom was still at work.
2 She told Lucy that her mom had to work late.
3 She added that her mom wouldn't be home till nine.
4 She also said her dad would probably want a pizza.
5 She told Lucy she would call again later.

p.164/1
1 The teacher asked Emily not to argue with Jacob.
2 She told Jacob and Emily to discuss their opinions quietly.
3 She told Emily not to use bad language in her classroom.
4 She asked Jacob to revise his essay.

p.164/2
1 Mike asked if Olivia had gone to Camden Lock Market.
2 Sophie asked where Olivia had stayed.
3 Jessie wanted to know if London restaurants were expensive.
4 Antonia wanted to know if you could buy cheap clothes and CDs in London.

p.166
1 Every week bottles and trash are thrown into our garden, or graffiti is sprayed on our wall.
2 Last week three bikes were stolen from the school yard.
3 This week so far two mobiles have been stolen from kids in my class – and it's only Wednesday.
4 I expect a few windows will be broken in our school before the end of the month.
5 A lot more must be done to stop thieves, bullies and vandalism.

Diese Wörterverzeichnisse findest du in deinem Englischbuch:

- Das **Vocabulary** (Vokabelverzeichnis – S. 170–191) enthält alle neuen Wörter und Wendungen aus Band 5, die du lernen musst. Sie stehen in der Reihenfolge, in der sie in den Units vorkommen.
- Das **Dictionary** (S. 192–226) enthält den Wortschatz der Bände 1–5 in alphabetischer Reihenfolge. Dort kannst du nachschlagen, was ein Wort bedeutet, wie man es ausspricht oder wie es geschrieben wird.

So ist das Vocabulary aufgebaut:

- Hier siehst du, wo die Wörter vorkommen.
  p. 10/3 = Seite 10, Abschnitt 3
  p. 14/P 2 = Seite 14, Übung 2
- Die Lautschrift zeigt dir, wie ein Wort ausgesprochen und betont wird.
- Eingerückte Wörter lernst du am besten zusammen mit dem vorausgehenden Wort, weil die beiden zusammengehören.
- Die blauen Kästen solltest du dir besonders gut ansehen.

p.10/3	**nearly** ['nɪəli]	fast, beinahe	= almost
p.14/P 2	**I see.** [ˌaɪ 'siː]	Ich verstehe. / Aha. / Ach so.	Jan's English is so good be English. – Oh, I ~. I didn't k
	witness ['wɪtnəs]	Zeuge, Zeugin	
p.15/P 4	(to) **rent** sth. [rent]	etwas mieten, etwas leihen	(to) ~ a flat, a car, a holid
	rent [rent]	Miete	How much ~ do you pay
	(to) **introduce** sb. **to** sb. [ˌɪntrə'djuːs]	jn. jm. vorstellen; jn. mit jm. bekanntmachen	This morning our class te sports teacher **to** us.

Introducing people

Tipps zum Wörterlernen findest du im Skills File auf Seite 135.

Abkürzungen:

n = *noun*		*v* = *verb*	
adj = *adjective*		*adv* = *adverb*	
prep = *preposition*		*conj* = *conjunction*	
pl = *plural*		*no pl* = *no plural*	
p. = page		pp. = pages	
sb. = somebody		sth. = something	
jn. = jemanden		jm. = jemandem	
AE = *American English*		*BE* = *British English*	
infml = *informal* (umgangssprachlich, informell)			

Symbole:

! Hier stehen Hinweise auf Besonderheiten, bei denen man leicht Fehler machen kann.

◄► ist das „Gegenteil"-Zeichen: **outdoors ◄► indoors**

~ Die **Tilde** in den Beispielsätzen steht für das neue Wort. Beispiel: **area** – Germany has an ~ of about 357,000 sq km.

Unit 1: Australia

a **barbecue**

p.6	**nationality** [ˌnæʃə'næləti]	Staatsangehörigkeit, Nationalität	
	the outback ['aʊtbæk]	*(Australien)* das Hinterland	
	the bush [bʊʃ]	der Busch *(unkultiviertes, „wildes" Land in Australien, Afrika)*	
	bush [bʊʃ]	Busch, Strauch	
	sleeping bag ['sliːpɪŋ bæg]	Schlafsack	
	barbecue ['bɑːbɪkjuː]	Grillfest, Grillparty	
	at someone's place	bei jemandem zu Hause	Are we going to meet at school or **at your** ~?
	not (...) either ['aɪðə, 'iːðə]	auch nicht; auch kein	Ben doesn't like barbecues, and Lea does**n't** ~. I haven't got any money. – I have**n't** got any ~.
p.7	**What's special about ...?**	Was ist das Besondere an ...?	**What's special** ~ Uluru?

PART A Australia – yesterday and today

p. 8/1 A

	desert ['dezət]	Wüste	
	area ['eəriə]	Fläche	Germany has an ~ of about 357,000 sq km.
	flag [flæg]	Flagge, Fahne	
	shape [ʃeɪp]	Form	different **shapes**: 
	cross [krɒs]	Kreuz	
	historical [hɪ'stɒrɪkl]	geschichtlich, historisch	
p. 8/1 B	**Aborigine** [ˌæbə'rɪdʒəni]	Ureinwohner/in *(Australiens)*	noun: **Aborigine** – adjective: **Aboriginal** [ˌæbə'rɪdʒənl]
	disease [dɪ'zi:z]	Krankheit	
	colony ['kɒləni]	Kolonie	! stress: <u>co</u>**lony** ['kɒləni] Australia was once a British ~.
	prisoner ['prɪznə]	Gefangene(r)	
	prison ['prɪzn]	Gefängnis	
	independent [ˌɪndɪ'pendənt]	unabhängig	Australia became ~ from Britain in 1901.

Year dates – Jahreszahlen

You write	You say	German
1608	sixteen oh eight	sechzehnhundertacht
1800	eighteen hundred	achtzehnhundert
1999	nineteen ninety nine	neunzehnhundertneunundneunzig
2009	two thousand and nine	zweitausendneun
2010	twenty ten	zweitausendzehn
the 18th century	the eighteenth century	das achtzehnte Jahrhundert
the 70s	the seventies	die siebziger Jahre
the 1970s	the nineteen seventies	die siebziger Jahre (des 20. Jahrhunderts)

	(to) **do business with** ['bɪznəs]	Geschäfte machen mit; Handel treiben mit	Germany **does** a lot of ~ **with** Russia and China. Does your company **do** much ~ **with** China?
p. 9/1 C	**outdoors** [ˌaʊt'dɔ:z]	im Freien, (nach) draußen	You can't play ~ when it's too cold. **outdoors** ◄► **indoors**
	because of [bɪ'kɒz_əv]	wegen	

because – because of

- We stayed inside **because** <u>it was raining</u>. … **weil** <u>es regnete</u>. **because** *(conj)*: before a <u>clause</u>
- We stayed inside **because of** <u>the rain</u>. … **wegen** <u>des Regens</u>. **because of** *(prep)*: before a <u>noun</u>

cancer ['kænsə]	Krebs *(Krankheit)*	

	(to) **avoid** [ə'vɔɪd]	vermeiden, aus dem Weg gehen	We wanted to ~ the traffic so we turned into a small road. Nobody likes Lucy. Everyone tries to ~ her.
	sunscreen ['sʌnskriːn]	Sonnenschutzmittel	Before you go in the sun you should put on some ~.
p.9/1 D	**reef** [riːf]	Riff	
	dolphin ['dɒlfɪn]	Delfin	! stress: **<u>dol</u>phin** ['dɒlfɪn] 
	whale [weɪl]	Wal(fisch)	
	by two degrees / ten per cent	um zwei Grad / zehn Prozent	House prices fell ~ eight per cent last year.
	recent ['riːsnt]	jüngste(r, s), aktuelle(r, s); vor kurzem *(geschehen, entstanden usw.)*	Their most ~ CD was released last month. I read about Obama in a ~ newspaper article. We've had a lot of accidents here in ~ weeks.
	recently ['riːsntli]	in letzter Zeit; neulich, vor kurzem	Have you seen Ann ~? (*not:* ~~in the last time~~)
p.10/3	**figure** ['fɪgə]	Zahl, Ziffer	The **~s** aren't 100 per cent correct. Please check them again. ! stress: **<u>fi</u>gure** ['fɪgə]
	bar chart ['bɑː tʃɑːt]	Balkendiagramm	
	pie chart ['paɪ tʃɑːt]	Tortendiagramm, Kreisdiagramm	
	percentage [pə'sentɪdʒ]	Prozentsatz, prozentualer Anteil	What ~ of your pocket money do you spend on sweets?
	(to) **divide** sth. **(into)** [dɪ'vaɪd]	etwas (auf)teilen (in)	The teacher **~d** the class **into** six groups.
	nearly ['nɪəli]	fast, beinahe	= almost
p.11/P 1	**leaf** [liːf], *pl* **leaves** [liːvz]	Blatt *(an Pflanzen)*	

PART B Two Australian teenagers

p.12/1	**nowhere** ['nəʊweə]	nirgendwo(hin)	It's the only hotel. There's ~ else to stay. Jeannie lives miles away from the nearest town <u>in the middle of ~</u>. (*etwa:* ... am Ende der Welt)
	on my/our/... own [əʊn]	allein, selbstständig *(ohne Hilfe)*	Did she go with Les? – No, she went **on her ~**. I don't need any help. I can do it **on my ~**.
	motorbike ['məʊtəbaɪk]	Motorrad	
	(to) **attach (to)** [ə'tætʃ]	anhängen, anheften (an) *(an Brief, Mail)*	You can ~ the photos and mail them to me. **I'm ~ing** some photos of Ashley's party.

p.13/4	**couch potato** ['kaʊtʃ pəˌteɪtəʊ] *(infml)*	Stubenhocker/in; *jemand, der viel vor dem Fernseher sitzt*	 a **couch potato**
p.14/P 1	**surprising** [sə'praɪzɪŋ]	überraschend, erstaunlich	They played really badly. It's not ~ that they lost. ! It was **surprising**. = Es war überrasch**end**. She was **surprised**. = Sie war überrasch**t**.
p.14/P 2	**I see.** [ˌaɪ 'siː]	Ich verstehe. / Aha. / Ach so.	Jan's English is so good because his mother is English. – Oh, **I** ~. I didn't know that.
	lifeguard station ['laɪfɡɑːd]	Station der Rettungsschwimmer/innen	
	witness ['wɪtnəs]	Zeuge, Zeugin	
p.14/P 3	**advice** *(no pl)* [əd'vaɪs]	Rat, Ratschläge	Take my ~: go and see a doctor. ! He gave me some ~ (= einen Rat) / lots of ~ (= viele Ratschläge). *Nie:* an ~~advice~~ / ~~advices~~
	(to) **advise** [əd'vaɪz]	beraten; raten *(einen Rat geben)*	He **~d** me to wear a hat in the sun. ! verb: (to) **advise** – noun: **advice**
p.15/P 4	(to) **rent** sth. [rent]	etwas mieten, etwas leihen	(to) ~ a flat / a car / a holiday flat / a DVD
	rent [rent]	Miete	How much ~ do you pay for your flat?
	How are you doing?	Wie geht's? *(zur Begrüßung)*	
	seat [siːt]	(Sitz-)Platz	
	(to) **introduce** sb. **to** sb. [ˌɪntrə'djuːs]	jn. jm. vorstellen; jn. mit jm. bekanntmachen	This morning our class teacher **~d** our new sports teacher **to** us.

Introducing people

	(to) **borrow** sth. **(from)** ['bɒrəʊ]	(sich) etwas (aus)leihen, borgen (von)	Can I ~ your dictionary? You'll get it back in a minute.
	(to) **lend** sb. sth. [lend], **lent, lent** [lent]	jm. etwas leihen, etwas an jn. verleihen	Can you ~ me £10 until tomorrow? – Sorry, I never ~ money.

(to) lend – (to) borrow

(to) **lend** = (to) give to

(to) **borrow** = (to) take from

PART C The Aboriginal people of Australia

p.16/1	**flat** [flæt]	flach, eben	We took a long walk along the ~, sandy beach. ! **flat** = **1.** *(n)* Wohnung; **2.** *(adj)* flach, eben
	cave [keɪv]	Höhle	
	landscape ['lændskeɪp]	Landschaft	
	owner ['əʊnə]	Besitzer/in	
p.16/2	(to) **settle** ['setl]	sich niederlassen, siedeln; besiedeln	Millions of immigrants **~d** in the US in the 19th century. North America **was** first **~d** by the English in the 16th century.
	settler ['setlə]	Siedler/in	When did the first **~s** come to America?
	belief [bɪ'li:f]	Glaube, Überzeugung	verb: (to) **believe** – noun: **belief**
	ancestor ['ænsestə]	Vorfahre/Vorfahrin	Grandpa says one of our **~s** was a pirate.
	plant [plɑ:nt]	Pflanze	
	(to) **plant** [plɑ:nt]	pflanzen, einpflanzen	
	that's why	deshalb, darum	It rained all day yesterday. **That's ~** we played at home.
	(to) **need to do** sth.	etwas tun müssen; etwas zu tun brauchen	(to) have to do sth.

'need' als Hilfsverb – 'need' als Vollverb

Hilfsverb

Du kennst bereits das **Hilfsverb** ***need***. Es kommt nur im *simple present* vor und hauptsächlich in verneinter Form.

You **needn't** wait for him.
*Du **brauchst nicht** auf ihn zu warten.*

Vollverb

Das **Vollverb** *(to)* ***need to*** *do sth.* kannst du auch in anderen Zeiten verwenden, und es kommt auch in bejahten Sätzen und in Fragen vor.

(to) **need to do** sth.: Verneinung und Fragebildung wie bei allen Vollverben mit einer Form von *do*

You **don't need to** wait for him.
*Du **brauchst nicht** auf ihn zu warten.*

I **didn't need to** tell her. She knew it already.
*Ich **musste** es ihr **nicht** erzählen. ...*

Everybody **needs to** sleep, eat and drink.
*Jeder **muss** schlafen, essen und trinken.*

Do we **need to** wear a helmet?
***Müssen** wir einen Helm tragen?*

	(to) **respect** [rɪ'spekt]	achten, respektieren	(to) **respect** other people's rights/opinions
	respect [rɪ'spekt]	Achtung, Respekt	When the boss died they closed the company for a day out of **~**. **out of respect** = aus Respekt
p.17/3	**generation** [ˌdʒenə'reɪʃn]	Generation	! stress: **gene<u>ra</u>tion** [ˌdʒenə'reɪʃn]
	racist ['reɪsɪst]	rassistisch; Rassist/in	
	race [reɪs]	Rasse	
	orphan ['ɔːfn]	Waise, Waisenkind	a child without parents
	in the back (of)	hinten, im hinteren Teil (von)	
	truck [trʌk], *BE auch:* **lorry** ['lɒri]	Lastwagen, LKW	a **truck/lorry**
	blanket ['blæŋkɪt]	Decke *(zum Zudecken)*	
	(to) **apologize (to** sb. **for** sth.**)** [ə'pɒlədʒaɪz]	sich (bei jm. für etwas) entschuldigen	(to) say sorry He **~d for** not writing sooner.
	apology [ə'pɒlədʒi]	Entschuldigung *(Bitte um Verzeihung)*	You were very rude and I expect an **~**.
	(to) **care about** sth. [keə]	etwas wichtig nehmen	! • I **care about** what I eat. (= What I eat is important to me.) • Many people do**n't care** if their food is fresh. (= Fresh food is not important to them.)
p.17/4	rabbit-**proof** ['ræbɪt pruːf]	kaninchen-sicher, kaninchen-fest	! Some other words with **-proof**: a **weatherproof/windproof/rainproof** jacket; a **waterproof** watch; a **fireproof** door; a **childproof** bottle
	calm [kɑːm]	ruhig, still	not nervous: a **~** person; quiet: a **~** sea
p.19/P 5	**film/book review** [rɪ'vjuː]	Film-/Buchkritik, Film-/Buchbesprechung	
	(to) **recommend** sth. **to** sb. [ˌrekə'mend]	jm. etwas empfehlen	Let's try this café. It must be good because John **~ed** it **to** me.

PART D In the outback

p.20	**now and then**	gelegentlich, ab und zu	Take a break **now and ~** and you'll work better.
	(to) **breathe (in/out)** [briːð]	(ein/aus)atmen	(to) **breathe in** ◄► (to) **breathe out**
	breath [breθ]	Atem	! pronunciation: **breath** *(noun)* [breθ] (to) **breathe** *(verb)* [briːð] (to) **take a deep breath** = tief Luft holen (to) **be out of breath** = außer Atem sein
p.21	(to) **shake** [ʃeɪk], **shook** [ʃʊk], **shaken** ['ʃeɪkən]	schütteln; zittern	You should **~** the bottle before you open it. Look, he's nervous: his hands are **shaking**.

	neck [nek]	Hals, Genick	! **Hals** = **1.** *(außen)* **neck**; **2.** *(innen)* **throat**
	(to) **repair** sth. [rɪ'peə]	etwas reparieren	
	fear (of sb./sth.**)** [fɪə]	Angst (vor jm./etwas)	Because of his ~ **of** flying, Ed never travels by plane.
	poison ['pɔɪzn]	Gift	
	poisonous ['pɔɪzənəs]	giftig	Be careful! That snake could be ~.
p.22	(to) **make** sb. **do** sth.	jn. dazu bringen, etwas zu tun	Funny films ~ me laugh, and sad films ~ me cry.
	cattle *(pl)* ['kætl]	Vieh, Rinder	! The **cattle** are in the field. = Das Vieh ist ...
p.23	**back** [bæk]	Rücken	**back** = **1.** Rücken – My **back** hurts. **2.** zurück – Let's go **back** to Sydney.
	(to) **bleed** [bli:d], **bled, bled** [bled]	bluten	You're **~ing**! – Yes, I've cut my finger.
	conscious ['kɒnʃəs]	bewusst; bei Bewusstsein	**conscious** ◄► **unconscious** (= bewusstlos)
p.24	**honest** ['ɒnɪst]	ehrlich	You can believe her. She's an ~ person. ! pronunciation: silent 'h' – **honest** ['ɒnɪst]
	kind [kaɪnd]	freundlich, nett	**kind** ◄► **unkind**

Opposites with the prefix *un-*

comfortable	uncomfortable	fair	unfair	healthy	unhealthy
conscious	unconscious	friendly	unfriendly	kind	unkind
cool	uncool	fortunately	unfortunately	safe	unsafe
countable	uncountable	happy	unhappy	tidy	untidy

Unit 2: The world of work

pp.32/33	**future** ['fju:tʃə]	Zukunft; Zukunfts-, zukünftige(r,s)	Have you got any plans for the ~?
	training ['treɪnɪŋ]	*(berufliche)* Ausbildung	He had to do special ~ to become a paramedic. He finished his ~ in 2008.
	(to) **train (as** sth.**)** [treɪn]	eine Ausbildung (zu/als etwas) machen	After school she **~ed as** a gardener. He **~ed** at London Bridge Hospital before he became a doctor.
	qualification [ˌkwɒlɪfɪ'keɪʃn]	Abschluss, Qualifikation	! stress: **qualification** [ˌkwɒlɪfɪ'keɪʃn]
	apprenticeship [ə'prentɪʃɪp]	Lehre, Ausbildung	She began her ~ as a hairdresser in 2009.
	apprentice [ə'prentɪs]	Auszubildende(r), Lehrling	
	decision [dɪ'sɪʒn]	Entscheidung	verb: (to) **decide** [dɪ'saɪd] – noun: **decision** ! (to) **make a decision** = eine Entscheidung treffen/fällen
	skill [skɪl]	Fähigkeit, Fertigkeit	What **~s** do you need as a shop assistant?
	police officer [pə'li:s‿ˌɒfɪsə]	Polizist/in, Polizeibeamter, -beamtin	
	instructor [ɪn'strʌktə]	Lehrer/in, Trainer/in	**fitness instructor** = Fitnesstrainer/in **driving instructor** = Fahrlehrer/in **ski instructor** = Skilehrer/in

	make-up artist ['ɑːtɪst]	Maskenbildner/in	a **make-up artist**
	childcare assistant ['tʃaɪldkeər‿əˌsɪstənt]	Kinderpfleger/in; Erzieher/in	
	childcare ['tʃaɪldkeə]	Kinderbetreuung	
	chef [ʃef]	Koch, Köchin *(Berufsbezeichnung)*	! English **chef** = German „Koch/Köchin“ English **boss** = German „Chef/Chefin“

	mechanic [mə'kænɪk]	Mechaniker/in	
	garage ['gærɑːʒ]	Autowerkstatt *(oft mit Tankstelle)*	
	customer adviser [əd'vaɪzə]	Kundenbetreuer/in, -berater/in	
p.33/1	(to) **work long hours**	lange arbeiten	
	(to) **serve** [sɜːv]	bedienen *(Kunden)*	I waited for ten minutes before the shop assistant **~d** me.
	artistic [ɑː'tɪstɪk]	künstlerisch	! He's **artistic**. = Er ist künstlerisch begabt. nouns: **art** (= Kunst), **artist** (= Künstler/in) adjective: **artistic**
	organized ['ɔːgənaɪzd]	(gut) organisiert	an ~ person (= eine gut organisierte Person) ~ crime (= das organisierte Verbrechen) ! stress: **organized** ['ɔːgənaɪzd] verb: (to) **organize** – adjective: **organized**
	pay [peɪ]	Bezahlung, Lohn	verb: (to) **pay** – noun: **pay** The ~ was good.

PART A Personality quiz

p.34	(to) **print** [prɪnt]	drucken	verb: (to) **print** – noun: **printer** (= Drucker)
	(to) **ask** sb. **to do** sth.	jn. (darum) bitten, etwas zu tun	She **~ed** me **to** lend her a book.

(to) ask/tell/expect/want sb. to do sth.

Nach ***ask, tell, expect, want*** steht oft ein **Objekt *(me, Daniel, us, …)*** + ***to*-Infinitiv**.

She **asked** me **to help** her.	Sie bat mich, ihr zu helfen. / Sie bat mich, dass ich ihr helfe.
She **told** Daniel **to come** home early.	Sie sagte Daniel, dass er früh nach Hause kommen soll.
Our teacher **expects** us **to do** our homework.	Unsere Lehrerin erwartet von uns, dass wir unsere Hausaufgaben machen.
My sister **wants** me **to turn down** the music.	Meine Schwester möchte, dass ich die Musik leiser stelle.

! Nach den entsprechenden deutschen Verben steht meist ein Nebensatz mit „dass“, aber auf die englischen Verben darf kein *that*-Satz folgen:

Ich möchte, **dass du mir hilfst**. — I want **you to help me.**
(*Nie*: I want ~~that you help me~~.)

I don't mind helping/ working/...	Es macht mir nichts aus zu helfen / zu arbeiten / ...	

(to) mind

I **don't mind helping** in our shop, but I hate getting up so early.	Es macht mir nichts aus, ...
I'd like to ask you a few questions, **if you don't mind**.	..., wenn Sie nichts dagegen haben.
Do you mind if I open the window?	Stört es Sie, ...
Would you mind waiting outside, please?	Würden Sie bitte draußen warten?

normal ['nɔːml]	normal, üblich	! stress: **<u>nor</u>mal** ['nɔːml]
reliable [rɪ'laɪəbl]	zuverlässig, verlässlich	Our car ist not very ~. There's always something wrong with it.
(to) **solve** [sɒlv]	lösen; aufklären	(to) ~ a problem / a puzzle / a crime / a case
p.35 **mostly** ['məʊstli]	hauptsächlich, überwiegend	Tomorrow it will be cold and ~ cloudy.
quality ['kwɒləti]	Qualität; Eigenschaft	These oranges are expensive, but very good ~. One of a customer adviser's most important **qualities** is friendliness.
confident ['kɒnfɪdənt]	selbstbewusst, (selbst)sicher	I'm very shy, and I feel nervous when I'm with other people. I'd like to be more ~.
energetic [ˌenə'dʒetɪk]	dynamisch, tatkräftig, energisch	I'm an active, ~ person who loves sports.
energy ['enədʒi]	Energie	
racing car ['reɪsɪŋ kɑː]	Rennwagen	
vet's assistant [ˌvets_ə'sɪstənt]	Tierarzthelfer/in	the **vet's assistant** 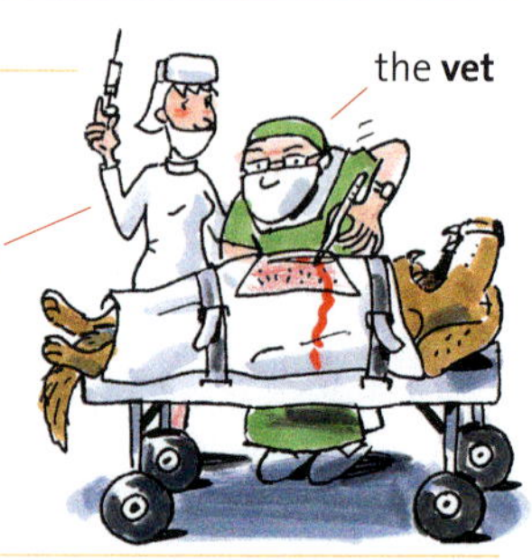 the **vet**
logical ['lɒdʒɪkl]	logisch	a ~ person („ein logisch denkender Mensch")
technology [tek'nɒlədʒi]	Technologie	! stress: **tech<u>no</u>logy** [tek'nɒlədʒi]
technician [tek'nɪʃn]	Techniker/in	! stress: **tech<u>ni</u>cian** [tek'nɪʃn]
builder ['bɪldə]	Bauarbeiter/in	a **builder** 
punctual ['pʌŋktʃuəl]	pünktlich	You're late again. You must try to be more ~.
office worker ['ɒfɪs wɜːkə]	Büroangestellte(r)	
p.35/2 **nurse** [nɜːs]	Krankenpfleger/in, -schwester	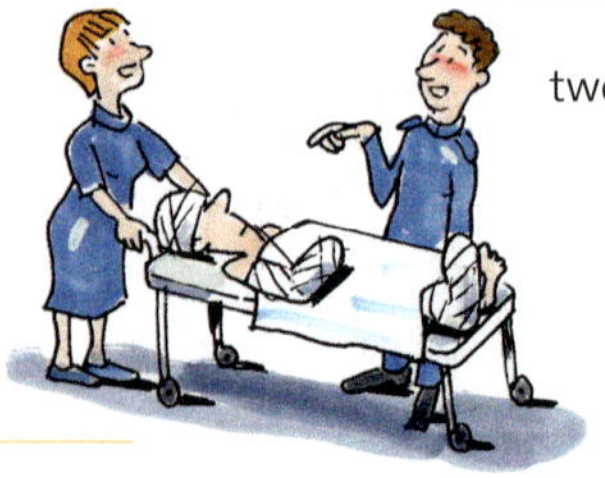 two **nurses**

p.36/P 3	**interest (in)** ['ɪntrəst]	Interesse (an)	Tell me about your hobbies and **~s**.
p.37/P 5	**application** [ˌæplɪ'keɪʃn]	Bewerbung	**letter of application** = Bewerbungsschreiben
	(to) **fill** sth. **in** [ˌfɪl_'ɪn]	etwas ausfüllen	
	form [fɔːm]	Formular	
	ink [ɪŋk]	Tinte	
	first name ['fɜːst neɪm]	Vorname	
	surname ['sɜːneɪm]	Nachname	= **family name**
	work experience *(no pl)* ['wɜːk_ɪkˌspɪəriəns]	Praktikum; Arbeits-, Praxis- erfahrung(en)	! English: I have done **work experience** in a bank. German: ... **ein Praktikum** in einer Bank ...
	to date	bis heute	We need ten people to help with the party, but **to ~** only six have volunteered.

PART B Applying for a job

p.38/1	(to) **apply for** sth. [ə'plaɪ]	sich um/für etwas bewerben; etwas beantragen	
	CV [siː 'viː] (curriculum vitae [kəˌrɪkjələm 'viːtaɪ])	Lebenslauf	curriculum vitae *ist ein lateinischer Begriff und heißt übersetzt „Lauf des Lebens"*
	birth [bɜːθ]	Geburt	Write down your address, **date of ~** (= Geburts- datum) and **place of ~** (= Geburtsort).
	postcode ['pəʊstkəʊd]	Postleitzahl	the **postcode** 
	secondary school ['sekəndri]	weiterführende Schule	
	primary school ['praɪməri]	Grundschule	
	first aid [ˌfɜːst_'eɪd]	Erste Hilfe	
	certificate [sə'tɪfɪkət]	Bescheinigung, Zertifikat	Do you get a ~ at the end of the course?
	moped licence ['məʊped ˌlaɪsns] *(BE)*	Mopedführerschein	**driving licence** = Führerschein
	reference ['refrəns]	Referenz, Empfehlung	I got a ~ when the work experience finished. ! stress: **<u>re</u>ference** ['refrəns]
p.38/2	**advertisement** [əd'vɜːtɪsmənt] *(infml:* **ad** [æd], *BE auch:* **advert** ['ædvɜːt])	Anzeige, Inserat; *(im Fernsehen)* Werbespot	You find job **~s** in newspapers or on the internet. Lots of people change channels during the **~s**.
	(to) **advertise** ['ædvətaɪz]	Werbung machen (für); inserieren	! English: **advertise** clothes/cars/... German: **<u>für</u>** Kleidung/Autos/... **werben**
	(to) **enclose** sth. [ɪn'kləʊz]	etwas *(einem Brief)* beilegen	I **enclose** my CV. *or* My CV **is enclosed**.
	reception [rɪ'sepʃn]	Rezeption, Empfang	Leave your hotel key at the ~ before you go out.
	(to) **be happy to do** sth.	gern bereit sein, etwas zu tun	We'll **be ~ to** help if you have any problems.
	contact ['kɒntækt]	Kontakt, Verbindung	
	(to) **contact** sb. ['kɒntækt]	sich mit jm. in Verbindung setzen / jn. kontaktieren	For more information on the job please ~ us on 07978-569-0897.

p.39/P 1	**similar (to)** ['sɪmələ]	ähnlich (wie)	A highway in the USA is ~ **to** an *Autobahn* in Germany. The brothers look very ~, almost like twins.
	nature ['neɪtʃə]	Natur	
	technical ['teknɪkl]	technisch	noun: **technician** („Techniker/in") adjective: **technical**
	college ['kɒlɪdʒ]	*hier:* berufliche Fach(hoch)-schule	After school she wants to go to a technical ~.
p.39/P 2	**level** ['levl]	(Lern-)Stand, Niveau, Grad	

PART C A reality TV show

p.40/1	**(job) interview**	Vorstellungsgespräch	
	candidate ['kændɪdət]	Kandidat/in, Bewerber/in	! stress: **candidate** ['kændɪdət]
	(to) **impress** [ɪm'pres]	beeindrucken	
	carefully ['keəfəli]	aufmerksam; vorsichtig; gründlich, sorgfältig	They listened ~. (= aufmerksam) Ride your bike ~. (= vorsichtig) He did his work ~. (= sorgfältig, gründlich)
	(to) **dress** [dres]	sich kleiden	Emily has very nice clothes and always **~es** well. ! „sich anziehen" im Sinne von „sich ankleiden, Kleidung anziehen" = (to) **get dressed**: After I got up, I **got dressed** and went to school.
	suitable ['su:təbl]	geeignet, passend	Jeans aren't ~ clothes for a job interview. Dress **suitably** when you go for a job interview.
	strength [streŋθ]	Stärke, Kraft	adjective: **strong** – noun: **strength**
	weakness ['wi:knəs]	Schwäche, Schwachpunkt	adjective: **weak** – noun: **weakness**
p.40/2	**assessment** [ə'sesmənt]	Einschätzung, Beurteilung	
	(to) **assess** [ə'ses]	einschätzen, beurteilen	Interviewers try to ~ a candidate's qualities.
	sheet [ʃi:t]	Blatt, Bogen *(Papier)*	a ~ of paper
p.40/3	**look** [lʊk]	(Gesichts-)Ausdruck	I knew something was wrong when I saw the ~ on her face.

He's **tying** his son's tie.

She's **tying** her hair back.

	tie [taɪ]	Krawatte, Schlips	
	(to) **tie** [taɪ]	binden	! -ing form: **tying**
	cheeky ['tʃi:ki]	frech, dreist	
p.41/P 1	**I'll let you know.**	Ich gebe dir/Ihnen Bescheid.	
	necessary ['nesəsəri]	nötig, notwendig	
p.43/P 5	**travel agent** ['trævl‿ˌeɪdʒənt]	Reisebürokaufmann/-kauffrau	We went to a **travel agent's** to ask about holidays in Spain. (= ins Reisebüro)

PART D How to be a teenage millionaire

p.44	**simple** ['sɪmpl]	einfach, nicht kompliziert	**simple** ◄► **complicated** ['kɒmplɪkeɪtɪd] = kompliziert
	more and more	immer mehr	**More and ~** teenagers have their own blogs.
	I **used to** be excited ... ['ju:st tə]	Früher war ich (immer) aufgeregt ...	

... used to be/do ...

Mit **used to ...** kannst du ausdrücken, dass etwas früher der Fall war, aber heute nicht mehr:

I **used to do** a lot of sport, but I haven't got the time now.	Ich habe früher (immer) viel Sport getrieben, ...
Dad **used to smoke**, but he gave up when I was born.	Dad hat (früher) geraucht, ...
We **used to live** in London, but now we live in Berlin.	Früher haben wir in London gewohnt, ...

! Frage und Verneinung mit **did** bzw. **didn't**:

Did you **use to cry** a lot when you were little?	Hast du viel geweint, als du klein warst?
He's changed a lot. He **didn't use to be** so shy.	... Er war früher nicht so schüchtern.

	cheque (for) [tʃek]	Scheck (über)	Ashley's mum was surprised when they received a **~ for** $ 2,700.
p.45	(to) **continue** [kən'tɪnju]	fortsetzen; weitermachen (mit)	After school you can ~ your education at college or university.
	(to) **react (to)** [ri'ækt]	reagieren (auf)	How did your parents ~ **to** your plans?
	for a while [waɪl]	für eine Weile, eine Zeit lang	I haven't seen you **for a ~**. Where've you been?
	ambitious [æm'bɪʃəs]	ehrgeizig	
	determined [dɪ'tɜ:mɪnd]	fest entschlossen	Dad has given up smoking and is ~ never to smoke again.
	stressful ['stresfl]	anstrengend, stressig	
	(to) **run** sth.	etwas leiten *(Hotel, Firma usw.)*	My aunt is a mechanic and **~s** her own garage.
	(to) **return (to)** [rɪ'tɜ:n]	zurückkehren (nach, zu)	He left the house at 7 and **~ed** three hours later.
	definite ['defɪnət]	fest, bestimmt; endgültig, eindeutig	Have you got any ~ plans for the future? I need a ~ answer by tomorrow.
p.46	**relationship** [rɪ'leɪʃnʃɪp]	Beziehung	
	greedy ['gri:di]	gierig, habgierig	 A ~ person is someone who wants more food or money than he/she really needs.
	(to) **sum** sth. **up** **(-mm-)** [ˌsʌm_'ʌp]	etwas zusammenfassen	At the end of her speech, she **~med up** her main ideas.

Unit 3: Teen world

p.48	**only child** [ˌəʊnli 'tʃaɪld]	Einzelkind	Does she have any brothers or sisters? – No, she's an **~ child**.
	ideal [aɪ'di:əl]	ideal	
	(to) **want to be** sth.	etwas werden wollen *(beruflich)*	When I finish school I **want to ~** a make-up artist.

PART A Mobile teens

p.50/1	(to) **communicate** [kə'mju:nɪkeɪt]	kommunizieren	
	communication [kəˌmju:nɪ'keɪʃn]	Kommunikation	

Verbs and their nouns

(to) **apply** **application**	sich bewerben Bewerbung
(to) **attract** **attraction**	anziehen, anlocken Attraktion
(to) **communicate** **communication**	kommunizieren Kommunikation
(to) **organize** ['ɔ:gənaɪz] **organization** [ˌɔ:gənaɪ'zeɪʃn]	organisieren Organisation
(to) **present** [prɪ'zent] **presentation** [ˌprezn'teɪʃn]	präsentieren Präsentation
(to) **produce** **production**	produzieren Produktion
(to) **revise** [aɪ] **revision** [ɪ]	wiederholen; überarbeiten Wiederholung; Überarbeitung
(to) **translate** **translation**	übersetzen Übersetzung

	generally ['dʒenrəli]	allgemein, im Allgemeinen, generell	Teenagers **~** use their mobiles to communicate with their friends.
	(to) **give** sth. **up**	auf etwas verzichten	Some people **~ up** sweets before Easter.
	alarm clock [ə'lɑ:m klɒk]	Wecker	 an **alarm clock**
	(to) **set the alarm clock (-tt-)** [set], **set, set**	den Wecker stellen	
	as usual ['ju:ʒuəl]	wie immer, wie üblich	We're waiting for Jo. He's late, **as ~**.
	(to) **go out with** sb.	mit jm. gehen *(als Freund/in)*	
	phone box ['fəʊn bɒks]	Telefonzelle	a **phone box** 
	not (...) at all [ət‿'ɔ:l]	überhaupt nicht, ganz und gar nicht; überhaupt kein/e ...	Do you think my plan is crazy? – No, **not at ~**. Sorry, I can't help you. I have**n't** got any money **at ~**.
p.51/1	(to) **be addicted (to** sth.**)** [ə'dɪktɪd]	abhängig (von etwas) sein, süchtig (nach etwas) sein	She**'s ~ to** chocolate – she eats it all the time.
	wedding ['wedɪŋ]	Hochzeit, Trauung	
	funeral ['fju:nərəl]	Trauerfeier, Beerdigung	

	secretly ['siːkrətli]	heimlich	• *(adv)* She **secretly** put some salt into his tea. • *(adj)* We had a **secret** meeting. (geheim) • *(n)* I can't tell you. It's a **secret**. (Geheimnis)
	unwanted [ˌʌn'wɒntɪd]	unerwünscht, ungewollt	(to) feel **unwanted** an **unwanted** child (ein ungewolltes Kind)
	(to) **go by** [ˌɡəʊ 'baɪ]	vergehen, vorübergehen *(Zeit)*	She said she'd be back in a minute, but a whole hour **went ~** before she returned.
	(to) **ask** sb. **out**	sich mit jm. verabreden; jn. einladen, mit einem auszugehen	If you really like him, why don't you **~** him **out**?
	(to) **dump** sb. [dʌmp] *(infml)*	mit jm. Schluss machen	She **~ed** her boyfriend but now she'd like to have him back.
	perhaps [pə'hæps]	vielleicht	= maybe
p.52/P1	**in reply to your** letter/ article/... [rɪ'plaɪ]	in Beantwortung Ihres Briefes/ Artikels/...	I am writing **in ~ to** your letter of 12 April.
	busy ['bɪzi]	beschäftigt	Would you like to go out tonight? – I'd love to, but I'm afraid I'm too **~**.
	face to face	von Angesicht zu Angesicht, persönlich	Can I talk to you **face to ~**? 
	(to) **get annoyed (with** sb.**/ about** sth.**)** [ə'nɔɪd]	sich ärgern (über jn./etwas)	**!** • I **got** really **annoyed with** him because he was late. = Ich habe mich über ihn geärgert ... • She was **annoyed**. = Sie war verärgert. • He's **annoying**. = Er geht mir auf die Nerven.
	(to) **ban (-nn-)** [bæn]	verbieten; ein (Aufenthalts-)Verbot erteilen	They've **~ned** smoking at our youth club. Sports stadiums should **~** people who use racist language.
	public ['pʌblɪk]	öffentliche(r,s)	
	complete [kəm'pliːt]	vollständig, völlig	I'm sorry. I **~ly** forgot that it's your birthday today. verb: (to) **complete** – adjective: **complete** – adverb: **completely**
	ridiculous [rɪ'dɪkjələs]	lächerlich, albern	 Jo has **~ed** his bus to school.
p.53/P3	(to) **miss** sth. [mɪs]	etwas verpassen	
	(to) **save** sth. [seɪv]	etwas (ab)speichern *(Daten, Telefonnummern)*	
	Hang on. [ˌhæŋ‿'ɒn] *(infml)*	Einen Augenblick. / Sofort. / *(am Telefon)* Bleiben Sie dran.	Are you coming? – **~ on**, I'll be there in a second. Can I talk to Tom? – **~ on**, I'll just see if he's here.
p.53/P4	**exchange rate** [ɪks'tʃeɪndʒ reɪt]	Wechselkurs	What's the **~ ~**? – 1.14 to the pound, I think.

cash [kæʃ]	Bargeld	! (to) **pay cash** = bar bezahlen
credit card ['kredɪt kɑːd]	Kreditkarte	(to) **pay by credit card** = mit Kreditkarte bezahlen ! stress: **credit card** ['kredɪt kɑːd]
note [nəʊt]	(Geld-)Schein, Banknote	My sister found a 10-euro ~ this morning.
(to) **block** sth. [blɒk]	etwas sperren	We couldn't get through because the street was **~ed** by a truck.
(to) **enter** sth. ['entə]	etwas eingeben *(Geheimzahl)*	~ your PIN, please.
receipt [rɪ'siːt]	Quittung; Kassenbon	

PART B Teens in trouble

p. 54/1 **troublemaker** ['trʌblmeɪkə]	Randalierer/in, Unruhestifter/in	
behaviour (towards sb.**)** [bɪ'heɪvjə]	Verhalten, Benehmen (gegenüber jm.)	His ~ **towards** me has changed. He's very friendly now.
(to) **behave** [bɪ'heɪv]	sich verhalten, sich benehmen	He's 16, but he still **~s** like a little child. **Behave yourself**, or you can go to your room.
order ['ɔːdə]	Befehl, Anweisung, Anordnung	
punishment ['pʌnɪʃmənt]	Bestrafung, Strafe	Feeling sick was a kind of ~ for eating too much.
(to) **punish** ['pʌnɪʃ]	bestrafen	When you did something wrong as a child, how were you **~ed**?

(to) **stick** sth. **up** [stɪk], **stuck, stuck** [stʌk]	etwas aufhängen *(und dabei mit Klebstoff befestigen)*	**stick** ~ a poster, photos, a sign, an advert, a list of names
(to) **stick**	(auf)kleben	Don't forget to ~ a stamp on your postcard.
(to) **spray** [spreɪ]	sprühen	verb: (to) **spray** – noun: **spray** (= Spray)
(to) **shoplift** ['ʃɒplɪft]	Ladendiebstahl begehen	
shoplifting ['ʃɒplɪftɪŋ]	Ladendiebstahl	

shoplifting

(to) **threaten** ['θretn]	(be)drohen	When my girlfriend saw my beard, she **~ed** to dump me. The long dry summers ~ the wild animals.
(to) **vandalize** ['vændəlaɪz]	mutwillig beschädigen, mutwillig zerstören	Cars and shopwindows in the city centre have been **~d** again.
vandalism ['vændəlɪzəm]	Vandalismus, Zerstörungswut	! stress: **vandalism** ['vændəlɪzəm]

	at a time	gleichzeitig, auf einmal	I can't listen to more than one person **at a ~**.
p.55/3	**shocking** ['ʃɒkɪŋ]	schockierend	! It was **shocking** to see so many homeless people on the streets. (= schockierend) Everybody was **shocked**. (= schockiert)
	discipline ['dɪsəplɪn]	Disziplin	
p.56/P 1	**finally** ['faɪnəli]	zuletzt, als letztes	We visited Boston, Chicago and ~ Denver.
p.57/P 2	**worrying** ['wʌriɪŋ]	beunruhigend, sorgenvoll	It can be ~ if you think somebody is following you. We had a ~ time when grandpa was ill.
p.57/P 3	**ugly** ['ʌgli]	hässlich	

PART C Get involved

p.58/1	**community** [kə'mju:nəti]	*(politische)* Gemeinde	
	spring [sprɪŋ]	Quelle	a **spring**

trash [træʃ] *(AE)*	Abfall, Müll	= rubbish *(BE)*
plastic ['plæstɪk]	Plastik	
such (a) [sʌtʃ]	so (ein/e), solch (ein/e); solche	The gold medal is a huge success for **~ a** young swimmer.

German 'so'

- ***so* + adjective**:
  Helen is **so nice/beautiful**. ... **so** nett/schön
  The book was **so good/interesting** that I read it twice. ... **so** gut/interessant
- ***such a*** (+ adjective) **+ noun**:
  Helen is **such a** nice **person**. ... **so** ein netter Mensch
  It was **such a** good **book** that I read it twice. ... **so** ein gutes Buch

It's a shame. [ʃeɪm]	Es ist ein Jammer / eine Schande.	**It's a ~** you can't come to our party.
turtle ['tɜ:tl]	Wasserschildkröte	a **turtle**

mainly ['meɪnli]	hauptsächlich	Turtles eat ~ sea grass.
the **Bible** ['baɪbl]	die Bibel	
(to) **hold** sth. [həʊld], **held** [held], **held** [held]	etwas veranstalten, abhalten *(Veranstaltung, Wettbewerb)*	The disco is **held** at the same time every week.
coin [kɔɪn]	Münze	
bill [bɪl] *(AE)*	(Geld-)Schein, Banknote	

some **coins** and **notes** *(BE)*/**bills** *(AE)*

	canned [kænd]	Dosen-; ... in Dosen	You can keep ~ food for a very long time.
	can [kæn]	Dose, Büchse	 a **can** of tomatoes · **cans** of cola
	(to) **store** [stɔː]	(ein)lagern, aufbewahren	The bottle should be **~d** in a cool and dark place.
	overnight [ˌəʊvəˈnaɪt]	über Nacht	It was too late to go home, so we stayed ~.
p. 60/P4	**alcohol** [ˈælkəhɒl]	Alkohol	

PART D The caller

p. 62	(to) **go red**	rot werden, erröten	He was so embarrassed that he **went** ~. 
	busy [ˈbɪzi]	besetzt *(Telefon, Leitung)*	I called you but your mobile was ~ .
	(to) **lie** [laɪ], **lied** [laɪd], **lied** [laɪd]	lügen	! -ing form: **lying** – She's **lying**.
	(to) **show off** (sth.)	angeben, prahlen (mit etwas)	Have you seen her new mobile? – Oh well, she just wants to **~ off**. She **~ed off** her new expensive mobile.
	Nice try.	Netter Versuch.	**Nice ~**. Maybe you'll be luckier next time.
	(to) **hang up** [ˌhæŋ‿ˈʌp], **hung** [hʌŋ], **hung** [hʌŋ]	*(den Telefonhörer)* auflegen	After a one-hour telephone call I said goodbye and **hung ~**.
p. 63	**old people's home**	Alten-, Seniorenheim	
	(to) **deserve** [dɪˈzɜːv]	verdienen *(zu Recht bekommen)*	We've worked very hard, so I think we ~ a break.
	knock [nɒk]	Klopfen	There was a ~ on the door. (= Es klopfte.)
	(to) **knock (at/on** sth.) [nɒk]	(an etwas) klopfen	He's **~ing** at the door. 
	prayer [ˈpreə]	Gebet	
	(to) **pray** [preɪ]	beten	
	(to) **dial** (*BE:* **-ll-**) [ˈdaɪəl]	*(Telefonnummer)* wählen	
	(to) **leave** sb. **alone**	jn. in Ruhe lassen	Go away and **leave** me ~.
	muddy [ˈmʌdi]	schlammig, matschig; schmutzig	 **mud**
	mud [mʌd]	Schlamm, Matsch	
p. 64	**footstep** [ˈfʊtstep]	Schritt	
	thrilling [ˈθrɪlɪŋ]	aufregend, spannend	The book was so ~ that I couldn't put it down.

Unit 4: Exploring cities

p.74	**official** [ə'fɪʃl]	offiziell, amtlich, Amts-	Canada has two ~ languages: French and English. ! stress: **official** [ə'fɪʃl]
	pollution [pə'lu:ʃn]	(Umwelt-)Verschmutzung	
	polluted [pə'lu:tɪd]	verseucht, verunreinigt	a **polluted** river

	contrast ['kɒntrɑ:st]	Kontrast, Gegensatz	! stress: **contrast** ['kɒntrɑ:st]
	financial [faɪ'nænʃl]	finanziell, Finanz-	! stress: **financial** [faɪ'nænʃl]
	a third	ein Drittel	= $1/3$
p.75	**unemployment** [ˌʌnɪm'plɔɪmənt]	Arbeitslosigkeit	~ rose in the town after the factory closed.
	suburb ['sʌbɜ:b]	Vorort	
	public transport *(no pl)* [ˌpʌblɪk 'trænspɔ:t]	öffentlicher Personennahverkehr, öffentliche Verkehrsmittel	It's cheaper to use ~ **transport** than to go by car. ! stress: **transport** ['trænspɔ:t]

PART A Mumbai

p.76/1	**positive** ['pɒzətɪv]	positiv	**positive** ◄► **negative** ['negətɪv]
	helpful ['helpfl]	hilfsbereit; hilfreich, nützlich	He is a very ~ person. Your advice was ~.
	typical (of) ['tɪpɪkl]	typisch (für)	! Alan arrived ten minutes late. – That's ~ **of** him. (*not:* ... typical ~~for~~ him)
	(to) **live on** sth.	von etwas leben; sich von etwas ernähren	I don't know how they can **live** ~ £ 55 a week. Giraffes **live** mainly ~ leaves.
	colourful ['kʌləfl]	farbenfroh, farbenprächtig, farbig	women in **colourful** saris

	sick [sɪk] *(besonders AE)*	krank	= ill *(besonders BE)*
p.77/2	(to) **adjust to** sth. [ə'dʒʌst]	sich an etwas anpassen; sich an etwas gewöhnen	After a while her eyes **~ed** to the dark. She easily **~ed** to the new situation at work.
	(to) **be familiar with** sth. [fə'mɪliə]	mit etwas vertraut sein; sich mit etwas auskennen	I need help with the new computer programme. **Are** you ~ **with** it?
	on board [ɒn 'bɔ:d]	an Bord	
	tiny ['taɪni]	winzig	
	(to) **hold on (to** sth.**)**	sich festhalten (an etwas)	
	frame [freɪm]	Rahmen; Gestell	
	(to) **lean out** [ˌli:n_'aʊt]	sich hinauslehnen	Don't ~ **out** of the window too far.

	passenger ['pæsɪndʒə]	Passagier/in, Fahrgast, Reisende(r)	**~s** to the airport please change at the next station.
	tight [taɪt]	dicht, eng	There wasn't much space in the car so we had to sit very ~. She was wearing a very ~ pair of jeans.
	Hindu ['hɪnduː]	Hindu; Hindu-	
	Muslim ['mʊzlɪm]	Muslim/Muslima, Muslimin; muslimisch	
	Christian ['krɪstʃən]	Christ/in; christlich	
p.78/P 1	**poverty** ['pɒvəti]	Armut	noun: **poverty** – adjective: **poor**
	homelessness ['həʊmləsnəs]	Obdachlosigkeit	noun: **homelessness** – adjective: **homeless**

Adjectives and their nouns

clever **cleverness**	schlau, klug Schlauheit, Klugheit	**ill** **illness**	krank Krankheit
friendly ! **friendl<u>i</u>ness**	freundlich Freundlichkeit	**sad** **sadness**	traurig Traurigkeit
happy ! **happ<u>i</u>ness**	glücklich Glück	**weak** **weakness**	schwach Schwäche

	fascinating ['fæsɪneɪtɪŋ]	faszinierend	adjective: **fascinating** noun: **fascination** [ˌfæsɪ'neɪʃn]
	fashionable ['fæʃnəbl]	modisch, schick	a **fashionable** restaurant/dress/area/idea/...
	glamorous ['glæmərəs]	glamourös	especially attractive and exciting: a **glamorous** movie star/job/...
p.79/P 3	**I'm not feeling great.**	Ich fühle mich nicht besonders wohl.	
	flu [fluː]	Grippe	I have a headache and a temperature. I think I have (the) ~.
	pain [peɪn]	Schmerz(en)	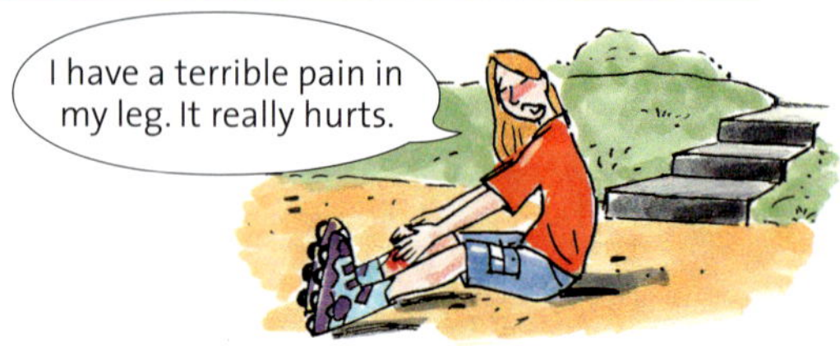
	virus ['vaɪrəs], *pl* **viruses** ['vaɪrəsəz]	Virus	! pronunciation: **virus** ['vaɪrəs]
	cream [kriːm]	Salbe; Creme	
	medicine ['medsn, 'medɪsn]	Medizin	You'll feel better after you've taken your ~. She's studying ~ at university.
	pill [pɪl]	Pille, Tablette	
	prescription [prɪ'skrɪpʃn]	Rezept *(für Medikamente)*	The doctor gave me a ~ for some pills.
	patient ['peɪʃnt]	Patient/in	! stress: **<u>pa</u>tient** ['peɪʃnt]

PART B Johannesburg

shacks in a slum

p.80/1	**impressive** [ɪm'presɪv]	beeindruckend, eindrucksvoll	
	running water	fließendes Wasser *(Leitungswasser)*	
	shack [ʃæk]	Hütte, Baracke	
	metal ['metl]	Metall	! stress: **metal** ['metl]

indoor – outdoor

indoor und **outdoor** stehen immer vor einem Nomen:

indoor toilet	Innentoilette	**outdoor activities**	Aktivitäten im Freien
indoor market	Markthalle	**outdoor temperature**	Außentemperatur
indoor swimming pool	Hallenbad	**outdoor swimming pool**	Freibad

	hero ['hɪərəʊ], *pl* **heroes** ['hɪərəʊz]	Held/in; Idol, Vorbild	Nelson Mandela is a ~ to many people in South Africa. She was really brave. I think she's a ~.
	unforgettable [ˌʌnfə'getəbl]	unvergesslich	Working as a volunteer in Johannesburg was an ~ experience.
p.81/2	(to) **recognize** sb./sth. ['rekəgnaɪz]	jn./etwas (wieder)erkennen	She looked completely different. I didn't ~ her.
	freedom ['fri:dəm]	Freiheit	
	confidence ['kɒnfɪdəns]	Selbstvertrauen; Zuversicht; Vertrauen	If you have ~, you'll do well in the interview. She had complete ~ in the doctors. noun: **confidence** – adjective: **confident**
	style [staɪl]	Stil	
	baggy ['bægi]	weit (geschnitten) *(Hose)*	trousers: **tight** ◂▸ **baggy**
	floppy hat ['flɒpi]	Schlapphut	
	political [pə'lɪtɪkl]	politisch	
	politics ['pɒlɪtɪks]	(die) Politik	**Politics** is interesting. ! stress: **politics** ['pɒlɪtɪks] noun: **politics** – adjective: **political**
	(to) **be about to do** sth.	im Begriff sein, etwas zu tun; kurz davor sein, etwas zu tun	I **was** ~ **to** go to bed when the doorbell rang.
	autograph ['ɔ:təgrɑ:f]	Autogramm	
p.83/P 3	**separate** ['seprət]	getrennt, separat	
	(to) **force** [fɔ:s]	zwingen, erzwingen	
	association [əˌsəʊsi'eɪʃn]	Verband, Vereinigung	
	relations *(pl)* [rɪ'leɪʃnz]	Beziehungen *(zwischen Ländern, Firmen, Organisationen)*	

an **autograph**

PART C Berlin: City survival kit

p.84	**survival** [sə'vaɪvl]	Überleben	**survival** of the fittest = das Überleben der Stärksten noun: **survival** – verb: (to) **survive**
	kit [kɪt]	Ausrüstung	**survival kit** = Überlebenspäckchen **first-aid kit** = Verbandskasten, Erste-Hilfe-Kasten **repair kit** = Flickzeug
	(to) **book** [bʊk]	buchen, reservieren	(to) ~ a room / a table / a flight / a holiday / a ticket / ...
	passport ['pɑːspɔːt]	(Reise-)Pass	
	somewhere to stay	ein Platz zum Übernachten	
	dormitory ['dɔːmətri] (*infml:* **dorm** [dɔːm])	Schlafsaal	

	double room [ˌdʌbl 'ruːm]	Doppelzimmer	**single room** [ˌsɪŋgl 'ruːm] = Einzelzimmer
	basement ['beɪsmənt]	Keller(geschoss)	
	You should have told me.	Du hättest es mir sagen sollen.	*(Look at the blue box on p. 191.)*
	(to) **fancy** sth. ['fænsi] *(infml)*	Lust auf/zu etwas haben	Do you ~ a cola? Can't we take the bus? I don't ~ walking all the way.
p.85	**on top (of** sth.**)** [ɒn 'tɒp]	oben, oben drauf (auf etwas)	Can I have some cake with cream **on** ~, please?
	(to) **queue** [kjuː]	sich anstellen, anstehen	We had to ~ for ages to get tickets. verb: (to) **queue** – noun: **queue**
p.86/P1	**certainly** ['sɜːtnli]	bestimmt, sicher(lich); gerne, selbstverständlich, klar	
	wake-up call	Weckanruf	

	pleasant ['pleznt]	angenehm	
	stay [steɪ]	Aufenthalt	noun: **stay** – verb: (to) **stay**

Have a ...

Have a pleasant stay.	Einen angenehmen Aufenthalt!
Have a good trip/journey.	Gute Reise!
Have a good holiday/weekend.	Schöne Ferien! / Schönes Wochenende!
Have a good time.	Viel Spaß!

fully booked	ausgebucht	
(to) **check in** [ˌtʃek‿'ɪn]	einchecken *(Hotel, Flughafen)*	(to) **check in** ◄► (to) **check out** (auschecken)
connection [kə'nekʃn]	Verbindung	

	(to) **connect (to/with)** [kə'nekt]	verbinden (mit)	verb: (to) **connect** – noun: **connection**
	at once	sofort	= immediately
p.86/P 2	(to) **leave a message**	eine Nachricht hinterlassen	
	(to) **take a message**	eine Nachricht entgegen-nehmen	Can I **take a message** for her/him? (= Soll ich ihr/ihm etwas ausrichten?)

'I would have left' / 'You should have left' – *would/should* + *have* + past participle

p.87/P4

A visit to the zoo **would have been** nice, but I didn't have the time.	Ein Besuch im Zoo **wäre** schön **gewesen** ...
Without your help, I **wouldn't have passed** the exam.	... **hätte** ich die Prüfung **nicht bestanden**.
He **would have gone** to the cinema, but his girlfriend didn't want to.	Er **wäre** ins Kino **gegangen**, ...

Mit ***I would*** **+** ***have*** **+ past participle** kannst du sagen, was <u>du</u> (anstelle von jemand anderem) in einer bestimmten Situation getan hättest:

In a situation like that, I **would have taken** the bus.	... **hätte** ich den Bus **genommen**.
I **wouldn't have waited** for Laura. I **would have left** without her.	Ich **hätte nicht** auf Laura **gewartet**. Ich **wäre** ohne sie **gegangen**.

Mit ***You should*** **+** ***have*** **+ past participle** kannst du sagen, was jemand in einer bestimmten Situation hätte tun sollen:

The washing machine doesn't work. – Oh, you **should have told** me.	... du **hättest** es mir **sagen sollen**.

	suit [su:t]	Anzug	
p.88/P 5	**talk** [tɔ:k]	Vortrag, Rede	
	(to) **give a talk (on** sth.**)**	einen Vortrag / eine Rede halten (über etwas)	
	(to) **introduce** sth. [ˌɪntrə'dju:s]	etwas einführen *(Thema, Mode, Methode)*	**!** (to) **introduce** sb. = jn. vorstellen (to) **introduce** sth. = etwas *(neu)* einführen
	visual ['vɪʒuəl]	visuell; optisch	**!** stress: <u>**vis**</u>**ual** ['vɪʒuəl]
	material [mə'tɪəriəl]	Material	**!** stress: **mat**<u>**er**</u>**ial** [mə'tɪəriəl]
	basic ['beɪsɪk]	grundlegend; Grund-, Haupt-	**basic** computer skills; the **basic** idea/problem/question
	(to) **draw** sb.'s **attention to** sth. [ə'tenʃn], **drew, drawn**	jn. auf etwas aufmerksam machen; jemandes Aufmerk-samkeit auf etwas lenken	I'm writing to you to **~ your ~ to** the number of accidents in Cork Street.
	Feel free to ask questions.	*etwa:* Ihr könnt jetzt gern Fragen stellen.	
	slide [slaɪd]	Folie *(bei einer Computer-präsentation)*; Dia	

Das **Dictionary** enthält den Wortschatz der Bände 1 bis 5 von *English G 21*.
Wenn du wissen möchtest, was ein Wort bedeutet, wie man es ausspricht oder wie es geschrieben wird, kannst du hier nachschlagen.

Im **Dictionary** werden folgende **Abkürzungen und Symbole** verwendet:

jm. = jemandem	sb. = somebody	*pl* = *plural*	*AE* = *American English*
jn. = jemanden	sth. = something	*no pl* = *no plural*	*infml* = *informal*

° Mit diesem Kringel sind Wörter markiert, die nicht zum Lernwortschatz gehören.
▸ Der Pfeil verweist auf Kästchen im **Vocabulary** (S. 170–191), in denen du weitere Informationen zu diesem Wort findest.

Die **Fundstellenangaben** zeigen, wo ein Wort zum ersten Mal vorkommt.
Die Ziffern in Klammern bezeichnen Seitenzahlen:

I = Band 1 • II = Band 2 • III = Band 3 • IV = Band 4 • V = Band 5
V 1 (6) = Band 5, Unit 1, Seite 6
V 1 (6/170) = Band 5, Unit 1, Seite 170 (im Vocabulary, zu Seite 6)

Tipps zur Arbeit mit einem Wörterbuch findest du im Skills File auf Seite 137.

Tipp

Auf der **Audio-CD im Workbook** findest du sowohl dieses englisch-deutsche Wörterverzeichnis als auch ein deutsch-englisches Wörterverzeichnis mit dem Lernwortschatz der Bände 1–5.

A

a [ə]
1. ein, eine I
2. once/twice a week einmal/zweimal pro Woche III • **a bit** ein bisschen, etwas II • **a few** ein paar, einige II • **a little** ein bisschen, wenig IV • **a lot (of)** eine Menge, viel, viele II • **He likes her a lot.** Er mag sie sehr. I

able ['eɪbl]: **be able to do sth.** etwas tun können; fähig sein / in der Lage sein, etwas zu tun III

Aboriginal [ˌæbə'rɪdʒənl] *(bezüglich der Ureinwohner Australiens)* Aborigine- V 1 (8/171)

Aborigine [ˌæbə'rɪdʒəni] Ureinwohner/in *(Australiens)* V 1 (8)

about [ə'baʊt]
1. über I
2. ungefähr II
3. be about to do sth. im Begriff sein, etwas zu tun; kurz davor sein, etwas zu tun V 4 (81)
about yourself über dich (selbst) III • **ask about sth.** nach etwas fragen I • **How about ...?** Wie wär's mit ...? III • **This is about Mr Green.** Es geht um Mr Green. I
What about ...? 1. Was ist mit ...? / Und ...? I; **2.** Wie wär's mit ...? I
What are you talking about? Wovon redest du? I • **What was the best thing about ...?** Was war das Beste an ...? II

above [ə'bʌv] oben; über, oberhalb (von) IV

°**academy** [ə'kædəmi] Akademie

accent ['æksənt] Akzent II

accident ['æksɪdənt] Unfall II

ache [eɪk] wehtun IV

across [ə'krɒs]
1. (quer) über III
2. hinüber, herüber III

act [ækt]
1. sich verhalten IV
2. aufführen, spielen I
°**Act out** ... Spiele/Spielt ... vor.

action film ['ækʃn fɪlm] Actionfilm V 1 (15)

active ['æktɪv] aktiv, tätig IV

activity [æk'tɪvəti] Aktivität, Tätigkeit I

actor ['æktə] Schauspieler/in II

actually ['æktʃuəli]
1. eigentlich; in Wirklichkeit III
2. nebenbei bemerkt; übrigens IV

ad [æd] *(infml)* Anzeige, Inserat; *(im Fernsehen)* Werbespot V 2 (38)

°**adapted** [ə'dæptɪd] adaptiert; bearbeitet

add (to) [æd] hinzufügen, ergänzen, addieren (zu) I

addicted [ə'dɪktɪd]: **be addicted (to sth.)** abhängig (von etwas) sein, süchtig (nach etwas) sein V 3 (51)

address [ə'dres] Adresse, Anschrift II

adjust to sth. [ə'dʒʌst] sich an etwas anpassen; sich an etwas gewöhnen V 4 (77)

admission [əd'mɪʃn] Eintritt, Eintrittspreis IV

adult ['ædʌlt] Erwachsene(r) III

advantage (over sb./sth.) [əd'vɑːntɪdʒ] Vorteil (gegenüber jm./etwas) IV

adventure [əd'ventʃə] Abenteuer IV

advert ['ædvɜːt] Anzeige, Inserat; *(im Fernsehen)* Werbespot V 2 (38)

advertise ['ædvətaɪz] Werbung machen (für); inserieren V 2 (38/179)

advertisement [əd'vɜːtɪsmənt] Anzeige, Inserat; *(im Fernsehen)* Werbespot V 2 (38)

°**advertiser** ['ædvətaɪzə] Inserent/in, Werbekunde/-kundin

advice *(no pl)* [əd'vaɪs] Rat, Ratschläge V 1 (14)

advise [əd'vaɪz] beraten; raten *(einen Rat geben)* V 1 (14)

adviser [əd'vaɪzə] Betreuer/in, Berater/in V 2 (33) • **customer adviser** Kundenbetreuer/in, -berater/in V 2 (33)

afraid [ə'freɪd]
1. be afraid (of) Angst haben (vor) I
2. I'm afraid leider II

African American [ˌæfrɪkən_ə'merɪkən] afro-amerikanisch; Afro-Amerikaner/in IV

°**Afrikaans** [ˌæfrɪ'kɑːns] Afrikaans *(eine von mehreren Amtssprachen in Südafrika, aus dem Niederländischen entstanden)*

after ['ɑːftə] nach *(zeitlich)* I
after that danach I

after ['ɑːftə] nachdem II

afternoon [ˌɑːftə'nuːn] Nachmittag I • **in the afternoon** nachmittags, am Nachmittag I • **on Friday afternoon** freitagnachmittags, am Freitagnachmittag I

again [ə'gen] wieder; noch einmal I

against [ə'genst] gegen III

age [eɪdʒ] Alter III • **kids my age** Kinder in meinem Alter / meines Alters V 1 (12)
agent: travel agent ['trævl‿ˌeɪdʒənt] Reisebürokaufmann/-kauffrau V 2 (43) • **travel agent's** Reisebüro V 2 (43)
ago [ə'gəʊ]: **a minute ago** vor einer Minute I
agree (on) [ə'griː] sich einigen (auf) I • **agree with sb./sth.** jm./etwas zustimmen; mit jm./etwas übereinstimmen II
aid: first aid [ˌfɜːst‿'eɪd] Erste Hilfe V 2 (38)
°**aim** [eɪm] zielen
air [eə] Luft III • °**air conditioning** *(no pl)* ['eə kənˌdɪʃnɪŋ] Klimatisierung, Klimaanlage
airport ['eəpɔːt] Flughafen III
alarm clock [ə'lɑːm klɒk] Wecker V 3 (50) • **set the alarm clock** den Wecker stellen V 3 (50/182)
album ['ælbəm] Album III
alcohol ['ælkəhɒl] Alkohol V 3 (60)
alive [ə'laɪv] am Leben, lebendig IV
all [ɔːl] alle; alles I • **2 all** [ˌtuː‿'ɔːl] 2 beide (2:2 unentschieden) III
all day den ganzen Tag (lang) I
all over the world auf der ganzen Welt III • **all right** gut, in Ordnung II • **all the time** die ganze Zeit I • **all the way** den ganzen Weg IV • °**all-white team** Team, das nur aus Weißen besteht
from all over the UK/the world/England aus dem gesamten Vereinigten Königreich / aus der ganzen Welt / aus ganz England III
not (...) at all [ət‿'ɔːl] überhaupt nicht, ganz und gar nicht; überhaupt kein/e V 3 (50) • **This is all wrong.** Das ist ganz falsch. I
°**allow time** [əˌlaʊ 'taɪm] Zeit einplanen
allowed [ə'laʊd]: **be allowed** erlaubt sein IV • **be allowed to do sth.** etwas tun dürfen III
almost ['ɔːlməʊst] fast, beinahe III
alone [ə'ləʊn] allein I • **leave sb. alone** jn. in Ruhe lassen V 3 (63)
along [ə'lɒŋ]: **along the street** entlang der Straße / die Straße entlang II
alphabet ['ælfəbet] Alphabet I
°**alphabetical** [ˌælfə'betɪkl] alphabetisch
already [ɔːl'redi] schon, bereits II
also ['ɔːlsəʊ] auch II
although [ɔːl'ðəʊ] obwohl III
always ['ɔːlweɪz] immer I

am [ˌeɪ‿'em]: **7 am** 7 Uhr morgens/vormittags I
amazing [ə'meɪzɪŋ] erstaunlich, unglaublich II
ambitious [æm'bɪʃəs] ehrgeizig V 2 (45)
ambulance ['æmbjələns] Krankenwagen III
American football [əˌmerɪkən 'fʊtbɔːl] Football I
amnesty ['æmnəsti] Amnestie, Begnadigung IV
an [ən] ein, eine I
°**Anangu** ['ænəŋgʊ] Anangu *(Selbstbezeichnung verschiedener australischer Aboriginevölker)*
ancestor ['ænsestə] Vorfahre/Vorfahrin V 1 (16)
and [ənd, ænd] und I • **and so on** *(short:* **etc.** [et'setərə]*)* und so weiter (usw.) IV
angel ['eɪndʒl] Engel II
angry (about sth. / with sb.) ['æŋgri] wütend, böse (über etwas / auf jn.) II
animal ['ænɪml] Tier II
anniversary [ˌænɪ'vɜːsəri] Jahrestag IV • **anniversary of sb.'s death** jemandes Todestag IV
announce [ə'naʊns] ankündigen, bekanntgeben III
announcement [ə'naʊnsmənt] Durchsage, Ansage; Ankündigung, Bekanntgabe III
annoy sb. [ə'nɔɪ] jn. ärgern, belästigen III
annoyed [ə'nɔɪd] verärgert V 3 (52/183) • **get annoyed (with sb.; at/about sth.)** sich ärgern (über jn. / über etwas) V 3 (52)
annoying [ə'nɔɪɪŋ]: **My dad is annoying.** Mein Vater geht mir auf die Nerven. III
anorak ['ænəræk] Anorak, Windjacke III
another [ə'nʌðə] ein(e) andere(r, s); noch ein(e) I • **another 45 p** weitere 45 Pence, noch 45 Pence II
answer ['ɑːnsə] antworten; beantworten I
answer (to) ['ɑːnsə] Antwort (auf) I
anti- ['ænti] anti- V 3 (54)
any ['eni] jede(r,s) (beliebige); irgendein(e) IV • **any ...?** (irgend)welche ...? I • **any time** jederzeit IV • **not (...) any** kein, keine I • **not (...) any more** nicht mehr III
anybody ['enibɒdi] (irgend)jemand II; jede(r) IV • **anybody else?** sonst noch jemand? IV • **not (...) anybody** niemand II

anyone ['eniwʌn] (irgend)jemand; jede(r) IV
anything ['eniθɪŋ] (irgend)etwas II; alles, was es auch sei / egal was IV
anything else irgendetwas anderes IV • **anything else?** sonst noch etwas? IV • **not (...) anything** nichts II
anyway ['eniweɪ]
1. sowieso I
2. trotzdem II
3. aber egal, ...; wie auch immer, ...; wie dem auch sei, ... III
anywhere ['eniweə] irgendwo(hin) II • **not (...) anywhere** nirgendwo(hin) II
apart [ə'pɒːt] auseinander, getrennt IV
°**apartheid** [ə'pɑːtaɪt] Apartheid *(bis 1994 Trennung von Schwarzen und Weißen in Südafrika)*
apartment [ə'pɑːtmənt] Wohnung IV
apologize (to sb. for sth.) [ə'pɒlədʒaɪz] sich (bei jm. für etwas) entschuldigen V 1 (17)
apology [ə'pɒlədʒi] Entschuldigung *(Bitte um Verzeihung)* V 1 (17/175)
appear [ə'pɪə] erscheinen IV
appetite ['æpɪtaɪt] Appetit III
apple ['æpl] Apfel I
application [ˌæplɪ'keɪʃn] Bewerbung V 2 (37) • **letter of application** Bewerbungsschreiben V 2 (37/179)
apply for sth. [ə'plaɪ] sich um/für etwas bewerben; etwas beantragen V 2 (38)
appointment [ə'pɔɪntmənt] Termin, Verabredung I • °**make appointments** einen Termin machen, eine Verabredung treffen
apprentice [ə'prentɪs] Auszubildende(r), Lehrling V 2 (32/176)
apprenticeship [ə'prentɪʃɪp] Lehre, Ausbildung V 2 (32)
April ['eɪprəl] April I
archive ['ɑːkaɪv] Archiv IV
are [ɑː] bist; sind; seid I • **How are you?** Wie geht es dir/Ihnen/euch? II • **The pencils are 35 p.** Die Bleistifte kosten 35 Pence. I • **You're joking, aren't you?** Du machst Witze, nicht wahr? / Das ist nicht dein Ernst, oder? II
area ['eəriə] Bereich; Gebiet, Gegend III; Fläche V 1 (8)
argue ['ɑːgjuː] sich streiten, sich zanken I
argument ['ɑːgjumənt]
1. Argument, Begründung III
2. Streit III

arm [ɑːm] Arm I
armchair ['ɑːmtʃeə] Sessel I
around [ə'raʊnd] um ... (herum); in ... umher, durch III • **around six** um sechs herum, gegen sechs III • **around the lake** um den See (herum) III • **around the town** in der Stadt umher, durch die Stadt **jump/run/walk around** herumspringen/-rennen / umherspazieren III
arrival (arr) [ə'raɪvl] Ankunft III
arrive [ə'raɪv] ankommen, eintreffen II
art [ɑːt] Kunst I
article ['ɑːtɪkl] (Zeitungs-)Artikel III
artificial [ˌɑːtɪ'fɪʃl] künstlich, Kunst- III
artist ['ɑːtɪst] Künstler/in III **make-up artist** Maskenbildner/in V 2 (33)
artistic [ɑː'tɪstɪk] künstlerisch V 2 (33)
as *(prep)* [əz, æz] als IV • **as a firefighter** als Feuerwehrmann, -frau IV
as *(conj)* [əz, æz] als, während II **as you can see** wie du sehen kannst II • **as if** als ob IV
as ... as [əz, æz] so ... wie II • **as big/exciting as** so groß/aufregend wie II • **just as ... as** genauso ... wie V 1 (16)
as usual ['juːʒuəl] wie immer, wie üblich V 3 (50)
°**ASBO** ['æzbəʊ] **(anti-social behaviour order)** einstweilige Verfügung wegen antisozialen Verhaltens
ask [ɑːsk] fragen I • **ask about sth.** nach etwas fragen I • **ask questions** Fragen stellen I • **ask sb. the way** jn. nach dem Weg fragen II • **ask sb. for directions** jn. nach dem Weg fragen; jn. um eine Wegbeschreibung bitten IV • **ask sb. out** sich mit jm. verabreden; jn. einladen, mit einem auszugehen V 3 (51) • **ask sb. to do sth.** jn. (darum) bitten, etwas zu tun V 2 (34)
► S.177 (to) ask/tell/expect/want sb. to do sth.
asleep [ə'sliːp]: **be asleep** schlafen I
°**aspect** ['æspekt] Aspekt, Seite
Assembly [ə'sembli] Versammlung *(morgendliche Schulversammlung, oft mit Andacht)* III
assess [ə'ses] einschätzen, beurteilen V 2 (40/180)
assessment [ə'sesmənt] Einschätzung, Beurteilung V 2 (40)
assistant [ə'sɪstənt]: **childcare assistant** Kinderpfleger/in V 2 (32) **dentist's assistant** Zahnarzthelfer/in V 2 (35) • **vet's assistant** Tierarzthelfer/in V 2 (35)
association [əˌsəʊsi'eɪʃn] Verband, Vereinigung V 4 (83)
at [ət, æt]: **at 7 Hamilton Street** in der Hamiltonstraße 7 I • **at 8.45** um 8.45 I • **at a time** gleichzeitig, auf einmal V 3 (54) • **at break** in der Pause *(zwischen Schulstunden)* II • **at first** zuerst, am Anfang IV **at home** daheim, zu Hause I • **at last** endlich, schließlich I • **at least** zumindest, wenigstens I **at night** nachts, in der Nacht I **at once** sofort V 4 (86) • **at school** in der Schule I • **at that table** an dem Tisch (dort) / an den Tisch (dort) I • **at the bottom (of)** unten, am unteren Ende (von) II **at the butcher's** beim Metzger/Fleischer III • **at the chemist's** beim Apotheker III • **at the end (of)** am Ende (von) I • **at the Shaws' house** im Haus der Shaws / bei den Shaws zu Hause I • **at the station** am Bahnhof I • **at the top (of)** oben, am oberen Ende, an der Spitze (von) I • **at the weekend** am Wochenende I • **at work** bei der Arbeit / am Arbeitsplatz I **not (...) at all** [ət_'ɔːl] überhaupt nicht, ganz und gar nicht; überhaupt kein/e V 3 (50)
ate [et, eɪt] *siehe* **eat**
athletics [æθ'letɪks] Leichtathletik III
Atlantic: **the Atlantic (Ocean)** [ətˌlæntɪk_'əʊʃn] der Atlantische Ozean, der Atlantik IV
attach (to) [ə'tætʃ] anhängen, anheften *(an Brief, Mail)* V 1 (12)
attack [ə'tæk] angreifen III
attack [ə'tæk] Angriff III
attention [ə'tenʃn] Aufmerksamkeit **draw sb's attention to sth.** jn. auf etwas aufmerksam machen; jemandes Aufmerksamkeit auf etwas lenken V 4 (88)
attitude (to, towards) ['ætɪtjuːd] Haltung (gegenüber), Einstellung (zu, gegenüber) IV
attract [ə'trækt] anziehen, anlocken V 3 (50/182)
attraction [ə'trækʃən] Attraktion IV
audience ['ɔːdiəns] Publikum; Zuschauer/innen, Zuhörer/innen II
August ['ɔːgəst] August I
aunt [ɑːnt] Tante I • **auntie** ['ɑːnti] Tante II
°**Aussie** ['ɒzi] *(infml)* Australier/in; australisch
°**Australian Rules football** *Australischer Nationalsport*
auto ['ɔːtəʊ] *(AE)* Auto, PKW IV
°**auto-rickshaw** ['ɔːtəʊ ˌrɪkʃɔː] Auto-Rikscha
autograph ['ɔːtəgrɑːf] Autogramm V 4 (81)
autumn ['ɔːtəm] Herbst I
avenue ['ævənjuː] Allee IV
average ['ævərɪdʒ] Durchschnitt, durchschnittlich, Durchschnitts- IV
avoid [ə'vɔɪd] vermeiden, aus dem Weg gehen V 1 (9)
away [ə'weɪ] weg, fort I
awesome ['ɔːsəm] *(AE, infml)* klasse, großartig IV
awful ['ɔːfl] furchtbar, schrecklich II

B

baby ['beɪbi] Baby I • **have a baby** ein Baby/Kind bekommen II
back [bæk] Rücken V 1 (23) • **in the back** hinten, im hinteren Teil V 1 (17)
back (to) [bæk] zurück (nach) I **Good to have you back.** Schön, dass du wieder da bist. IV
back door [ˌbæk 'dɔː] Hintertür II
background ['bækgraʊnd] Hintergrund II • **background file** *etwa:* Hintergrundinformation(en) II
backpack ['bækpæk] *(AE)* Rucksack IV
°**backwards** ['bækwədz] nach hinten
bacon ['beɪkən] Schinkenspeck II
bad [bæd] schlecht, schlimm • **bad timing** schlechtes Timing III • **be bad at sth.** in etwas schlecht sein, etwas schlecht können III
badly ['bædli]: **do badly (in)** schlecht abschneiden (in) III
badminton ['bædmɪntən] Badminton, Federball I • **badminton racket** Badmintonschläger III
bag [bæg] Tasche, Beutel, Tüte I **sleeping bag** ['sliːpɪŋ bæg] Schlafsack V 1 (6)
bagel ['beɪgl] Bagel *(ringförmiges Gebäck)* IV
baggy ['bægi] weit (geschnitten) *(Hose)* V 4 (81)
bagpipes *(pl)* ['bægpaɪps] Dudelsack III
°**bait** [beɪt] Köder

bakery ['beɪkəri] Bäckerei III
ball [bɔːl]
1. Ball I
2. Ball *(Tanzveranstaltung)* IV
ban (-nn-) [bæn] verbieten; ein (Aufenthalts-)Verbot erteilen V 3 (52)
banana [bə'nɑːnə] Banane I
band [bænd] Band, (Musik-)Gruppe I
bank [bæŋk] Bank, Sparkasse I
bank robber ['bæŋk ˌrɒbə] Bankräuber/in I
°**Bantu** [bæn'tuː] *Sammelbegriff für über 400 verschiedene Volksgruppen Süd- und Mittelafrikas*
bar [bɑː]
1. Bar II
2. **bar chart** ['bɑː tʃɑːt] Balkendiagramm V 1 (10)
barbecue ['bɑːbɪkjuː] Grillfest, Grillparty V 1 (6)
°**bark** [bɑːk] bellen
baseball ['beɪsbɔːl] Baseball I
baseball cap Baseballmütze II
basement ['beɪsmənt] Keller(geschoss) V 4 (84)
basic ['beɪsɪk] grundlegend; Grund-, Haupt- V 4 (88)
basket ['bɑːskɪt] Korb I • **a basket of apples** ein Korb Äpfel I
basketball ['bɑːskɪtbɔːl] Basketball I
bath [bɑːθ] Bad, Badewanne II
have a bath baden, ein Bad nehmen II
bathroom ['bɑːθruːm] Badezimmer I
bay [beɪ] Bucht III
be [biː], **was/were, been** sein I
be with sb. mit jemandem zusammen sein IV
beach [biːtʃ] Strand II • **on the beach** am Strand II
bean [biːn] Bohne IV
bear [beə] Bär II
beard [bɪəd] Bart IV
beat [biːt], **beat, beaten** schlagen; besiegen III
beaten ['biːtn] *siehe* **beat**
beautiful ['bjuːtɪfl] schön I
beauty ['bjuːti] Schönheit III
became [bɪ'keɪm] *siehe* **become**
because [bɪ'kɒz] weil I • **because of** [bɪ'kɒz‿əv] wegen V 1 (9)
► S.171 because – because of
become [bɪ'kʌm], **became, become** werden II
bed [bed] Bett I • **Bed and Breakfast (B&B)** [ˌbed‿ən 'brekfəst] Frühstückspension I • **go to bed** ins Bett gehen I

bedroom ['bedruːm] Schlafzimmer I
beef [biːf] Rindfleisch III
been [biːn] *siehe* **be**
before [bɪ'fɔː] vor *(zeitlich)* I
before [bɪ'fɔː] bevor II
beg (for) (-gg-) [beg] betteln (um); (eindringlich) bitten (um) IV
began [bɪ'gæn] *siehe* **begin**
begin (-nn-) [bɪ'gɪn], **began, begun** beginnen, anfangen (mit) III
beginning [bɪ'gɪnɪŋ] Beginn, Anfang; Einleitung II
begun [bɪ'gʌn] *siehe* **begin**
behave [bɪ'heɪv] sich verhalten, sich benehmen V 3 (54/184) • **Behave yourself!** Benimm dich! V 3 (54/184)
behaviour [bɪ'heɪvjə] Verhalten, Benehmen V 3 (54)
behind [bɪ'haɪnd] hinter II
belief [bɪ'liːf] Glaube, Überzeugung V 1 (16)
believe [bɪ'liːv] glauben III
bell [bel] Klingel, Glocke III
belong to [bɪ'lɒŋ] gehören (zu) IV
below [bɪ'ləʊ] unten; unter, unterhalb (von) IV
bench [bentʃ] (Sitz-)Bank IV
best [best] am besten II • **the best ...** der/die/das beste ...; die besten I • **What was the best thing about ...?** Was war das Beste an ...? II • **Best wishes** *etwa:* Alles Gute / Mit besten Grüßen *(als Briefschluss)* IV
better ['betə] besser I • °**better lock the door** mach besser/lieber die Tür zu • **like sth. better** etwas lieber mögen II
between [bɪ'twiːn] zwischen II
°**beyond the story** [bɪ'jɒnd] über die Geschichte hinaus
Bible: the Bible ['baɪbl] die Bibel V 3 (58) • °**Bible school** Bibelschule
big [bɪg] groß I • **big wheel** [ˌbɪg 'wiːl] Riesenrad III
bike [baɪk] Fahrrad I • **bike ride** (Rad-)Fahrt II • **ride a bike** Rad fahren I
bill [bɪl]
1. Rechnung III
2. *(AE)* Geldschein V 3 (58)
°**billycan** ['bɪlikæn] Kochtopf, -geschirr
bin [bɪn] Mülltonne II
biography [baɪ'ɒgrəfi] Biografie III
biology [baɪ'ɒlədʒi] Biologie I
bird [bɜːd] Vogel I
birth [bɜːθ] Geburt V 2 (38) • **date of birth** Geburtsdatum V 2 (38)
place of birth Geburtsort V 2 (38/179)

birthday ['bɜːθdeɪ] Geburtstag I
Happy birthday. Herzlichen Glückwunsch zum Geburtstag. I • **My birthday is in May.** Ich habe im Mai Geburtstag. I • **My birthday is on 13th June.** Ich habe am 13. Juni Geburtstag. I • **When's your birthday?** Wann hast du Geburtstag? I
biscuit ['bɪskɪt] Keks, Plätzchen I
bit [bɪt]
1. **a bit** ein bisschen, etwas II
2. °**bit** kleines Teil, Stückchen
black [blæk] schwarz I
blame sb. (for) [bleɪm] jm. die Schuld geben (an); jm. Vorwürfe machen (wegen) III
blanket ['blæŋkɪt] Decke *(zum Zudecken)* V 1 (17)
bled [bled] *siehe* **bleed**
bleed [bliːd], **bled, bled** bluten V 1 (23)
bleep [bliːp] piepsen II
bleep [bliːp] Piepton II
blew [bluː] *siehe* **blow**
block [blɒk] (Häuser-, Wohn-)Block IV
block sth. [blɒk] etwas sperren V 3 (53)
blog [blɒg] *(von web log)* Blog *(Internet-Tagebuch)* IV
blond [blɒnd] blond, hell IV
blood [blʌd] Blut IV
bloody ['blʌdi] blutig V 4 (82)
blow [bləʊ], **blew, blown** wehen, blasen III
blown [bləʊn] *siehe* **blow**
blue [bluː] blau I
board [bɔːd]
1. (Wand-)Tafel I • **on the board** an der/die Tafel I • **bulletin board** *(AE)* schwarzes Brett, Anschlagtafel IV • **notice board** *(BE)* Anschlagtafel, schwarzes Brett I
2. **on board** an Bord V 4 (77)
boat [bəʊt] Boot, Schiff I
body ['bɒdi] Körper I
bodyguard ['bɒdigɑːd] Bodyguard, Leibwächter/in IV
bold print [ˌbəʊld 'prɪnt] Fettdruck III
°**Bollywood** ['bɒliwʊd] *indische Unterhaltungsfilmindustrie*
°**bone** [bəʊn] Knochen
book [bʊk] Buch I • **book review** [rɪ'vjuː] Buchkritik, Buchbesprechung V 1 (19)
book [bʊk] buchen, reservieren V 4 (84)
booked [bʊkt]: **fully booked** ausgebucht V 4 (86)
boot [buːt] Stiefel I

°**boot camp** ['bu:t kæmp] Erziehungslager *(für junge Straftäter/innen)*
border ['bɔ:də] Grenze IV
bored [bɔ:d] gelangweilt IV
boring ['bɔ:rɪŋ] langweilig I
born [bɔ:n]**: be born** geboren sein/werden II
borough ['bʌrə, *AE:* 'bɜ:rəʊ] (Stadt-)Bezirk IV
borrow sth. (from) ['bɒrəʊ] (sich) etwas (aus)leihen, (sich) borgen (von) V 1 (15)
▶ S.174 (to) lend – (to) borrow
boss [bɒs] Chef/in, Boss III
both [bəʊθ] beide I
bottle ['bɒtl] Flasche I • **a bottle of milk** eine Flasche Milch I
childproof bottle kindersichere Flasche V 1 (17/175)
bottom ['bɒtəm] unteres Ende II
at the bottom (of) unten, am unteren Ende (von) II
bought [bɔ:t] *siehe* **buy**
bowl [bəʊl] Schüssel I • **a bowl of cornflakes** eine Schale Cornflakes I
box [bɒks] Kasten, Kästchen, Kiste I • **phone box** Telefonzelle V 3 (50)
sandwich box Brotdose I
boy [bɔɪ] Junge I
boyfriend ['bɔɪfrend] (fester) Freund IV
°**bracket** ['brækɪt] Klammer *(in Texten)*
brainstorm ['breɪnstɔ:m] brainstormen *(so viele Ideen wie möglich sammeln)* III
brave [breɪv] tapfer, mutig III
bread *(no pl)* [bred] Brot I
break [breɪk] Pause I • **at break** in der Pause *(zwischen Schulstunden)* II • **take a break** eine Pause machen IV
break [breɪk]**, broke, broken** (zer-)brechen; kaputt gehen IV
break a journey eine Reise unterbrechen III
breakable ['breɪkəbl] zerbrechlich IV
breakdance ['breɪkdɑ:ns] Breakdance IV
breakfast ['brekfəst] Frühstück I
have breakfast frühstücken I
breath [breθ] Atem V 1 (20/175) • **out of breath** außer Atem V 1 (20/175)
take a deep breath tief Luft holen V 1 (20/175)
breathe (in/out) [bri:ð] (ein/aus)atmen V 1 (20)
bridge [brɪdʒ] Brücke I
bridle path ['braɪdl pɑ:θ] Reitweg III
bright [braɪt] hell, leuchtend II
brilliant ['brɪliənt] genial, toll III
bring [brɪŋ]**, brought, brought** (mit-, her)bringen I
British ['brɪtɪʃ] britisch; Brite, Britin II
brochure ['brəʊʃə] Prospekt, Broschüre II
broke [brəʊk] *siehe* **break**
broken ['brəʊkən] *siehe* **break**
broken ['brəʊkən] gebrochen; zerbrochen, kaputt, defekt II
brother ['brʌðə] Bruder I
brought [brɔ:t] *siehe* **bring**
brown [braʊn] braun I
budgie ['bʌdʒi] Wellensittich I
°**bugger** ['bʌgə] Kerl
build [bɪld]**, built, built** bauen II
builder ['bɪldə] Bauarbeiter/in V 2 (35)
building ['bɪldɪŋ] Gebäude II
built [bɪlt] *siehe* **build**
bulletin board ['bʊlətɪn bɔ:d] *(AE)* schwarzes Brett, Anschlagtafel IV
bully ['bʊli] einschüchtern, tyrannisieren II
bully ['bʊli] (Schul-)Tyrann III
bunk (bed) [bʌŋk] Etagenbett, Koje II
burger ['bɜ:gə] Burger IV
burn [bɜ:n] brennen; verbrennen IV
bus [bʌs] Bus I • **bus stop** ['bʌs stɒp] Bushaltestelle III
bush [bʊʃ] Busch, Strauch V 1 (6/170)
the bush [bʊʃ] der Busch *(unkultiviertes, „wildes" Land in Australien, Afrika)* V 1 (6)
business ['bɪznəs] Geschäft; Handel IV • **do business with** Geschäfte machen mit; Handel treiben mit V 1 (8) • **Mind your own business.** Das geht dich nichts an! / Kümmere dich um deine eigenen Angelegenheiten! II • **start a business** eine Firma gründen V 2 (44)
busy ['bɪzi]
1. belebt, verkehrsreich; hektisch III
2. beschäftigt V 3 (52)
3. besetzt *(Telefon, Leitung)* V 3 (62)
but [bət, bʌt]
1. aber I
2. sondern IV
butcher ['bʊtʃə] Fleischer/in, Metzger/in III • **at the butcher's** beim Fleischer/Metzger III
butter ['bʌtə] Butter III
button ['bʌtn] Knopf III
buy [baɪ]**, bought, bought** kaufen I
by [baɪ]
1. von I
2. an; (nahe) bei II
3. by car/train/bike/... mit dem Auto/Zug/Rad/... II
4. bis spätestens; nicht später als
by ten o'clock bis (spätestens) zehn Uhr III
5. by the way übrigens II
6. by two degrees / ten per cent um zwei Grad / zehn Prozent V 1 (9)
7. go by vergehen, vorübergehen *(Zeit)* V 3 (51)
Bye. [baɪ] Tschüs! I

C

cab [kæb] Taxi IV • **get a cab** ein Taxi nehmen IV
cabin ['kæbɪn] Hütte III
cable ['keɪbl] Kabel *(auch kurz für Kabelfernsehen)* IV
café ['kæfeɪ] *(kleines)* Restaurant, Imbissstube, Café II
cafeteria [ˌkæfə'tɪəriə] Cafeteria; *(USA)* Schulmensa IV
cage [keɪdʒ] Käfig I
cake [keɪk] Kuchen, Torte I
calendar ['kælɪndə] Kalender I
call [kɔ:l]
1. rufen; anrufen I
2. nennen I
call sb. names jn. mit Schimpfwörtern hänseln, jm. Schimpfwörter nachrufen III
call [kɔ:l] Anruf, Telefongespräch I
wake-up call Weckanruf V 4 (86)
called [kɔ:ld]**: be called** heißen, genannt werden III
caller ['kɔ:lə] Anrufer/Anruferin V 3 (62)
calm [kɑ:m] ruhig, still V 1 (17)
calm down [ˌkɑ:m 'daʊn] sich beruhigen II
calorie ['kæləri] Kalorie IV
came [keɪm] *siehe* **come**
camel ['kæml] Kamel II
camera ['kæmərə] Kamera, Fotoapparat I
camp [kæmp] zelten III
camp [kæmp] Camp, (Ferien-)Lager IV
can [kən, kæn]
1. können I
2. dürfen I
Can I help you? Kann ich Ihnen helfen? / Was kann ich für Sie tun? *(im Geschäft)* I
can [kæn] Dose, Büchse V 3 (58/186)
canal [kə'næl] Kanal III

cancer ['kænsə] Krebs *(Krankheit)* V 1 (9)
candidate ['kændɪdət] Kandidat/in, Bewerber/in V 2 (40)
°**cane toad** ['keɪn təʊd] Agakröte
canned [kænd] Dosen-; ... in Dosen V 3 (58)
canoe [kə'nuː] Kanu III
canoe [kə'nuː] paddeln, Kanu fahren III
canteen [kæn'tiːn] Kantine, Schulmensa II
canyon ['kænjən] Schlucht IV
cap [kæp] Mütze, Kappe II
capital ['kæpɪtl] Hauptstadt III
capital letter [ˌkæpɪtl 'letə] Großbuchstabe III
°**captain** ['kæptɪn] Kapitän/in
caption ['kæpʃn] Bildunterschrift III
car [kɑː] Auto I • **car park** Parkplatz III • **racing car** ['reɪsɪŋ kɑː] Rennwagen V 2 (35)
caravan ['kærəvæn] Wohnwagen II
card [kɑːd] (Spiel-, Post-)Karte I
credit card ['kredɪt kɑːd] Kreditkarte V 3 (53)
care about sth. [keə] etwas wichtig nehmen V 1 (17)
career [kə'rɪə] Karriere III
°**careers teacher** *Lehrer/in, der/die Berufsberatung anbietet*
careful ['keəfl]
1. vorsichtig II
2. sorgfältig, gründlich II
3. aufmerksam V 2 (40)
careless ['keələs] nachlässig; unvorsichtig, leichtsinnig V 4 (82)
caretaker ['keəteɪkə] Hausmeister/in II
carrot ['kærət] Möhre, Karotte I
cartoon [kɑː'tuːn] Cartoon (Zeichentrickfilm; Bilderwitz) II
case [keɪs] Fall II
cash [kæʃ] Bargeld V 3 (53) • **pay cash** bar bezahlen V 3 (53/184)
castle ['kɑːsl] Burg, Schloss II
cat [kæt] Katze I
catch [kætʃ], **caught, caught** fangen; erwischen II
cathedral [kə'θiːdrəl] Kathedrale, Dom III
cattle *(pl)* ['kætl] Rinder V 1 (22)
°**cattle station** Rinderfarm
caught [kɔːt] *siehe* **catch**
cause [kɔːz] verursachen IV
cause (of sth.) [kɔːz] Grund, Ursache (für etwas) IV
cave [keɪv] Höhle V 1 (16) • °**cave painting** Höhlenmalerei
CD [ˌsiː'diː] CD I • **CD player** CD-Spieler I

ceilidh ['keɪli] *Musik- und Tanzveranstaltung, vor allem in Schottland und Irland* III
cellphone ['selfəʊn] *(AE)* Handy, Mobiltelefon IV
Celsius (C) ['selsiəs] Celsius IV
cent (c) [sent] Cent I • **per cent (%)** [pə 'sent] Prozent III
centimetre (cm) ['sentɪmiːtə] Zentimeter III
central ['sentrəl] Zentral-, Mittel- III
centre ['sentə] Zentrum, Mitte I
city centre Stadtzentrum, Innenstadt I • **sports centre** Sportzentrum I
century ['sentʃəri] Jahrhundert II
certainly ['sɜːtnli] bestimmt, sicher(lich); gerne, selbstverständlich, klar V 4 (86)
certificate [sə'tɪfɪkət] Zertifikat, Bescheinigung V 2 (38)
chair [tʃeə] Stuhl I
champion ['tʃæmpiən] Meister/in, Champion I
championship ['tʃæmpiənʃɪp] Meisterschaft III
chance [tʃɑːns] Chance, Möglichkeit IV
change [tʃeɪndʒ]
1. (sich) ändern; (sich) verändern IV
2. wechseln IV
3. umsteigen III
4. sich umziehen IV
change [tʃeɪndʒ]
1. (Ver-)Änderung, Wechsel IV
2. Wechselgeld I; Kleingeld IV
channel ['tʃænl] Kanal, Sender IV
hop channels zappen IV
character ['kærəktə]
1. Charakter, Wesen IV
2. Person, Figur *(in Roman, Film, Theaterstück)* IV
chart [tʃɑːt] Diagramm V 1 (10)
charts [tʃɑːts] Charts, Hitliste III
chat (-tt-) [tʃæt] plaudern; chatten II
chat room ['tʃæt ruːm] Chatroom III
cheap [tʃiːp] billig I
check [tʃek]
1. (über)prüfen, kontrollieren I
2. **check in** einchecken *(Hotel, Flughafen)* V 4 (86)
3. **check out** auschecken *(Hotel)* V 4 (86)
°**checklist** ['tʃeklɪst] Checkliste
checkpoint ['tʃekpɔɪnt] Kontrollpunkt *(hier auch: zur Selbstüberprüfung)* I
cheek [tʃiːk] Wange IV
cheeky ['tʃiːki] frech, dreist V 2 (40)
cheer [tʃɪə] jubeln, Beifall klatschen II

cheerleader ['tʃɪəliːdə] Cheerleader *(Stimmungsanheizer/in bei Sportereignissen)* IV
cheese [tʃiːz] Käse I • **cream cheese** Frischkäse IV
chef [ʃef] Koch, Köchin *(Berufsbezeichnung)* V 2 (33)
chemist ['kemɪst] Drogerie, Apotheke II • **at the chemist's** beim Apotheker III
cheque (for) [tʃek] Scheck (über) V 2 (45)
cherry ['tʃeri] Kirsche II
chicken ['tʃɪkɪn] Huhn; (Brat-)Hähnchen I
child [tʃaɪld], *pl* **children** ['tʃɪldrən] Kind I • **only child** Einzelkind V 3 (48)
childcare ['tʃaɪldkeə] Kinderbetreuung V 2 (32/176) • **childcare assistant** Kinderpfleger/in V 2 (32)
childproof ['tʃaɪldpruːf] kindersicher *(Flasche, Verschluss)* V 1 (17/175)
°**children's home** [ˌtʃɪldrənz 'həʊm] Kinderheim
chips *(pl)* [tʃɪps]
1. *(BE)* Pommes frites I
2. **(potato) chips** *(AE)* Kartoffelchips IV
chocolate ['tʃɒklət] Schokolade I
°**choice** [tʃɔɪs] Wahl
choir ['kwaɪə] Chor I
choose [tʃuːz], **chose, chosen** (sich) aussuchen, (aus)wählen I
chorus ['kɔːrəs] Refrain III
chose [tʃəʊz] *siehe* **choose**
chosen ['tʃəʊzn] *siehe* **choose**
°**chrissake: for chrissake** ['kraɪseɪk] **(= for Christ's sake)** *(infml) etwa:* verdammt noch mal *(wörtlich: um Christus willen)*
Christian ['krɪstʃən] Christ/in; christlich V 4 (77)
Christmas ['krɪsməs] Weihnachten I
church [tʃɜːtʃ] Kirche I
cinema ['sɪnəmə] Kino I • **go to the cinema** ins Kino gehen II
circle ['sɜːkl] Kreis IV
circus ['sɜːkəs] (runder) Platz III
citizen ['sɪtɪzn] (Staats-)Bürger/in, Staatsangehörige(r) IV
city ['sɪti] (Groß-)Stadt I • **city centre** Stadtzentrum, Innenstadt I
civil ['sɪvl]: **civil rights** *(pl)* Bürgerrechte IV • **civil war** Bürgerkrieg IV
°**claim an island (for sb.)** [kleɪm] eine Insel in Besitz nehmen (für jn.)

clap (-pp-) [klæp] (Beifall) klatschen IV
°**clarification** [ˌklærəfɪ'keɪʃn] Klärung
class [klɑːs]
1. (Schul-)Klasse I
2. Unterricht; Kurs IV
class teacher Klassenlehrer/in I
classical ['klæsɪkl] klassisch III
classmate ['klɑːsmeɪt] Klassenkamerad/in, Mitschüler/in I
classroom ['klɑːsruːm] Klassenzimmer I
clean [kliːn] sauber II
clean [kliːn] sauber machen, putzen I • **I clean my teeth.** Ich putze mir die Zähne. I
cleaner ['kliːnə] Putzfrau, -mann II
°**clean-up** ['kliːn‿ʌp] Reinemachen
clear [klɪə] klar, deutlich I
clever ['klevə] schlau, klug I
cleverness ['klevənəs] Klugheit, Schlauheit IV
click on sth. [klɪk] etwas anklicken II
cliff [klɪf] Klippe, Felsen III
climb [klaɪm] klettern; hinaufklettern (auf) I • **Climb a tree.** Klettere auf einen Baum. I
clinic ['klɪnɪk] Klinik II
clock [klɒk] (Wand-, Stand-, Turm-) Uhr I • **alarm clock** [ə'lɑːm klɒk] Wecker V 3 (50)
clone [kləʊn] Klon III
close (to) [kləʊs] nahe (bei, an) III
°**be close** sich nahe stehen • **That was close.** Das war knapp. II
close [kləʊz] schließen, zumachen I
closed [kləʊzd] geschlossen II
°**closing phrase** ['kləʊzɪŋ freɪz] Grußformel *(am Briefende)*
clothes *(pl)* [kləʊðz, kləʊz] Kleider, Kleidung(sstücke) II
cloud [klaʊd] Wolke II
cloudless ['klaʊdləs] wolkenlos IV
cloudy ['klaʊdi] bewölkt II
clown [klaʊn] Clown/in II
club [klʌb] Klub; Verein I
°**clue** [kluː] Hinweis
coach [kəʊtʃ] Trainer/in, Coach III
coast [kəʊst] Küste III
code: dress code ['dres kəʊd] Kleiderordnung IV
coffee ['kɒfi] Kaffee IV • **coffee to go** Kaffee zum Mitnehmen IV
coin [kɔɪn] Münze V 3 (58)
cola ['kəʊlə] Cola I
cold [kəʊld] kalt I • **be cold** frieren I
cold [kəʊld]
1. Kälte IV
2. Erkältung II
have a cold erkältet sein, eine Erkältung haben II
collect [kə'lekt] sammeln I
collection [kə'lekʃn] Sammlung IV
collector [kə'lektə] Sammler/in II
college ['kɒlɪdʒ] berufliche Fach(hoch)schule V 2 (39)
colony ['kɒləni] Kolonie V 1 (8)
colour ['kʌlə] kolorieren, färben, bunt an-, ausmalen III
colour ['kʌlə] Farbe I • **What colour is ...?** Welche Farbe hat ...? I
colourful ['kʌləfl] farbenfroh, farbenprächtig, farbig V 4 (76)
column ['kɒləm] Säule III
°**combine** [kəm'baɪn] kombinieren, verbinden
come [kʌm], **came, come** kommen I • °**come for sth./sb.** kommen, um etwas/jn. zu holen • **come home** nach Hause kommen I
come in hereinkommen I
Come on. 1. Na los, komm. II; **2.** Ach komm! / Na hör mal! II
°**We've come a long way.** Wir sind weit gekommen. *(Wir haben viel erreicht.)*
comedy ['kɒmədi] Komödie IV
comfortable ['kʌmftəbl] bequem, behaglich IV • **Make yourself comfortable.** Machs dir bequem. IV
comic ['kɒmɪk] Comic-Heft I
°**command** [kə'mɑːnd] Befehl, Aufforderung
comment ['kɒment] Kommentar, Bemerkung IV
Commonwealth ['kɒmənwelθ]**: the Commonwealth** *Gemeinschaft der Länder des ehemaligen Britischen Weltreichs* III
communicate [kə'mjuːnɪkeɪt] sich verständigen, kommunizieren V 3 (50)
communication [kəˌmjuːnɪ'keɪʃn] Kommunikation V 3 (50/182)
community [kə'mjuːnəti] *(politische)* Gemeinde V 3 (58) • **community hall** Gemeindehalle, Gemeindesaal; Gemeinschaftshalle, Gemeinschaftssaal III
company ['kʌmpəni] Firma, Gesellschaft III
compare [kəm'peə] vergleichen IV
comparison [kəm'pærɪsn] Steigerung; Vergleich II
competition [ˌkɒmpə'tɪʃn] Wettbewerb, Wettkampf IV
complain (about sth.) [kəm'pleɪn] sich (über etwas) beschweren, sich (über etwas) beklagen III
complete [kəm'pliːt] vollständig, völlig V 3 (52)
°**complete** [kəm'pliːt] vervollständigen, ergänzen
complicated ['kɒmplɪkeɪtɪd] kompliziert V 2 (44/181)
computer [kəm'pjuːtə] Computer I
concert ['kɒnsət] Konzert III • **rock concert** Rockkonzert V 3 (60)
conclusion [kən'kluːʒn] Schluss(folgerung) IV • **draw conclusions** Schlüsse ziehen, schlussfolgern IV
°**conditioning: air conditioning** *(no pl)* ['eə kənˌdɪʃnɪŋ] Klimatisierung, Klimaanlage
confidence ['kɒnfɪdəns] Selbstvertrauen; Vertrauen V 4 (81)
confident ['kɒnfɪdənt] selbstbewusst, (selbst)sicher; zuversichtlich V 2 (35)
connect (to/with) [kə'nekt] verbinden (mit) V 4 (86/190)
connection [kə'nekʃn] Verbindung V 4 (86)
conscious ['kɒnʃəs] bewusst; bei Bewusstsein V 1 (23)
contact ['kɒntækt] Kontakt, Verbindung V 2 (38) • **contacts** *(pl) Liste von Bekannten/Kontakten (im Handy, im Mailprogramm)* V 3 (53)
contact sb. ['kɒntækt] sich mit jm. in Verbindung setzen V 2 (38/179)
contain [kən'teɪn] enthalten IV
context ['kɒntekst] Zusammenhang, Kontext IV • °**from the context** aus dem Zusammenhang, aus dem Kontext
continent ['kɒntɪnənt] Kontinent V 4 (74)
continue [kən'tɪnju] fortsetzen; weitermachen (mit) V 2 (45)
contrast ['kɒntrɑːst] Kontrast, Gegensatz V 4 (74)
control: remote control [rɪˌməʊt kən'trəʊl] Fernbedienung IV
conversation [ˌkɒnvə'seɪʃn] Gespräch, Unterhaltung IV
cook [kʊk] kochen, zubereiten II
cook [kʊk] Koch/Köchin III
cooker ['kʊkə] Herd I
cookie ['kʊkɪ] *(AE)* Keks IV
cool [kuːl]
1. kühl II
2. cool I
copy ['kɒpi] kopieren; abschreiben II
copy ['kɒpi]
1. Kopie, Abschrift II
2. Exemplar III
°**coral** ['kɒrəl] Koralle
corner ['kɔːnə] Ecke I • **on the corner of Green Street and London**

Road Green Street, Ecke London Road II
cornflakes ['kɔːnfleɪks] Cornflakes I
correct [kə'rekt] berichtigen, korrigieren II
correct [kə'rekt] richtig III
cost [kɒst], **cost, cost** kosten IV
cotton ['kɒtn] Baumwolle IV
couch [kaʊtʃ] Couch, Sofa V 1 (13)
couch potato *(infml)* Stubenhocker/in *(jd., der viel vor dem Fernseher sitzt)* V 1 (13)
could [kəd, kʊd]
1. he could ... er konnte ... II
2. he could ... er könnte ... III
count [kaʊnt] zählen II
countable ['kaʊntəbl] zählbar IV
countdown ['kaʊntdaʊn] Countdown III
counter ['kaʊntə] Theke, Ladentisch IV
country ['kʌntri] Land *(auch als Gegensatz zur Stadt)* II • **in the country** auf dem Land II
countryside ['kʌntrisaɪd] Land(schaft), Natur IV
couple ['kʌpl]: **a couple of weeks** ein paar Wochen IV
course [kɔːs] Kurs, Lehrgang III
course: of course [əv 'kɔːs] natürlich, selbstverständlich I
court [kɔːt]
1. Platz, Court *(für Squash, Badminton, Tennis)* III
2. Gericht(shof) IV
cousin ['kʌzn] Cousin, Cousine I
cover ['kʌvə] (CD-)Hülle I
cow [kaʊ] Kuh II
crash (into) [kræʃ] zusammenstoßen (mit); hineinfahren (in) IV
crazy ['kreɪzi] verrückt III
cream [kriːm] Sahne; Creme IV; Salbe V 4 (79) • **cream cheese** Frischkäse IV
°**create** [kri'eɪt] erzeugen
credit card ['kredɪt kɑːd] Kreditkarte V 3 (53) • **pay by credit card** mit Kreditkarte bezahlen V 3 (53/184)
cricket ['krɪkɪt] Kricket *(Schlagballspiel)* V 1 (13)
crime [kraɪm] Kriminalität; Verbrechen IV • **crime film** Krimi IV
crime series Krimiserie IV • **crime story** Krimi IV
crisps *(pl)* [krɪsps] Kartoffelchips I
crocodile ['krɒkədaɪl] Krokodil II
cross [krɒs] Kreuz V 1 (8)
cross [krɒs] überqueren II • **cross a time zone** eine Zeitzone passieren/durchqueren IV
cross [krɒs]: **be cross (with)** böse, sauer sein (auf) I

crowd [kraʊd] (Menschen-)Menge, Masse; *(infml auch:)* Clique, Gruppe IV
crowded ['kraʊdɪd] überfüllt, voll IV
cruel ['kruːəl] grausam IV
crush [krʌʃ]: **have a crush on sb.** in jn. verknallt sein III
cry [kraɪ] weinen IV
°**cry** [kraɪ] Schrei
°**crystal clear** [ˌkrɪstl 'klɪə] kristallklar
culture ['kʌltʃə] Kultur IV • **culture shock** Kulturschock V 4 (76)
cup [kʌp]
1. Tasse III
2. Pokal III
a cup of tea eine Tasse Tee III
cupboard ['kʌbəd] Schrank I
curriculum vitae [kəˌrɪkjələm 'viːtaɪ] **(CV)** Lebenslauf V 2 (38)
curry ['kʌri] Curry(gericht) III
curtain ['kɜːtn] Vorhang IV
customer ['kʌstəmə] Kunde, Kundin II • **customer adviser** Kundenbetreuer/in, -berater/in V 2 (33)
cut (-tt-) [kʌt], **cut, cut** schneiden III • °**cut sb.'s pay** jm. den Lohn kürzen • **cut sth. off** etwas abtrennen, abschneiden III • **cut the grass** Rasen mähen IV
CV [siː 'viː] **(curriculum vitae)** Lebenslauf V 2 (38)
cycle ['saɪkl] (mit dem) Rad fahren II • **cycle path** Radweg II

D

dad [dæd] Papa, Vati; Vater I
daily ['deɪli] täglich IV
°**dam** [dæm] (Stau)Damm
°**damn** [dæm] *(infml)* verdammt
dance [dɑːns] tanzen I
dance [dɑːns] Tanz I • **dance floor** Dancefloor, Tanzfläche IV
dancer ['dɑːnsə] Tänzer/in II
dancing ['dɑːnsɪŋ] Tanzen I
dancing lessons Tanzstunden, Tanzunterricht I
danger ['deɪndʒə] Gefahr III • **in danger** in Gefahr V 1 (9)
dangerous ['deɪndʒərəs] gefährlich II
dark [dɑːk] dunkel I
date [deɪt] Datum I • **date of birth** Geburtsdatum V 2 (38) • **to date** bis heute V 2 (37)
daughter ['dɔːtə] Tochter I
day [deɪ] Tag I • **one day** eines Tages I • **days of the week** Wochentage I • **day out** Tagesausflug III

dead [ded] tot I
deal [diːl]: **It's a deal.** Abgemacht! III • **make a deal** ein Abkommen / eine Abmachung treffen III
dear [dɪə] Schatz, Liebling I • **Oh dear!** Oje! II
dear [dɪə]: **Dear Jay ...** Lieber Jay, ... I • **Dear Sir or Madam** Sehr geehrte Damen und Herren *(Anrede in Briefen)* IV
death [deθ] Tod IV
debate [dɪ'beɪt] debattieren IV
debate [dɪ'beɪt] Debatte IV
December [dɪ'sembə] Dezember I
decide (on sth.) [dɪ'saɪd] (etwas) beschließen; sich (für etwas) entscheiden IV
decision [dɪ'sɪʒn] Entscheidung V 2 (32) • **make a decision** eine Entscheidung treffen/fällen V 2 (32/176)
deep [diːp] tief IV
deer, *pl* **deer** [dɪə] Reh, Hirsch II
definite ['defɪnət] fest, bestimmt; endgültig, eindeutig V 2 (45)
°**definition** [ˌdefɪ'nɪʃn] Definition
degree [dɪ'griː] Grad II
deli ['deli] Deli *(Lebensmittelgeschäft und Fastfoodrestaurant)* IV
delicious [dɪ'lɪʃəs] köstlich, lecker II
dentist ['dentɪst] Zahnarzt, -ärztin IV • **dentist's assistant** Zahnarzthelfer/in V 2 (35)
department store [dɪ'pɑːtmənt stɔː] Kaufhaus II
departure (dep) [dɪ'pɑːtʃə] Abfahrt, Abflug; Abreise III
depressed [dɪ'prest] deprimiert, niedergeschlagen IV
depressing [dɪ'presɪŋ] deprimierend, trostlos IV
describe sth. (to sb.) [dɪ'skraɪb] (jm.) etwas beschreiben II
description [dɪ'skrɪpʃn] Beschreibung II
desert ['dezət] Wüste V 1 (8)
deserve [dɪ'zɜːv] verdienen *(zu Recht bekommen)* V 3 (63)
design [dɪ'zaɪn] entwerfen, gestalten II
design [dɪ'zaɪn] Design; Gestaltung; Entwurf V 2 (37)
designer [dɪ'zaɪnə] Designer/in V 3 (48) • **fashion designer** Modedesigner/in V 4 (81)
desk [desk] Schreibtisch I
destroy [dɪ'strɔɪ] zerstören III
detail ['diːteɪl] Detail, Einzelheit II
detective [dɪ'tektɪv] Detektiv/in I
private detective [ˌpraɪvət dɪ'tektɪv] Privatdetektiv/in V 2 (35)

determined [dɪ'tɜːmɪnd]**: be determined (to do sth.)** (fest) entschlossen sein (etwas zu tun) V 2 (45)
dial (*BE:* **-ll-**) ['daɪəl] *(Telefonnummer)* wählen V 3 (63)
°**dialogue** ['daɪəlɒg] Dialog
°**diamond** ['daɪəmənd] Diamant
diary ['daɪəri] Tagebuch; Terminkalender I
dice, *pl* **dice** [daɪs] Würfel II
°**dictate** [dɪk'teɪt] diktieren
dictionary ['dɪkʃənri] Wörterbuch, *(alphabetisches)* Wörterverzeichnis I
did [dɪd] *siehe* **do** • **Did you go ...?** Bist du ... gegangen? / Seid ihr ... gegangen? I • **we didn't sing** wir sangen nicht / wir haben nicht gesungen I
°**didgeridoo** [ˌdɪdʒəri'duː] Didgeridoo
die (of) *(-ing form:* **dying***)* [daɪ]
1. sterben (an) II
°**2.** *(infml)* kaputtgehen
°**3.** *(infml)* ausgehen, ersterben
difference ['dɪfrəns] Unterschied IV
different (from) ['dɪfrənt] verschieden, unterschiedlich; anders (als) I
difficult ['dɪfɪkəlt] schwierig, schwer I
°**dingo** ['dɪŋgəʊ], *pl* **dingoes** ['dɪŋgəʊz] Dingo *(australischer Wildhund)*
dining room ['daɪnɪŋ ruːm] Esszimmer I
dinner ['dɪnə] Abendessen, Abendbrot I • **have dinner** Abendbrot essen I
dinosaur ['daɪnəsɔː] Dinosaurier IV
directions *(pl)* [də'rekʃnz] Wegbeschreibung(en) IV
director: film director ['fɪlm dəˌrektə] Regisseur/in IV
dirty ['dɜːti] schmutzig II
disabled [dɪs'eɪbld] (körper)behindert III
disadvantage [ˌdɪsəd'vɑːntɪdʒ] Nachteil IV
disagree (with) [ˌdɪsə'griː] nicht übereinstimmen (mit); anderer Meinung sein (als) III
disappear [ˌdɪsə'pɪə] verschwinden II
disappoint [ˌdɪsə'pɔɪnt] enttäuschen IV
disappointed (about/in) [ˌdɪsə'pɔɪntɪd] enttäuscht (von/über) IV
discipline ['dɪsəplɪn] Disziplin V 3 (55)
disc jockey (DJ) ['dɪsk dʒɒki, 'diː dʒeɪ] Diskjockey (DJ)
disco ['dɪskəʊ] Disko I
discover [dɪ'skʌvə] entdecken; herausfinden IV
discriminate against sb. [dɪ'skrɪmɪneɪt] jn. diskriminieren, jn. benachteiligen IV
discrimination (against) [dɪˌskrɪmɪ'neɪʃn] Diskriminierung (von), Benachteiligung (von) IV
°**discuss** [dɪ'skʌs] besprechen; diskutieren (über)
discussion [dɪ'skʌʃn] Diskussion II
disease [dɪ'ziːz] Krankheit V 1 (8)
dish [dɪʃ] Gericht *(Speise)* III
dishwasher ['dɪʃwɒʃə] Geschirrspülmaschine I
display [dɪ'spleɪ]**: be on display** ausgestellt sein/werden IV
divide sth. into sth. [dɪ'vaɪd] etwas (auf)teilen (in) V 1 (10)
divorced [dɪ'vɔːst] geschieden I
DJ ['diː dʒeɪ] Diskjockey III
DJ ['diː dʒeɪ] *(Musik/CDs/Platten)* auflegen *(in der Disko)* III
do [duː], **did, done** tun, machen I
Do you like ...? Magst du ...? I
do a gig einen Auftritt haben, ein Konzert geben III • **do a good job** gute Arbeit leisten II • **do a project** ein Projekt machen, durchführen II • **do an exercise** eine Übung machen II • **do badly/well (in)** schlecht/gut abschneiden (in) III • **do research** recherchieren IV **do sport** Sport treiben I • **do work experience** ein Praktikum machen V 2 (37/179) • **How are you doing?** Wie geht's? V 1 (15)
doable ['duːəbl] machbar IV
doctor ['dɒktə] Doktor; Arzt/Ärztin II • **to the doctor's** zum Arzt III
°**document** ['dɒkjumənt] dokumentieren
documentary [ˌdɒkju'mentri] Dokumentarfilm, -beitrag IV
dog [dɒg] Hund I
dollar ($) ['dɒlə] Dollar IV
dolphin ['dɒlfɪn] Delfin V 1 (9)
done [dʌn] *siehe* **do**
don't [dəʊnt]**: Don't listen to Dan.** Hör/Hört nicht auf Dan. I • **I don't know.** Ich weiß es nicht. I • **I don't like ...** Ich mag ... nicht. / Ich mag kein(e) ... I
door [dɔː] Tür I • **fireproof door** ['faɪəpruːf] feuerfeste Tür V 1 (17/175)
doorbell ['dɔːbel] Türklingel I
dorm [dɔːm] *(infml)* Schlafsaal V 4 (84)
dormitory ['dɔːmətri] Schlafsaal V 4 (84)
dossier ['dɒsieɪ] Mappe, Dossier *(des Sprachenportfolios)* I
double ['dʌbl] zweimal, doppelt, Doppel- I • °**double circle** Doppelkreis, „Kugellager" *(als Gesprächskreis)* • **double room** [ˌdʌbl 'ruːm] Doppelzimmer V 4 (84)
down [daʊn] hinunter, herunter, nach unten I • **down there** dort unten II • **fall down** hinfallen II **turn sth. down** etwas leiser stellen IV
°**Down Under** [ˌdaʊn‿'ʌndə] *umgangssprachliche Bezeichnung für Australien*
download [ˌdaʊn'ləʊd] runterladen, downloaden III
downloadable [ˌdaʊn'ləʊdəbl] herunterladbar, zum Herunterladen IV
downstairs [ˌdaʊn'steəz] unten; nach unten I
downtown [ˌdaʊn'taʊn] (im/in das) Stadtzentrum IV • **the downtown bus** der Bus Richtung Stadtzentrum IV
°**drag on (-gg-)** [dræg] sich hinziehen
°**dragon boat** ['drægən bəʊt] Drachenboot • °**dragon boat racing** Drachenbootrennen
°**drain** [dreɪn]**: blood drains from sb.'s face** jd. wird blass
drama ['drɑːmə]
1. Schauspiel, darstellende Kunst I
2. Fernsehspiel; Drama IV
drank [dræŋk] *siehe* **drink**
draw [drɔː], **drew, drawn**
1. zeichnen III
2. draw conclusions Schlüsse ziehen, schlussfolgern IV
3. draw sb's attention to sth. jn. auf etwas aufmerksam machen; jemandes Aufmerksamkeit auf etwas lenken V 4 (88)
draw [drɔː] Unentschieden III
Our last match was a draw, 2–2. *(you say: two all)* Unser letztes Spiel war ein Unentschieden, 2:2. III
drawing ['drɔːɪŋ] Zeichnung III
drawn [drɔːn] *siehe* **draw**
dream [driːm] Traum I • **dream house** Traumhaus I
dream (of, about) [driːm] träumen (von) III
dreamer ['driːmə] Träumer/in V 2 (34)
°**Dreamtime** ['driːmtaɪm] *in der Mythologie der Aborigines die Zeit der Schöpfung*
dress [dres] Kleid I
dress [dres] sich kleiden; sich anziehen V 2 (40)

dress code ['dres kəʊd] Kleiderordnung IV
dressed [drest]: **get dressed** sich anziehen I
drew [dru:] *siehe* **draw**
°**drill instructor** ['drɪl_ɪn,strʌktə] Ausbilder/in *(beim Militär)*
drink [drɪŋk] Getränk I
drink [drɪŋk], **drank, drunk** trinken I
drinkable ['drɪŋkəbl] trinkbar, Trink- IV
drive [draɪv], **drove, driven** *(ein Auto / mit dem Auto)* fahren II
drive [draɪv] (Auto-)Fahrt III
driven ['drɪvn] *siehe* **drive**
driver ['draɪvə] Fahrer/in II
driving instructor ['draɪvɪŋ_ɪn,strʌktə] Fahrlehrer/in V 2 (32/176)
driving licence ['draɪvɪŋ ,laɪsns] Führerschein V 2 (38/179)
drop (-pp-) [drɒp]
1. fallen lassen I
2. drop sb. off jn. absetzen *(aussteigen lassen)* IV
drove [drəʊv] *siehe* **drive**
drug [drʌg] Droge, Rauschgift; Medikament IV • **be on drugs** *(gewohnheitsmäßig)* Drogen nehmen IV
drum [drʌm] Trommel III • **drums** *(pl)* [drʌmz] Schlagzeug III • **play the drums** Schlagzeug spielen III
drunk [drʌŋk] *siehe* **drink**
drunk [drʌŋk] betrunken IV
°**duck-billed platypus** [,dʌkbɪld 'plætɪpəs] Schnabeltier
dump sb. [dʌmp] mit jm. Schluss machen V 3 (51)
during *(prep)* ['djuərɪŋ] während IV
dustbin ['dʌstbɪn] Mülltonne II
DVD [,di: vi:' di:] DVD I

E

each [i:tʃ] jeder, jede, jedes (einzelne) I • **each other** [i:tʃ_'ʌðə] einander, sich (gegenseitig) III
°**eagle** ['i:gl] Adler
ear [ɪə] Ohr I
earache ['ɪəreɪk] Ohrenschmerzen II
early ['ɜ:li] früh I
earn [ɜ:n] verdienen IV
earring ['ɪərɪŋ] Ohrring I
earth [ɜ:θ] Erde IV • **on earth** auf der Erde IV
earthquake ['ɜ:θkweɪk] Erdbeben IV
east [i:st] Osten; nach Osten; östlich III
eastbound ['i:stbaʊnd] Richtung Osten III
Easter ['i:stə] Ostern; Oster- IV
easy ['i:zi] leicht, einfach I
easy-going [,i:zi'gəʊɪŋ] gelassen, locker III
eat [i:t], **ate, eaten** essen I
eaten ['i:tn] *siehe* **eat**
editor ['edɪtə] Redakteur/in III
education [,edʒʊ'keɪʃn] Bildung IV
°**e.g.** [,i:'dʒi:] *(from Latin: exempli gratia)* z.B.
egg [eg] Ei II
either ['aɪðə, 'i:ðə]: **not (...) either** auch nicht; auch kein V 1 (6)
elect sb. sth. [ɪ'lekt] jn. zu etwas wählen IV
election [ɪ'lekʃn] Wahl *(von Kandidaten bei einer Abstimmung)* IV
electric [ɪ'lektrɪk] elektrisch, Elektro- III
electricity [ɪ,lek'trɪsəti] Strom, Elektrizität III
electronic [ɪ,lek'trɒnɪk] elektronisch III
elementary school [,elɪ'mentri sku:l] *(USA) Grundschule für 6- bis 11-Jährige* IV
elephant ['elɪfənt] Elefant I
elevator ['elɪveɪtə] *(AE)* Fahrstuhl, Aufzug II
else [els]: **anything else** irgendetwas anderes IV • **anything else?** sonst noch etwas? IV • **anybody else?** ... sonst noch jemand? IV
somebody else jemand anders IV
somewhere else woanders IV
what else? was (sonst) noch? IV
who else? wen (sonst) noch? IV
e-mail, email ['i:meɪl] E-Mail I
embarrassed [ɪm'bærəst]: **I'm embarrassed.** Es ist mir peinlich. IV
empty ['empti] leer I
°**emu** ['i:mju:] Emu
enclose sth. [ɪn'kləʊz] etwas *(einem Brief)* beilegen V 2 (38)
end [end] enden; beenden III
end [end] Ende, Schluss I • **at the end (of)** am Ende (von) I • **in the end** schließlich, zum Schluss III
ending ['endɪŋ] Ende, (Ab-)Schluss *(einer Geschichte, eines Films usw.)* III
endless ['endləs] endlos IV
enemy ['enəmi] Feind/in II
energetic [,enə'dʒetɪk] aktiv, tatkräftig V 2 (35)
energy ['enədʒi] Energie V 2 (35/178)
engine ['endʒɪn] Motor IV • **search engine** Suchmaschine *(im Internet)* IV
engineer [,endʒɪ'nɪə] Ingenieur/in II
°**engineering** [,endʒɪ'nɪərɪŋ] Maschinenbau
English ['ɪŋglɪʃ] Englisch; englisch I
enjoy [ɪn'dʒɔɪ] genießen II • **Enjoy yourself.** Viel Spaß / Amüsier dich gut! III
enough [ɪ'nʌf] genug I
enter ['entə]
1. betreten; eintreten (in) III
2. eingeben *(Geheimzahl)* V 3 (53)
entry ['entri] Eintrag, Eintragung *(im Wörterbuch/Tagebuch)* III
equipment [ɪ'kwɪpmənt] Ausrüstung III
eraser [ɪ'reɪsər] *(AE)* Radiergummi IV
escape (from sb./sth.) [ɪ'skeɪp] fliehen (vor jm./aus etwas); entkommen III
especially [ɪ'speʃəli] besonders IV
essay (about, on) ['eseɪ] Aufsatz (über) I
etc. [et'setərə] und so weiter (usw.) IV
ethnic ['eθnɪk] ethnisch, Volks- IV
°**eucalyptus** [,ju:kə'lɪptəs] Eukalyptus
euro (€) ['jʊərəʊ] Euro I
even ['i:vn]
1. sogar II • **even if** sogar wenn IV
2. not even (noch) nicht einmal III
He didn't even open the letter. Er hat den Brief nicht einmal geöffnet. III
evening ['i:vnɪŋ] Abend I • **in the evening** abends, am Abend I
on Friday evening freitagabends, am Freitagabend I
event [ɪ'vent] Ereignis; Veranstaltung IV
ever? ['evə] je? / jemals? / schon mal? II
every ['evri] jeder, jede, jedes I
everybody ['evribɒdi] jeder, alle II
everyday *(adj)* ['evrideɪ] Alltags-; alltägliche(r, s) III
everyone ['evrɪwʌn] jeder, alle IV
everything ['evriθɪŋ] alles I
everywhere ['evriweə] überall III
exact [ɪg'zækt] exakt, genau IV
exactly [ɪg'zæktli] genau III
example [ɪg'zɑ:mpl] Beispiel III
for example zum Beispiel III
excellent ['eksələnt] ausgezeichnet, hervorragend IV
except [ɪk'sept] außer IV
exchange [ɪks'tʃeɪndʒ]: **exchange rate** Wechselkurs V 3 (53) • **exchange student** Austauschschüler/in III

excited [ɪk'saɪtɪd] begeistert, aufgeregt III
exciting [ɪk'saɪtɪŋ] aufregend, spannend I
Excuse me, ... [ɪk'skjuːz miː] Entschuldigung, ... / Entschuldigen Sie, ... I
exercise ['eksəsaɪz]
1. Übung, Aufgabe I
2. *(no pl)* (körperliche) Bewegung, Training IV
exercise book ['eksəsaɪz bʊk] Schulheft, Übungsheft I
expect [ɪk'spekt] erwarten III
expect sb. to do sth. von jm. erwarten, dass er/sie etwas tut V 2 (34/177)
► S.177 (to) ask/tell/expect/want sb. to do sth.
expensive [ɪk'spensɪv] teuer I
experience [ɪk'spɪəriəns] Erfahrung(en), Erlebnis IV • **in my experience** meiner Erfahrung nach; nach meiner Erfahrung IV
work experience *(no pl)* ['wɜːk‿ɪk,spɪəriəns] Praktikum; Arbeits-, Praxiserfahrung(en) V 2 (37)
do work experience ein Praktikum machen V 2 (37/179)
experience [ɪk'spɪəriəns] erfahren, erleben IV
explain sth. to sb. [ɪk'spleɪn] jm. etwas erklären, erläutern II
explanation [,eksplə'neɪʃn] Erklärung II
explore [ɪk'splɔː] erkunden, erforschen I
explorer [ɪk'splɔːrə] Entdecker/in, Forscher/in II
explosion [ɪk'spləʊʒn] Explosion IV
extra ['ekstrə] zusätzlich I
extracurricular activities (*kurz:* **extracurriculars)** [,ekstrəkə'rɪkjələz] *schulische Angebote außerhalb des regulären Unterrichts, oft als Arbeitsgemeinschaften* IV
eye [aɪ] Auge I

F

face [feɪs] Gesicht I • **face to face** von Angesicht zu Angesicht, persönlich V 3 (52)
fact [fækt] Tatsache, Fakt III
factory ['fæktri] Fabrik II
failure *(n)* ['feɪljə] ungenügend *(USA, Schulnote)* IV
fair [feə] fair, gerecht II
faithfully ['feɪθfəli]: **Yours faithfully** Mit freundlichen Grüßen *(Briefschluss bei namentlich unbekanntem Empfänger)* IV
fall [fɔːl], **fell, fallen** fallen, stürzen; hinfallen II • **fall down** hinfallen II • **fall in love (with sb.)** sich verlieben (in jn.) IV • **fall off** herunterfallen (von) II
°**fall** [fɔːl]: **the fall of the Wall** der Fall der Mauer *(in Berlin 1989)*
fallen ['fɔːlən] *siehe* **fall**
false [fɔːls] falsch IV
familiar [fə'mɪliə]: **be familiar with sth.** vertraut sein mit; sich auskennen mit V 4 (77)
family ['fæməli] Familie I • **family name** Nachname, Familienname V 2 (37) • **family tree** (Familien-)Stammbaum I
famous (for) ['feɪməs] berühmt (für, wegen) II
fan [fæn] Fan I
fancy sth. ['fænsi] Lust auf/zu etwas haben V 4 (84)
fantastic [fæn'tæstɪk] fantastisch, toll I
far [fɑː] weit (entfernt) II • **so far** bisher, bis jetzt IV
farm [fɑːm] Bauernhof, Farm II
farmer ['fɑːmə] Bauer/Bäuerin, Landwirt/in; (Fisch-)Züchter/in III
farmhouse ['fɑːmhaʊs] Farmhaus, Bauernhaus IV
farming ['fɑːmɪŋ] Landwirtschaft IV
fascinating ['fæsɪneɪtɪŋ] faszinierend V 4 (78)
fascination [,fæsɪ'neɪʃn] Faszination V 4 (78/188)
fashion ['fæʃn] Mode II • **fashion designer** ['fæʃn dɪ,zaɪnə] Modedesigner/in V 4 (81)
fashionable ['fæʃnəbl] modisch, schick V 4 (78)
fast [fɑːst] schnell II • **fast food** [,fɑːst 'fuːd] Fastfood III
fat [fæt] fett IV
father ['fɑːðə] Vater I
fault [fɔːlt]: **It's not my fault.** Es ist nicht meine Schuld. III
favour ['feɪvə]: **Would you do me a favour?** Würdest du mir einen Gefallen tun? IV
favourite ['feɪvərɪt] Lieblings- I **my favourite colour** meine Lieblingsfarbe I
favourite Liebling V 3 (63)
fear (of) [fɪə] Angst (vor) V 1 (21)
February ['februəri] Februar I
fed [fed] *siehe* **feed** • **be fed up (with sth.)** [,fed‿'ʌp] die Nase voll haben (von etwas) II
feed [fiːd], **fed, fed** füttern I
feel [fiːl], **felt, felt** sich fühlen; fühlen; sich anfühlen II • **Feel free to ask questions.** Ihr könnt jetzt gern Fragen stellen. V 4 (88) • **I feel sick.** Mir ist schlecht. IV • **I'm not feeling great.** Ich fühle mich nicht besonders wohl. V 4 (79)
feeling ['fiːlɪŋ] Gefühl III
feet [fiːt] *Plural von „foot"*
fell [fel] *siehe* **fall**
felt [felt] *siehe* **feel**
felt tip ['felt tɪp] Filzstift I
female ['fiːmeɪl] weiblich III
fence [fens] Zaun IV
ferry ['feri] Fähre III
festival ['festɪvl] Fest, Festival, Festspiele III
few [fjuː]: **a few** ein paar, einige II
fiction: science fiction [,saɪəns 'fɪkʃn] Sciencefiction V 1 (15)
fiddle ['fɪdl] *(infml)* Fiedel, Geige III
play the fiddle Geige spielen III
field [fiːld] Feld, Acker, Weide II
in the field auf dem Feld II
fight (for) [faɪt], **fought, fought** kämpfen (für, um) III
fight [faɪt] Kampf; Schlägerei IV
figure ['fɪgə] Zahl, Ziffer V 1 (10)
file [faɪl] **background file** *etwa:* Hintergrundinformation(en) II
grammar file *Grammatikanhang* I
skills file *Anhang mit Lern- und Arbeitstechniken* I • **sound file** Tondatei, Soundfile III
fill in [,fɪl‿'ɪn] ausfüllen; einsetzen V 2 (37)
film [fɪlm] Film I • **film director** Regisseur/in IV • **film review** Filmkritik, Filmbesprechung V 1 (19)
film star Filmstar I • **film studio** Filmstudio III • **action film** Actionfilm V 1 (15)
film [fɪlm] filmen III
film-maker ['fɪlmmeɪkə] Filmemacher/in III
final ['faɪnl] letzte(r, s); End- III
final score Endstand III
final ['faɪnl] Finale, Endspiel III
finally ['faɪnəli] zuletzt, als letztes V 3 (56)
financial [faɪ'nænʃl] finanziell, Finanz- V 4 (74)
find [faɪnd], **found, found** finden I
find out (about) herausfinden (über) I
finder ['faɪndə] Finder I
fine [faɪn]
1. gut, schön; in Ordnung II
2. *(gesundheitlich)* gut II
I'm/He's fine. Es geht mir/ihm gut. II

finger ['fɪŋgə] Finger I
finish ['fɪnɪʃ] beenden, zu Ende machen; enden I
fire ['faɪə] Feuer, Brand II • **fire safety** Verhalten im Brandfall IV **fire station** Feuerwache IV • **put out a fire** ein Feuer löschen IV
firefighter ['faɪəfaɪtə] Feuerwehrfrau, -mann IV
fireman/-woman ['faɪəmən, 'faɪə,wʊmən] Feuerwehrmann/-frau II
fireproof ['faɪəpru:f] feuerfest *(Tür)* V 1 (17/175)
first [fɜ:st]
1. erste(r, s) I
2. zuerst, als Erstes I
at first zuerst, am Anfang IV • **be first** der/die Erste sein I • **first aid** [,fɜ:st_'eɪd] Erste Hilfe V 2 (38)
first-aid kit Erste-Hilfe-Kasten, Verbandskasten V 4 (84/190) • **first floor** erster Stock *(BE)* / Erdgeschoss *(AE)* IV • **first half** erste Halbzeit III • **first name** Vorname V 2 (37)
fish [fɪʃ] fischen, angeln III
fish, *pl* **fish** [fɪʃ] Fisch I
°**fishbowl** ['fɪʃbəʊl] Fishbowl *(gesteuerte Diskussionsform)*
fist [fɪst] Faust IV
fit (-tt-) [fɪt] passen I • **fit in** hineinpassen; sich einfügen, sich anpassen IV
fit [fɪt] fit V 1 (13)
fitness ['fɪtnəs] Fitness IV • **fitness instructor** [ɪn'strʌktə] Fitnesstrainer/in V 2 (32)
flag [flæg] Flagge, Fahne V 1 (8)
flash [flæʃ] Lichtblitz III
flat [flæt] Wohnung I
flat [flæt] flach V 1 (16) • **flat screen** ['flæt skri:n] Flachbildschirm IV
flew [flu:] *siehe* **fly**
flight [flaɪt] Flug II • **a 14-hour flight** ein 14-stündiger Flug, ein 14-Stunden-Flug III
floor [flɔ:]
1. Fußboden I
2. Stock(werk) IV • **first floor** erster Stock *(BE)* / Erdgeschoss *(AE)* IV • **ground floor** *(BE)* Erdgeschoss IV • **on the second floor** im zweiten Stock *(BE)* / im ersten Stock *(AE)* IV
floppy hat ['flɒpi] Schlapphut V 4 (81)
°**flow chart** ['fləʊ tʃɑ:t] Flussdiagramm
flown [fləʊn] *siehe* **fly**
flu [flu:] Grippe V 4 (79)
flute [flu:t] Querflöte III

fly [flaɪ], **flew, flown** fliegen II
°**fly** [flaɪ] Fliege
fog [fɒg] Nebel II
foggy ['fɒgi] neblig II
folk (music) ['fəʊk ,mju:zɪk] Folk *(englische, schottische, irische oder nordamerikanische Volksmusik des 20. Jahrhunderts)* III
follow ['fɒləʊ] folgen; verfolgen I **follow the rules** Regeln befolgen V 3 (52)
°**following** ['fɒləʊɪŋ]: **the following ...** die folgenden ...
food [fu:d]
1. Essen; Lebensmittel I
2. Futter I
foot [fʊt], *pl* **feet** [fi:t] Fuß I; Fuß *(Längenmaß: 30,48 cm)* IV
football ['fʊtbɔ:l] Fußball I • **football boots** Fußballschuhe, -stiefel I
footstep ['fʊtstep] Schritt V 3 (64)
for [fə, fɔ:] für I • **for a while** für eine Weile, eine Zeit lang V 2 (45) **for breakfast/lunch/dinner** zum Frühstück/Mittagessen/Abendbrot I • **for example** zum Beispiel III **for lots of reasons** aus vielen Gründen I • **for miles** meilenweit II • **for sale** *(auf Schild)* zu verkaufen IV • **for the first time** zum ersten Mal IV • **for 20 minutes** seit 20 Minuten; 20 Minuten lang IV • **for three days** drei Tage (lang) I • **just for fun** nur zum Spaß I • **What for?** Wofür? II **What's for homework?** Was haben wir als Hausaufgabe auf? I
force [fɔ:s] zwingen, erzwingen V 4 (83)
foreground ['fɔ:graʊnd] Vordergrund II
foreign ['fɒrən] ausländisch, fremd IV • **foreign language** Fremdsprache IV
forest ['fɒrɪst] Wald II
forgave [fə'geɪv] *siehe* **forgive**
forget (-tt-) [fə'get], **forgot, forgotten** vergessen I
forgive [fə'gɪv], **forgave, forgiven** vergeben, verzeihen IV
forgiven [fə'gɪvn] *siehe* **forgive**
forgot [fə'gɒt] *siehe* **forget**
forgotten [fə'gɒtn] *siehe* **forget**
fork [fɔ:k] Gabel III
form [fɔ:m]
1. (Schul-)Klasse I • **form teacher** Klassenlehrer/in I
2. Formular V 2 (37)
°**form** [fɔ:m] bilden
°**formal letter** ['fɔ:ml] formeller/förmlicher Brief

fortunately ['fɔ:tʃənətli] zum Glück IV
forum ['fɔ:rəm] Forum V 2 (40)
forward ['fɔ:wəd]
°**1.** vorwärts
2. look forward to sth. sich auf etwas freuen IV
fought [fɔ:t] *siehe* **fight**
found [faʊnd] *siehe* **find**
found [faʊnd] gründen IV
fox [fɒks] Fuchs II
frame [freɪm] Rahmen; Gestell V 4 (77)
free [fri:]
1. frei I • **free time** Freizeit, freie Zeit I
2. kostenlos I
Feel free to ask questions. Ihr könnt jetzt gern Fragen stellen. V 4 (88)
freedom ['fri:dəm] Freiheit V 4 (81)
French [frentʃ] Französisch I
French fries *(AE)* [fraɪz] Pommes Frites IV
fresh [freʃ] frisch IV
Friday ['fraɪdeɪ, 'fraɪdi] Freitag I
fridge [frɪdʒ] Kühlschrank I
friend [frend] Freund/in I • **online friend** Internetfreund/in V 1 (12)
friendliness ['frendlinəs] Freundlichkeit IV
friendly ['frendli] freundlich III
fries [fraɪz]: **French fries** *(AE)* Pommes Frites IV
frog [frɒg] Frosch II
from [frəm, frɒm]
1. aus I
2. von I
from all over the UK/the world/England aus dem gesamten Vereinigten Königreich / aus der ganzen Welt / aus ganz England III
from Monday to Friday von Montag bis Freitag III • **I'm from ...** Ich komme aus ... / Ich bin aus ... I
Where are you from? Wo kommst du her?
front [frʌnt]: **in front of** vor *(räumlich)* I • **front door** [,frʌnt 'dɔ:] Wohnungstür, Haustür I
fruit [fru:t] Obst, Früchte; Frucht I
fruit salad ['fru:t ,sæləd] Obstsalat I
fruity ['fru:ti] fruchtig V 4 (82)
full [fʊl] voll I
fully ['fʊli]: **fully booked** ausgebucht V 4 (86)
fun [fʌn] Spaß I • **have fun** Spaß haben, sich amüsieren I • **Have fun!** Viel Spaß! I • **just for fun** nur zum Spaß I • **Riding is fun.** Reiten macht Spaß. I

funeral ['fju:nərəl] Trauerfeier, Beerdigung V 3 (51)
funny ['fʌni] witzig, komisch I
future ['fju:tʃə] Zukunft; Zukunfts-, zukünftig V 2 (32)

G

°**gallery** ['gæləri] (Bilder-)Galerie
game [geɪm] Spiel I
gang [gæŋ] Gang, (Jugend-)Bande V 3 (57)
gangster ['gæŋstə] Gangster/in V 4 (81)
garage ['gærɑ:ʒ]
1. Garage II
2. Autowerkstatt V 2 (33)
garbage ['gɑ:rbɪdʒ] *(AE)* Müll, Abfall IV
garden ['gɑ:dn] Garten I
gardener ['gɑ:dnə] Gärtner/in IV
gas [gæs]
1. Gas IV
2. *(AE)* Benzin IV • **gas station** *(AE)* Tankstelle IV
gate [geɪt]
1. Tor III
2. Flugsteig III
°**gateway (to)** ['geɪtweɪ] Tor (zu), Zugang (zu)
gave [geɪv] *siehe* **give**
°**Gazette** [gə'zet] Blatt, Anzeiger
°**GCSE (General Certificate of Secondary Education)** [sə'tɪfɪkət] *Schulabschlussprüfungen für 16-Jährige in England, Wales und Nordirland, vergleichbar der mittleren Reife oder der Fachoberschulreife*
gear [gɪə] Ausrüstung IV
°**geek** [gi:k] Freak
general ['dʒenrəl] allgemeine(r,s) III
generally ['dʒenrəli] allgemein, im Allgemeinen, generell V 3 (50)
generation [,dʒenə'reɪʃn] Generation V 1 (17) • °**Y generation** *Generation, die nach 1980 geboren wurde*
geography [dʒi'ɒgrəfi] Geografie, Erdkunde I
German ['dʒɜ:mən] Deutsch; deutsch; Deutsche(r) I
Germany ['dʒɜ:məni] Deutschland I
get (-tt-) [get], **got, got**
1. bekommen, kriegen II
2. holen, besorgen II
3. gelangen, (hin)kommen I
4. **get angry/hot/...** wütend/heiß/... werden II
5. **get dressed** [drest] sich anziehen I
6. **get off (the train/bus)** (aus dem Zug/Bus) aussteigen I • **get on (the train/bus)** (in den Zug/Bus) einsteigen I
7. **get up** aufstehen I
get a cab ein Taxi nehmen IV
get involved sich engagieren (für, bei); sich beteiligen (an) IV • **get on well/badly with sb.** sich gut/schlecht mit jm. verstehen IV
get ready (for) sich fertig machen (für), sich vorbereiten (auf) I
°**Get real!** *(infml)* Komm auf den Boden! / Werd vernünftig! • **get sth. off the ground** etwas auf den Weg bringen; etwas auf die Beine stellen III • **get things ready** Dinge fertig machen, vorbereiten I
get to know sb. jn. kennenlernen IV
getting by in English [,getɪŋ 'baɪ] *etwa:* auf Englisch zurechtkommen I
ghost [gəʊst] Geist, Gespenst II
gig [gɪg] *(infml)* Gig, Auftritt III
do a gig einen Auftritt haben, ein Konzert geben III
giraffe [dʒə'rɑ:f] Giraffe II
girl [gɜ:l] Mädchen I
girlfriend ['gɜ:lfrend] (feste) Freundin IV
give [gɪv], **gave, given** geben I
give a talk (on sth.) einen Vortrag/eine Rede halten (über etwas) V 4 (88/191) • **give sth. up** auf etwas verzichten V 3 (50) • **give up** aufgeben, resignieren IV
given ['gɪvn] *siehe* **give**
glad [glæd] froh, dankbar III
glamorous ['glæmərəs] glamourös V 4 (78)
glass [glɑ:s] Glas I • **a glass of water** ein Glas Wasser I
glasses *(pl)* ['glɑ:sɪz] (eine) Brille I
glue [glu:] (auf-, ein)kleben II
glue [glu:] Klebstoff I • **glue stick** Klebestift I
go [gəʊ], **went, gone** gehen I; fahren II • **go by** vergehen, vorübergehen *(Zeit)* V 3 (51) • **go by car/train/bike/...** mit dem Auto/Zug/Rad/... fahren II • **go for a walk** spazieren gehen, einen Spaziergang machen II • **go home** nach Hause gehen I • **go on** 1. weitermachen I, 2. weiterreden III • **Go on.** Mach/Erzähl weiter. I • **go on a trip** einen Ausflug machen II
go on holiday in Urlaub fahren II
go red rot werden, erröten V 3 (62)
go riding reiten gehen I • **go shopping** einkaufen gehen I • **go sightseeing** auf Sightseeingtour gehen, sich Sehenswürdigkeiten ansehen V 4 (74) • **go swimming** schwimmen gehen I • **go to bed** ins Bett gehen I • **go to the cinema** ins Kino gehen II • **go together** zusammenpassen, -gehören II • **go well** gut (ver)laufen, gutgehen III • **go with** gehören zu, passen zu III • **go out with sb.** mit jm. gehen *(als Freund/in)* V 3 (50) • **coffee to go** Kaffee zum Mitnehmen IV • **Let's go.** Auf geht's! I
goal [gəʊl] Tor *(im Sport)* III • **score a goal** ein Tor schießen, einen Treffer erzielen III
goalkeeper ['gəʊlki:pə] Torwart, Torfrau III
gold [gəʊld] Gold IV
golden ['gəʊldən] goldene(r,s) IV
golf [gɒlf] Golf III
gone [gɒn] *siehe* **go**
good [gʊd]
1. gut I
2. brav II
Good afternoon. Guten Tag. *(nachmittags)* I • **Good luck (with ...)!** Viel Glück (bei/mit ...)! I
Good morning. Guten Morgen. I
Good to have you back. Schön, dass du wieder da bist. IV • **be good at sth.** gut in etwas sein; etwas gut können III
Goodbye. [,gʊd'baɪ] Auf Wiedersehen. I • **say goodbye** sich verabschieden I
got [gɒt] *siehe* **get**
got [gɒt]: **I've got ...** Ich habe ... I
I haven't got a chair. Ich habe keinen Stuhl. I
government ['gʌvənmənt] Regierung IV
governor ['gʌvənə] Gouverneur/in *(Oberhaupt eines US-Bundesstaates)* IV
grab sth. (-bb-) [græb] sich etwas schnappen IV
grade [greɪd]
1. Klasse, Jahrgangsstufe IV
2. (Schul-)Note, Zensur IV
°**graduate** *(AE)* ['grædʒueɪt] den Schulabschluss machen *(an einer amerikanischen Highschool)*
graffiti [grə'fi:ti] Graffiti V 3 (54)
grammar ['græmə] Grammatik I
grammar file *Grammatikanhang* I
grand [grænd] eindrucksvoll, beeindruckend IV
grandad ['grændæd] Opa III
grandchild ['græntʃaɪld], *pl* **grandchildren** Enkel/in I

grandfather ['grænfɑːðə] Großvater I
grandma ['grænmɑː] Oma I
grandmother ['grænmʌðə] Großmutter I
grandpa ['grænpɑː] Opa I
grandparents ['grænpeərənts] Großeltern I
granny ['græni] Oma II
grape [greɪp] Weintraube IV
°**graph: suspense graph** [sə'spens grɑːf] Spannungskurve
grass [grɑːs] Gras, Rasen IV • **cut the grass** Rasen mähen IV
great [greɪt] großartig, toll I
great-grandfather [ˌgreɪt 'grænfɑːðə] Urgroßvater III
great-grandmother [ˌgreɪt 'grænmʌðə] Urgroßmutter III
greedy ['griːdi] gierig, habgierig V 2 (46)
green [griːn] grün I
grew [gruː] *siehe* **grow**
grey [greɪ] grau II
°**groan** [grəʊn] stöhnen
ground [graʊnd] (Erd-)Boden III
ground floor *(BE)* Erdgeschoss IV
get sth. off the ground etwas auf den Weg bringen; etwas auf die Beine stellen III
grounded ['graʊndɪd]: **be grounded** Ausgehverbot/Hausarrest haben III
group [gruːp] Gruppe I • **group word** Oberbegriff II
grow [grəʊ], **grew, grown**
1. *(Getreide usw.)* anbauen, anpflanzen II
2. grow up [ˌgrəʊ‿'ʌp] erwachsen werden; aufwachsen III
grown [grəʊn] *siehe* **grow**
grumble ['grʌmbl] murren, nörgeln I
°**guard** [gɑːd] Wächter/in
guess [ges] raten, erraten, schätzen III • **Guess what!** [ˌges 'wɒt] Stell dir vor! / Stellt euch vor! IV
guest [gest] Gast I
guide [gaɪd]: **(tour) guide** (Fremden-)Führer/in, Reiseleiter/in IV
guilty ['gɪlti] schuldbewusst; schuldig IV
guinea pig ['gɪni pɪg] Meerschweinchen I
guitar [gɪ'tɑː] Gitarre I • **play the guitar** Gitarre spielen I
°**Gujarati** [ˌguːdʒə'rɑːti] Gujarati *(in Gujarat, Indien, gesprochene Sprache)*
gun [gʌn] Gewehr IV
guy [gaɪ] *(infml)* Typ, Kerl IV
guys *(pl)* [gaɪz] *(AE, infml)* Leute III

gym [dʒɪm] Sporthalle, Turnhalle; Fitnessstudio IV

H

had [hæd] *siehe* **have** *und* **have got**
hair *(no pl)* [heə] Haar, Haare I
hairdresser ['heədresə] Friseur/in III
hairy ['heəri] haarig, behaart V 4 (82)
half [hɑːf], *pl* **halves** [hɑːvz] Hälfte III • **first half** erste Halbzeit III
half of ... die Hälfte der/des ... IV
half [hɑːf]: **half an hour** eine halbe Stunde III • **half past 11** halb zwölf (11.30/23.30) I • **three and a half days** dreieinhalb Tage IV
half-pipe ['hɑːfpaɪp] Halfpipe III
half-time [ˌhɑːf 'taɪm] Halbzeit(pause) III
hall [hɔːl] Flur, Diele I • **study hall** ['stʌdɪ hɔːl] *Zeit zum selbstständigen Arbeiten/Lernen in der Schule* IV
halves [hɑːvz] *Plural von „half"*
hamburger ['hæmbɜːgə] Hamburger I
hamster ['hæmstə] Hamster I
hand [hænd] Hand I
handball ['hændbɔːl] Handball III
hang [hæŋ], **hung, hung:**
Hang on. Einen Augenblick. / Sofort. / *(am Telefon)* Bleiben Sie dran. V 3 (53) • **hang out (with friends)** *(infml)* rumhängen, abhängen (mit Freunden/Freundinnen) III • **hang up** *(den Telefonhörer)* auflegen V 3 (62)
happen (to) ['hæpən] geschehen, passieren (mit) I
happiness ['hæpinəs] Glück IV
happy ['hæpi] glücklich, froh I
Happy birthday. Herzlichen Glückwunsch zum Geburtstag. I
happy ending Happyend II • **be happy to do sth.** gern bereit sein, etwas zu tun V 2 (38)
harbour ['hɑːbə] Hafen II
hard [hɑːd] hart; schwer, schwierig II • **work hard** hart arbeiten II
hard-working [ˌhɑːd 'wɜːkɪŋ] fleißig, tüchtig III
hat [hæt] Hut II
hate [heɪt] hassen, gar nicht mögen I
have [həv, hæv], **had, had** haben, besitzen II • **have a baby** ein Baby/Kind bekommen II • **have a bath** baden, ein Bad nehmen II
have a cold erkältet sein, eine Erkältung haben II • **have a crush on sb.** in jn. verknallt sein III
Have a good holiday. Schöne Ferien! V 4 (86) • **Have a good time.** Viel Spaß! V 4 (86) • **have a look at sth.** sich etwas ansehen, einen Blick werfen auf etwas IV • **have a picnic** ein Picknick machen I
have a sauna in die Sauna gehen II • **have a shower** (sich) duschen I • **have a sore throat** Halsschmerzen haben II • **have a temperature** Fieber haben II • **have breakfast/dinner** frühstücken / Abendbrot essen I • **have ... for breakfast** zum Frühstück essen/trinken I • **have fun** Spaß haben, sich amüsieren I • **have sleepovers** Schlafpartys veranstalten III • **have to do** tun müssen I
Good to have you back. Schön, dass du wieder da bist. IV
► S.190 Have a ...
have got: I've got ... [aɪv 'gɒt] Ich habe ... I • **I haven't got a chair.** Ich habe keinen Stuhl. I
he [hiː] er I
head [hed] Kopf I • **head teacher** Schulleiter/in III
headache ['hedeɪk] Kopfschmerzen II
heading ['hedɪŋ] Überschrift, Titel IV
headless ['hedləs] kopflos IV
headline ['hedlaɪn] Schlagzeile IV
headphones *(pl)* ['hedfəʊnz] Kopfhörer III
health [helθ] Gesundheit IV
healthy ['helθi] gesund II
hear [hɪə], **heard, heard** hören I
heard [hɜːd] *siehe* **hear**
heart [hɑːt] Herz II
heaven ['hevn] Himmel *(im religiösen Sinn)* IV
hedgehog ['hedʒhɒg] Igel II
held [held] *siehe* **hold**
helicopter ['helɪkɒptə] Hubschrauber, Helikopter II
Hello. [hə'ləʊ] Hallo. / Guten Tag. I
helmet ['helmɪt] Helm III
help [help] helfen I • **Can I help you?** Kann ich Ihnen helfen? / Was kann ich für Sie tun? *(im Laden)* I
help [help] Hilfe I
helpful ['helpfl]
1. nützlich, hilfreich IV
2. hilfsbereit V 4 (76)
helpless ['helpləs] hilflos IV
her [hə, hɜː]
1. ihr, ihre I
2. sie; ihr I

here [hɪə]
1. hier I
2. hierher I
Here you are. Bitte sehr. / Hier bitte. I
hero ['hɪərəʊ] Held/in; Idol, Vorbild V 4 (80)
hers [hɜːz] ihrer, ihre, ihrs II
herself [hə'self, hɜː'self] sich (selbst) III
Hi! [haɪ] Hallo! I • **Say hi to Dilip for me.** Grüß Dilip von mir. I
°**hickory** ['hɪkəri] Hickorynussbaum (*nordamerikanischer Walnussbaum*)
hid [hɪd] *siehe* **hide**
hidden ['hɪdn] *siehe* **hide**
hide [haɪd], **hid, hidden** verstecken; sich verstecken I
high [haɪ] hoch III
highlight ['haɪlaɪt] Highlight V 4 (88)
high school ['haɪ skuːl] *(USA)* Schule für 14- bis 18-Jährige IV
highway ['haɪweɪ] *(USA) Fernstraße (oft mit vier oder mehr Spuren)* IV
hijacker ['haɪdʒækə] (Flugzeug-)Entführer/in IV
hike [haɪk] wandern IV
hike [haɪk] Wanderung, Marsch IV • **go on a hike** wandern gehen IV
hill [hɪl] Hügel II
hilly ['hɪli] hügelig III
him [hɪm] ihn; ihm I
himself [hɪm'self] sich (selbst) III
°**Hindi** ['hɪndi] Hindi
Hindu ['hɪnduː] Hindu; Hindu- V 4 (77)
hip hop ['hɪp hɒp] Hip Hop III
hippo ['hɪpəʊ] Flusspferd II
his [hɪz]
1. sein, seine I
2. seiner, seine, seins II
historical [hɪ'stɒrɪkl] geschichtlich, historisch V 1 (8)
history ['hɪstri] Geschichte I
hit (-tt-) [hɪt] **hit, hit** schlagen II
hit [hɪt] Hit III
hobby ['hɒbi] Hobby I
hockey ['hɒki] Hockey I • **hockey shoes** Hockeyschuhe I
hold [həʊld], **held, held**
1. halten II
2. veranstalten, abhalten *(Veranstaltung, Wettbewerb)* V 3 (58)
3. **hold on (to sth.)** sich festhalten (an etwas) V 4 (77)
hole [həʊl] Loch IV
holiday ['hɒlədeɪ]
1. Feiertag IV
2. **holiday(s)** Ferien I
holiday flat Ferienwohnung II
be on holiday in Urlaub sein; Ferien haben/machen II • **go on holiday** in Urlaub fahren II
a two-week holiday ein zweiwöchiger Urlaub III • **Have a good holiday.** Schöne Ferien! V 4 (86)
► S.190 Have a ...
home [həʊm] Heim, Zuhause I
at home daheim, zu Hause I
°**children's home** Kinderheim
come home nach Hause kommen I • **get home** nach Hause kommen I • **go home** nach Hause gehen I • **old people's home** Alten-, Seniorenheim V 3 (63)
homeless ['həʊmləs] obdachlos IV
homelessness ['həʊmləsnəs] Obdachlosigkeit V 4 (78)
hometown ['həʊmtaʊn] Heimatstadt, -ort IV
homework *(no pl)* ['həʊmwɜːk] Hausaufgabe(n) I • **do homework** die Hausaufgabe(n) machen I
What's for homework? Was haben wir als Hausaufgabe auf? I
honest ['ɒnɪst] ehrlich V 1 (24)
°**honour** ['ɒnə] ehren
Hooray! [hu'reɪ] Hurra! II
hop channels [ˌhɒp 'tʃænəlz] zappen IV
hope [həʊp] hoffen II
hope [həʊp] Hoffnung III
horrible ['hɒrəbl] scheußlich, grauenhaft II
horse [hɔːs] Pferd I
hospital ['hɒspɪtl] Krankenhaus II
hostel ['hɒstl] Herberge, Wohnheim III
hot [hɒt] heiß I • **hot chocolate** heiße Schokolade I
hotel [həʊ'tel] Hotel II
hotline ['hɒtlaɪn] Hotline II
hour ['aʊə] Stunde II • **half an hour** eine halbe Stunde III • **a 14-hour flight** ein 14-stündiger Flug, ein 14-Stunden-Flug III • **a 24-hour supermarket** ein Supermarkt, der 24 Stunden geöffnet ist III
hours *(pl)* ['aʊəz]
1. Öffnungszeiten IV
2. **work long hours** lange arbeiten V 2 (33)
house [haʊs] Haus I • **at the Shaws' house** im Haus der Shaws / bei den Shaws zu Hause I
how [haʊ] wie I • **How about ...?** Wie wär's mit ...? III • **How am I doing?** Wie komme ich voran? *(Wie sind meine Fortschritte?)* III
How are you? Wie geht es dir/ Ihnen/euch? II • **How are you doing?** Wie geht's? V 1 (15) • **How do you know ...?** Woher weißt/ kennst du ...? I • **how long?** seit wann? / wie lange? IV • **how many?** wie viele? I • **how much?** wie viel? I • **How much is/are ...?** Was kostet/kosten ...? / Wie viel kostet/kosten ...? I • **How old are you?** Wie alt bist du? I • **how to do sth.** wie man etwas tut / tun kann / tun soll IV • **How was ...?** Wie war ...? I
huge [hjuːdʒ] riesig, sehr groß III
human ['hjuːmən] Menschen-, menschlich IV
hundred ['hʌndrəd] hundert I
hung [hʌŋ] *siehe* **hang**
hungry ['hʌŋgri] hungrig III
I'm hungry. Ich habe Hunger III
hunt [hʌnt] jagen III
hunt [hʌnt] Jagd III
hurry ['hʌri] eilen; sich beeilen II
hurry up sich beeilen I
hurry ['hʌri]: **be in a hurry** in Eile sein, es eilig haben I
hurt [hɜːt], **hurt, hurt** wehtun; verletzen I
hurt [hɜːt] verletzt II
husband ['hʌzbənd] Ehemann II
hutch [hʌtʃ] (Kaninchen-)Stall I

I

I [aɪ] ich I • **I'm** [aɪm] ich bin I
I'm from ... Ich komme aus ... / Ich bin aus ... I • **I'm sorry.** Tut mir leid. / Entschuldigung. I
ice [aɪs]: **ice cream** (Speise-)Eis I
ice hockey Eishockey III • **ice rink** Schlittschuhbahn II
icy ['aɪsi] eisig V 4 (82)
idea [aɪ'dɪə] Idee, Einfall I
ideal [aɪ'diːəl] ideal V 3 (48)
if [ɪf]
1. falls, wenn II
2. ob II
as if als ob IV • **even if** sogar wenn IV
ill [ɪl] krank II
illegal [ɪ'liːgl] illegal, ungesetzlich IV
illness ['ɪlnəs] Krankheit IV
°**imaginary journey** [ɪ'mædʒɪnəri] Phantasiereise
imagination [ɪˌmædʒɪ'neɪʃn] Fantasie, Vorstellung IV
imagine sth. [ɪ'mædʒɪn] sich etwas vorstellen III
immediately [ɪ'miːdiətli] sofort IV

immigrant ['ɪmɪgrənt] Einwanderer/Einwanderin IV
important (to) [ɪm'pɔ:tnt] wichtig (für) II
impossible [ɪm'pɒsəbl] unmöglich II
impress [ɪm'pres] beeindrucken V 2 (40)
impressed [ɪm'prest] beeindruckt IV
impressive [ɪm'presɪv] beeindruckend, eindrucksvoll V 4 (80)
improve [ɪm'pru:v] verbessern IV
in [ɪn] in I • **in ... Street** in der ...straße I • **in danger** in Gefahr V 1 (9) • **in English** auf Englisch I **in front of** vor *(räumlich)* I • **in here** hier drinnen I • **in the afternoon** nachmittags, am Nachmittag I • **in the country** auf dem Land II • **in the end** schließlich, zum Schluss III • **in the evening** abends, am Abend I • **in the field** auf dem Feld II • **in the morning** am Morgen, morgens I **in the photo** auf dem Foto I • **in the picture** auf dem Bild I • **in the world** (auf) der Welt IV • **in the yard** auf dem Hof II • **in time** rechtzeitig II • **in 1919** 1919, im Jahre 1919 IV
independent [ˌɪndɪ'pendənt] unabhängig V 1 (8)
indoor ['ɪndɔ:] *(nur vor Nomen)* Hallen-; im Gebäude V 4 (80) • **indoor market** Markthalle V 4 (80/189) **indoor swimming pool** Hallenbad V 4 (80/189) • **indoor toilet** Innentoilette V 4 (80)
▸ S.189 indoor – outdoor
indoors [ˌɪn'dɔ:z] drinnen, nach drinnen V 1 (9/171)
industrial [ɪn'dʌstriəl] industriell, Industrie- IV
industry ['ɪndəstri] Industrie IV
infinitive [ɪn'fɪnətɪv] Infinitiv *(Grundform des Verbs)* I
information (about/on) *(no pl)* [ˌɪnfə'meɪʃn] Information(en) (über) II
ink [ɪŋk] Tinte V 2 (37)
inside [ˌɪn'saɪd]
1. innen (drin), drinnen I
2. nach drinnen II
3. innerhalb IV
4. **inside the car** ins Auto (hinein), ins Innere des Autos II
install [ɪn'stɔ:l] installieren, einrichten II
instant messages *(pl)* [ˌɪnstənt 'mesɪdʒɪz] *Nachrichten, die man im Internet austauscht (in Echtzeit)* III
instructions *(pl)* [ɪn'strʌkʃnz]
1. (Gebrauchs-)Anweisung(en), Anleitung(en) II
°2. Hinweise zur Einnahme *(bei Medikamenten)*
instructor [ɪn'strʌktə] Lehrer/in, Trainer/in V 2 (32) • **driving instructor** Fahrlehrer/in V 2 (32/176) **fitness instructor** Fitnesstrainer/in V 2 (32/176) • **ski instructor** Skilehrer/in V 2 (32/176)
instrument ['ɪnstrəmənt] Instrument III
interest (in) ['ɪntrəst] Interesse (an) V 2 (36)
interested ['ɪntrəstɪd]: **be interested (in)** interessiert sein (an), sich interessieren (für) III
interesting ['ɪntrəstɪŋ] interessant I
international [ˌɪntə'næʃnəl] international III
internet ['ɪntənet] Internet III • **on the internet** im Internet IV • **surf the internet** im Internet surfen III
interview ['ɪntəvju:]
1. Interview I
2. **(job) interview** Vorstellungsgespräch, Bewerbungsgespräch V 2 (40)
interview ['ɪntəvju:] interviewen, befragen II
interviewer ['ɪntəvju:ə] Interviewer/in, Befrager/in V 2 (41)
into ['ɪntə, 'ɪntʊ] in ... (hinein) I
introduce [ˌɪntrə'dju:s]
1. **introduce sb. to sb.** jn. jm. vorstellen; jn. mit jm. bekanntmachen V 1 (15)
▸ S.173 Introducing people
2. **introduce sth.** etwas einführen *(Thema, Mode, Methode)* V 4 (88)
introduction (to) [ˌɪntrə'dʌkʃn] Einführung (in) III
invitation (to) [ˌɪnvɪ'teɪʃn] Einladung (zu) I
invite (to) [ɪn'vaɪt] einladen (zu) I
involved [ɪn'vɒlvd]: **get involved** sich engagieren (für, bei); sich beteiligen (an) IV
is [ɪz] ist I
island ['aɪlənd] Insel II
°**issue** ['ɪʃu:] (Streit-)Frage, Thema, Angelegenheit
it [ɪt] er/sie/es I • **It's £1.** Er/Sie/Es kostet 1 Pfund. I • **It says here: ...** Hier steht: ... / Es heißt hier: ... II
its [ɪts] sein/seine; ihr/ihre I
itself [ɪt'self] sich (selbst) III

J

jacket ['dʒækɪt] Jacke, Jackett II **rainproof jacket** ['reɪnpru:f] regendichte Jacke V 1 (17/175) • **weatherproof jacket** ['weðəpru:f] wetterfeste Jacke V 1 (17/175) • **windproof jacket** ['wɪndpru:f] winddichte Jacke V 1 (17/175)
jail [dʒeɪl] Gefängnis IV
jam: traffic jam ['træfɪk dʒæm] (Verkehrs-)Stau IV
January ['dʒænjuəri] Januar I
jazz [dʒæz] Jazz III
jealous (of) ['dʒeləs] neidisch (auf); eifersüchtig (auf) III
jealousy ['dʒeləsi] Eifersucht IV
jeans *(pl)* [dʒi:nz] Jeans I
Jewish ['dʒu:ɪʃ] jüdisch IV
job [dʒɒb] Aufgabe, Job I • **job interview** Vorstellungsgespräch, Bewerbungsgespräch V 2 (40) °**job profile** Anforderungsprofil, Tätigkeitsprofil
jobless ['dʒɒbləs] arbeitslos IV
join sb. [dʒɔɪn] sich jm. anschließen; bei jm. mitmachen II
joke [dʒəʊk] Witz I
joke [dʒəʊk] scherzen, Witze machen II
journalist ['dʒɜ:nəlɪst] Journalist/in IV
journey ['dʒɜ:ni] Fahrt, Reise III **Have a good journey.** Gute Reise! V 4 (86)
judge (by) [dʒʌdʒ] beurteilen, einschätzen (nach) IV
judo ['dʒu:dəʊ] Judo I • **do judo** Judo machen I
jug [dʒʌg] Krug I • **a jug of milk** ein Krug Milch I
juice [dʒu:s] Saft I
juicy ['dʒu:si] saftig V 4 (82)
July [dʒu'laɪ] Juli I
jumble sale ['dʒʌmbl seɪl] Wohltätigkeitsbasar I
jump [dʒʌmp] springen II • **jump around** herumspringen III
June [dʒu:n] Juni I
junior ['dʒu:niə] Junioren-, Jugend- I
just [dʒʌst]
1. (einfach) nur, bloß I • **It's just a game.** Es ist nur/bloß ein Spiel. III
2. einfach III • **I just can't find my keys.** Ich kann einfach meine Schlüssel nicht finden. III • **Just don't listen to them.** Hör einfach nicht hin. III
3. gerade (eben), soeben II • **just then** genau in dem Moment / gerade dann III

4. just as ... as genauso ... wie V 1 (16)
5. just like your mother genau wie deine Mutter III

K

kangaroo [ˌkæŋgə'ruː] Känguru II
keep [kiːp], **kept, kept** (be)halten; aufbewahren III • **keep in touch** in Verbindung bleiben, Kontakt halten III • **keep sth. warm/cool/open/...** etwas warm/kühl/offen/... halten II
kept [kept] *siehe* **keep**
ketchup ['ketʃəp] Ketschup V 3 (58)
key [kiː] Schlüssel II • **key ring** Schlüsselring II • **key word** Stichwort, Schlüsselwort I
keyboard ['kiːbɔːd] Keyboard *(elektronisches Tasteninstrument)* III
kick [kɪk] treten IV
kid [kɪd] Kind, Jugendliche(r) I
kill [kɪl] töten I
kilogram (kg) ['kɪləgræm], **kilo** ['kiːləʊ] Kilogramm, Kilo (kg) III
a 150-kilogram bear ein 150 Kilogramm schwerer Bär III
kilometre (km) ['kɪləmiːtə] Kilometer III • **a ten-kilometre walk** eine Zehn-Kilometer-Wanderung III
kind [kaɪnd] freundlich, nett V 1 (24)
kind (of) [kaɪnd] Art III • **What kind of car ...?** Was für ein Auto ...? III
kindergarten ['kɪndəgɑːtn] Kindergarten; *(USA)* Vorschule *(für 5- bis 6-Jährige)* IV
king [kɪŋ] König I
kingdom: the United Kingdom (UK) [juˌnaɪtɪd 'kɪŋdəm, juː'keɪ] das Vereinigte Königreich III
kiss [kɪs] Kuss IV
kiss [kɪs] küssen IV
kit [kɪt] Ausrüstung V 4 (84) • **first-aid kit** Erste-Hilfe-Kasten, Verbandskasten V 4 (84/190) • **repair kit** Flickzeug V 4 (84/190) • **survival kit** Überlebenspäckchen V 4 (84)
kitchen ['kɪtʃɪn] Küche I
kite [kaɪt] Drachen I
kiwi ['kiːwiː] Kiwi II
knee [niː] Knie I
knew [njuː] *siehe* **know**
knife [naɪf], *pl* **knives** [naɪvz] Messer III
knock [nɒk] Klopfen V 3 (63)
knock (at/on sth.) [nɒk] (an etwas) klopfen V 3 (63/186)
know [nəʊ], **knew, known**
1. wissen I
2. kennen I
know about sth. von etwas wissen; über etwas Bescheid wissen II • **get to know** kennenlernen IV • **How do you know ...?** Woher weißt du ...? / Woher kennst du ...? I • **I don't know.** Ich weiß es nicht. I • **I'll let you know.** Ich gebe dir/Ihnen Bescheid V 2 (41) • **..., you know.** ..., wissen Sie. / ..., weißt du. I • **You know what, Sophie?** Weißt du was, Sophie? I
known [nəʊn]
1. *siehe* **know**
2. bekannt IV
koala [kəʊ'ɑːlə] Koala V 1 (6)
°**kwaito** ['kwaɪtəʊ] *südafrikanische Popmusik zum Tanzen, Text meist eher gesprochen als gesungen*

L

°**label** ['leɪbl] beschriften, etikettieren
°**label** ['leɪbl] Firmenmarke, Etikett
laid [leɪd] *siehe* **lay the table**
lain [leɪn] *siehe* **lie**
lake [leɪk] (Binnen-)See II
lamb [læm] Lamm(fleisch) III
lamp [læmp] Lampe I
land [lænd] landen II
land [lænd] Land, Grund und Boden II
landscape ['lændskeɪp] Landschaft V 1 (16)
lane [leɪn] Gasse, Weg III
language ['læŋgwɪdʒ] Sprache I
foreign language Fremdsprache IV
laptop ['læptɒp] Laptop V 1 (12)
large [lɑːdʒ] groß II
lasagne [lə'zænjə] Lasagne I
last [lɑːst] letzte(r, s) I • **the last day** der letzte Tag I • **at last** endlich, schließlich I
last (for) [lɑːst] dauern IV
late [leɪt] spät; zu spät I • **be late** zu spät sein/kommen I • **Sorry, I'm late.** Entschuldigung, dass ich zu spät bin/komme. I
later ['leɪtə] später I
latest ['leɪtɪst] neueste(r, s) III
laugh [lɑːf] lachen I • **laugh at sb.** jn. auslachen IV
laughable ['lɑːfəbl] lächerlich IV
laughter ['lɑːftə] Gelächter II
°**lavatory** ['lævətri] *(veraltet oder gehoben)* Toilette
law [lɔː] Gesetz IV
lay [leɪ] *siehe* **lie**
lay the table [leɪ], **laid, laid** den Tisch decken I
°**layer: ozone layer** ['əʊzəʊn ˌleɪə] Ozonschicht
°**layout** ['leɪaʊt] Layout, Anordnung, Aufbau
leader ['liːdə] Leiter/in, (An-)Führer/in III
leaf [liːf], *pl* **leaves** [liːvz] Blatt *(an Pflanzen)* V 1 (11)
lean out [ˌliːn‿'aʊt] sich hinauslehnen V 4 (77)
learn [lɜːn] lernen I • **learn sth. about sth.** etwas über etwas erfahren, etwas über etwas herausfinden II
least [liːst] am wenigsten III • **at least** zumindest, wenigstens I
leather ['leðə] Leder III
leave [liːv], **left, left**
1. (weg)gehen; abfahren II
2. verlassen II
3. zurücklassen II
4. leave a message eine Nachricht hinterlassen V 4 (86)
5. leave sb. alone jn. in Ruhe lassen V 3 (63)
6. leave sth. out etwas weglassen/auslassen IV
leaves [liːvz] *Plural von „leaf"*
left [left] *siehe* **leave**
left [left] linke(r, s) II • **look left** nach links schauen II • **on the left** links, auf der linken Seite II • **turn left** (nach) links abbiegen II
leg [leg] Bein I
legal ['liːgl] legal, gesetzlich IV
leisure ['leʒə] Freizeit • **leisure centre** Freizeitzentrum, -park II
lemon ['lemən] Zitrone III
lemonade [ˌlemə'neɪd] Limonade I
lend sb. sth. [lend], **lent, lent** jm. etwas leihen, etwas an jn. verleihen V 1 (15/174)
► S.174 (to) lend – (to) borrow
lent [lent] siehe **lend**
less [les] weniger IV
lesson ['lesn] (Unterrichts-)Stunde I • **lessons** *(pl)* Unterricht I
let [let], **let, let** lassen II • **Let's ...** Lass uns ... / Lasst uns ... I • **Let's go.** Auf geht's! I • **Let's look at the list.** Sehen wir uns die Liste an. / Lasst uns die Liste ansehen. I
let sb. do sth. jm. erlauben, etwas zu tun; zulassen, dass jd. etwas tut III • **I'll let you know.** Ich gebe dir/Ihnen Bescheid V 2 (41)
letter ['letə]
1. Buchstabe I • **capital letter** [ˌkæpɪtl 'letə] Großbuchstabe III
2. letter (to) Brief (an) II • °**letter**

to the editor Leserbrief • **letter of application** Bewerbungsschreiben V 2 (37/179)

lettuce ['letɪs] (Kopf-)Salat II

level ['levl] (Lern-)Stand, Niveau, Grad V 2 (39) • **°UV level** Grad der UV-Strahlenbelastung

library ['laɪbrəri] Bibliothek, Bücherei I

licence ['laɪsns]**: driving licence** Führerschein V 2 (38/179) • **moped licence** Mopedführerschein V 2 (38)

license plate ['laɪsns pleɪt] *(AE)* Nummernschild IV

lie *(-ing form:* **lying***)* [laɪ] lügen V 3 (62)

lie *(-ing form:* **lying***)* [laɪ]**, lay, lain** liegen IV

life [laɪf], *pl* **lives** [laɪvz] Leben I

lifeguard ['laɪfgɑːd] Rettungsschwimmer/in V 1 (14) • **lifeguard station** Station der Rettungsschwimmer/innen V 1 (14)

lift [lɪft] Fahrstuhl, Aufzug II

light [laɪt] Licht III • **traffic light** (Verkehrs-)Ampel IV

like [laɪk] wie I • **What was the weather like?** Wie war das Wetter? II • **like that / like this** so IV

like [laɪk] mögen, gernhaben I
like sth. better etwas lieber mögen II • **I like swimming/dancing.** Ich schwimme/tanze gern. I • **I'd like ... (= I would like ...)** Ich hätte gern ... / Ich möchte gern ... I • **I'd like to talk about ... (= I would like to talk about ...)** Ich möchte/würde gern über ... reden I • **Would you like ...?** Möchtest du ...? / Möchten Sie ...? I • **Would you like some?** Möchtest du etwas/ein paar? / Möchten Sie etwas/ein paar? I

likeable ['laɪkəbl] liebenswert, nett, sympathisch IV

°**likely** ['laɪkli] wahrscheinlich

line [laɪn]
1. Zeile II
°2. Linie
3. (U-Bahn-)Linie III
4. *(AE)* Schlange, Reihe *(wartender Menschen)* IV

link [lɪŋk] verbinden, verknüpfen I

link [lɪŋk] Verbindung, Verknüpfung III

linking word ['lɪŋkɪŋ wɜːd] Bindewort II

lion ['laɪən] Löwe II

list [lɪst] Liste I

list [lɪst] auflisten, aufzählen II

listen (to) ['lɪsn] zuhören; sich etwas anhören I • **listen for sth.** auf etwas horchen, achten III

listener ['lɪsənə] Zuhörer/in II

listing ['lɪstɪŋ]**: TV listings** *(pl)* das Fernsehprogramm IV

little ['lɪtl]
1. klein I
2. wenig IV

live [lɪv] leben, wohnen I • **live on sth.** von etwas leben; sich von etwas ernähren V 4 (76)

live music [laɪv] Livemusik II

lives [laɪvz] *Plural von „life"*

living room ['lɪvɪŋ ruːm] Wohnzimmer I

local ['ləʊkl] Orts-, örtlich II; Lokal-, IV • **local paper** Lokalzeitung IV

location [ləʊ'keɪʃn]
1. (Wohn-)Ort III
2. (Veranstaltungs-)Ort III
3. Drehort

lock [lɒk] abschließen; sperren III

lock [lɒk] Schleuse III

logical ['lɒdʒɪkl] logisch V 2 (35)

logo ['ləʊgəʊ] Logo III

lonely ['ləʊnli] einsam III

long [lɒŋ] lang I • **work long hours** lange arbeiten V 2 (33)

look [lʊk]
1. schauen, gucken I
2. look different/great/old anders/toll/alt aussehen I
look after sth./sb. auf etwas/jn. aufpassen; sich um etwas/jn. kümmern II • **look at** ansehen, anschauen I • **look for** suchen II
look forward to sich auf etwas freuen IV • **look left/right** nach links/rechts schauen II • **look round** sich umsehen I • **look sth. up** etwas nachschlagen III • **look up (from)** hochsehen, aufschauen (von) II

look [lʊk]
1. look (at) Blick (auf) • **have a look at sth.** sich etwas ansehen, einen Blick werfen auf etwas IV
2. (Gesichts-)Ausdruck V 2 (40)

lorry ['lɒri] Lastkraftwagen III

lose [luːz]**, lost, lost** verlieren II

lost [lɒst] *siehe* **lose**

lot [lɒt]**: a lot (of) / lots (of)** eine Menge, viel, viele II • **Thanks a lot!** Vielen Dank! I • **He likes her a lot.** Er mag sie sehr. I • **lots more** viel mehr I

°**lottery** ['lɒtəri] Lotterie

loud [laʊd] laut I

love [lʌv] lieben, sehr mögen II
would love to do sth. etwas gern tun wollen V 1 (12)

love [lʌv] Liebe II • **Love ...** Liebe Grüße, ... *(Briefschluss)* I • **fall in love (with sb.)** sich verlieben (in jn.) IV

luck [lʌk]**: Good luck (with ...)!** Viel Glück (bei/mit ...)! I

luckily ['lʌkɪli] zum Glück, glücklicherweise II

lucky ['lʌki]**: be lucky (with)** Glück haben (mit) III

lunch [lʌntʃ] Mittagessen I
lunch break Mittagspause I

°**lunchtime** ['lʌntʃtaɪm] Mittagszeit

lyrics *(pl)* ['lɪrɪks] Liedtext(e), Songtext(e) III

M

machine [mə'ʃiːn] Maschine, Gerät; *hier:* Automat III • **ticket machine** Fahrkartenautomat III

mad [mæd] verrückt I • **be mad about sth.** verrückt nach/auf etwas sein III

madam: Dear Sir or Madam [sɜː, sə; 'mædəm] Sehr geehrte Damen und Herren *(Anrede in Briefen)* IV

made [meɪd] *siehe* **make**

magazine [ˌmægə'ziːn] Zeitschrift, Magazin I

mail [meɪl] schicken, senden *(per Post oder E-mail)*; mailen III • **mail sb.** jn. anmailen II

mailbox ['meɪlbɒks] Mailbox V 3 (52)

main [meɪn] Haupt- III

mainly ['meɪnli] hauptsächlich V 3 (58)

majority [mə'dʒɒrəti] Mehrheit IV

make [meɪk]**, made, made** machen; bauen I • **make a deal** ein Abkommen / eine Abmachung treffen III • **make a decision** eine Entscheidung treffen/fällen V 2 (32/176) • **make a mess** alles durcheinanderbringen, alles in Unordnung bringen I • **make a point** ein Argument vorbringen III • **make a speech** eine Rede halten IV • °**make it** (es) überleben • °**make notes** sich Notizen machen • **make sb. do sth.** jn. dazu bringen etwas zu tun V 1 (22) °**make sth. up** sich etwas ausdenken • **make sure that** sich vergewissern, dass ...; dafür sorgen, dass ... IV • **Make yourself comfortable.** Machs dir bequem. IV

make-up ['meɪkʌp] Make-up II
make-up artist ['ɑːtɪst] Maskenbildner/in V 2 (33)

male [meɪl] männlich III

man [mæn], *pl* **men** [men] Mann I
°**manage sth.** ['mænɪdʒ] etwas regeln
manager ['mænədʒə]
1. Manager/in III
°**2.** Geschäftsführer/in, Leiter/in
°**manatee** [ˌmænə'tiː] Seekuh
many ['meni] viele I • **how many?** wie viele? I
map [mæp] Landkarte, Stadtplan II
°**Marathi** [mə'rɑːti] Marathi *(in West- und Zentralindien gesprochene Sprache)*
March [mɑːtʃ] März I
march [mɑːtʃ] Marsch, Demonstration IV
mark [mɑːk] *(BE)* (Schul-)Note, Zensur IV
mark sth. up [ˌmɑːk_'ʌp] etwas markieren, kennzeichnen II
market ['mɑːkɪt] Markt II
marmalade ['mɑːməleɪd] (Orangen-)Marmelade I
married (to) ['mærɪd] verheiratet (mit) I
match [mætʃ] Spiel, Wettkampf I
°**match** [mætʃ]
1. passen zu
2. zuordnen
°**Match the letters and numbers.** Ordne die Buchstaben den Zahlen zu.
match day ['mætʃ deɪ] Spieltag V 2 (41)
mate [meɪt] *(infml)* Freund/in, Kumpel III
material [mə'tɪəriəl] Material V 4 (88)
maths [mæθs] Mathematik I
matter ['mætə]: **What's the matter?** Was ist los? / Was ist denn? II
°**mattress** ['mætrəs] Matratze
°**maximum** ['mæksɪməm] maximal
May [meɪ] Mai I
may [meɪ] dürfen III
maybe ['meɪbi] vielleicht I
mayor ['meə] Bürgermeister/in IV
me [miː] mir; mich I • **Me too.** Ich auch. I • **more than me** mehr als ich II • **That's me.** Das bin ich. I
Why me? Warum ich? I
meal [miːl] Mahlzeit, Essen III
mean [miːn], **meant, meant**
1. bedeuten III
2. meinen *(sagen wollen)* II
meaning ['miːnɪŋ] Bedeutung III
meant [ment] *siehe* **mean**
meat [miːt] Fleisch I
mechanic [mə'kænɪk] Mechaniker/in V 2 (33)
medal ['medl] Medaille III
media *(pl)* ['miːdiə] Medien III
mediation [ˌmiːdi'eɪʃn] Vermittlung, Sprachmittlung, Mediation II
medicine ['medsn, 'medɪsn] Medizin V 4 (79)
medium ['miːdiəm] mittel(groß) II
meet [miːt], **met, met**
1. treffen; kennenlernen I
2. sich treffen I
Nice to meet you. Nett, dich kennenzulernen. III
meeting ['miːtɪŋ] Versammlung, Besprechung IV
member (of) ['membə] Mitglied (von, in) IV
men [men] *Plural von „man"*
menu ['menjuː] Speisekarte II
mess [mes]: **be a mess** sehr unordentlich sein; fürchterlich aussehen II • **make a mess** alles durcheinanderbringen, alles in Unordnung bringen I
message ['mesɪdʒ] Nachricht III
instant messages *Nachrichten, die man im Internet austauscht (in Echtzeit)* III • **leave a message** eine Nachricht hinterlassen V 4 (86)
take a message eine Nachricht entgegennehmen V 4 (86/191)
Can I take a message for her/him? Kann ich ihr/ihm etwas ausrichten? V 4 (86/191) • **text message** SMS III
met [met] *siehe* **meet**
metal ['metl] Metall V 4 (80)
metre ['miːtə] Meter II
mice [maɪs] *Plural von „mouse"*
microphone ['maɪkrəfəʊn] Mikrofon III
middle (of) ['mɪdl] Mitte I; Mittelteil II • **middle school** *(USA) Schule für 11- bis 14-Jährige* IV • **in the middle of nowhere** *(infml) etwa:* am Ende der Welt V 1 (12)
midnight ['mɪdnaɪt] Mitternacht III
might [maɪt]: **you might need help** du könntest (vielleicht) Hilfe brauchen III
mild [maɪld] mild III
mile [maɪl] Meile *(= ca. 1,6 km)* II
for miles meilenweit II
°**military-style** ['mɪlətriˌstaɪl] im Militärstil
milk [mɪlk] Milch I
million ['mɪljən] Million III
millionaire [ˌmɪljə'neə] Millionär/in IV
mime [maɪm] pantomimisch darstellen, vorspielen II
mind [maɪnd]: **I don't mind helping/working/...** Es macht mir nichts aus zu helfen/zu arbeiten/... V 2 (34) • **Do you mind?** Stört es Sie? V 2 (34/178) • **if you don't mind** wenn Sie nichts dagegen haben V 2 (34/178) • **Would you mind waiting outside?** Würden Sie bitte draußen warten? V 2 (34/178)
Mind your own business. Das geht dich nichts an! / Kümmere dich um deine eigenen Angelegenheiten! II • **Never mind.** *etwa:* Nicht so wichtig. / Ist (doch) egal. / Das willst du gar nicht wissen. IV
► S.178 (to) mind
mind map ['maɪnd mæp] Mindmap („Gedankenkarte", „Wissensnetz") I
mine [maɪn] meiner, meine, meins II
°**minimum** ['mɪnɪməm] Minimum
minister ['mɪnɪstə] Pfarrer/in, Pastor/in IV
minority [maɪ'nɒrəti] Minderheit IV
mints *(pl)* [mɪnts] Pfefferminzbonbons I
minus ['maɪnəs] minus IV
minute ['mɪnɪt] Minute I • **Wait a minute.** Warte mal! / Moment mal! II
mirror ['mɪrə] Spiegel II
miss [mɪs]
1. vermissen II
2. verpassen V 3 (53)
3. Miss a turn. Einmal aussetzen. II
Miss White [mɪs] Frau White *(unverheiratet)* I
missing ['mɪsɪŋ]: **be missing** fehlen II
mistake [mɪ'steɪk] Fehler I
mix [mɪks] mischen, mixen III
mix [mɪks] Mix, Mischung III
°**mixed-race** [ˌmɪkst'reɪs] gemischtrassische(r,s)
mixture ['mɪkstʃə] Mischung III
mobile (phone) ['məʊbaɪl] Mobiltelefon, Handy I
model ['mɒdl] Modell*(-flugzeug, -schiff usw.)* I; (Foto-)Modell II
role model Vorbild V 2 (46)
modern ['mɒdən] modern III
mole [məʊl] Maulwurf II
mom [mɒm, *AE:* mɑːm] *(AE)* Mama, Mutti; Mutter III
moment ['məʊmənt] Moment III
Monday ['mʌndeɪ, 'mʌndi] Montag I • **Monday morning** Montagmorgen I
money ['mʌni] Geld I • **raise money (for)** [reɪz] Geld sammeln (für) IV
monitor ['mɒnɪtə] Bildschirm, Monitor III

monkey ['mʌŋki] Affe II
monster ['mɒnstə] Ungeheuer, Monster II
month [mʌnθ] Monat I
monument ['mɒnjumənt] Denkmal, Monument IV
moon [mu:n] Mond II
moped ['məʊped] Moped V 2 (38) **moped licence** Mopedführerschein V 2 (38)
more [mɔ:] mehr I • **more and more** immer mehr V 2 (44) • **lots more** viel mehr I • **more than** mehr als II • **more than me** mehr als ich II • **more boring (than)** langweiliger (als) II • **no more music** keine Musik mehr I • **not (...) any more** nicht mehr III
morning ['mɔ:nɪŋ] Morgen, Vormittag I • **in the morning** morgens, am Morgen I • **Monday morning** Montagmorgen I • **on Friday morning** freitagmorgens, am Freitagmorgen I
mosque [mɒsk] Moschee III
most [məʊst] (der/die/das) meiste ...; am meisten II • **most people** die meisten Leute I • **(the) most boring** der/die/das langweiligste ...; am langweiligsten II
mostly ['məʊstli] hauptsächlich, überwiegend V 2 (35)
motel [məʊ'tel] Motel IV
mother ['mʌðə] Mutter I
motorbike ['məʊtəbaɪk] Motorrad V 1 (12)
mountain ['maʊntən] Berg II
mouse [maʊs], *pl* **mice** [maɪs] Maus I
mouth [maʊθ] Mund I
move [mu:v]
1. bewegen; sich bewegen II **Move back one space.** Geh ein Feld zurück. II • **Move on one space.** Geh ein Feld vor. II
2. move (to) umziehen (nach, in) II • **move in** einziehen II • **move out** ausziehen II
movement ['mu:vmənt] Bewegung II
movie ['mu:vi] Film III
MP3 player [ˌempi:'θri: ˌpleɪə] MP3-Spieler I
Mr ... ['mɪstə] Herr ... I
Mrs ... ['mɪsɪz] Frau ... I
Ms ... [mɪz, məz] Frau ... II
much [mʌtʃ] viel I • **how much?** wie viel? I • **How much is/are ...?** Was kostet/kosten ...? / Wie viel kostet/kosten ...? I • **like/love sth. very much** etwas sehr mögen / sehr lieben II
mud [mʌd] Schlamm, Matsch V 3 (63/186)
muddy ['mʌdi] schlammig, matschig, schmutzig V 3 (63)
muesli ['mju:zli] Müsli IV
multi- ['mʌlti] viel-, mehr-; multi-, Multi- IV • **multi-coloured** mehrfarbig IV • **multi-millionaire** Multimillionär/in IV
multiple choice [ˌmʌltɪpl 'tʃɔɪs] Multiple-Choice II
mum [mʌm] Mama, Mutti; Mutter I
°**Mumbaikar** [ˌmʊm'baɪkɑ:] Bewohner/in Mumbais
murder ['mɜ:də] Mord IV
museum [mju'zi:əm] Museum I
mushroom ['mʌʃrʊm, -ru:m] Pilz III
music ['mju:zɪk] Musik I
musical ['mju:zɪkl] Musical I
musician [mju:'zɪʃn] Musiker/in III
Muslim ['mʊzlɪm] Muslim/Muslima, Muslimin; muslimisch V 4 (77)
must [mʌst]
1. müssen I
2. mustn't do nicht tun dürfen II
must [mʌst] Muss IV
°**must-see sights** Sehenswürdigkeiten, die man unbedingt sehen sollte
my [maɪ] mein/e I
myself [maɪ'self] mir/mich (selbst) III
mystery ['mɪstri] Geheimnis, Rätsel IV

N

name [neɪm] Name I • **call sb. names** jn. mit Schimpfwörtern hänseln, jm. Schimpfwörter nachrufen III • **family name** Nachname, Familienname V 2 (37) • **first name** Vorname V 2 (37) • **My name is ...** Ich heiße ... / Mein Name ist ... I • **What's your name?** Wie heißt du? I
name [neɪm] nennen; benennen II **name after** benennen nach IV
nation ['neɪʃn] Nation IV
national ['næʃnəl] national III **national park** Nationalpark IV
nationality [ˌnæʃə'nælɪti] Staatsangehörigkeit, Nationalität V 1 (6)
Native American [ˌneɪtɪv‿ə'merɪkən] Amerikanische(r) Ureinwohner/in, Indianer/in IV
natural ['nætʃrəl] Natur-, natürlich IV
nature ['neɪtʃə] Natur V 2 (39)
near [nɪə] in der Nähe von, nahe (bei) I
nearly ['nɪəli] fast, beinahe V 1 (10)
neat [ni:t] gepflegt II • **neat and tidy** schön ordentlich II
necessary ['nesəsəri] nötig, notwendig V 2 (41)
neck [nek] Hals, Genick V 1 (21)
need [ni:d] brauchen, benötigen I **need to do sth.** etwas tun müssen; etwas zu tun brauchen V 1 (16)
► S.174 'need' als Hilfsverb/als Vollverb
needn't do ['ni:dnt] nicht tun müssen, nicht zu tun brauchen II
negative ['negətɪv] negativ V 4 (76/187)
neighbour ['neɪbə] Nachbar/in I
nephew ['nefju:, 'nevju:] Neffe IV
nervous ['nɜ:vəs] nervös, aufgeregt I
network ['netwɜ:k]
1. (Fernseh-/Radio-) Sendernetz IV
°**2.** (Wörter-)Netz
never ['nevə] nie, niemals I **Never mind.** [ˌnevə 'maɪnd] *etwa:* Nicht so wichtig. / Ist (doch) egal. / Das willst du gar nicht wissen. IV
new [nju:] neu I
news *(no pl)* [nju:z] Nachrichten, Neuigkeiten III • **That's good news.** Das sind gute Nachrichten. III
newspaper ['nju:speɪpə] Zeitung I
newsreader ['nju:zˌri:də] Nachrichtensprecher/in IV
next [nekst]**: be next** der/die Nächste sein I • **the next morning/day** am nächsten Morgen/Tag I **What have we got next?** Was haben wir als Nächstes? I
next to [nekst] neben II
nice [naɪs] schön, nett I • **Nice to meet you.** Nett, dich/euch/Sie kennenzulernen. III • **Nice try.** Netter Versuch. V 3 (62)
niece [ni:s] Nichte IV
night [naɪt] Nacht, später Abend I **at night** nachts, in der Nacht I **on Friday night** freitagnachts, Freitagnacht I
nightclub ['naɪtklʌb] Nachtklub III
nil [nɪl] null III
no [nəʊ] nein I
no [nəʊ] kein, keine I • **no more music** keine Musik mehr I • **no one** niemand IV • **No smoking!** Rauchen verboten! III • **No way!** Auf keinen Fall! / Kommt nicht in Frage! II
nobody ['nəʊbədi] niemand II
nod (-dd-) [nɒd] nicken (mit) II
noise [nɔɪz] Geräusch; Lärm I

noisy ['nɔɪzi] laut, lärmend II
°**nomophobia** [ˌnɒmə'fəʊbiə] *die Angst, kein Mobiltelefon zu haben*
non-violent [ˌnɒn'vaɪələnt] gewaltlos, gewaltfrei IV
normal ['nɔːml] normal, üblich V 2 (34)
north [nɔːθ] Norden; nach Norden; nördlich III
northbound ['nɔːθbaʊnd] Richtung Norden III
north-east [ˌnɔːθ'iːst] Nordosten; nach Nordosten; nordöstlich III
north-west [ˌnɔːθ'west] Nordwesten; nach Nordwesten; nordwestlich III
nose [nəʊz] Nase I
not [nɒt] nicht I • **not (...) any** kein, keine I • **not (...) any more** nicht mehr III • **not (...) anybody** niemand II • **not (...) anything** nichts II • **not (...) anywhere** nirgendwo(hin) II • **not (...) at all** überhaupt nicht, ganz und gar nicht; überhaupt kein/e V 3 (50) **not (...) either** auch nicht; auch kein V 1 (6) • **not even** (noch) nicht einmal III • **not (...) yet** noch nicht II
note [nəʊt]
1. Mitteilung, Notiz I • °**make notes** sich Notizen machen
take notes sich Notizen machen I
2. (Geld-)Schein, Banknote V 3 (53)
nothing ['nʌθɪŋ] nichts II
notice ['nəʊtɪs] bemerken IV
notice board ['nəʊtɪs bɔːd] Anschlagtafel, schwarzes Brett I
°**novel** ['nɒvl] Roman
November [nəʊ'vembə] November I
now [naʊ] nun, jetzt I • **now and then** gelegentlich, ab und zu V 1 (20)
nowhere ['nəʊweə] nirgendwo(hin) V 1 (12) • **in the middle of nowhere** *(infml) etwa:* am Ende der Welt V 1 (12)
number ['nʌmbə] Zahl, Ziffer, Nummer I • **number plate** Nummernschild IV
°**nun** [nʌn] Nonne
nurse [nɜːs] Krankenpfleger/in, Krankenschwester V 2 (35)
nut [nʌt] Nuss IV

O

o [əʊ] null I
ocean ['əʊʃn] Ozean IV
o'clock [ə'klɒk]: **eleven o'clock** elf Uhr I
October [ɒk'təʊbə] Oktober I
°**odd** [ɒd]: **What word is the odd one out?** Welches Wort passt nicht dazu / gehört nicht dazu?
of [əv, ɒv] von I • **two kilos of oranges** zwei Kilo Orangen III
of course [əv 'kɔːs] natürlich, selbstverständlich I
off [ɒf]: **a week/day/month ... off** eine Woche / einen Tag / einen Monat ... frei IV • **cut sth. off** etwas abtrennen, abschneiden III
fall off herunterfallen (von) II
get off (the train/bus) (aus dem Zug/Bus) aussteigen I • **get sth. off the ground** etwas auf den Weg bringen; etwas auf die Beine stellen III • **take sth. off** etwas ausziehen *(Kleidung)* II • **take 10 c off** 10 Cent abziehen I • **tear sth. off** etwas abreißen IV • **turn sth. off** etwas ausschalten III
offer ['ɒfə] anbieten IV
offer ['ɒfə] Angebot IV
office ['ɒfɪs]
1. Büro V 2 (35) • **office worker** Büroangestellte(r) V 2 (35)
2. **ticket office** Kasse *(für den Verkauf von Eintrittskarten)* IV; Fahrkartenschalter III
officer ['ɒfɪsə]
1. **police officer** Polizist/in, Polizeibeamter, -beamtin V 2 (32)
°2. *Anrede für einen Polizisten / eine Polizistin, wenn man den Rang nicht weiß*
official [ə'fɪʃl] offiziell, amtlich, Amts- V 4 (74)
often ['ɒfn] oft, häufig I
Oh dear! [əʊ 'dɪə] Oje! II
Oh well ... [əʊ 'wel] Na ja ... / Na gut ... I
oil [ɔɪl] Öl III
oily ['ɔɪli] ölig V 4 (82)
OK [əʊ'keɪ] okay, gut, in Ordnung I
I'll/You'll/She'll/ ... be OK. Mir/ Dir/Ihr/ ... wird nichts passieren. IV
old [əʊld] alt I • **old people's home** Alten-, Seniorenheim V 3 (63) • **a sixteen-year-old** ein/e Sechzehnjährige/r III • **a sixteen-year-old girl** ein sechzehnjähriges Mädchen III
old-fashioned [ˌəʊld'fæʃnd] altmodisch III
Olympic Games [əˌlɪmpɪk 'geɪmz] *(kurz:* **the Olympics** [ə'lɪmpɪks]*)* Olympische Spiele; die Olympiade IV
on [ɒn]
1. auf I
2. weiter III
3. an, eingeschaltet *(Radio, Licht usw.)* II
and so on *(short:* **etc.** [et'setərə]*)* und so weiter (usw.) IV • **be on** gezeigt werden, laufen *(im Fernsehen/Kino)* IV • **be on holiday** in Urlaub sein; Ferien haben/machen II • **go on holiday** in Urlaub fahren II • **on a shift** in einer Schicht IV • **on board** an Bord V 4 (77)
on 13th June am 13. Juni I • **on Friday** am Freitag I • **on Friday afternoon** freitagnachmittags, am Freitagnachmittag I **on Friday evening** freitagabends, am Freitagabend I • **on Friday morning** freitagmorgens, am Freitagmorgen I • **on Friday night** freitagnachts, Freitagnacht I • **on the beach** am Strand II • **on the board** an die Tafel I • **on the corner of Green Street and London Road** Green Street, Ecke London Road II • **on the internet** im Internet IV • **on the left** links, auf der linken Seite II • **on the phone** am Telefon I **on the plane** im Flugzeug II • **on the radio** im Radio I • **on the right** rechts, auf der rechten Seite II • **on the train** im Zug I • **on TV** im Fernsehen I **straight on** geradeaus weiter II • **What page are we on?** Auf welcher Seite sind wir? I
once [wʌns]
1. einmal III • **once a week** einmal pro Woche III
2. einst, früher einmal III
3. **at once** sofort V 4 (86)
one [wʌn] eins, ein, eine I • **one day** eines Tages I • **a new one** ein neuer / eine neue / ein neues II • **my old ones** meine alten II
no one niemand IV
one-day ticket [ˌwʌn deɪ 'tɪkɪt] Tages(fahr)karte III
onion ['ʌnjən] Zwiebel III
online [ˌɒn'laɪn] online, Online- III
online friend Internetfreund/in V 1 (12)
only ['əʊnli]
1. nur, bloß I
2. erst III
3. **the only guest** der einzige Gast I • **only child** Einzelkind V 3 (48)
onto ['ɒntə, 'ɒntʊ] auf (... hinauf) III
open ['əʊpən] öffnen, aufmachen I
open ['əʊpən] offen, geöffnet II

open-air [ˌəʊpən‿ˈeə] im Freien; Freilicht- III
opening [ˈəʊpənɪŋ]: **opening hours** Öffnungszeiten IV • °**opening sentence** Einleitungssatz
opera [ˈɒprə] Oper III
operation (on) [ˌɒpəˈreɪʃn] Operation (an) III
opinion [əˈpɪnjən] Meinung III • **in my opinion** meiner Meinung nach III
opposite [ˈɒpəzɪt] Gegenteil I
or [ɔː] oder I
orange [ˈɒrɪndʒ] orange(farben) I
orange [ˈɒrɪndʒ] Orange, Apfelsine I • **orange juice** [ˈɒrɪndʒ dʒuːs] Orangensaft I
order [ˈɔːdə] bestellen IV
order [ˈɔːdə]
1. Befehl, Anweisung, Anordnung V 3 (54)
°2. Reihenfolge • °**in the right order** in der richtigen Reihenfolge • °**word order** Wortstellung
organization [ˌɔːgənaɪˈzeɪʃn] Organisation V 3 (50/182)
organize [ˈɔːgənaɪz] ordnen, organisieren III
organized [ˈɔːgənaɪzd] (gut) organisiert V 2 (33)
original *(n; adj)* [əˈrɪdʒənl] Original; Original- IV
orphan [ˈɔːfn] Waise, Waisenkind V 1 (17)
other [ˈʌðə] andere(r, s) I • **the others** die anderen I • **the other way round** anders herum II
Ouch! [aʊtʃ] Autsch! I
our [ˈaʊə] unser, unsere I
ours [ˈaʊəz] unserer, unsere, unseres II
ourselves [aʊəˈselvz] uns (selbst) III
out heraus, hinaus; draußen II
out of ... aus ... (heraus/hinaus) I
out of breath [breθ] außer Atem V 1 (20/175) • **day out** Tagesausflug III
outback [ˈaʊtbæk]: **the outback** *(Australien)* das Hinterland V 1 (6)
outdoor [ˈaʊtdɔː] *(nur vor Nomen)* Außen-; im Freien, Freiluft- V 4 (80/189) • **outdoor activities** Aktivitäten im Freien V 4 (80/189)
outdoor swimming pool Freibad V 4 (80/189) • **outdoor temperature** Außentemperatur V 4 (80/189)
► S.189 indoor – outdoor
outdoors [ˌaʊtˈdɔːz] im Freien, (nach) draußen V 1 (9)
outfit [ˈaʊtfɪt] Outfit *(Kleidung; Ausrüstung)* II
°**outline** [ˈaʊtlaɪn] Gliederung
outside [ˌaʊtˈsaɪd]
1. draußen I
2. nach draußen II
3. **outside his room** vor seinem Zimmer; außerhalb seines Zimmers I
over [ˈəʊvə]
1. über, oberhalb von I
2. **be over** vorbei/zu Ende sein I
over there da drüben, dort drüben I • **over to ...** hinüber zu/nach ... II
all over the world auf der ganzen Welt III • **from all over the UK/the world/England** aus dem gesamten Vereinigten Königreich / aus der ganzen Welt / aus ganz England III
°**overcrowding** [ˌəʊvəˈkraʊdɪŋ] Überfüllung, Übervölkerung
overnight [ˌəʊvəˈnaɪt] über Nacht V 3 (58)
own [əʊn]
1. **our own pool** unser eigenes Schwimmbad II
2. **on my/our/... own** [əʊn] allein, selbstständig *(ohne Hilfe)* V 1 (12)
owner [ˈəʊnə] Besitzer/in V 1 (16)
°**Oz** [ɒz] *(infml)* Australien
°**ozone layer** [ˈəʊzəʊn ˌleɪə] Ozonschicht

P

Pacific [pəˈsɪfɪk]: **the Pacific (Ocean)** der Pazifische Ozean, der Pazifik IV
pack [pæk] packen, einpacken II
packet [ˈpækɪt] Päckchen, Packung, Schachtel I • **a packet of mints** ein Päckchen/eine Packung Pfefferminzbonbons I
paddle [ˈpædl] paddeln III
paddle [ˈpædl] Paddel III
pads *(pl)* [pædz] (Knie- usw.) Schützer III
page [peɪdʒ] (Buch-, Heft-)Seite I
What page are we on? Auf welcher Seite sind wir? I
paid [peɪd] *siehe* **pay**
pain [peɪn] Schmerz V 4 (79)
painful [ˈpeɪnfl] schmerzhaft IV
paint [peɪnt] (an)malen I
painter [ˈpeɪntə] Maler/in II
pair [peə]: **a pair (of)** ein Paar II
palace [ˈpæləs] Palast, Schloss III
panic [ˈpænɪk]: **Don't panic!** Keine Panik. / Bleib ruhig. IV
pants *(pl)* [pænts] *(AE)* Hose IV
paper [ˈpeɪpə]
1. Papier I
2. Zeitung II • **local paper** Lokalzeitung IV
paragraph [ˈpærəgrɑːf] Absatz *(in einem Text)* II
Paralympics [ˌpærəˈlɪmpɪks] Paralympische Spiele *(Olympische Spiele für Sportler/innen mit körperlicher Behinderung)* III
paramedic [ˌpærəˈmedɪk] Sanitäter/in II
paraphrase [ˈpærəfreɪz] umschreiben, anders ausdrücken III
parcel [ˈpɑːsl] Paket I
parents [ˈpeərənts] Eltern I
park [pɑːk] Park I • **park ranger** *Ranger sind eine Art Aufseher/in in Nationalparks, die auch Führungen machen und als Wald- und Wildhüter/innen arbeiten* IV
parliament [ˈpɑːləmənt] Parlament III
parrot [ˈpærət] Papagei I
part [pɑːt] Teil I • **take part (in)** teilnehmen (an) III
partner [ˈpɑːtnə] Partner/in I
party [ˈpɑːti] Party I
pass [pɑːs] (herüber)reichen, weitergeben I • °**pass out** ohnmächtig werden • **pass round** herumgeben I • °**pass sth. on** etwas weitergeben
passenger [ˈpæsɪndʒə] Passagier/in, Fahrgast, Reisende(r) V 4 (77)
passport [ˈpɑːspɔːt] (Reise-)Pass V 4 (84)
past [pɑːst] Vergangenheit I
past [pɑːst] vorbei (an), vorüber (an) II • **half past 11** halb zwölf (11.30/23.30) I • **quarter past 11** Viertel nach elf (11.15/23.15) I
pasta *(no pl)* [ˈpæstə] Pasta, Nudeln, Teigwaren IV
path [pɑːθ] Pfad, Weg II • **bridle path** Reitweg III
patient [ˈpeɪʃnt] Patient/in V 4 (79)
pavement [ˈpeɪvmənt] Gehweg, Bürgersteig IV
pay (for) [peɪ], **paid, paid** bezahlen II • **pay by credit card** mit Kreditkarte bezahlen V 3 (53/184) • **pay cash** bar bezahlen V 3 (53/184)
pay [peɪ] Bezahlung, Lohn V 2 (33)
PE [ˌpiː‿ˈiː], **Physical Education** [ˌfɪzɪkəl‿edʒuˈkeɪʃn] Turnen, Sportunterricht I
pea [piː] Erbse III
pen [pen] Kugelschreiber, Füller I
pence (p) *(pl)* [pens] Pence *(Plural von „penny")*

pencil ['pensl] Bleistift I • **pencil case** ['pensl keɪs] Federmäppchen I • **pencil sharpener** ['pensl ʃɑ:pnə] Bleistiftanspitzer I
penny ['peni] *kleinste britische Münze* I
people ['pi:pl] Menschen, Leute I
old people's home Alten-, Seniorenheim V 3 (63)
pepper ['pepə] Pfeffer III
per [pɜ:, pə] pro III • **per cent (%)** [pə 'sent] Prozent III
percentage [pə'sentɪdʒ] Prozentsatz, prozentualer Anteil V 1 (10)
perfect ['pɜ:fɪkt] perfekt; ideal; vollkommen IV
perhaps [pə'hæps] vielleicht V 3 (51)
period ['pɪəriəd] (Unterrichts-/Schul-)Stunde IV
person ['pɜ:sn] Person II
personal ['pɜ:sənl] persönliche(r, s) III
°**personality** [,pɜ:sə'næləti] Persönlichkeit
pet [pet] Haustier I • **pet shop** Tierhandlung I
petrol ['petrəl] Benzin IV • **petrol station** Tankstelle IV
phone [fəʊn] Telefon I • **on the phone** am Telefon I • **phone box** Telefonzelle V 3 (50) • **phone call** Anruf, Telefongespräch I • **phone number** Telefonnummer I
phone [fəʊn] telefonieren, anrufen I
photo ['fəʊtəʊ] Foto I • **in the photo** auf dem Foto I • **take photos** Fotos machen, fotografieren I
°**photocopy** ['fəʊtəʊkɒpi] Fotokopie
°**phrase** [freɪz] Ausdruck, (Rede-)Wendung
piano [pi'ænəʊ] Klavier, Piano I
play the piano Klavier spielen I
pick [pɪk]
°**1. pick out** aussuchen, auswählen
2. pick sb. up jn. abholen III
3. pick sth. up etwas hochheben, aufheben II
°**pick** [pɪk]: **pick of the day** das Beste von heute
picnic ['pɪknɪk] Picknick I • **have a picnic** ein Picknick machen I
picture ['pɪktʃə] Bild I • **in the picture** auf dem Bild I • **picture story** Bildergeschichte IV
pie [paɪ] Obstkuchen; Pastete II
pie chart Tortendiagramm, Kreisdiagramm V 1 (10)
piece [pi:s]: **a piece of** ein Stück I
a piece of paper ein Stück Papier I
pig [pɪg] III
pill [pɪl] Pille, Tablette V 4 (79)
pink [pɪŋk] pink(farben), rosa I
pipe [paɪp] Pfeife III
pirate ['paɪrət] Pirat, Piratin I
pitch [pɪtʃ] Spielfeld III
pizza ['pi:tsə] Pizza I
place [pleɪs] Ort, Platz I • **at someone's place** bei jemandem zu Hause V 1 (6) • **place of birth** Geburtsort V 2 (38/179) • **take place** stattfinden IV
°**placemat** ['pleɪsmæt] Set, Platzdeckchen
plan [plæn] Plan I
plan (-nn-) [plæn] planen I
plane [pleɪn] Flugzeug II • **on the plane** im Flugzeug II
planet ['plænɪt] Planet II
plant [plɑ:nt] Pflanze V 1 (16)
plant [plɑ:nt] pflanzen, einpflanzen V 1 (16/174)
plantation [plɑ:n'teɪʃn] Plantage IV
plastic ['plæstɪk] Plastik V 3 (58)
plate [pleɪt] Teller I • **a plate of chips** ein Teller Pommes frites I
license plate *(AE)* Nummernschild IV • **number plate** *(BE)* Nummernschild IV
platform ['plætfɔ:m] Bahnsteig, Gleis III
°**platypus: duck-billed platypus** [,dʌkbɪld 'plætɪpəs] Schnabeltier
play [pleɪ] spielen I • **play football** Fußball spielen I • **play the drums** Schlagzeug spielen III • **play the fiddle** Geige spielen III • **play the guitar** Gitarre spielen I • **play the piano** Klavier spielen I
play [pleɪ] Theaterstück I
player ['pleɪə] Spieler/in I
pleasant ['pleznt] angenehm V 4 (86)
please [pli:z] bitte *(in Fragen und Aufforderungen)* I
plot [plɒt] Handlung *(eines Romans, Films, Theaterstücks)* IV
plug [plʌg] Stecker III
plus [plʌs] plus IV
pm [,pi:‿'em]: **7 pm** 7 Uhr abends / 19 Uhr I
pocket ['pɒkɪt] Tasche *(an Kleidungsstück)* II • **pocket money** Taschengeld II
poem ['pəʊɪm] Gedicht I
point [pɔɪnt] Punkt II • **make a point** ein Argument vorbringen III • **10.4 (ten point four)** 10,4 (zehn Komma vier) III
point (at/to sth.) [pɔɪnt] zeigen, deuten (auf etwas) II
poison ['pɔɪzn] Gift V 1 (21)
poisonous ['pɔɪzənəs] giftig V 1 (21/176)
police *(pl)* [pə'li:s] Polizei I • **police officer** Polizist/in, Polizeibeamter, -beamtin V 2 (32) • **police station** Polizeiwache, Polizeirevier II
policeman [pə'li:smən] Polizist II
policewoman [pə'li:swʊmən] Polizistin II
°**policy** ['pɒləsi] Politik, Vorgehensweise
polite [pə'laɪt] höflich IV
political [pə'lɪtɪkl] politisch V 4 (81)
politics ['pɒlɪtɪks] (die) Politik V 4 (81)
polluted [pə'lu:tɪd] verseucht, verunreinigt V 4 (74/187)
pollution [pə'lu:ʃn] (Umwelt-)Verschmutzung V 4 (74)
poltergeist ['pəʊltəgaɪst] Poltergeist I
ponytail ['pəʊniteɪl] Pferdeschwanz *(Frisur)* III
pool [pu:l] (Schwimm-)Becken III
poor [pɔ:, pʊə]
1. arm I • **poor Sophie** (die) arme Sophie I
°**2.** schlecht, armselig
pop (music) [pɒp] Pop(musik) III
popcorn ['pɒpkɔ:n] Popcorn II
popular (with) ['pɒpjulə] populär, beliebt (bei) III
population [,pɒpju'leɪʃn] Bevölkerung, Einwohner(zahl) IV
pork [pɔ:k] Schweinefleisch III
°**port** [pɔ:t] (Handels-,Fracht-)Hafen, Hafenstadt
positive ['pɒzətɪv] positiv V 4 (76)
possibility [,pɒsə'bɪləti] Möglichkeit, Chance IV
possible ['pɒsəbl] möglich II
post [pəʊst] Post *(Briefe, Päckchen, ...)* III • **post office** ['pəʊst‿ɒfɪs] Postamt II
post [pəʊst] posten *(ins Netz stellen)* V 1 (6)
postcard ['pəʊstkɑ:d] Postkarte II
postcode ['pəʊstkəʊd] Postleitzahl V 2 (38)
poster ['pəʊstə] Poster I
potato [pə'teɪtəʊ], *pl* **potatoes** Kartoffel I • **potato chips** *(AE)* Kartoffelchips IV • **couch potato** *(infml)* Stubenhocker/in *(jd., der viel vor dem Fernseher sitzt)* V 1 (13)
°**pouch** [paʊtʃ] Beutel
poultry ['pəʊltri] Geflügel IV
pound (£) [paʊnd] Pfund *(britische Währung)* I
°**pour** [pɔ:] strömen; schütten, gießen
poverty ['pɒvəti] Armut V 4 (78)

practice ['præktɪs] *hier:* Übungsteil I
practise ['præktɪs] üben; trainieren I
pray [preɪ] beten V 3 (63/186)
prayer ['preə] Gebet V 3 (63)
prejudice ['predʒudɪs] Vorurteil IV
prejudiced ['predʒədɪst]**: be prejudiced (against)** voreingenommen sein (gegen), Vorurteile haben (gegenüber) IV
°**prepaid** [ˌpri:'peɪd] vorausbezahlt
prepare (for) [prɪ'peə] vorbereiten; sich vorbereiten (auf) II
prescription [prɪ'skrɪpʃn] Rezept *(für Medikamente)* V 4 (79)
present ['preznt]
1. Gegenwart I
2. Geschenk I
present [prɪ'zent] präsentieren V 3 (50/182)
presentation [ˌprezn'teɪʃn] Präsentation, Vorstellung I
presenter [prɪ'zentə] Moderator/in II
president ['prezɪdənt] Präsident/in IV
press [pres] drücken III
pretty ['prɪti] hübsch I
pretty healthy/good/... ['prɪti] ziemlich gesund/gut/... II
price [praɪs] (Kauf-)Preis I
primary school ['praɪməri sku:l] Grundschule V 2 (38)
prime time ['praɪm taɪm] Hauptsendezeit IV
print [prɪnt] drucken V 2 (34)
print: bold print [ˌbəʊld 'prɪnt] Fettdruck III
printer ['prɪntə] Drucker V 2 (34)
prison ['prɪzn] Gefängnis V 1 (8/171)
prisoner ['prɪznə] Gefangene(r) V 1 (8)
private detective [ˌpraɪvət dɪ'tektɪv] Privatdetektiv/in V 2 (35)
prize [praɪz] Preis, Gewinn I
probably ['prɒbəbli] wahrscheinlich II
problem ['prɒbləm] Problem II
produce [prə'dju:s] produzieren, herstellen III
product ['prɒdʌkt] Produkt IV
production [prə'dʌkʃn] Produktion, Herstellung IV
profile ['prəʊfaɪl] Porträt, Steckbrief III; Profil V 2 (36)
programme ['prəʊgræm]
1. Programm I
2. (Fernseh-)Sendung IV
project (about, on) ['prɒdʒekt] Projekt (über, zu) I • **do a project** ein Projekt machen, durchführen II

promise ['prɒmɪs] versprechen II
pronunciation [prəˌnʌnsi'eɪʃn] Aussprache I
proof *(no pl)* [pru:f] Beweis(e) II
protect sb. (from sth.) [prə'tekt] jn. (be)schützen (vor etwas) III
protest [prə'test] protestieren IV
protest ['prəʊtest] Protest IV
°**protester** [prə'testə] Demonstrant/in
proud (of sb./sth.) [praʊd] stolz (auf jn./etwas) II
province ['prɒvɪns] Provinz III
PS [ˌpi:‿'es] **(postscript** ['pəʊstskrɪpt]**)** PS *(Nachschrift unter Briefen)* III
pub [pʌb] Kneipe, Lokal II
public ['pʌblɪk] öffentlich V 3 (52)
public transport *(no pl)* öffentliche Verkehrsmittel, öffentlicher Personennahverkehr V 4 (75)
publish ['pʌblɪʃ] veröffentlichen III
pull [pʊl] ziehen I
pullover ['pʊləʊvə] Pullover II
punctual ['pʌŋktʃuəl] pünktlich V 2 (35)
punish ['pʌnɪʃ] bestrafen V 3 (54/184)
punishment ['pʌnɪʃmənt] Bestrafung, Strafe V 3 (54)
purple ['pɜ:pl] violett; lila I
purse [pɜ:s] Geldbörse II
push [pʊʃ] drücken, schieben, stoßen I
put (-tt-) [pʊt]**, put, put** legen, stellen, *(etwas wohin)* tun I • °**put down an animal** ein Tier einschläfern • **put out a fire** ein Feuer löschen IV • **put sth. on** etwas anziehen *(Kleidung)* II • °**put sth. on the wall** etwas an die Wand hängen • °**put sth. together** etwas zusammenstellen, zusammenfügen • °**Put up your hand.** Heb deine Hand. / Hebt eure Hand.
puzzled ['pʌzld] verwirrt II
pyjamas *(pl)* [pə'dʒɑ:məz] Schlafanzug II
pyramid ['pɪrəmɪd] Pyramide IV

Q

qualification [ˌkwɒlɪfɪ'keɪʃn] Abschluss, Qualifikation V 2 (32)
quality ['kwɒləti] Qualität; Eigenschaft V 2 (35)
quarter ['kwɔ:tə]**: quarter past 11** Viertel nach 11 (11.15/23.15) I
quarter to 12 Viertel vor 12 (11.45/23.45) I
queen [kwi:n] Königin III

question ['kwestʃn] Frage I • **ask questions** Fragen stellen I
°**question word** Fragewort
°**questionnaire** [ˌkwestʃə'neə] Fragebogen
queue [kju:] *(BE)* Schlange, Reihe *(wartender Menschen)* IV
queue [kju:] sich anstellen, anstehen V 4 (85)
quick [kwɪk] schnell I
quiet ['kwaɪət] leise, still, ruhig I
quite bad/quick/good ... [kwaɪt] ziemlich schlimm/schnell/gut/... II
quiz [kwɪz]**,** *pl* **quizzes** ['kwɪzɪz] Quiz, Ratespiel I
°**quotation mark** [kwəʊ'teɪʃn mɑ:k] Anführungszeichen

R

rabbit ['ræbɪt] Kaninchen I
rabbit-proof kaninchen-sicher, kaninchen-fest V 1 (17)
race [reɪs] Rasse V 1 (17/175)
racing car ['reɪsɪŋ kɑ:] Rennwagen V 2 (35)
racist ['reɪsɪst] rassistisch; Rassist/in V 1 (17)
racket ['rækɪt]**: badminton racket** Badmintonschläger III
radio ['reɪdiəʊ] Radio I • **on the radio** im Radio I
raft [rɑ:ft] Schlauchboot *(wildwassertauglich)* IV
rafting ['rɑ:ftɪŋ] Rafting *(Wildwasserfahren mit dem Schlauchboot)* IV
railway ['reɪlweɪ] Eisenbahn II
rain [reɪn] Regen II
rain [reɪn] regnen II
°**rainfall** ['reɪnfɔ:l] Regen, Niederschlag
rainforest ['reɪnfɒrɪst] Regenwald V 1 (9)
rainproof ['reɪnpru:f] regendicht *(Kleidung)* V 1 (17/175)
rainy ['reɪni] regnerisch II
raise [reɪz]
1. raise money (for) Geld sammeln (für) IV
°**2. raise sth.** etwas (hoch)heben
ran [ræn] *siehe* **run**
rang [ræŋ] *siehe* **ring**
ranger ['reɪndʒə]**: (park) ranger** *eine Art Aufseher/in in Nationalparks, die auch Führungen machen und als Wald- und Wildhüter/innen arbeiten* IV
rap [ræp] Rap *(rhythmischer Sprechgesang)* I

rapids *(pl)* ['ræpɪdz] Stromschnellen III

rate: **exchange rate** [ɪks'tʃeɪndʒ reɪt] Wechselkurs V 3 (53)

°**ray** [reɪ] (Licht-)Strahl • °**ultraviolet rays** [ˌʌltrə'vaɪələt] ultraviolette Strahlen

RE [ˌɑːr_'iː], **Religious Education** [rɪˌlɪdʒəs_edʒu'keɪʃn] Religion, Religionsunterricht I

react (to) [ri'ækt] reagieren (auf) V 2 (45)

read [riːd], **read, read** lesen I **read on** weiterlesen III • °**read out** vorlesen • °**Read out loud.** Lies laut vor. • °**Read the poem to a partner.** Lies das Gedicht einem Partner / einer Partnerin vor.

read [red] *siehe* **read**

reader ['riːdə] Leser/in II

ready ['redi] bereit, fertig I • **get ready (for)** sich fertig machen (für), sich vorbereiten (auf) I • **get things ready** Dinge fertig machen, vorbereiten I

real [rɪəl] echt, wirklich I

realistic [ˌriːə'lɪstɪk] realistisch, wirklichkeitsnah III

reality [ri'æləti] Wirklichkeit, Realität IV

really ['rɪəli] wirklich I

reason ['riːzn] Grund, Begründung I • **for lots of reasons** aus vielen Gründen I

receipt [rɪ'siːt] Quittung; Kassenbon V 3 (53)

receive [rɪ'siːv] empfangen IV

recent ['riːsnt] jüngste(r, s), aktuelle(r, s); vor kurzem *(geschehen, entstanden usw.)* V 1 (9)

recently ['riːsntli] in letzter Zeit; neulich, vor kurzem V 1 (9/172)

reception [rɪ'sepʃn] Rezeption, Empfang *(in einem Hotel)* V 2 (38)

°**receptionist** [rɪ'sepʃənɪst] Rezeptionist/in; Empfangsdame

recognize sb./sth. ['rekəgnaɪz] jn./etwas (wieder)erkennen V 4 (81)

recommend sth. to sb. [ˌrekə'mend] jm. etwas empfehlen V 1 (19)

record [rɪ'kɔːd] *(Musik / einen Film)* aufnehmen III

record ['rekɔːd] Schallplatte III

recorder [rɪ'kɔːdə] Blockflöte III

recording [rɪ'kɔːdɪŋ] Aufnahme, Aufzeichnung III

recycled [ˌriː'saɪkld] wiederverwertet, wiederverwendet, recycelt II

recycling [ˌriː'saɪklɪŋ] Wiederverwertung, Recycling II

red [red] rot I • **go red** rot werden, erröten V 3 (62)

reef [riːf] Riff V 1 (9)

refer to (**-rr-**) [rɪ'fɜː] sich beziehen auf III

reference ['refrəns] Referenz, Empfehlung V 2 (38)

reggae ['regeɪ] Reggae III

regular ['regjələ] normal *(Größenangabe bei Getränken, Fastfood)* IV

rehearsal [rɪ'hɜːsl] Probe *(am Theater)* I

rehearse [rɪ'hɜːs] proben *(am Theater)* I

relations *(pl)* [rɪ'leɪʃnz] Beziehungen *(zwischen Ländern, Firmen, Organisationen)* V 4 (83)

relationship [rɪ'leɪʃnʃɪp] Beziehung V 2 (46)

relax [rɪ'læks] (sich) entspannen, sich ausruhen II

relaxed [rɪ'lækst] locker, entspannt III

release [rɪ'liːs] *(CD, Film)* herausbringen, auf den Markt bringen III

reliable [rɪ'laɪəbl] zuverlässig, verlässlich V 2 (34)

remember sth./sb. [rɪ'membə]
1. sich an etwas/jn. erinnern I
2. sich etwas/jn. merken I
3. einer Person/Sache gedenken V 4 (83)

remote control [rɪˌməʊt kən'trəʊl] Fernbedienung IV

rent [rent] Miete V 1 (15)

rent sth. [rent] etwas mieten, etwas leihen V 1 (15)

repair sth. [rɪ'peə] etwas reparieren V 1 (21) • **repair kit** Flickzeug V 4 (84/190)

repeat [rɪ'piːt] Wiederholung *(einer Fernsehsendung)* IV

reply [rɪ'plaɪ]: **in reply to your letter/article/...** in Beantwortung Ihres Briefes/Artikels/... V 3 (52)

report (on) [rɪ'pɔːt] Bericht, Reportage (über) I

report (to sb.) [rɪ'pɔːt] (jm.) berichten II

represent [ˌreprɪ'zent] repräsentieren, vertreten III

°**request** [rɪ'kwest] Bitte

rerun ['riːrʌn] *(AE)* Wiederholung *(einer Fernsehsendung)* IV

rescue helicopter ['reskjuː ˌhelɪkɒptə] Rettungshubschrauber II

research (on) *(no pl)* [rɪ'sɜːtʃ, 'riːsɜːtʃ] Recherche, Nachforschung(en) IV **do research** recherchieren IV

respect [rɪ'spekt] achten, respektieren V 1 (16)

respect [rɪ'spekt] Achtung, Respekt V 1 (16/175) • **out of respect** aus Achtung, aus Respekt V 1 (16/175)

rest [rest] Rest II

restaurant ['restrɒnt] Restaurant II

result [rɪ'zʌlt] Ergebnis, Resultat I

return (to) [rɪ'tɜːn] zurückkehren (nach, zu) V 2 (45)

return ticket [rɪ'tɜːn ˌtɪkɪt] Rückfahrkarte II

°**reunification** [ˌriːˌjuːnɪfɪ'keɪʃn] Wiedervereinigung

review [rɪ'vjuː]: **film/book review** Film-/Buchkritik, Film-/Buchbesprechung V 1 (19)

revise [rɪ'vaɪz]
1. überarbeiten III
2. wiederholen III

revision [rɪ'vɪʒn] Wiederholung *(des Lernstoffs)* I

rhino ['raɪnəʊ] Nashorn II

rice [raɪs] Reis III

rich [rɪtʃ] reich II

ridden ['rɪdn] *siehe* **ride**

riddle ['rɪdl] Rätsel III

ride [raɪd], **rode, ridden** reiten I **go riding** reiten gehen I • **ride a bike** Rad fahren I

ride [raɪd]: **(bike) ride** (Rad-)Fahrt II **take a ride** eine Fahrt machen III

ridiculous [rɪ'dɪkjələs] lächerlich, albern V 3 (52)

right [raɪt] richtig I • **all right** [ɔːl 'raɪt] gut, in Ordnung II • **be right** Recht haben I • **That's right.** Das ist richtig. / Das stimmt. I • **You need a school bag, right?** Du brauchst eine Schultasche, stimmt's? / nicht wahr? I

right [raɪt] rechte(r, s) II • **look right** nach rechts schauen II • **on the right** rechts, auf der rechten Seite II • **turn right** (nach) rechts abbiegen II

right [raɪt]: **right now** jetzt sofort; jetzt gerade I

right [raɪt] Recht IV

rim [rɪm] Kante IV

ring [rɪŋ] Ring II

ring [rɪŋ], **rang, rung** klingeln, läuten II

ringtone ['rɪŋtəʊn] Klingelton III

rise [raɪz], **rose, risen** (auf)steigen IV

risen ['rɪzn] *siehe* **rise**

river ['rɪvə] Fluss II

RnB [ˌɑːr_ən'biː] RnB *(Rhythm and Blues; Form des Blues, in der Rhythmus eine große Rolle spielt; moderner RnB enthält Rap- und Hip Hop-Elemente)* III

road [rəʊd] Straße I • **Park Road** [ˌpɑːk 'rəʊd] Parkstraße I

rock [rɒk]
1. Fels, Felsen III

2. rock concert Rockkonzert V 3 (60) • **rock star** Rockstar V 3 (48)
rock and roll [ˌrɒk‿ən ˈrəʊl] Rock and Roll IV
rode [rəʊd] *siehe* **ride**
role [rəʊl] Rolle III • **role play** Rollenspiel II • **role model** Vorbild V 2 (46)
roll [rəʊl] Brötchen I
Roman [ˈrəʊmən] römisch; Römer, Römerin II
romance [rəʊˈmæns, ˈrəʊmæns] Romanze; Romantik IV
room [ruːm] Raum, Zimmer I
double room Doppelzimmer V 4 (84) • **single room** Einzelzimmer V 4 (84/190)
rose [rəʊz] *siehe* **rise**
round [raʊnd] rund II
round [raʊnd] um ... (herum); in ... umher II • **the other way round** anders herum II
route [ruːt] Strecke, Route IV
royal [ˈrɔɪəl] königlich III
rubber [ˈrʌbə] Radiergummi I
rubbish [ˈrʌbɪʃ] (Haus-)Müll, Abfall II
rucksack [ˈrʌksæk] Rucksack III
rude [ruːd] unhöflich, unverschämt II
rule [ruːl] Regel, Vorschrift IV
follow the rules Regeln befolgen V 3 (52)
ruler [ˈruːlə] Lineal I
run [rʌn] (Wett-)Lauf II
run (-nn-) [rʌn], **ran, run**
1. laufen, rennen I • **run around** herumrennen III
2. run sth. etwas leiten, führen *(Hotel, Firma usw.)* V 2 (45)
°3. the soup kitchen is running low on ... der Suppenküche geht bald ... aus
rung [rʌŋ] *siehe* **ring**
runner [ˈrʌnə] Läufer/in II
running [ˈrʌnɪŋ]: **running shoes** Laufschuhe III • **running track** Laufbahn *(Sport)* III • **running water** fließendes Wasser V 4 (80)
rush hour [ˈrʌʃ‿aʊə] Hauptverkehrszeit III

S

sad [sæd] traurig II
saddle [ˈsædl] Sattel III
sadness [ˈsædnəs] Traurigkeit IV
safe (from) [seɪf] sicher, in Sicherheit (vor) II
safety [ˈseɪfti] Sicherheit IV • **fire safety** Verhalten im Brandfall IV
said [sed] *siehe* **say**
sailor [ˈseɪlə] Seemann, Matrose II
salad [ˈsæləd] Salat *(als Gericht oder Beilage)* I
sale [seɪl] (Aus-, Schluss-)Verkauf IV • **for sale** *(auf Schild)* zu verkaufen IV
salmon [ˈsæmən], *pl* **salmon** Lachs III
salt [sɔːlt] Salz III • **salt water** Salzwasser V 1 (9)
same [seɪm]: **the same ...** der-/die-/dasselbe ...; dieselben ... I • **be/look the same** gleich sein/aussehen I
sandwich [ˈsænwɪtʃ] Sandwich, *(zusammengeklapptes)* belegtes Brot I • **sandwich box** Brotdose I
sang [sæŋ] *siehe* **sing**
°sank [sæŋk] *siehe* **sink**
sat [sæt] *siehe* **sit**
satellite [ˈsætəlaɪt] Satellit IV
Saturday [ˈsætədeɪ, ˈsætədi] Samstag, Sonnabend I
sauna [ˈsɔːnə] Sauna II • **have a sauna** in die Sauna gehen II
sausage [ˈsɒsɪdʒ] (Brat-, Bock-) Würstchen, Wurst I
save [seɪv]
1. retten II
2. sparen II
3. etwas (ab)speichern *(Daten, Telefonnummern)* V 3 (53)
saw [sɔː] *siehe* **see**
saxophone [ˈsæksəfəʊn] Saxophon III
say [seɪ], **said, said** sagen I • **It says here: ...** Hier steht: ... / Es heißt hier: ... II • **say goodbye** sich verabschieden I • **Say hi to Dilip for me.** Grüß Dilip von mir. I • **say sorry** sich entschuldigen II
scan a text (-nn-) [skæn] einen Text schnell nach bestimmten Wörtern/Informationen absuchen II
°scar [skɑː] Narbe
scared [skeəd] verängstigt II • **be scared (of)** Angst haben (vor) I
scarf [skɑːf], *pl* **scarves** [skɑːvs] Schal III
scary [ˈskeəri] unheimlich; gruselig I
scene [siːn] Szene I
schedule [*AE:* ˈskedʒuːl, *BE:* ˈʃedjuːl] *(AE)*
1. Stundenplan IV
2. Fahrplan IV
school [skuːl] Schule I • **at school** in der Schule I • **school bag** Schultasche I • **°School of the Air** *Fernunterricht über Kurzwellenfunk in den dünn besiedelten Gebieten Australiens, für die Primarstufe und die untere Sekundarstufe* • **school subject** Schulfach I • **primary school** Grundschule V 2 (38) • **secondary school** weiterführende Schule V 2 (38)
science [ˈsaɪəns] Naturwissenschaft I • **science fiction** Sciencefiction V 1 (15)
score [skɔː] Spielstand; Punktestand III • **final score** Endstand III • **What's the score now? – 2–0.** *(you say:* **two nil**) Wie steht es jetzt? *(beim Sport)* – 2:0 III
score (a goal) [skɔː] ein Tor schießen, einen Treffer erzielen III
scream [skriːm] schreien III
screen [skriːn]: **flat screen** Flachbildschirm IV
°screw up [ˌskruː‿ˈʌp] *(infml)* Mist bauen; alles vermasseln
sea [siː] Meer, *(die)* See I • **sea snake** Seeschlange V 1 (9)
search (for) [sɜːtʃ] suchen (nach), durchsuchen IV
search engine [ˈsɜːtʃ‿endʒɪn] Suchmaschine *(im Internet)* IV
seat [siːt] (Sitz-)Platz V 1 (15)
second [ˈsekənd] zweite(r, s) I
second floor zweiter Stock *(BE)* / erster Stock *(AE)* IV • **second-hand** [ˌsekənd ˈhænd] gebraucht; aus zweiter Hand III
secondary school [ˈsekəndri skuːl] weiterführende Schule V 2 (38)
secret [ˈsiːkrət] geheim V 3 (51/183)
secret [ˈsiːkrət] Geheimnis V 3 (51/183)
secretly [ˈsiːkrətli] heimlich V 3 (51)
section [ˈsekʃn] Abschnitt, Teil, (Themen-)Bereich III
°security forces *(pl)* [sɪˈkjʊərəti ˌfɔːsɪz] Sicherheitskräfte
see [siː], **saw, seen**
1. sehen I
2. see sb. jn. besuchen, jn. aufsuchen II
I see. Ich verstehe. / Aha. / Ach so. V 1 (14) • **See?** Siehst du? I • **See you.** Tschüs. / Bis bald. I • **Wait and see!** Wart's ab! III
seem (to be / to do) [siːm] (zu sein / zu tun) scheinen IV
seen [siːn] *siehe* **see**
segregate [ˈsegrɪgeɪt] trennen *(nach Rasse, Religion, Geschlecht)* IV
segregation [ˌsegrɪˈgeɪʃn] (Rassen-)Trennung IV
sell [sel], **sold, sold** verkaufen II
be sold out ausverkauft sein; vergriffen sein III

semester [sɪ'mestə] Semester *(Schulhalbjahr in den USA)* IV
semi-final [ˌsemi'faɪnl] Halbfinale III
send (to) [send], **sent, sent** schicken, senden (an) II
sent [sent] *siehe* **send**
sentence ['sentəns] Satz I
separate ['seprət] getrennt, separat V 4 (83)
September [sep'tembə] September I
series, *pl* **series** ['sɪəri:z] (Sende-)Reihe, Serie II
serious ['sɪəriəs] ernst, ernsthaft IV
seriously? ['sɪəriəsli] im Ernst? IV
serve [sɜ:v] bedienen *(Kunden)* V 2 (33)
°**service** ['sɜ:vɪs] Dienst
°**Sesotho** [ses'u:tu:] *Sprache in Südafrika*
set the alarm clock (-tt-) [set], **set, set** den Wecker stellen V 3 (50/182)
settle ['setl] sich niederlassen, siedeln;besiedeln V 1 (16)
settler ['setlə] Siedler/in V 1 (16/174)
setup ['setʌp] Setup II
sex [seks] Geschlecht III
shack [ʃæk] Hütte, Baracke V 4 (80)
shadow ['ʃædəʊ] Schatten IV
shake [ʃeɪk], **shook, shaken** schütteln; zittern V 1 (21)
shaken ['ʃeɪkən] *siehe* **shake**
shame [ʃeɪm]: **It's a shame.** Es ist ein Jammer / eine Schande. V 3 (58)
shampoo [ʃæm'pu:] Shampoo, Haarwaschmittel III
shape [ʃeɪp] Form V 1 (8)
share sth. (with sb.) [ʃeə]
1. sich etwas teilen (mit jm.) I
°**2.** etwas (mit jm.) gemeinsam haben
she [ʃi:] sie I
sheep, *pl* **sheep** [ʃi:p] Schaf II
sheet [ʃi:t] Blatt, Bogen *(Papier)* V 2 (40)
shelf [ʃelf], *pl* **shelves** [ʃelvz] Regal(brett) I
shift [ʃɪft] Schicht *(bei der Arbeit)* IV
shine [ʃaɪn], **shone, shone** scheinen *(Sonne)* II
ship [ʃɪp] Schiff I
shirt [ʃɜ:t] Hemd I
shock [ʃɒk] Schock V 4 (76)
shocked [ʃɒkt] schockiert IV
shocking ['ʃɒkɪŋ] schockierend V 3 (55)
shoe [ʃu:] Schuh I
shone [ʃɒn] *siehe* **shine**
shook [ʃʊk] *siehe* **shake**
shoot [ʃu:t], **shot, shot**
1. schießen, erschießen III
°**2.** fotografieren
shop [ʃɒp] Laden, Geschäft I
shop assistant ['ʃɒp‿əˌsɪstənt] Verkäufer/in I • **shop window** Schaufenster II
shop (-pp-) [ʃɒp] einkaufen (gehen) I
shoplift ['ʃɒplɪft] Ladendiebstahl begehen V 3 (54)
shoplifting ['ʃɒplɪftɪŋ] Ladendiebstahl V 3 (54/184)
shopping ['ʃɒpɪŋ] (das) Einkaufen I
go shopping einkaufen gehen I
shopping list Einkaufsliste I
short [ʃɔ:t] kurz I; klein *(Person)* IV
shorts *(pl)* [ʃɔ:ts] Shorts, kurze Hose I
shot [ʃɒt] *siehe* **shoot**
should [ʃəd, ʃʊd]: **You should have told me.** Du hättest es mir sagen sollen. V 4 (84) • **Why should I ... ?** Warum sollte ich ... ? III
shoulder ['ʃəʊldə] Schulter I
shout [ʃaʊt] schreien, rufen I
show [ʃəʊ] Show, Vorstellung I
show [ʃəʊ], **showed, shown**
1. zeigen I
2. show (sth.) off (mit etwas) angeben V 3 (62)
shower ['ʃaʊə] Dusche I • **have a shower** (sich) duschen I
shown [ʃəʊn] *siehe* **show**
shut up [ˌʃʌt‿'ʌp], **shut, shut** den Mund halten II
shy [ʃaɪ] schüchtern, scheu II
sick [sɪk]
1. I feel sick. Mir ist schlecht. IV
2. *(besonders AE)* krank V 4 (76)
side [saɪd] Seite II
sidewalk ['saɪdwɔ:k] *(AE)* Gehweg, Bürgersteig IV
sights *(pl)* [saɪts] Sehenswürdigkeiten II
sightseeing ['saɪtsi:ɪŋ] Sightseeing *(Besichtigung der lokalen Sehenswürdigkeiten)* V 4 (74)
sign [saɪn] Schild, Zeichen III
sign [saɪn] unterschreiben IV
silence ['saɪləns] Stille; Schweigen III
silent letter [ˌsaɪlənt 'letə] „stummer" Buchstabe *(nicht gesprochener Buchstabe)* II
silly ['sɪli] albern, dumm I
similar (to) ['sɪmələ] ähnlich wie V 2 (39)
simple ['sɪmpl] einfach, nicht kompliziert V 2 (44)
since [sɪns]
1. da, weil IV
2. since April 4th seit dem 4. April IV
sincerely [sɪn'sɪəli]: **Yours sincerely** Mit freundlichen Grüßen/Herzliche Grüße *(Briefschluss bei namentlich bekanntem Empfänger)* IV
sing [sɪŋ], **sang, sung** singen I
singer ['sɪŋə] Sänger/in II
single ['sɪŋgl] ledig, alleinstehend I
single (ticket) einfache Fahrkarte *(nur Hinfahrt)* III • **single room** Einzelzimmer V 4 (84/190)
single ['sɪŋgl] Single III
°**sink** [sɪŋk], **sank, sunk** sinken; versenken
sink [sɪŋk] Spüle, Spülbecken I
sir [sɜ:, sə]: **Dear Sir or Madam** Sehr geehrte Damen und Herren *(Anrede in Briefen)* IV
°**sis** [sɪs] *(infml) kurz für* **sister**
sister ['sɪstə] Schwester I • **sister city** *(AE)* Partnerstadt IV
sit (-tt-) [sɪt], **sat, sat** sitzen; sich setzen I • **sit down** sich hinsetzen II • **Sit with me.** Setz dich zu mir. / Setzt euch zu mir. I
size [saɪz] Größe I
skate [skeɪt] Inliner/Skateboard fahren I
skateboard ['skeɪtbɔ:d] Skateboard I
skater ['skeɪtə] Skateboardfahrer/in III
skates *(pl)* [skeɪts] Inliner I
sketch [sketʃ] Sketch I
ski [ski:] Ski fahren/laufen III
ski [ski:] Ski III • **ski instructor** ['ski:‿ɪnˌstrʌktə] Skilehrer/in V 2 (32/176) • **ski slope** ['ski: sləʊp] Skipiste III
skill [skɪl] Fähigkeit, Fertigkeit V 2 (32)
skills file ['skɪlz faɪl] *Anhang mit Lern- und Arbeitstechniken* I
skim a text (-mm-) [skɪm] einen Text überfliegen *(um den Inhalt grob zu erfassen)* III
skin [skɪn] Haut IV
skinny ['skɪni] mager IV
skirt [skɜ:t] Rock II
sky [skaɪ] Himmel II
°**skydiving** ['skaɪdaɪvɪŋ] Fallschirmspringen
skyline ['skaɪlaɪn] Skyline *(Horizont; Silhouette)* IV
skyscraper ['skaɪskreɪpə] Wolkenkratzer IV
slave [sleɪv] Sklave, Sklavin II
sledge [sledʒ] Schlitten III
sleep [sli:p], **slept, slept** schlafen I
sleep [sli:p] Schlaf III

sleeping bag ['sliːpɪŋ bæg] Schlafsack V 1 (6)
sleepless ['sliːpləs] schlaflos IV
sleepover ['sliːpəʊvə] Schlafparty III
slept [slept] *siehe* **sleep**
slide [slaɪd] Folie *(bei einer Computerpräsentation)*; Dia V 4 (88)
°**Slip! Slop! Slap!** [slɪp, slɒp, slæp] *kurz für:* Schlüpf in ein Hemd! Trag Sonnenschutz auf! Setz einen Hut auf! *(als Schutzmaßnahmen gegen UV-Strahlung)*
slogan ['sləʊgən] Slogan V 4 (81)
slow [sləʊ] langsam II
slum [slʌm] Slum, Elendsviertel V 4 (74)
small [smɔːl] klein I
smart [smɑːt] clever, schlau II
smell [smel] riechen II
smell [smel] Geruch II
smile [smaɪl] lächeln I • **smile at sb.** jn. anlächeln II
smile [smaɪl] Lächeln II
smoke [sməʊk] rauchen III • **No smoking!** Rauchen verboten. III
smoke [sməʊk] Rauch III
snack [snæk] Snack, Imbiss II
snake [sneɪk] Schlange I • **sea snake** ['siː sneɪk] Seeschlange V 1 (9)
°**snakebite** ['sneɪkbaɪt] Schlangenbiss
°**snorkel** ['snɔːkl] schnorcheln
snow [snəʊ] Schnee II
snowball ['snəʊbɔːl] Schneeball IV
snowshoe ['snəʊʃuː] Schneeschuh III
snowshoeing ['snəʊʃuːɪŋ] Schneeschuhwandern III
so [səʊ]
1. also; deshalb, daher I • **So?** Und? / Na und? II
°2. sodass
3. **so sweet** so süß I • **so far** bisher, bis jetzt IV
3. **so that** sodass, damit III
4. **Do you really think so?** Meinst du wirklich? / Glaubst du das wirklich? II
▶ S.185 German 'so'
soap [səʊp] Seife I • **soap opera** ['səʊp‿ɒprə] *(kurz:* **soap***)* Seifenoper IV
soccer ['sɒkə] Fußball IV
social ['səʊʃl] sozial, Sozial- IV
sock [sɒk] Socke, Strumpf I
soda ['səʊdə] *(AE)* Limonade IV
sofa ['səʊfə] Sofa I
soft [sɒft] weich IV • **soft drink** alkoholfreies Getränk IV
software ['sɒftweə] Software II
sold [səʊld] *siehe* **sell** • **be sold out** ausverkauft sein; vergriffen sein III
soldier ['səʊldʒə] Soldat/in IV
solve [sɒlv] lösen V 2 (34)
some [səm, sʌm] einige, ein paar I
some cheese/juice etwas Käse/Saft I
somebody ['sʌmbədi] jemand I
Find/Ask somebody who ... Finde/Frage jemanden, der ... II • **somebody else** jemand anders IV
°**somehow** ['sʌmhaʊ] irgendwie
someone ['sʌmwʌn] jemand IV
something ['sʌmθɪŋ] etwas II
sometimes ['sʌmtaɪmz] manchmal I
somewhere ['sʌmweə] irgendwo(hin) II • **somewhere else** woanders IV • **somewhere to stay** ein Platz zum Übernachten V 4 (84)
son [sʌn] Sohn I
song [sɒŋ] Lied, Song I
soon [suːn] bald I
sore [sɔː]**: have a sore throat** Halsschmerzen haben II
sorry ['sɒri]**: (I'm) sorry.** Entschuldigung. / Tut mir leid. I • **Sorry, I'm late.** Entschuldigung, dass ich zu spät bin/komme. I • **Sorry?** Wie bitte? I • **say sorry** sich entschuldigen II
sort [sɔːt] Art, Sorte II
SOS [ˌes‿əʊ‿'es] SOS *(internationales Funknotsignal)* V 3 (58)
sound [saʊnd] klingen, sich *(gut usw.)* anhören I
sound [saʊnd] Laut; Klang I
sound file ['saʊnd faɪl] Tondatei, Soundfile III
soundtrack ['saʊndtræk] Soundtrack, Filmmusik V 1 (19)
soup [suːp] Suppe II
source [sɔːs] Quelle *(von Information, Energie usw.)* IV
south [saʊθ] Süden; nach Süden; südlich III
southbound ['saʊθbaʊnd] Richtung Süden III
south-east [ˌsaʊθ'iːst] Südosten; nach Südosten; südöstlich III
south-west [ˌsaʊθ'west] Südwesten; nach Südwesten; südwestlich III
souvenir [ˌsuːvə'nɪə] Souvenir, Mitbringsel IV
space [speɪs] Platz *(Raum)* IV
Move back one space. Geh ein Feld zurück. II • **Move on one space.** Geh ein Feld vor. II
spaghetti [spə'geti] Spaghetti II
sparkling water ['spɑːklɪŋ] Mineralwasser mit Kohlensäure, Sprudel IV
speak (to) [spiːk]**, spoke, spoken** sprechen (mit), reden (mit) II
special ['speʃl]**: a special day** ein besonderer Tag I • **What's special about ...?** Was ist das Besondere an ...? V 1 (7)
specific [spə'sɪfɪk] bestimmte(r,s), spezifische(r,s) IV
speech [spiːtʃ] Rede IV • **make a speech** eine Rede halten IV
spell [spel] buchstabieren I
spelling ['spelɪŋ] (Recht-)Schreibung, Schreibweise III
spend [spend]**, spent, spent: spend money (on)** Geld ausgeben (für) II • **spend time (on)** Zeit verbringen (mit) II
spent [spent] *siehe* **spend**
°**spice** [spaɪs] Gewürz
spicy ['spaɪsi] würzig, scharf gewürzt III
splash [splæʃ] spritzen IV
spoke [spəʊk] *siehe* **speak**
spoken ['spəʊkən] *siehe* **speak**
spoon [spuːn] Löffel III
sport [spɔːt] Sport; Sportart I
do sport *(BE)* Sport treiben I
sports centre Sportzentrum I
sports hall Sporthalle III
sportsman ['spɔːtsmən] Sportler IV
sportswoman ['spɔːtswʊmən] Sportlerin IV
sporty ['spɔːti] sportlich III
spot (-tt-) [spɒt] entdecken III
spotlight ['spɒtlaɪt] Spotlight IV
spray [spreɪ] sprühen V 3 (54/184)
spring [sprɪŋ]
1. Frühling I
2. Quelle V 3 (58)
spy [spaɪ] Spion/in I
square [skweə] Platz III • **square km (sq km)** Quadratkilometer IV
squeeze [skwiːz] drücken; (aus-)pressen III
squirrel ['skwɪrəl] Eichhörnchen II
stadium ['steɪdiəm] Stadion III
stage [steɪdʒ] Bühne III
stairs *(pl)* [steəz] Treppe; Treppenstufen I
stamp [stæmp] Briefmarke I
stand [stænd]**, stood, stood** stehen; sich (hin)stellen II
star [stɑː]
1. Stern II
2. (Film-, Pop-)Star I • **rock star** ['rɒk stɑː] Rockstar V 3 (48)
start [stɑːt] starten, anfangen, beginnen (mit) I • **start a business** eine Firma gründen V 2 (44)
start [stɑːt] Start IV
state [steɪt] Staat III

statement ['steɪtmənt] Aussage, Feststellung III
station ['steɪʃn] Bahnhof I • **at the station** am Bahnhof I • **fire station** Feuerwache IV • **gas station** *(AE)* Tankstelle IV • **lifeguard station** ['laɪfgɑːd] Station der Rettungsschwimmer/innen V 1 (14) **petrol station** *(BE)* Tankstelle IV °**sheep station** Schaffarm
statue ['stætʃuː] Statue II
stay [steɪ]
1. bleiben I • **stay out** draußen bleiben, wegbleiben III
2. wohnen, übernachten II • **stay with** wohnen bei III • **somewhere to stay** ein Platz zum Übernachten V 4 (84)
stay [steɪ] Aufenthalt V 4 (86)
Have a pleasant stay. Einen angenehmen Aufenthalt! V 4 (86)
steak [steɪk] Steak III
steal [stiːl], **stole, stolen** stehlen II
steel [stiːl] Stahl III • **steel drum** Steeldrum III
°**steer** [stɪə] junger Ochse
step [step]
1. Schritt I
2. Treppenstufe IV
stereo ['steriəʊ] Stereoanlage I
stew [stjuː] Eintopf(gericht) III
°**stick** [stɪk] Stock
stick [stɪk], **stuck, stuck**
1. (auf)kleben V 3 (54/184)
2. **stick sth. up** etwas aufhängen *(und dabei mit Klebstoff befestigen)* V 3 (54)
3. **stick out of sth.** aus etwas herausragen, herausstehen III
sticker ['stɪkə] Sticker IV
still [stɪl] (immer) noch I
stole [stəʊl] *siehe* **steal**
stolen ['stəʊlən]
1. *siehe* **steal**
2. gestohlene(r) V 1 (17)
stomach ['stʌmək] Magen II
stomach ache Magenschmerzen, Bauchweh II
stone [stəʊn] Stein II
stood [stʊd] *siehe* **stand**
stop (-pp-) [stɒp]
1. aufhören I
2. anhalten I
Stop that! Hör auf damit! / Lass das! I
stop [stɒp] Halt IV
store [stɔː] (ein)lagern, aufbewahren V 3 (58)
storm [stɔːm] Sturm; Gewitter II
stormy ['stɔːmi] stürmisch II
story ['stɔːri] Geschichte, Erzählung I

straight on [streɪt‿'ɒn] geradeaus weiter II
°**straighten up (one's life)** [ˌstreɪtn‿'ʌp] (sein Leben) in Ordnung bringen
strange [streɪndʒ] seltsam, sonderbar; fremd III
strawberry ['strɔːbəri] Erdbeere II
street [striːt] Straße I • **at 7 Hamilton Street** in der Hamiltonstraße 7 I
strength [streŋθ] Stärke, Kraft V 2 (40)
stress [stres] Betonung III
stressful ['stresfl] anstrengend, stressig V 2 (45)
strict [strɪkt] streng III
strike [straɪk] Streik III • **be on strike** streiken, sich im Streik befinden III • **go on strike** streiken, in den Streik treten III
strong [strɒŋ] stark II
structure ['strʌktʃə] strukturieren, aufbauen II
stuck [stʌk] *siehe* **stick**
student ['stjuːdənt] Schüler/in; Student/in I • **exchange student** Austauschschüler/in III
studio ['stjuːdiəʊ] Studio III
study ['stʌdi] studieren; sorgfältig durchlesen; lernen IV • **study hall** *Zeit zum selbstständigen Arbeiten/ Lernen in der Schule* IV • **study skills** *(pl)* Lern- und Arbeitstechniken I
stuff [stʌf] Zeug, Kram II
stupid ['stjuːpɪd] blöd, dämlich II
style [staɪl] Stil V 4 (81)
subject ['sʌbdʒɪkt] Schulfach I
suburb ['sʌbɜːb] Vorort V 4 (75)
subway ['sʌbweɪ]: **the subway** *(AE)* die U-Bahn II
succeed (in sth.) [sək'siːd] Erfolg haben, erfolgreich sein (mit etwas, bei etwas) IV
success [sək'ses] Erfolg III
successful [sək'sesfl] erfolgreich III
such (a) [sʌtʃ] so (ein/e), solch (ein/e); solche V 3 (58)
► S.185 German 'so'
suddenly ['sʌdnli] plötzlich, auf einmal I
suffer (from sth.) ['sʌfə] (an/unter etwas) leiden IV
sugar ['ʃʊgə] Zucker II
°**suggest** [sə'dʒest] vorschlagen
suggestion [sə'dʒestʃən] Vorschlag IV
suit [suːt] Anzug V 4 (87)
suitable ['suːtəbl] geeignet, passend V 2 (40)
suitcase ['suːtkeɪs] Koffer II

sum sth. up (-mm-) [ˌsʌm‿'ʌp] etwas zusammenfassen V 2 (46)
summarize sth. ['sʌməraɪz] etwas zusammenfassen IV
summary ['sʌməri] Zusammenfassung IV
summer ['sʌmə] Sommer I
sun [sʌn] Sonne II
Sunday ['sʌndeɪ, 'sʌndi] Sonntag I
sung [sʌŋ] *siehe* **sing**
sunglasses *(pl)* ['sʌnglɑːsɪz] (eine) Sonnenbrille I
°**sunk** [sʌŋk] siehe **sink**
sunny ['sʌni] sonnig II
sunscreen ['sʌnskriːn] Sonnenschutzmittel V 1 (9)
°**sunsmart: get sunsmart** ['sʌnsmɑːt] *etwa: schütze dich intelligent gegen die Sonne*
super ['suːpə] super IV
supermarket ['suːpəmɑːkɪt] Supermarkt II
superstar ['suːpəstɑː] Superstar V 4 (81)
support [sə'pɔːt] unterstützen IV
support a team eine Mannschaft unterstützen; Fan einer Mannschaft sein III
supporter [sə'pɔːtə] Anhänger/in, Fan III
sure [ʃʊə, ʃɔː] klar, sicher IV • **be sure** sicher sein II • **make sure that ...** sich vergewissern, dass ...; dafür sorgen, dass ... IV
surf [sɜːf]: **surf the internet** im Internet surfen III
surfboard ['sɜːfbɔːd] Surfbrett II
surfing ['sɜːfɪŋ]: **go surfing** wellenreiten gehen, surfen gehen II
surname ['sɜːneɪm] Nachname V 2 (37)
surprise [sə'praɪz] Überraschung III
surprise sb. [sə'praɪz] jn. überraschen III
surprised (at sth.) [sə'praɪzd] überrascht (über/von etwas) III
surprising [sə'praɪzɪŋ] überraschend, erstaunlich V 1 (14)
survey (on) ['sɜːveɪ] Umfrage, Untersuchung (über) II
survival [sə'vaɪvl] Überleben V 4 (84) • **survival kit** Überlebenspäckchen V 4 (84)
survive [sə'vaɪv] überleben II
°**suspense** [sə'spens] Spannung
°**suspense graph** [sə'spens grɑːf] Spannungskurve
swam [swæm] *siehe* **swim**
swap sth. (for sth.) (-pp-) [swɒp] etwas (ein)tauschen (für etwas/ gegen etwas) IV

°**Swati Snacks** ['swɒtɪ snæks] *Fastfoodrestaurant in Mumbai, das traditionelle indische Küche anbietet*
sweat [swet] schwitzen IV
sweat [swet] Schweiß IV
sweatshirt ['swetʃɜːt] Sweatshirt I
sweet [swiːt] süß I
sweetheart ['swiːthɑːt] Liebling, Schatz II
sweets *(pl)* [swiːts] Süßigkeiten I
swim (-mm-) [swɪm]**, swam, swum** schwimmen I • **go swimming** schwimmen gehen I
swimmer ['swɪmə] Schwimmer/in II
swimming ['swɪmɪŋ]**: swimming pool** [puːl] Schwimmbad, Schwimmbecken I • **swimming trunks** *(pl)* [trʌŋks] Badehose III **indoor swimming pool** Hallenbad V 4 (80/189) • **outdoor swimming pool** Freibad V 4 (80/189)
swimsuit ['swɪmsuːt] Badeanzug III
swum [swʌm] *siehe* **swim**
syllable ['sɪləbl] Silbe I
synonym ['sɪnənɪm] Synonym *(Wort mit gleicher oder sehr ähnlicher Bedeutung)* IV
system ['sɪstəm] System IV

T

table ['teɪbl] Tisch I
table tennis ['teɪbl tenɪs] Tischtennis I • **table tennis bat** Tischtennisschläger III
take [teɪk]**, took, taken**
1. nehmen I
2. (weg-, hin)bringen I
3. dauern, *(Zeit)* brauchen III
take a break eine Pause machen IV • **take a deep breath** tief Luft holen V 1 (20/175) • **take a message** eine Nachricht entgegennehmen V 4 (86/191) • **Can I take a message for her/him?** Soll ich ihr/ihm etwas ausrichten? V 4 (86/191)
take a ride eine Fahrt machen III
take notes sich Notizen machen I
take out herausnehmen I • **take part (in)** teilnehmen (an) III
take photos Fotos machen, fotografieren I • **take place** stattfinden IV • **take sth. off** etwas ausziehen *(Kleidung)* II • **take 10 c off** 10 Cent abziehen I • **take sth. over** etwas übernehmen; etwas in seine Gewalt bringen IV • °**Take turns.** Wechselt euch ab. • **We'll take them.** *(beim Einkaufen)* Wir nehmen sie. I

taken ['teɪkən] *siehe* **take**
talent ['tælənt] Talent, Begabung III
talk (to sb. about sth.) [tɔːk] (mit jm. über etwas) reden, sich (mit jm. über etwas) unterhalten I
talk [tɔːk] Vortrag, Rede V 4 (88)
give a talk (on sth.) einen Vortrag/ eine Rede halten (über etwas) V 4 (88/191)
tall [tɔːl] hoch *(Bäume, Türme usw.)*; groß *(Person)* IV
tattoo [tə'tuː] Tattoo IV
taught [tɔːt] *siehe* **teach**
taxi ['tæksi] Taxi III
tea [tiː] Tee; *(auch:) leichte Nachmittags- oder Abendmahlzeit* I
teach [tiːtʃ]**, taught, taught** unterrichten, lehren I
teacher ['tiːtʃə] Lehrer/in I • **head teacher** Schulleiter/in III
team [tiːm] Team, Mannschaft I
tear [tɪə] Träne IV
tear sth. off [teə]**, tore, torn** etwas abreißen IV
teaspoon ['tiːspuːn] Teelöffel III
°**techie** ['teki] *(infml)* Technikfreak, -narr
technical ['teknɪkl] technisch V 2 (39)
technician [tek'nɪʃn] Techniker/in V 2 (35)
°**technique** [tek'niːk] Technik, Methode
technology [tek'nɒlədʒi] Technologie V 2 (35)
teddy ['tedi] Teddybär III
teen [tiːn] Teenager-, Jugend- III
teenager ['tiːneɪdʒə] Teenager, Jugendliche(r) II
teeth [tiːθ] *Plural von „tooth"*
telephone ['telɪfəʊn] Telefon I
telephone number Telefonnummer I • **What's your telephone number?** Was ist deine Telefonnummer? I
television (TV) ['telɪvɪʒn] Fernsehen I
tell (about) [tel]**, told, told** erzählen (von), berichten (über) I • **Tell me your names.** Sagt mir eure Namen. I • **tell sb. the way** jm. den Weg beschreiben II • **tell sb. to do sth.** jm. sagen, dass er/sie etwas tun soll V 2 (34/177)
► S.177 (to) ask/tell/expect/want sb. to do sth.
temperature ['temprətʃə] Temperatur II • **have a temperature** Fieber haben II
tennis ['tenɪs] Tennis I
tense [tens] (grammatische) Zeit, Tempus III

tent [tent] Zelt IV
term [tɜːm] Trimester II
terrible ['terəbl] schrecklich, furchtbar I
terrified ['terɪfaɪd]**: be terrified (of)** schreckliche Angst haben (vor) IV
°**terrifying** ['terɪfaɪɪŋ] furchtbar
°**territory** ['terətri] Bundesterritorium *(in Australien, hat weniger Autonomie als ein Staat)*
terrorist ['terərɪst] Terrorist/in; Terror-, terroristisch IV
test [test] Test, Prüfung II
text [tekst] Text I • **text message** SMS III • **skim a text** einen Text überfliegen *(um den Inhalt grob zu erfassen)* III
text sb. [tekst] jm. eine SMS schicken III
than [ðæn, ðən] als II • **more than** mehr als II • **more than me** mehr als ich II
thank [θæŋk]**: Thank you.** Danke (schön). I • **Thanks.** Danke. I **Thanks a lot!** Vielen Dank! I **Thanks very much!** Danke sehr! / Vielen Dank! II
that [ðət, ðæt]
1. das (dort) I
2. jene(r, s) I
That's me. Das bin ich. I • **That's right.** Das ist richtig. / Das stimmt. I • **That's up to you.** Das liegt bei dir. / Das kannst/musst du (selbst) entscheiden. III • **that's why** deshalb, darum V 1 (16)
that [ðət, ðæt] der, die, das; die *(Relativpronomen)* III
that [ðət, ðæt] dass I • **so that** sodass, damit III
that far/good/bad/... [ðæt] so weit/ gut/schlecht/... III
the [ðə, ði] der, die, das; die I
theatre ['θɪətə] Theater II
°**theft** [θeft] Diebstahl
their [ðeə] ihr, ihre *(Plural)* I
theirs [ðeəz] ihrer, ihre, ihrs II
them [ðəm, ðem] sie; ihnen I
°**theme park worker** ['θiːm pɑːk] *jd., der in einem Freizeitpark arbeitet*
themselves [ðəm'selvz] sich (selbst) III
then [ðen] dann, danach I • **now and then** gelegentlich, ab und zu V 1 (20)
there [ðeə]
1. da, dort I
2. dahin, dorthin I
down there dort unten II • **over there** da drüben, dort drüben I
there are es sind (vorhanden); es gibt I • **there's** es ist (vorhanden);

es gibt I • **there isn't a ...** es ist kein/e ...; es gibt kein/e ... I
thermometer [θə'mɒmɪtə] Thermometer II
these [ðiːz] diese, die (hier) I
they [ðeɪ] sie *(Plural)* I
thief [θiːf], *pl* **thieves** [θiːvz] Dieb/in II
thing [θɪŋ] Ding, Sache I • **What was the best thing about ...?** Was war das Beste an ...? II
think [θɪŋk], **thought, thought** glauben, meinen, denken I
think about 1. nachdenken über II; 2. denken über, halten von II
think of 1. denken über, halten von II; 2. denken an; sich ausdenken II
third [θɜːd] dritte(r, s) I
third [θɜːd]: **a third** ein Drittel V 4 (74)
this [ðɪs]
1. dies (hier) I
2. diese(r, s) I
This is Isabel. Hier spricht Isabel. / Hier ist Isabel. *(am Telefon)* II
this morning/afternoon/evening heute Morgen/Nachmittag/Abend I • **this way** hier entlang, in diese Richtung II
those [ðəʊz] die (da), jene (dort) I
thought [θɔːt] *siehe* **think**
thought [θɔːt] Gedanke IV
thoughtful ['θɔːtfl] nachdenklich; aufmerksam, rücksichtsvoll V 4 (82)
thousand ['θaʊznd] tausend I
threaten ['θretn] (be)drohen V 3 (54)
°**three-part** dreiteilige(r, s)
threw [θruː] *siehe* **throw**
thrilling ['θrɪlɪŋ] aufregend, spannend V 3 (64)
throat [θrəʊt] Hals, Kehle II
°**throat lozenges** ['lɒzɪndʒɪz] Halspastillen, Lutschtabletten
through [θruː] durch II
throw [θrəʊ], **threw, thrown** werfen I • **throw up** sich übergeben IV
thrown [θrəʊn] *siehe* **throw**
°**thump** [θʌmp] pochen
Thursday ['θɜːzdeɪ, 'θɜːzdi] Donnerstag I
°**tick** [tɪk] Häkchen
°**tick** [tɪk] ankreuzen, ein Häkchen machen
ticket ['tɪkɪt]
1. Eintrittskarte I
2. Fahrkarte II
ticket machine Fahrkartenautomat III • **ticket office** Kasse *(für den Verkauf von Eintrittskarten)* IV; Fahrkartenschalter III
one-day ticket Tages(fahr)karte III • **return ticket** Rückfahrkarte II
single (ticket) einfache Fahrkarte *(nur Hinfahrt)* III
tidy ['taɪdi] aufräumen I
tidy ['taɪdi] ordentlich, aufgeräumt II
tie [taɪ] Krawatte V 2 (40)
tie *(-ing form:* **tying***)* [taɪ] binden V 2 (40/180)
tiger ['taɪgə] Tiger II
tight [taɪt]
1. fest IV
2. dicht, eng V 4 (77)
till [tɪl] bis *(zeitlich)* I
time [taɪm]
1. Zeit; Uhrzeit I
2. **time(s)** Mal(e); -mal II
at a time gleichzeitig, auf einmal V 3 (54) • **any time** jederzeit IV
cross a time zone [zəʊn] eine Zeitzone passieren IV • **for the first time** zum ersten Mal IV • **Have a good time.** Viel Spaß! V 4 (86) • **in time** rechtzeitig II • **three times** dreimal III • **What's the time?** Wie spät ist es? I
°**timeline** ['taɪmlaɪn] Zeitachse, Zeitleiste
timetable ['taɪmteɪbl]
1. Stundenplan I
2. Fahrplan II
timing ['taɪmɪŋ]: **bad timing** schlechtes Timing III
°**tinned** [tɪnd] Dosen-
tiny ['taɪni] winzig V 4 (77)
tip [tɪp]
1. Tipp II
2. Spitze IV
tired ['taɪəd] müde I • **be tired of sth.** genug von etwas haben, etwas satt haben IV
title ['taɪtl] Titel, Überschrift I
to [tə, tu]
1. zu, nach I • **to Jenny's** zu Jenny I • °**to the front** nach vorn
2. **an e-mail to** eine E-Mail an I
write to schreiben an I
3. **quarter to 12** Viertel vor 12 (11.45/23.45) I
4. **try to help/to play/...** versuchen, zu helfen/zu spielen/... I
5. um zu II
6. **from Monday to Friday** von Montag bis Freitag III
°**toad: cane toad** ['keɪn təʊd] Agakröte
toast [təʊst] Toast(brot) I
tobacco [tə'bækəʊ] Tabak II
today [tə'deɪ] heute I
°**to-do list** [tə 'duː lɪst] Erledigungsliste
toe [təʊ] Zeh I
together [tə'geðə] zusammen I
toilet ['tɔɪlət] Toilette I
told [təʊld] *siehe* **tell**
tomato [tə'mɑːtəʊ], *pl* **tomatoes** Tomate II
tomorrow [tə'mɒrəʊ] morgen I
tomorrow's weather das Wetter von morgen II
tonight [tə'naɪt] heute Nacht, heute Abend I • **tonight's programme** das Programm von heute Abend; das heutige Abendprogramm II
too [tuː]: **from Bristol too** auch aus Bristol I • **Me too.** Ich auch. I
too much/big/... [tuː] zu viel/groß/... I
took [tʊk] *siehe* **take**
tool [tuːl] Werkzeug IV
tooth [tuːθ], *pl* **teeth** [tiːθ] Zahn I
toothache ['tuːθeɪk] Zahnschmerzen II
toothless ['tuːθləs] zahnlos IV
top [tɒp]
1. Spitze, oberes Ende I • **at the top (of)** oben, am oberen Ende, an der Spitze (von) I • **on top (of sth.)** [ɒn 'tɒp] oben, oben drauf (auf etwas) V 4 (85)
2. Top, Oberteil I
topic ['tɒpɪk] Thema, Themenbereich I • **topic sentence** *Satz, der in das Thema eines Absatzes einführt* II
tore [tɔː] *siehe* **tear**
torn [tɔːn] *siehe* **tear**
tornado [tɔː'neɪdəʊ] Tornado, Wirbelsturm II
tortoise ['tɔːtəs] Schildkröte I
touch [tʌtʃ] berühren, anfassen II
touch [tʌtʃ]: **keep in touch** in Verbindung bleiben, Kontakt halten III
°**tough** [tʌf] zäh
tour [tʊə]: **tour (of the house)** Rundgang, Tour (durch das Haus) I • **tour guide** (Fremden-)Führer/in, Reiseleiter/in IV
tourist ['tʊərɪst] Tourist/in II
tourist information Fremdenverkehrsamt II
towards sb./sth. [tə'wɔːdz] auf jn./etwas zu II
towel ['taʊəl] Handtuch IV
tower ['taʊə] Turm I
town [taʊn] (Klein-)Stadt I
°**township** ['taʊnʃɪp] *Bezeichnung für die während der Apartheid in Südafrika eingerichteten Wohngegenden für die nicht weiße Bevölkerung*
track [træk]
1. Stück, Titel, Track *(auf einer CD)*

III
°2. Pfad
°**tractor** ['træktə] Traktor
tradition [trə'dɪʃn] Tradition IV
traditional [trə'dɪʃənl] traditionell III
traffic ['træfɪk] Verkehr II • **traffic jam** (Verkehrs-)Stau IV • **traffic light** (Verkehrs-)Ampel IV
°**trail** [treɪl] Spur
train [treɪn] Zug I • **on the train** im Zug I
train [treɪn]
1. trainieren III
2. **train (as sth.)** eine Ausbildung (zu/als etwas) machen V 2 (32/176)
trainers *(pl)* ['treɪnəz] Turnschuhe II
training ['treɪnɪŋ]
1. (berufliche) Ausbildung V 2 (32)
2. **training session** ['seʃn] Trainingsstunde, -einheit III
tram [træm] Straßenbahn III
translate (from ... into) [træns'leɪt] übersetzen (aus ... ins) III
translation [træns'leɪʃn] Übersetzung III
°**transparency** [træns'pærənsi] Folie *(für Overheadprojektoren)*
transport ['trænspɔːt] Beförderung, Transport III • **public transport** *(no pl)* [ˌpʌblɪk 'trænspɔːt] öffentliche Verkehrsmittel, öffentlicher Personennahverkehr V 4 (75)
trash [træʃ] *(AE)* Abfall, Müll V 3 (58)
travel (-ll-) ['trævl] reisen II
travel agent ['trævl‿ˌeɪdʒənt] Reisebürokaufmann/-kauffrau V 2 (43) • **travel agent's** Reisebüro V 2 (43/180)
Travelcard ['trævlkɑːd] Tages-/Wochen-/Monatsfahrkarte *(der Londoner Verkehrsbetriebe)* III
tree [triː] Baum I
trendy ['trendi] modisch, schick III
trick [trɪk]
1. (Zauber-)Kunststück, Trick I **do tricks** (Zauber-)Kunststücke machen I
2. Streich II
trip [trɪp] Reise; Ausflug I • **go on a trip** einen Ausflug machen II
trouble ['trʌbl] Schwierigkeiten, Ärger II • **be in trouble** in Schwierigkeiten sein; Ärger kriegen II
troublemaker ['trʌblmeɪkə] Randalierer/in, Unruhestifter/in V 3 (54)
trousers *(pl)* ['traʊzəz] Hose II
truck [trʌk] Lastwagen V 1 (17)
true [truː] wahr II
trumpet ['trʌmpɪt] Trompete III
try [traɪ]
1. versuchen I
2. probieren, kosten I
try and do sth. / try to do sth. versuchen, etwas zu tun I • **try on** anprobieren *(Kleidung)* I
try [traɪ] Versuch V 3 (62) • **Nice try.** Netter Versuch. V 3 (62)
T-shirt ['tiːʃɜːt] T-Shirt I
tsunami [tsuː'nɑːmi] Tsunami IV
tube [tjuːb]: **the Tube** *(no pl)* die Londoner U-Bahn III
Tuesday ['tjuːzdeɪ, 'tjuːzdi] Dienstag I
tune [tjuːn] Melodie III
tunnel ['tʌnl] Tunnel II
turkey ['tɜːki] Truthahn, Pute/Puter III
turn [tɜːn]
1. sich umdrehen II • **turn left/right** (nach) links/rechts abbiegen II • **turn to sb.** sich jm. zuwenden; sich an jn. wenden I
2. **turn sth. on/off** etwas ein-, ausschalten III
3. **turn sth. down/up** etwas leiser/lauter stellen IV
turn [tɜːn]: **It's your turn.** Du bist dran / an der Reihe. I • **Miss a turn.** Einmal aussetzen. II • °**Take turns.** Wechselt euch ab. • **Whose turn is it?** Wer ist dran / an der Reihe? II
turtle ['tɜːtl] Wasserschildkröte V 3 (58)
°**tusk** [tʌsk] Hauer *(Eckzahn eines Wildschweines)*
TV [tiː'viː] Fernsehen I • **on TV** im Fernsehen I • **watch TV** fernsehen I • **TV listings** *(pl)* das Fernsehprogramm IV
twice [twaɪs] zweimal • **twice a week** zweimal pro Woche III
twin [twɪn]: **twin brother** Zwillingsbruder I • **twins** *(pl)* Zwillinge I **twin town** Partnerstadt IV
two all [ˌtuː‿'ɔːl] 2 beide (2:2 unentschieden) III
type [taɪp] Typ III
typical (of) ['tɪpɪkl] typisch (für) V 4 (76)

U

ugly ['ʌgli] hässlich V 3 (57)
°**ultraviolet rays** [ˌʌltrəˌvaɪələt 'reɪz] ultraviolette Strahlen
unbelievable [ˌʌnbɪ'liːvəbl] unglaublich IV
uncle ['ʌŋkl] Onkel I
unclear [ˌʌn'klɪə] unklar III
uncomfortable [ʌn'kʌmftəbl] unbequem, unbehaglich IV
unconscious [ʌn'kɒnʃəs] bewusstlos V 1 (23/176)
uncool [ˌʌn'kuːl] *(infml)* uncool III
uncountable [ʌn'kaʊntəbl] unzählbar IV
under ['ʌndə] unter I • °**Down Under** [ˌdaʊn‿'ʌndə] *(infml)* (in/nach) Australien
underground ['ʌndəgraʊnd]: **the underground** die U-Bahn II
°**underline** [ˌʌndə'laɪn] unterstreichen
°**underlined** [ˌʌndə'laɪnd] unterstrichen
understand [ˌʌndə'stænd], **understood, understood** verstehen, begreifen I
understandable [ˌʌndə'stændəbl] verständlich IV
understood [ˌʌndə'stʊd] *siehe* **understand**
unemployment [ˌʌnɪm'plɔɪmənt] Arbeitslosigkeit V 4 (75)
unfair [ˌʌn'feə] unfair, ungerecht III
unforgettable [ˌʌnfə'getəbl] unvergesslich V 4 (80)
unforgivable [ˌʌnfə'gɪvəbl] unverzeihlich V 4 (82)
unfortunately [ʌn'fɔːtʃənətli] leider IV
unfriendly [ʌn'frendli] unfreundlich III
unhappy [ʌn'hæpi] unglücklich III
unhealthy [ʌn'helθi] ungesund III
uniform ['juːnɪfɔːm] Uniform I
unit ['juːnɪt] Lektion, Kapitel I
united: **the United Kingdom (UK)** [juˌnaɪtɪd 'kɪŋdəm] ([ˌjuː 'keɪ]) das Vereinigte Königreich *(Großbritannien und Nordirland)* III • **the United States (US)** [juˌnaɪtɪd 'steɪts] ([ˌjuː‿'es]) die Vereinigten Staaten *(von Amerika)* III
university [ˌjuːnɪ'vɜːsəti] Universität IV
unkind [ˌʌn'kaɪnd] unfreundlich V 1 (24/127)
unlock [ˌʌn'lɒk] aufschließen; entsperren III
unreadable [ʌn'riːdəbl] unleserlich IV
unsafe [ʌn'seɪf] nicht sicher, gefährlich III
untidy [ʌn'taɪdi] unordentlich III
until [ən'tɪl] bis III
unwanted [ˌʌn'wɒntɪd] unerwünscht, ungewollt V 3 (51)
up [ʌp] hinauf, herauf, nach oben I **up the hill** den Hügel hinauf II **That's up to you.** Das liegt bei dir. / Das kannst/musst du (selbst) entscheiden. III

°**uprising** ['ʌpraɪzɪŋ] Aufstand
upset (about) [ˌʌp'set] aufgebracht, gekränkt, mitgenommen (wegen) III
upset sb. (-tt-) [ʌp'set], **upset, upset** jn. ärgern, kränken, aus der Fassung bringen III
upstairs [ˌʌp'steəz] oben; nach oben I
us [əs, ʌs] uns I
use [ju:z] benutzen, verwenden I
used to ['ju:st tə]: **I used to be excited.** Früher war ich (immer) aufgeregt. V 2 (44)
► S.181 ... used to be/do ...
useful ['ju:sfl] nützlich III
usual ['ju:ʒuəl]: **as usual** wie immer, wie üblich V 3 (50)
usually ['ju:ʒuəli] meistens, gewöhnlich, normalerweise I
°**ute** [ju:t] *kleiner Geländewagen mit offener Ladefläche*
°**UV level** ['levl] Grad der UV-Strahlenbelastung

V

vacation [və'keɪʃn, *AE:* veɪ'keɪʃn] *(AE)* Urlaub, Ferien III
valley ['væli] Tal II
valuable ['væljuəbl] wertvoll IV
vandalism ['vændəlɪzəm] Vandalismus, Zerstörungswut V 3 (54)
vandalize ['vændəlaɪz] mutwillig beschädigen, mutwillig zerstören V 3 (54)
vegetable ['vedʒtəbl] *(ein)* Gemüse III
vegetarian [ˌvedʒə'teəriən] vegetarisch; Vegetarier/in IV
version ['vɜ:ʃn] Version, Fassung IV
very ['veri] sehr I • **like/love sth. very much** etwas sehr mögen/sehr lieben II • **Thanks very much!** Danke sehr! / Vielen Dank! II
vet [vet] Tierarzt/-ärztin V 2 (35)
vet's assistant [ˌvets_ə'sɪstənt] Tierarzthelfer/in V 2 (35)
victim ['vɪktɪm] Opfer III
video ['vɪdiəʊ] Video III
view [vju:] Aussicht, Blick II
°**view** [vju:] betrachten; *(im Fernsehen/Kino)* anschauen
viewer ['vju:ə] Zuschauer/in IV
village ['vɪlɪdʒ] Dorf I
violence ['vaɪələns] Gewalt; Gewalttätigkeit IV
violent ['vaɪələnt] gewalttätig; gewaltsam IV
violin [ˌvaɪə'lɪn] Violine, Geige III
virus ['vaɪrəs], *pl* **viruses** ['vaɪrəsəz] Virus V 4 (79)
visit ['vɪzɪt] besuchen II
visit ['vɪzɪt] Besuch II
visitor ['vɪzɪtə] Besucher/in, Gast I
visual ['vɪʒuəl] visuell; optisch V 4 (88)
vitae: curriculum vitae [kəˌrɪkjələm 'vi:taɪ] **(CV)** Lebenslauf V 2 (38)
vocabulary [və'kæbjələri] Vokabelverzeichnis, Wörterverzeichnis I
voice [vɔɪs] Stimme IV
volleyball ['vɒlibɔ:l] Volleyball I
volume ['vɒlju:m] Lautstärke IV
volunteer [ˌvɒlən'tɪə] sich freiwillig melden, sich bereit erklären IV
volunteer [ˌvɒlən'tɪə] Freiwillige(r) IV
vote for sb. [vəʊt] für jn. stimmen IV
°**voter** ['vəʊtə] Wähler/in

W

wait (for) [weɪt] warten (auf) I **Wait a minute.** Warte mal! / Moment mal! II • **I can't wait to see ...** ich kann es kaum erwarten, ... zu sehen I • **Wait and see!** Wart's ab! III
waiter ['weɪtə] Kellner II
waiting room ['weɪtɪŋ ru:m] Wartezimmer IV
waitress ['weɪtrəs] Kellnerin II
wake up [ˌweɪk_'ʌp], **woke, woken** aufwachen III • **wake sb. (up)** jn. (auf)wecken III
wake-up call ['weɪk_ʌp ˌkɔ:l] Weckanruf V 4 (86)
walk [wɔ:k] (zu Fuß) gehen I **walk around** herumlaufen, umherspazieren III • **walk around the town** in der Stadt umhergehen, durch die Stadt gehen III **walk off** weggehen IV
walk [wɔ:k] Spaziergang II • **a ten-kilometre walk** eine Zehn-Kilometer-Wanderung III • **go for a walk** spazieren gehen, einen Spaziergang machen II
wall [wɔ:l] Wand; Mauer II
want [wɒnt] (haben) wollen I **want to do sth.** etwas tun wollen I • **want sb. to do sth.** wollen, dass jm. etwas tut IV • **want to be sth.** etwas werden wollen *(beruflich)* V 3 (48)
► S.177 (to) ask/tell/expect/want sb. to do sth.
war [wɔ:] Krieg IV
wardrobe ['wɔ:drəʊb] Kleiderschrank I
warm [wɔ:m] warm II
warn sb. (about sth.) [wɔ:n] jn. (vor etwas) warnen III
was [wəz, wɒz]: **(I/he/she/it) was** *siehe* **be**
wash [wɒʃ] waschen I • **I wash my face.** Ich wasche mir das Gesicht. I
washing machine ['wɒʃɪŋ məˌʃi:n] Waschmaschine I
watch [wɒtʃ] beobachten, sich etwas ansehen; zusehen I **watch TV** fernsehen I
watch [wɒtʃ] Armbanduhr I
water ['wɔ:tə] Wasser I • **running water** fließendes Wasser *(Leitungswasser)* V 4 (80) • **salt water** Salzwasser V 1 (9)
waterproof ['wɔ:təpru:f] wasserdicht *(Kleidung, Uhr)* V 1 (17/175)
wave [weɪv] winken II
way [weɪ]
1. Weg II • **all the way** den ganzen Weg IV • **ask sb. the way** jn. nach dem Weg fragen II • **on the way (to)** auf dem Weg (zu/nach) II • **tell sb. the way** jm. den Weg beschreiben II • °**We've come a long way.** Wir sind weit gekommen. *(Wir haben viel erreicht.)*
2. Richtung II • **the other way round** anders herum II • **the wrong way** in die falsche Richtung II • **this way** hier entlang, in diese Richtung II • **which way?** in welche Richtung? / wohin? II
3. Art und Weise III • **the way you ...** so wie du ..., auf dieselbe Weise wie du ... IV
4. by the way übrigens II
5. No way! Auf keinen Fall! / Kommt nicht in Frage! II
we [wi:] wir I
weak [wi:k] schwach II
weakness ['wi:knəs] Schwäche, Schwachpunkt V 2 (40)
wear [weə], **wore, worn** tragen, anhaben *(Kleidung)* I
weather ['weðə] Wetter II
weatherproof ['weðəpru:f] wetterfest *(Kleidung)* V 1 (17/175)
webcam ['webkæm] Webcam III
website ['websaɪt] Website II
wedding ['wedɪŋ] Hochzeit, Trauung V 3 (51)
Wednesday ['wenzdeɪ, 'wenzdi] Mittwoch I
week [wi:k] Woche I • **days of the week** Wochentage I • **a two-week holiday** ein zweiwöchiger Urlaub III

weekend [ˌwiːk'end] Wochenende I
at the weekend am Wochenende I
welcome ['welkəm]
1. **Welcome (to Bristol).** Willkommen (in Bristol). I
2. **You're welcome.** Gern geschehen. / Nichts zu danken. I
welcome sb. (to) ['welkəm] jn. begrüßen, willkommen heißen (in) I
They welcome you to ... Sie heißen dich in ... willkommen I
well [wel]
1. gut II
2. *(gesundheitlich)* gut; gesund, wohlauf II
do well (in) gut abschneiden (in) III • **go well** gut (ver)laufen, gutgehen III • **You did well.** Das hast du gut gemacht. II • **Oh well ...** Na ja ... / Na gut ... I • **Well, ...** Nun, ... / Also, ... I • °**Well done!** [ˌwel 'dʌn] Gut gemacht!
Welsh [welʃ] walisisch; Walisisch II
went [went] *siehe* **go**
were [wə, wɜː]: **(we/you/they) were** *siehe* **be**
west [west] Westen; nach Westen; westlich III
westbound ['westbaʊnd] Richtung Westen III
western ['westən] westlich, West- III
wet [wet] nass III
whale [weɪl] Wal(fisch) V 1 (9)
what [wɒt]
1. was I
2. welche(r, s) I
What about ...? 1. Was ist mit ...? / Und ...? I; 2. Wie wär's mit ...? I
What are you talking about? Wovon redest du? I • **What colour is ...?** Welche Farbe hat ...? I
What for? Wofür? II • **What have we got next?** Was haben wir als Nächstes? I • **What kind of car ...?** Was für ein Auto ...? III • **What page are we on?** Auf welcher Seite sind wir? I • **What's for homework?** Was haben wir als Hausaufgabe auf? I • **What's the matter?** Was ist los? / Was ist denn? II • **What's the time?** Wie spät ist es? I • **What's your name?** Wie heißt du? I • **What's your telephone number?** Was ist deine Telefonnummer? I • **What was the weather like?** Wie war das Wetter? II • **I don't know what to do.** Ich weiß nicht, was ich machen soll. IV

whatever [wɒt'evə] was (auch) immer IV
wheel [wiːl] Rad III • **big wheel** Riesenrad III
wheelchair ['wiːltʃeə] Rollstuhl I
when [wen] wann I • **When's your birthday?** Wann hast du Geburtstag? I
when [wen]
1. wenn I
2. als I
whenever [wen'evə] wann immer IV
where [weə]
1. wo I
2. wohin I
Where are you from? Wo kommst du her? I
wherever [weər'evə] wo auch immer IV
which [wɪtʃ]: **Which picture ...?** Welches Bild ...? I • **which way?** in welche Richtung? / wohin? II
which [wɪtʃ] der, die, das; die *(Relativpronomen)* III
while [waɪl] während III
while [waɪl]: **for a while** für eine Weile, eine Zeit lang V 2 (45)
whisky ['wɪski] Whisky II
whisper ['wɪspə] flüstern I
whistle ['wɪsl] pfeifen II
whistle ['wɪsl] (Triller-)Pfeife III
white [waɪt] weiß I
who [huː]
1. wer I
2. wen/wem II
who [huː] der, die, das; die *(Relativpronomen)* III • **Find/Ask somebody who ...** Finde/Frage jemanden, der ... II
whoever [huː'evə] wer auch immer IV
whole [həʊl] ganze(r, s), gesamte(r, s) III
whole-grain ['həʊlgreɪn] Vollkorn- IV
whose? [huːz] wessen? II • **Whose are these?** Wem gehören diese? II
Whose turn is it? Wer ist dran / an der Reihe? II
why [waɪ] warum I • **that's why** deshalb, darum V 1 (16) • **Why me?** Warum ich? I • **Why should I ... ?** Warum sollte ich ... ? III
wide [waɪd] weit, breit IV
wife [waɪf], *pl* **wives** [waɪvz] Ehefrau II
wild [waɪld] wild II
will [wɪl]: **you'll be cold (= you will be cold)** du wirst frieren; ihr werdet frieren II • **you won't be cold** [wəʊnt] **(= you will not be cold)** du wirst nicht frieren; ihr werdet nicht frieren II

win (-nn-) [wɪn], **won, won** gewinnen I
win [wɪn] Sieg III
wind [wɪnd] Wind I
window ['wɪndəʊ] Fenster I
windproof ['wɪndpruːf] winddicht V 1 (17/175)
windy ['wɪndi] windig I
wine [waɪn] Wein IV
wing [wɪŋ] Flügel IV
winner ['wɪnə] Gewinner/in, Sieger/in II
winter ['wɪntə] Winter I
°**wish** [wɪʃ] wünschen
wish [wɪʃ]: **Best wishes** *etwa:* Alles Gute / Mit besten Grüßen *(als Briefschluss)* IV
with [wɪð]
1. mit I
2. bei I
be with sb. mit jemandem zusammen sein IV • **go with** gehören zu, passen zu III • **Sit with me.** Setz dich zu mir. / Setzt euch zu mir. I
without [wɪ'ðaʊt] ohne I
witness ['wɪtnəs] Zeuge/Zeugin V 1 (14)
wives [waɪvz] *Plural von „wife"*
woke [wəʊk] *siehe* **wake**
woken ['wəʊkən] *siehe* **wake**
wolf [wʊlf], *pl* **wolves** [wʊlvz] Wolf II
woman ['wʊmən], *pl* **women** ['wɪmɪn] Frau I
won [wʌn] *siehe* **win**
wonder ['wʌndə] sich fragen, gern wissen wollen II
won't [wəʊnt]: **you won't be cold (= you will not be cold)** du wirst nicht frieren; ihr werdet nicht frieren II
wood [wʊd] Holz III
woodpecker ['wʊdpekə] Specht II
woods *(pl)* [wʊdz] Wald, Wälder III
word [wɜːd] Wort I • **word building** Wortbildung II
°**word order** Wortstellung
wore [wɔː] *siehe* **wear**
work [wɜːk]
1. arbeiten I
2. funktionieren III
work hard hart arbeiten II • **work long hours** lange arbeiten V 2 (33)
work on sth. an etwas arbeiten I
work out gut ausgehen IV
work sth. out etwas herausarbeiten, herausfinden IV • °**work sth. through** etwas durcharbeiten

work [wɜːk] Arbeit I • **at work** bei der Arbeit / am Arbeitsplatz I
work experience *(no pl)* Praktikum; Arbeits-, Praxiserfahrung(en) V 2 (37) • **do work experience** ein Praktikum machen V 2 (37/179)
worker ['wɜːkə] Arbeiter/in II
office worker ['ɒfɪs wɜːkə] Büroangestellte(r) V 2 (35)
workplace ['wɜːkpleɪs] Arbeitsplatz IV
worksheet ['wɜːkʃiːt] Arbeitsblatt I
workshop ['wɜːkʃɒp] Workshop, Lehrgang III
world [wɜːld] Welt I • **all over the world** auf der ganzen Welt III
from all over the world aus der ganzen Welt III • **in the world** (auf) der Welt IV
worn [wɔːn] *siehe* **wear**
worried (about) ['wʌrid] beunruhigt (wegen), besorgt (wegen/um) IV
worry ['wʌri] Sorge, Kummer II
worry (about) ['wʌri] sich Sorgen machen (wegen, um) I • **Don't worry.** Mach dir keine Sorgen. I
worrying ['wʌriɪŋ] beunruhigend, sorgenvoll V 3 (57)
worse [wɜːs] schlechter, schlimmer II
worst [wɜːst]**: (the) worst** am schlechtesten, schlimmsten; der/die/das schlechteste, schlimmste II
would [wəd, wʊd]**: I/you/... would ...** ich würde / du würdest / ... III • **I'd like ... (= I would like ...)** Ich hätte gern ... / Ich möchte gern ... I
Would you like ...? Möchtest du ...? / Möchten Sie ...? I • **Would you like some?** Möchtest du etwas/ein paar? / Möchten Sie etwas/ein paar? I • **I'd like to talk about ... (= I would like to talk about ...)** Ich möchte über ... reden / Ich würde gern über ... reden I
write [raɪt]**, wrote, written** schreiben I • **write down** aufschreiben I • **write to** schreiben an I
writer ['raɪtə] Schreiber/in; Schriftsteller/in II
written ['rɪtn] *siehe* **write**
wrong [rɒŋ] falsch, verkehrt I
be wrong 1. falsch sein I; **2.** sich irren, Unrecht haben II • **the wrong way** in die falsche Richtung II
wrote [rəʊt] *siehe* **write**

Y

yard [jɑːd] Hof II • **in the yard** auf dem Hof II
yawn [jɔːn] gähnen II
year [jɪə]
1. Jahr I
2. Jahrgangsstufe I
a sixteen-year-old ein/e Sechzehnjährige/r III • **a sixteen-year-old girl** ein sechzehnjähriges Mädchen III
yellow ['jeləʊ] gelb I
°**yelp** [jelp] aufjaulen
yes [jes] ja I
yesterday ['jestədeɪ, 'jestədi] gestern I • **yesterday morning/afternoon/evening** gestern Morgen/Nachmittag/Abend I • **yesterday's homework** die Hausaufgaben von gestern II
yet [jet]**: not (...) yet** noch nicht II
yet? schon? II
°**Y generation** [ˌdʒenə'reɪʃn] *Generation, die nach 1980 geboren wurde*
°**YMCA** [ˌwaɪ‿emsiː‿'eɪ] **(Young Men's Christian Association)** CVJM, Christlicher Verein junger Männer/Menschen *(internationale Jugendorganisation, überkonfessionell christlich geprägt)*
yoga ['jəʊgə] Yoga I
you [juː]
1. du; Sie I
2. ihr I • **you two** ihr zwei I
3. dir; dich; euch I
4. man III
young [jʌŋ] jung I
your [jɔː]
1. dein/e I
2. Ihr I
3. euer/eure I
yours [jɔːz]
1. deiner, deine, deins II
2. Ihrer, Ihre, Ihrs II
3. eurer, eure, eures II
yourself [jɔː'self] dir/dich (selbst) III
yourselves [jɔː'selvz] euch (selbst) III
youth [juːθ] Jugend, Jugend- III
youth group Jugendgruppe IV
youth hostel Jugendherberge III
yuck [jʌk] igitt III

Z

zebra ['zebrə] Zebra II
zero ['zɪərəʊ] null I
zone [zəʊn] Zone, Gebiet IV
zoo [zuː] Zoo IV
°**Zulu** ['zuːluː] Zulu *(Sprache der Zulu, südafrikanisches Volk)*

English sounds (Englische Laute)

Die Lautschrift in den eckigen Klammern zeigt dir, wie ein Wort ausgesprochen wird.
In der folgenden Übersicht findest du alle Lautzeichen.

Vokale (Selbstlaute)

[i:]	green	[ʊ]	book	[ɪə]	here
[i]	happy	[ʌ]	mum	[eə]	where
[ɪ]	in	[ɜ:]	T-shirt	[ʊə]	tour
[e]	yes	[ə]	a partner		
[æ]	black	[eɪ]	skate		
[ɑ:]	park	[aɪ]	time		
[ɒ]	song	[ɔɪ]	boy		
[ɔ:]	morning	[əʊ]	old		
[u:]	blue	[aʊ]	now		

Konsonanten (Mitlaute)

[b]	box	[l]	hello	[ʒ]	television
[p]	play	[r]	red	[tʃ]	teacher
[d]	dad	[w]	we	[dʒ]	Germany
[t]	ten	[j]	you	[θ]	thanks
[g]	good	[f]	full	[ð]	this
[k]	cat	[v]	very	[h]	he
[m]	mum	[s]	sister	[x]	loch
[n]	no	[z]	please		
[ŋ]	sing	[ʃ]	shop		

Betonung

['] und [ˌ] sind **Betonungszeichen**
Sie stehen immer vor der betonten Silbe

['] zeigt die Hauptbetonung
[ˌ] zeigt die Nebenbetonung

Beispiel
mobile phone [ˌməʊbaɪl 'fəʊn]
Hauptbetonung auf **phone**
Nebenbetonung auf der ersten Silbe **mobile**

Der „Bindebogen"

Der **Bindebogen** [‿] zeigt an, dass zwei Wörter beim Sprechen aneinandergebunden und wie ein Wort ausgesprochen werden.

Beispiel
What colour is ...? [ˌwɒt 'kʌlər‿ɪz]
Mum and Dad [ˌmʌm‿ən 'dæd]
This is ... ['ðɪs‿ɪz]

The English alphabet (Das englische Alphabet)

a	[eɪ]	**h**	[eɪtʃ]	**o**	[əʊ]	**v**	[vi:]
b	[bi:]	**i**	[aɪ]	**p**	[pi:]	**w**	['dʌblju:]
c	[si:]	**j**	[dʒeɪ]	**q**	[kju:]	**x**	[eks]
d	[di:]	**k**	[keɪ]	**r**	[ɑ:]	**y**	[waɪ]
e	[i:]	**l**	[el]	**s**	[es]	**z**	[zed]
f	[ef]	**m**	[em]	**t**	[ti:]		
g	[dʒi:]	**n**	[en]	**u**	[ju:]		

First names (Vornamen)
Abby ['æbi]
Adnan ['ɑːdˌnɑːn, ˌɑːd'nɑːn]
Akeem [ɑː'kiːm, ɒ'kiːm]
Alex ['ælɪks]
Alfie ['ælfi]
Amy ['eɪmi]
Andrew ['ændruː]
Ashley ['æʃli]
Balu [bə'luː]
Ben [ben]
Berry ['beri]
Beyoncé [bɪ'jɒnseɪ]
Binita [bə'niːtə, bɪ'niːtə]
Brad [bræd]
Brian ['braɪən]
Carla ['kɑːlə]
Carolyn ['kærəlɪn]
Chloe ['kləʊi]
Colm [kɒlm, 'kɒləm]
Daisy ['deɪzi]
Dan [dæn]
Darren ['dærən]
Dave [deɪv]
David ['deɪvɪd]
Deepa ['diːpə]
Delaney [dɪ'leɪni]
Desmond ['dezmənd]
Dolly ['dɒli]
Drew [druː]
Elin ['elɪn]
Emily ['eməli]
Emma ['emə]
Ethan ['iːθən]
Ewan ['juːən]
Framji ['fræmdʒi]
Grace [greɪs]
Gracie ['greɪsi]
Hannah ['hænə]
Jake [dʒeɪk]
James [dʒeɪmz]
Jeannie ['dʒiːni]
Jeremy ['dʒerəmi]
Jonathan ['dʒɒnəθən]
Joseph ['dʒəʊzɪf, 'dʒəʊsef]
Karen ['kærən]
Katy ['keɪti]
Keira ['kɪərə]
Keisha ['kiːʃə]
Kirsty ['kɜːsti]
Kishore [ˌkɪ'ʃɔːr]
Kitty ['kɪti]
Laura ['lɔːrə]
Letitia [lə'tɪʃə]
Lily ['lɪli]
Lina ['liːnə]
Lindsay ['lɪndzi]
Lucy ['luːsi]
Luke [luːk]
Madonna [mə'dɒnə]
Mahatma [mə'hɑːtmə]
Mani ['mæni]
Margaret ['mɑːgrət, 'mɑːgrɪt]
Mark [mɑːk]
Mia ['miːə]
Michael ['maɪkl]
Missy ['mɪsi]
Molly ['mɒli]
Morris ['mɒrɪs]
Nelson ['nelsən]
Niall [niːl, 'naɪəl]
Nicole [nɪ'kɒl, nɪ'kəʊl]
Oscar ['ɒskə]
Pearl [pɜːl]
Phil [fɪl]
Poppy ['pɒpɪ]
Reece [riːs]
Rob [rɒb]
Robert ['rɒbət]
Rochelle [rɒ'ʃel]
Rohan ['rəʊən]
Rubin ['ruːbɪn]
Sandra ['sændrə, 'sɑːndrə]
Shane [ʃeɪn]
Shireen [ʃə'riːn]
Simon ['saɪmən]
Sinita [sɪ'niːtə]
Suketu [sʊ'keɪtu]
Sunny ['sʌni]
Tay [teɪ]
Tyson ['taɪsn]
Uma ['uːmə]
Victor ['vɪktə]
Zach [zæk]
Zoe ['zəʊi]

Family names / Surnames (Familiennamen)
Armstrong ['ɑːmstrɒŋ]
Beckam ['bekəm]
Bond [bɒnd]
Brown [braʊn]
Coman ['kəʊmən]
Connor ['kɒnə]
Cook [kʊk]
Denham ['denəm]
Gandhi ['gændi, 'gɑːndi]
Good [gʊd]
Gubbins ['gʌbɪnz]
Isaacson ['aɪzəksn]
Lulla ['lʌlə]
Mandela [mæn'delə]
McQueen [mə'kwiːn]
Mehta ['metə]
Mellon ['melən]
Murray ['mʌri]
Otambo [əʊ'tæmbəʊ]
Parton ['pɑːtn]
Pitt [pɪt]
Preston ['prestən]
Qualls [kwɒlz]
Ravenhill ['reɪvənhɪl]
Saunders ['sɔːndəz]
Smith [smɪθ]
Tutu ['tuːtuː]
waRona [wə'rəʊnə]
Whitbred ['wɪtbred]
Williams ['wɪljəmz]
Wilson ['wɪlsn]
Yates [jeɪts]

Place names (Ortsnamen)
Alice Springs [ˌælɪs 'sprɪŋz]
Atlanta [ət'læntə]
Bangkok [ˌbæŋ'kɒk]
Berlin [bɜː'lɪn]
Bloemfontein ['bluːmfənˌteɪn]
Bombay [ˌbɒm'beɪ]
Bondi Beach [ˌbɒndaɪ 'biːtʃ]
Brisbane ['brɪzbən]
Bristol ['brɪstl]
Broome [bruːm]
Buenos Aires [ˌbweɪnɒs 'aɪriz]
Cambridge ['keɪmbrɪdʒ]
Canberra ['kænbərə]
Cape Town ['keɪp taʊn]
Cardiff ['kɑːdɪf]
The **Chauncy School** ['tʃɔːnsi skuːl]
Checkpoint Charlie [ˌtʃekpɔɪnt 'tʃɑːli]
Chicago [ʃɪ'kɑːgəʊ]
Cologne [kə'ləʊn]
Darwin ['dɑːwɪn]
Detroit [də'trɔɪt, dɪ'trɔɪt]
Dublin ['dʌblɪn]
Eno ['iːnəʊ]
Eugene [juː'dʒiːn]
Galway ['gɔːlweɪ]
Great Barrier Reef [ˌgreɪt ˌbæriə 'riːf]
Hamburg ['hæmbɜːg]
Harston ['hɑːstən]
Hertford ['hɑːtfəd]
Hertfordshire ['hɑːtfədʃə]
Hollywood ['hɒliwʊd]
Hong Kong [ˌhɒŋ 'kɒŋ]
Joburg ['dʒəʊbɜːg]
Johannesburg [dʒəʊ'hænɪsbɜːg]
Jozi ['dʒəʊzi]
Kent [kent]
London ['lʌndən]
Los Angeles [lɒs 'ændʒəliːz]
Melbourne ['melbən]
Mumbai [ˌmʊm'baɪ]
Nashville ['næʃvɪl]
New Delhi [ˌnjuː 'deli]
New Mexico [ˌnjuː 'meksɪkəʊ]
New Orleans [ˌnjuː 'ɔːrlənz]
New York [ˌnjuː 'jɔːk]
Oregon ['ɒrɪgən]
Port Jackson [ˌpɔːt 'dʒæksən]
Pretoria [pri'tɔːrɪə]
Queensland ['kwiːnzlənd]
Rio De Janeiro [ˌriːəʊ də ʒə'nɪərəʊ]
San Francisco [ˌsæn frən'sɪskəʊ]
Sandton ['sændtən]
Swindon ['swɪndən]
Sydney ['sɪdni]
Tasmania [tæz'meɪniə]
Toronto [tə'rɒntəʊ]
Uluru ['uːləruː, ʊlə'ruː]
Victoria [vɪk'tɔːriə]
Ware [weə]
Weeki Wachee Springs [ˌwiːki ˌwɑːtʃi 'sprɪŋz]
Wiltshire ['wɪltʃə]

Other names (Andere Namen)
Batman ['bætmæn]
Bluebell ['bluːbel]
Daintree ['deɪntri]
FIFA ['fiːfə]
Flipper ['flɪpə]
IMAX ['aɪmæks]
Kakadu NP (National Park) [ˌkækə'duː]
Rosebank ['rəʊzbæŋk]
Rusty ['rʌsti]
San Souci [ˌsæn suː'si]
Simpson Desert ['sɪmpsn]
Sting [stɪŋ]
Tamla Motown [ˌtæmlə 'məʊtaʊn]
Tin Annie [ˌtɪn 'æni]
Torres Strait Islander [ˌtɒrəs ˌstreɪt 'aɪləndə]
Value Click Media [ˌvæljuː ˌklɪk 'miːdiə]

Country/Continent	Adjective	Person	People
Africa ['æfrɪkə] *Afrika*	African ['æfrɪkən]	an African	the Africans
America [ə'merɪkə] *Amerika*	American [ə'merɪkən]	an American	the Americans
Asia ['eɪʃə, 'eɪʒə] *Asien*	Asian ['eɪʃn, 'eɪʒn]	an Asian	the Asians
Australia [ɒ'streɪliə] *Australien*	Australian [ɒ'streɪliən]	an Australian	the Australians
Austria ['ɒstriə] *Österreich*	Austrian ['ɒstriən]	an Austrian	the Austrians
Belgium ['beldʒəm] *Belgien*	Belgian ['beldʒən]	a Belgian	the Belgians
Bosnia-Herzegovina [ˌbɒzniə ˌhɜtsəgə'viːnə] *Bosnien-Herzegowina*	Bosnian ['bɒzniən]	a Bosnian	the Bosnians
Canada ['kænədə] *Kanada*	Canadian [kə'neɪdiən]	a Canadian	the Canadians
China ['tʃaɪnə] *China*	Chinese [ˌtʃaɪ'niːz]	a Chinese	the Chinese
Croatia [krəʊ'eɪʃə] *Kroatien*	Croatian [krəʊ'eɪʃn]	a Croatian	the Croatians
the Czech Republic [ˌtʃek rɪ'pʌblɪk] *Tschechien, die Tschechische Republik*	Czech [tʃek]	a Czech	the Czechs
Denmark ['denmɑːk] *Dänemark*	Danish ['deɪnɪʃ]	a Dane [deɪn]	the Danes
England ['ɪŋglənd] *England*	English ['ɪŋglɪʃ]	an Englishman/-woman	the English
Europe ['jʊərəp] *Europa*	European [ˌjʊərə'piːən]	a European	the Europeans
Finland ['fɪnlənd] *Finnland*	Finnish ['fɪnɪʃ]	a Finn [fɪn]	the Finns
France [frɑːns] *Frankreich*	French [frentʃ]	a Frenchman/-woman	the French
Germany ['dʒɜːməni] *Deutschland*	German ['dʒɜːmən]	a German	the Germans
(Great) Britain ['brɪtn] *Großbritannien*	British ['brɪtɪʃ]	a Briton ['brɪtn]	the British
Greece [griːs] *Griechenland*	Greek [griːk]	a Greek	the Greeks
India ['ɪndiə] *Indien*	Indian ['ɪndiən]	an Indian	the Indians
Ireland ['aɪələnd] *Irland*	Irish ['aɪrɪʃ]	an Irishman/-woman	the Irish
Italy ['ɪtəli] *Italien*	Italian [ɪ'tæliən]	an Italian	the Italians
Japan [dʒə'pæn] *Japan*	Japanese [ˌdʒæpə'niːz]	a Japanese	the Japanese
the Netherlands ['neðələndz] *die Niederlande, Holland*	Dutch [dʌtʃ]	a Dutchman/-woman	the Dutch
Malaysia [mə'leɪʒə, mə'leɪziə] *Malaysia*	Malaysian [mə'leɪʒn, mə'leɪziən]	a Malaysian	the Malaysians
New Zealand [ˌnjuː 'ziːlənd] *Neuseeland*	New Zealand [ˌnjuː 'ziːlənd]	a New Zealander	the New Zealanders
Nigeria [naɪ'dʒɪəriə] *Nigeria*	Nigerian [naɪ'dʒɪəriən]	a Nigerian	the Nigerians
Norway ['nɔːweɪ] *Norwegen*	Norwegian [nɔː'wiːdʒən]	a Norwegian	the Norwegians
Pakistan [ˌpækɪ'stæn, ˌpɑːkɪ'stɑːn] *Pakistan*	Pakistani [ˌpækɪ'stæni, ˌpɑːkɪ'stɑːni]	a Pakistani	the Pakistanis
Poland ['pəʊlənd] *Polen*	Polish ['pəʊlɪʃ]	a Pole [pəʊl]	the Poles
Portugal ['pɔːtʃʊgl] *Portugal*	Portuguese [ˌpɔːtʃu'giːz]	a Portuguese	the Portuguese
Russia ['rʌʃə] *Russland*	Russian ['rʌʃn]	a Russian	the Russians
Scotland ['skɒtlənd] *Schottland*	Scottish ['skɒtɪʃ]	a Scotsman/-woman, a Scot [skɒt]	the Scots, the Scottish
Singapore [ˌsɪŋə'pɔː, ˌsɪŋgə'pɔː] *Singapur*	Singaporean [ˌsɪŋə'pɔːriən, sɪŋgə-]	a Singaporean	the Singaporeans
Slovakia [sləʊ'vɑːkiə, sləʊ'vækiə] *die Slowakei*	Slovak ['sləʊvæk]	a Slovak	the Slovaks
Slovenia [sləʊ'viːniə] *Slowenien*	Slovenian [sləʊ'viːniən], Slovene ['sləʊviːn]	a Slovene, a Slovenian	the Slovenes, the Slovenians
Spain [speɪn] *Spanien*	Spanish ['spænɪʃ]	a Spaniard ['spænɪəd]	the Spaniards
Sweden ['swiːdn] *Schweden*	Swedish ['swiːdɪʃ]	a Swede [swiːd]	the Swedes
Switzerland ['swɪtsələnd] *die Schweiz*	Swiss [swɪs]	a Swiss	the Swiss
Turkey ['tɜːki] *die Türkei*	Turkish ['tɜːkɪʃ]	a Turk [tɜːk]	the Turks
the United Kingdom (the UK) [juˌnaɪtɪd 'kɪŋdəm, ˌjuː'keɪ] *das Vereinigte Königreich (Großbritannien und Nordirland)*	British ['brɪtɪʃ]	a Briton ['brɪtn]	the British
the United States of America (the USA) [juˌnaɪtɪd ˌsteɪts_əv_ə'merɪkə, juː_es_'eɪ] *die Vereinigten Staaten von Amerika*	American [ə'merɪkən]	an American	the Americans
Wales [weɪlz] *Wales*	Welsh [welʃ]	a Welshman/-woman	the Welsh

Key to 'How am I doing?'

Unit 1 ▸ p. 25

1 Brisbane, Canberra, Melbourne, Sydney, Perth 3 of these, 1 point each
2 kangaroo, koala, crocodile, emu, wombat, platyus, cane toad 3 of these, 1 point each
3 wear a hat, use sunscreen, wear a shirt, wear sunglasses 2 of these, 1 point each
4 surfing, Australian Rules football, cricket, tennis, swimming, rugby 3 of these, 1 point each

One point for each correct answer to questions 5–13.

5 C autumn
6 B outback
7 D the Whites.
8 B were taken away by Whites.
9 a) Kim said (that) she would have/she'd have a great time Down Under.
b) Jess said (that) she just loved kangaroos.
c) Tom said (that) Frank had visited Sydney last year.
d) Lara said (that) they/we could go again next year.
10 C avoid
11 B Can I borrow it?
12 D repair
13 B attach

The chart on the right is a pie chart. It shows what percentage of the Australian population lives where. It is divided into three parts. The largest group (69%) lives in cities. The next largest group lives near cities and the smallest group lives far from cities. So we can say that 31% of the population don't live in cities.
1 point for each answer – 7 points

Getting ready for a test 1 ▸ pp. 26–31

1 LISTENING Travelling to Australia ▸ p. 28

1 B Gate 17
2 C chicken with a salad or pasta
3 A just over there
4 B $ 52.50
5 C 07:00–10:30

2 LISTENING Shark attack ▸ p. 29

a) 1 C New South Wales
2 A surfing
3 D leg
4 B 5 seconds
5 C Jon swam back to the beach
6 C scariest

b) 1 Jon's friends probably saved his life when they used/tied/put a rope round his leg and stopped the bleeding.
2 Jon is lucky. He will always have a big scar but he won't lose his leg/survived/is alive.
3 Experts say that sharks don't normally attack/hurt/kill/harm people.
4 The experts also say that more people die in road accidents in Australia every day than from shark attacks in ten years.
5 You should always swim in groups so your friends can help you. And never in the (early) morning or evening because that's when sharks usually feed.

3 LISTENING Young Australians and the internet ▸ p. 30

1 False
2 True
3 False
4 True
5 True
6 False

4 WRITING An online magazine for young Europeans ▸ p. 30

(individuelle Lösung)

Key to 'How am I doing?'

Unit 2

▸ p. 47

One point for each correct answer to questions 1–11

1 a) similar
   b) reliable
   c) cheeky
   d) ambitious
   e) punctual
2 You get one point for each correct pair.
   a) calm, organized
   b) punctual, reliable
   c) energetic, confident
3 a) ... to come for an interview next week.
   b) ... not to worry if next week wasn't possible.
   c) ... could come in two weeks.
   d) ... needed directions for getting to the office building.
4 a) nurse
   b) mechanic
   c) travel agent
   d) childcare assistant
   e) customer adviser
   f) fitness instructor
5 Possible answers (maximum number of points: 4): Personal statement, Education, Qualifications, Other skills, Work experience, Hobbies and interests, References
6 B you don't know the name of the person you're writing to.
7 A at the beginning of the letter.
8 B long verb forms.
9 A usually a good idea.
10 A your CV.
11 B Yours sincerely ...

Key to 'How am I doing?'

Unit 3 ▸ p. 65

One point for each correct answer to questions 1–10 and 13, one point for one of the phrases to question 12, and two points for each correct sentence to question 11.

1 C antisocial behaviour
2 D cleaning up trash
3 B want to volunteer
4 C note
5 B contacts
6 a) store it in the fridge
  b) dump someone
  c) communicate with someone
  d) enter your PIN
7 a) Don't forget to set your alarm clock.
  b) If you really like her, you should ask her out.
  c) Hang on, I'll be with you in a minute.
  d) Knock on the door before you enter the room.
8 a) Well, he's my friend, but yesterday I didn't like his behaviour at all.
  b) He was late for school as usual.
  c) You're right, I agree with you completely.
9 a) I hate boring lessons.
  b) Jo found an interesting job.
  c) I was surprised when she phoned yesterday.
10 C The girl was helping an old lady.
11 Two points for each correct sentence
  a) A boy who vandalized a park yesterday was taken to the police station.
  b) His name cannot/can't be printed in the newspapers because he is under 16.
  c) He will be taken to court tomorrow morning.
  d) I think he must be punished.
12 One point for one of these phrases
  a) express an opinion:
  I think ... / I feel ... / In my opionion ... / First ... / Second ... / And finally ...
  b) agree with an opinion:
  I agree (with you). / That's true. / That's a good point. / You're right. / ...
  c) disagree with an opinion:
  I don't agree (with you). / No, that's not right. / I don't think you can say that. / Sorry, but I think ... / I see what you mean but ... / Yes, but ... / ...
  d) ask for clarification:
  Could/Can you say that again? / Sorry, but I don't understand what you mean. / Can/Could you explain that? / ...
13 B – C – A (introduction – your arguments for or against – conclusion)

Key to 'How am I doing?'

Getting ready for a test 2

▸ pp. 66–73

1 READING Choosing a book ▸ p. 68

1 Student A: Book 7
2 Student B: Book 5
3 Student C: Book 6
4 Student D: Book 1
5 Student E: Book 4

2 MEDIATION A note to your friend ▸ p. 69

(individuelle Lösung)

3 READING Dev Patel ▸ pp. 66–67

a) 1 C The young English actor Dev Patel.
2 C quite surprising
3 B becomes a millionaire.
4 C had only played a small role in a TV series.
5 A has Indian parents but grew up in England.
6 B Acting.
7 D He replied to a newspaper advertisement.

b) 8 looked more like a 'slumdog' (wasn't too strong and handsome).
9 his daughter.
10 he didn't think he'd/he would get the part.
11 he grew up five years in those five months.
12 they are happy.

4 SPEAKING Describing a picture ▸ p. 72

(individuelle Lösung)

5 SPEAKING Hobbies and interests ▸ p. 72

(individuelle Lösung)

Unit 4

▸ p. 89

One point for each correct answer

1 A in the 1660s
2 C Bollywood
3 A gold
4 B townships
5 C four
6 C crowded
7 A If you had come early, you would have met Pam.
8 C If I had scored one more goal, we would have won the match.
9 Best order: B–D–A–C
one point for the best order
10 a) fashionable
b) tiny
c) contrast
11 a) Are you familiar with this area?
b) Lots of people in the world live on less than 1 US dollar a day.
c) Don't lean out of the window – it's dangerous.
d) I need your help. Can you come at once?
12 a) Pia and Linn want a double room in the hotel.
b) They can't get a room there because it is fully booked.
c) Not far away is a hostel where they can stay but only in a dormitory.
d) There are lots of people waiting outside the museum so Pia and Linn have to queue.
13 a) colourful
b) hopeful
c) successful

Illustrationen

Silke Bachmann, Hamburg (S. 15; S. 24; S. 56; S. 87; S. 97; S. 118 unten; S. 119 (u. 108 TF 6)); **Roland Beier**, Berlin (S. 9; S. 14; S. 52; S. 61; S. 134–139; S. 141–191); **Carlos Borrell**, Berlin (vordere und hintere Umschlaginnenseite; S. 74 (M); S. 112/113); **Dylan Gibson**, Pitlochry (S. 34; S. 108 TF 4 (u. 114); S. 114–116); **Christian Görke**, Berlin (S. 10; S. 11; S. 94; S. 111; S. 118 oben; S. 139 oben); **Graham-Cameron Illustration**, UK: **Eoin Coveney** (S. 62–63); **Alfred Schüssler**, Frankfurt/Main (S. 110)

Bildquellen

A1 Pix, Taufkirchen (Inhalt oben 2. v. li. (u. 32): REO); **Alamy**, Abingdon (Inhalt oben re. (u. 75): Thomas Cockrem, Inhalt U2 theme park: Teddy (M), theme park worker: Images-USA; Inhalt U3 crowd (u. 50): moodboard (RF) (M), Inhalt U4 (u. 74): frans lemmens; S. 8 Mitte li.: The London Art Archive, Mitte re.: The Print Collector; S. 12 unten (u. 135): Horizon International Images Limited; S. 13 Mitte li.: Buzz Pictures; S. 14 Bondi Beach warning sign caution notice: frank'n'focus (M); S. 16 Mitte li.: PCL, unten li.: WorldFoto; S. 17 unten: Photos 12; S. 20 li.: David Noble Photography; S. 30 unten re.: Brownstock Inc. (RF); S. 32 unten re.: Digital Vision (RF); S. 33 unten: Brownstock Inc.; S. 36 oben: Picture Partners, Bild 3: Image Source White; S. 41 Mitte (u. 91 u. 92) football (M): artpartner-images.com; S. 42 unten: Agencja FREE; S. 48 Mitte: Radius Images (RF); S. 49 oben: Steve Skjold; S. 53 re. (u. 101): Digital Vision (RF); S. 54: Janine Wiedel Photolibrary; S. 58 tin: FB-StockPhoto; S. 60: Radius Images (RF); S. 64 re.: image100 (RF); S. 72 unten: Digital Vision (RF); S. 74 Bild B: Tibor Bognar; S. 75 Bild D: Eric Nathan, Bild F: Peter Horree; S. 76 Deepa: Idealink Photography, Sunny: PhotosIndia.com LLC (RF), oben re.: Ron Boon, Mitte re.: Dinodia Images, unten re.: Julio Etchart; S. 79 oben: PhotosIndia.com RM 16; S. 80 oben: Tom Whipps, unten: West Africa Photography; S. 82 unten: AfriPics; S. 86: Geoff Williamson SuperPrime; S. 95 oben: Denkou Images; S. 108 TF 9 (u. 130): Greatstock Photographic Library/MonkeyApple (RF); S. 109 Bild 4: David Page, unten: Alex Maddox; S. 112 unten re.: Horizon International Images Limited; S. 129 cinema: Imagestate Media Partners Limited - Impact Photos/ Christopher Cormack; S. 129 unten re.: Dinodia Images; S. 130 oben re.: Imagestate Media Partners Limited - Impact Photos/Alain Evrard, 2. Reihe li.: Radius Images (RF), 3. Reihe re.: Gallo Images/Max Paddler (RF), 5. Reihe li.: Fancy (RF), 6. Reihe li.: Gallo Images (RF), 7. Reihe li.: Blend Images/Klaus Tiedge (RF); S. 131 unten li.: Constantinos Pliakos (RF), unten re.: Robert Harding Picture Library Ltd./Robert Cundy); **Argus**, Hamburg (S. 69: Peter Frischmuth); **Associated Press**, Frankfurt/Main (S. 77 unten: Gurinder Osan); **Chuck Braverman. Art and Design** (S. 55; S. 56 oben: © 2004 New Video Group, Inc.); **CartoonStock**, Bath (S. 51: Dave Carpenter); **Cinetext**, Frankfurt/Main (S. 129 Bollywood dancers: Cinetext Bildarchiv); **Corbis**, Düsseldorf (Inhalt U3 girl (M); S. 6 Bild 1: Dennis Degnan; S. 7 Bild 2: Aurora Open/Lars Schneider (RF); S. 8 unten li.: PoodlesRock; S. 9 Mitte re.: Oliver Strewe; S. 12 2. v. oben: John Simmons (RF); S. 16 unten re.: Catherine Karnow; S. 41 unten: Corbis Super RF (RF); S. 42 oben (u. 99): Simon Jarratt (RF); S. 48 li.: Peter M. Fisher, re.: James Marshall; S. 74 Bild A: Frédéric Soltan; S. 130 Mandela: Sygma/Yves Forestier; S. 132 unten: Peter Turnley); **Cornelsen Verlag**, Berlin (S. 40 oben: Michael Weihrauch); **Rob Cousins**, Bristol (Inhalt U3 blonde girl (M) (u. 50); 43 (u. 100)); **Ismail Farouk** (S. 131 oben re.: http://flickr.com/photos/ismailfarouk); **Fotolia**, New York (S. 56 unten: Klaus-Peter Adler); **Fotosearch**, Waukesha (S. 108 TF 5 (u. 117) (RF)); **GeoBeats, Inc.**, Rockville (S. 78); **Getty Images**, München (Inhalt 3. v. li. (u. 49): Allan Shoemake (RF); S. 6/7 background: Ted Mead; S. 7 Bild 3: Bec Parsons, Bild 6: Doug Armand; S. 9 oben: Jeff Hunter (RF); S. 12 oben girl: Jack Hollingsworth (RF) (M), 3. v. oben: Chris McGrath; S. 13 oben: Anthony Ong (RF); S. 13 unten li.: James Knowler, unten re.: Tony Lewis; S. 19 unten: ColorBlind Images (RF); S. 22 oben: Ian Waldie; S. 29 li.: Annie Griffiths Belt; S. 32 Mitte li.: Andersen Ross; S. 36 Bild 1: Image Source (RF); S. 53 Mitte (u. 101): Jason Dewey; S. 72 oben: Adrian Weinbrech; S. 77 oben: AFP; S. 81 oben u. unten: Per-Anders Pettersson; S. 83 oben li. u. re.: Time Life Pictures, unten: AFP; S. 93 unten li.: Popperfoto, unten re.: Getty Images Sport/Gallo Images; S. 108 TF 2 (u. 111): Getty Images News/Handout; S. 113 unten re.: Getty Images Sport/Quinn Rooney; S. 133 unten Mitte: AFP); **Bonnie Glänzer**, Berlin (S. 44 unten); **Guardian News & Media Ltd 2008** (S. 17 oben: Barbara McMahon); **The Hickory Daily Record**, Hickory (logo used by permission of The Hickory Daily Record, boys: Robert Reed); **David Hoffman Photo Library**, London (S. 32 oben re.); **iStockphoto**, Calgary (S. 6 oben: Renee Lee; S. 9 unten.: Nicola Stratford; S. 19 reporter: Paul Kline, Bild 1: ranplatt, Bild 2: Jacob Wackerhausen, Bild 3: Duncan Walker, Bild 4: blue_iq; S. 21 oben: Timothy Ball; S. 26 unten li.: Gene Chutka, unten re.: Jeffrey Smith; S. 27 (u. 113): susan flashman; S. 28 oben: Carlos Santa Maria; S. 28 Mitte li.: Elnur Amikishiyev; S. 29 re.: Chuck Babbitt; S. 30 oben: Pali Rao, unten li. screen (M): zak, question mark (M): Zeffss1; S. 34 Bild A: wrangel, Bild B: btrenkel, S. 40 unten: dawn liljenquist; S. 49 unten: Andresr; S. 66 unten re.: Diane White Rosier; S. 67 li.: Chris Schmidt, re.: Suzanne Tucker; S. 68 li.: Søren Sielemann, 2. v. li.: Rich Legg, Mitte: Chris Schmidt, 2. v. re.: ronen, re: Suzanne Tucker; S. 76 Pearl: Silvia Jansen, Rohan: Vikram Raghuvanshi; S. 79 unten: Chris Hepburn; S. 80 Mitte: Steven Allan; S. 87 li. (M) u. re. (M): Joselito Briones; S. 108 TF 1 (u. 109): James Bowyer, TF 8 (u. 128 u. 129): RENE DROUYER; S. 109 Bild 1: Linda & Colin McKie, Bild 2 u. 3: david franklin; S. 110: Paul Morton; S. 130 2. Reihe re.: Henrique NDR Martins, 3. Reihe li.: Cliff Parnell; S. 131 oben li.: Adam James Kazmierski; S. 133 oben 2. v. re.: snowkoala, unten li.: suhhui kuk, unten re.: Westbury); **Lonely Planet Images**, London (S. 130 5. Reihe re.: Richard I'Anson); **Masterfile**, Düsseldorf (S. 33 Mitte: Ron Fehling); **melalouise.net**, East St Kilda (S. 16 oben re.); **Newspix**, Surry Hills NSW (S. 18 (u. 95): Sam Ruttyn); **Okapia**, Frankfurt/Main (S. 22 unten: Hans Reinhard; S. 90); **Photofusion Picture Library**, London (S. 32 unten li.: Melanie Friend); **Photolibrary**, London (S. 53 li. (u. 101): Banana Stock; S. 112 oben: Jörg Reuther); **Picture-Alliance**, Frankfurt/Main (S. 9 Mitte li.

(u. 113): NHPA/photoshot/Dave Watts; S. 13 Mitte re.: dpa – Report; S. 34 Bild D: dpa – Report; S. 36 Bild 2: OKAPIA /Christine Steimer; S. 70: empics; S. 93 oben: Sven Simon; S. 111 unten: NHPA/photoshot; S. 128 unten: dpa); **Picture Desk**, London (S. 71 oben u. unten: Film 4/ Celador Films/Pathe International/The Kobal Collection; S. 129 unten li.: Pathe Pictures LTC/The Kobal Collection); **Daniel Raven-Ellison**, Thatcham (S. 82 Bild A u. B); **Marion Schönenberger**, Berlin (S. 84–85); **Shooting Jozi**, a project of Global Studio 2007 and the individuals who participated (S. 105 (u. 82 Mitte)); **Jakob Schröck**, Berlin (S. 88); **Shutterstock**, New York (Inhalt oben li. (u. 11): Tap10, Inhalt U1 (u. 16): Ronald Sumners; S. 7 Bild 4: Merryl McNaughton, Bild 5: BlueSoul Photography; S. 8 oben li.: Andrei Marincas, re.: Dimitrios Kaisaris; S. 12 oben trees: aliciahh (M); S. 14 Bondi Beach warning sign general warnings and live saving services: Graham Prentice (M); S. 16 Mitte re.: Kaspars Grinvalds; S. 20 re.: Ashley Whitworth; S. 21 Mitte: aliciahh, unten: ILYA GENKIN; S. 26 oben: Rob Wilson; S. 28 Mitte (u. Mitte re.): Robyn Mackenzie, unten li. (u. unten re.): Joe Gough, unten Mitte: Nayashkova Olga; S. 34 Bild C: Ilja Mašik; S. 41 oben: Yuri Arcurs; S. 57: Terry Chan; S. 61: Andresr; S. 64 li.: Pavel Sazonov; S. 66 oben li.: Robert Ranson, oben re.: Rick Becker-Leckrone, unten li.: Amy Myers; S. 74 South African flag (M): Andrew Chin, Indian flag (M): Andrew Chin, German flag (M): ARTEKI; S. 76 Balu: Mandy Godbehear; S. 108 TF 3 (u. 113): Patsy A. Jacks, TF 7: Laurent Renault, TF 10 (u. 133): Jenna Layne Voigt; S. 112 unten li.: tororo reaction; S. 113 unten li.: hocus-focus; S. 128 Mitte: Map Resources; S. 130 background pattern: Ferin, oben li.: Anke van Wyk, 2. Reihe Mitte: Johan Gerber, 6. Reihe re.: 1171, unten re.: michaeljung; S. 132 oben: Louie Schoeman; S. 133 oben 2. v. li.: Mike Liu, oben re.: Alexey Goosev; S. 142: Holger Mette); **vario-images**, Bonn (S. 58 snorkeling (M)); **Visum Foto**, Hamburg (S. 32 Mitte re.: Bernd Arnold); **Volunteer Manatee** (S. 58 Logo used with permission of Volunteer Manatee. Volunteer Services of Manatee County, Inc.); **Martynka Wawrzyniak**, New York (S. 44 oben; S. 45)

Titelbild

Corbis, Düsseldorf (sign and bus: Corbis Edge/Theo Allofs (M)), **Corel Library** (Hintergrund flag (M)), **Plainpicture**, Hamburg (jeans with map (M): Sina Preikschat)

Textquellen

S. 17 *Children were stolen for a racist policy. Now a nation says sorry.* Adapted from "Snatched from home for a racist ideal. Now a nation says sorry" by Barbara McMahon, 11.2.2008. http://www.guardian.co.uk/world/2008/feb/11/australia. Copyright Guardian News & Media Ltd 2008; **S. 20–23** *In the outback.* Abridged and adapted from „Children of the Wind - A Prayer for Blue Delaney" by Kirsty Murray. Allen & Unwin, Crows Nest, Australia, 2005 (www.allenandunwin.com); **S. 54** *ASBO boy.* Abridged and adapted from „ASBO made me give up life as a yob". From http://www.mirror.co.uk/news/top-stories/2007/11/13/asbo-made-me-give-up-life-as-a-yob-115875-20099323/ by Jeremy Armstrong, 13.11.2007. Mirror Syndication International, London; **S. 58** *Springs Clean-up.* Text adapted from http://manateens.blogspot.com/ (Stand 15.06.2009) used with permission of Volunteer ManaTEE. Volunteer Services of Manatee County, Inc., *Hickory Soup Kitchen.* Adapted from "Students soup up kitchen" by Sarah Newell Williamson, 6.8.2008. http://www2.hickoryrecord.com/content/2008/aug/06/students-soup-kitchen/. Used with permission of The Hickory Daily Record, Hickory; **S. 61** *Ein Beitrag für sich und die Gesellschaft.* Auszug aus der Informationsbroschüre "Für mich und für andere" http://www.bmfsfj.de/bmfsfj/generator/RedaktionBMFSFJ/Broschuerenstelle/Pdf-Anlagen/Fuer-mich-und-fuer-andere-FSJ-FOEJ GFD,property=pdf,bereich=bmfsfj,sprache=de,rwb=true.pdf. Herausgegeben vom Bundesministerium für Familie, Senioren, Frauen und Jugend. Berlin, 2008; **S. 62–63** *The caller.* Abridged and adapted. Reprinted by permission of Carus Publishing Company, from DARE TO BE SCARED: THIRTEEN STORIES TO CHILL AND THRILL by Daniel D. San Souci, text © 2003 by Robert D. San Souci; **S. 77** *Mumbai rush hour.* Abridged and adapted from "Mumbai" by Suketu Mehta. Copyright © 1997 by Suketu Mehta. Originally published by Granta Books. Reprinted by permission of William Morris Endeavor Entertainment, LLC on behalf of the Author; **S. 81** *We've come a long, long way.* Adapted from travel and leisure article from go2southafrica.com. http://www.go2southafrica.com/About-South-Africa/About-South-Africa/Johannesburg-Travel-&-Leisure-Article/ (Stand 4.3.2009). Used with permission; **S. 118–120** *Bus attack Part 1, Bus attack Part 2.* Abridged and adapted from case study 4, taken from http://www.restorativejustice.org.uk/Media/pdf/Case%20Study%20-%20Bus%20Co.pdf (30.06.2009). Used by permission of Restorative Justice Consortium, London; S. 121–127 Famous. Abridged and adapted from "TOTALLY OVER YOU" Copyright © Mark Ravenhill, 2003. All rights whatsoever in this play are strictly reserved and application for performance etc., must be made before rehearsal to Casarotto Ramsey & Associates Ltd., 7–12 Noel Street, London W1F 8GQ. No performance may be given unless a license has been obtained; **S. 131–132** *A tour of Soweto.* Abridged and adapted from "Many Stones" by Carolyn Coman. (Front Street, an imprint of Boyds Mills Press, 2000). Reprinted with the permission of Boyds Mills Press, Inc. Text copyright © by Carolyn Coman; **S. 137** Auszug aus „English G 2000 Wörterbuch - Das Wörterbuch zum Lehrwerk". Herausgegeben von der Langenscheidt-Redaktion Wörterbücher und der Cornelsen-Redaktion Englisch. © 2002 Cornelsen Verlag GmbH & Co. OHG, Berlin und Langenscheidt KG, Berlin und München.

Liedquelle

S. 117 *Nine to five.* Text, OT: Dolly Parton. © Velvet Apple Music. Neue Welt Musikverlag GmbH, Hamburg.

Infinitive	Simple past form	Past participle	
(to) **be**	**was/were**	**been**	sein
(to) **beat**	**beat**	**beaten**	schlagen; besiegen
(to) **become**	**became**	**become**	werden
(to) **begin**	**began**	**begun**	beginnen, anfangen (mit)
(to) **bleed** [iː]	**bled** [e]	**bled** [e]	bluten
(to) **blow**	**blew**	**blown**	wehen, blasen
(to) **break**	**broke**	**broken**	(zer)brechen; kaputt gehen
(to) **bring**	**brought**	**brought**	(mit-, her)bringen
(to) **build**	**built**	**built**	bauen
(to) **buy**	**bought**	**bought**	kaufen
(to) **catch**	**caught**	**caught**	fangen; erwischen
(to) **choose** [uː]	**chose** [əʊ]	**chosen** [əʊ]	(aus)wählen; (sich) aussuchen
(to) **come**	**came**	**come**	kommen
(to) **cost**	**cost**	**cost**	kosten
(to) **cut**	**cut**	**cut**	schneiden
(to) **do**	**did**	**done** [ʌ]	tun, machen
(to) **draw**	**drew**	**drawn**	zeichnen
(to) **drink**	**drank**	**drunk**	trinken
(to) **drive** [aɪ]	**drove**	**driven** [ɪ]	*(ein Auto)* fahren
(to) **eat**	**ate** [et, eɪt]	**eaten**	essen
(to) **fall**	**fell**	**fallen**	(hin)fallen, stürzen
(to) **feed**	**fed**	**fed**	füttern
(to) **feel**	**felt**	**felt**	(sich) fühlen; sich anfühlen
(to) **fight**	**fought**	**fought**	kämpfen
(to) **find**	**found**	**found**	finden
(to) **fly**	**flew**	**flown**	fliegen
(to) **forget**	**forgot**	**forgotten**	vergessen
(to) **forgive**	**forgave**	**forgiven**	vergeben, verzeihen
(to) **get**	**got**	**got**	bekommen; holen; werden; (hin)kommen
(to) **give**	**gave**	**given**	geben
(to) **go**	**went**	**gone** [ɒ]	gehen, fahren
(to) **grow**	**grew**	**grown**	wachsen; anbauen, anpflanzen
(to) **hang**	**hung**	**hung**	hängen
(to) **have (have got)**	**had**	**had**	haben, besitzen
(to) **hear** [ɪə]	**heard** [ɜː]	**heard** [ɜː]	hören
(to) **hide** [aɪ]	**hid** [ɪ]	**hidden** [ɪ]	(sich) verstecken
(to) **hit**	**hit**	**hit**	schlagen
(to) **hold**	**held**	**held**	halten
(to) **hurt**	**hurt**	**hurt**	wehtun; verletzen
(to) **keep**	**kept**	**kept**	(be)halten
(to) **know** [nəʊ]	**knew** [njuː]	**known** [nəʊn]	wissen; kennen
(to) **lay** the table	**laid**	**laid**	den Tisch decken
(to) **leave**	**left**	**left**	(weg)gehen; abfahren; verlassen; zurücklassen

Infinitive	Simple past form	Past participle	
(to) **lend**	**lent**	**lent**	verleihen
(to) **let**	**let**	**let**	lassen
(to) **lie** [aɪ]	**lay** [eɪ]	**lain** [eɪ]	liegen
(to) **lose** [uː]	**lost** [ɒ]	**lost** [ɒ]	verlieren
(to) **make**	**made**	**made**	machen; bauen; bilden
(to) **mean** [iː]	**meant** [e]	**meant** [e]	bedeuten; meinen
(to) **meet**	**met**	**met**	(sich) treffen
(to) **pay**	**paid**	**paid**	bezahlen
(to) **put**	**put**	**put**	legen, stellen, *(wohin)* tun
(to) **read** [iː]	**read** [e]	**read** [e]	lesen
(to) **ride** [aɪ]	**rode**	**ridden** [ɪ]	reiten; *(Rad)* fahren
(to) **ring**	**rang**	**rung**	klingeln, läuten
(to) **rise** [aɪ]	**rose**	**risen** [ɪ]	(auf)steigen
(to) **run**	**ran**	**run**	rennen, laufen
(to) **say** [eɪ]	**said** [e]	**said** [e]	sagen
(to) **see**	**saw**	**seen**	sehen; besuchen, aufsuchen
(to) **sell**	**sold**	**sold**	verkaufen
(to) **send**	**sent**	**sent**	schicken, senden
(to) **set** the alarm clock	**set**	**set**	den Wecker stellen
(to) **shake**	**shook**	**shaken**	schütteln; zittern
(to) **shine**	**shone** [ɒ]	**shone** [ɒ]	scheinen *(Sonne)*
(to) **shoot** [uː]	**shot**	**shot**	schießen, erschießen
(to) **show**	**showed**	**shown**	zeigen
(to) **shut up**	**shut**	**shut**	den Mund halten
(to) **sing**	**sang**	**sung**	singen
(to) **sit**	**sat**	**sat**	sitzen; sich setzen
(to) **sleep**	**slept**	**slept**	schlafen
(to) **speak**	**spoke**	**spoken**	sprechen
(to) **spend**	**spent**	**spent**	*(Zeit)* verbringen; *(Geld)* ausgeben
(to) **stand**	**stood**	**stood**	stehen; sich (hin)stellen
(to) **steal**	**stole**	**stolen**	stehlen
(to) **stick**	**stuck**	**stuck**	(auf)kleben
(to) **swim**	**swam**	**swum**	schwimmen
(to) **take**	**took**	**taken**	nehmen; (weg-, hin)bringen; dauern, *(Zeit)* brauchen
(to) **teach**	**taught**	**taught**	unterrichten, lehren
(to) **tear sth. off** [eə]	**tore**	**torn**	etwas abreißen
(to) **tell**	**told**	**told**	erzählen, berichten
(to) **think**	**thought**	**thought**	denken, glauben, meinen
(to) **throw**	**threw**	**thrown**	werfen
(to) **understand**	**understood**	**understood**	verstehen
(to) **upset**	**upset**	**upset**	ärgern, kränken, aus der Fassung bringen
(to) **wake** up	**woke**	**woken**	aufwachen; wecken
(to) **wear** [eə]	**wore** [ɔː]	**worn** [ɔː]	tragen *(Kleidung)*
(to) **win**	**won** [ʌ]	**won** [ʌ]	gewinnen
(to) **write**	**wrote**	**written**	schreiben

Was DU im Klassenzimmer sagen kannst / What YOU can say in the classroom

Du brauchst Hilfe / You need help

Tut mir leid, ich habe das nicht verstanden.	**Sorry, I don't understand.**
Können Sie/Kannst du das bitte noch einmal sagen?	**Can you say that again, please?**
Können Sie/Kannst du bitte lauter sprechen.	**Can you speak louder, please?**
Kann ich eine Frage stellen?	**Can I ask a question, please?**
Können Sie/Kannst du mir bitte helfen?	**Can you help me, please?**
Was bedeutet ...?	**What does ... mean?**
Ist ... das richtige Wort für ... ?	**Is ... the right word for ...?**
Ich habe ... – ist das auch richtig?	**I've got ... – is that right too?**
Können Sie ... bitte buchstabieren?	**Can you spell ..., please?**
Wie spricht man das erste Wort in Zeile 2 aus?	**How do you say the first word in line 2?**
Können Sie es bitte an die Tafel schreiben?	**Can you write that on the board, please?**
Können wir das bitte noch einmal hören?	**Can we listen to that again, please?**
Tut mir leid, ich finde es nicht. Auf welcher Seite sind wir?	**Sorry, I can't find it. What page are we on?**
Was haben wir (als Hausaufgabe) auf?	**What's for homework?**

Du hast ein Problem / You're in trouble

Entschuldigung, dass ich zu spät komme/meine Hausaufgaben nicht gemacht habe, Herr .../Frau ...	**Sorry, I'm late / I haven't done my homework, Mr/Mrs/Ms/Miss ...**
Tut mir leid, dass ich mein Schulheft vergessen habe.	**Sorry, I've forgotten my exercise book.**
Ich bin noch nicht fertig.	**I haven't finished yet.**
Entschuldigung, ich habe nicht zugehört/ das weiß ich nicht.	**Sorry, I wasn't listening / I don't know.**
Ich kann Nummer 3 nicht lösen.	**I can't do number 3.**

Über Texte reden / Talking about texts

Die Geschichte/Das Theaterstück/Das Gedicht/ Das Lied/Der Film handelt von ...	**The story/play/poem/ song/film is about ...**
Die Handlung spielt während/in ...	**The action takes place during/in ...**
In Zeile 15–20 steht, dass ...	**In lines 15–20 it says that ...**
Die Hauptfigur ist ...	**The main character is ...**
Der Mann/Die Frau/... scheint sehr einsam/zornig/ traurig/... zu sein.	**The man/woman/... seems to be very lonely/angry/ sad/...**
Die Beziehung zwischen ... und ... ist sonderbar/...	**The relationship between ... and ... is strange/...**
Es war lustig/unheimlich/langweilig/... als ...	**It was funny/scary/boring/... when ...**
Ich fand es gut/nicht gut als ...	**I liked it/didn't like it when ...**
Ich fand den Schluss überraschend/enttäuschend/ blöd/... , weil ...	**I found the ending surprising/disappointing/ stupid/... because ...**
Ich finde die Geschichte ist lustig/aufregend/...,weil ...	**I think the story is funny/exciting/... because ...**
Die Geschichte hat mich glücklich/wütend/... gemacht.	**The story made me (feel) happy/angry/...**

In einer Diskussion / In a discussion

Meiner Meinung nach ...	**In my opinion ...**
Ich will dir ein Beispiel geben: ...	**Let me give you an example: ...**
Erstens ... /Zweitens ... /Und schließlich ...	**First ... / Second ... / And finally ...**
Ich stimme (...) zu/nicht zu, weil ...	**I agree/disagree (with ...) because ...**
Ja, du hast Recht./Genau!	**Yes, you're right. / Exactly!**
Was Tim sagt, ist richtig/falsch.	**What Tim says is right/wrong.**
Du sagst ..., aber ...	**You say ..., but ...**
Was genau meinst du?	**What do you mean exactly?**
Du könntest Recht haben, aber ...	**You may be right, but ...**
Ich bin mir nicht sicher. Vielleicht ...	**I'm not so sure. Maybe/Perhaps ...**
Was meinst du (zu ...)?	**What do you think (about ...)?**

Bei der Partner- oder Gruppenarbeit	Working with a partner or in a group
Kann ich mit ... arbeiten?	**Can I work with ...?**
Was machen wir als Erstes?	**What are we going to do first?**
Lass/Lasst uns die Aufgabe noch einmal lesen.	**Let's read the task again.**
Wer ist dran? – Ich bin/Du bist dran, das zu schreiben/ die Fragen zu stellen.	**Whose turn is it? – It's my/your turn to write/ ask questions.**
Ich finde, wir sollten/könnten ...	**I think we should/could ...**
Hast du eine Idee/einen Vorschlag?	**Have you got any ideas?**
Mir gefällt deine Idee sehr gut. / Das klingt gut.	**I really like your idea. / That sounds good.**
Wo können wir etwas finden zu ...?	**Where can we find out about ...?**
Was hast du im Internet gefunden?	**What did you find on the internet?**
Was hältst du von meinem Text/Bild/...?	**What do you think of my text/picture/...?**
Ich verstehe nicht, was du meinst. / Ich bin mir da nicht sicher.	**I don't understand what you mean. / I'm not sure about that.**
Lass/Lasst uns ... auf unser Poster schreiben.	**Let's write ... on our poster.**
Lass/Lasst uns das Bild hier hinsetzen/-kleben.	**Let's put the picture here.**
Wie viel Zeit haben wir (noch)?	**How much (more) time do we have?**
Wir haben nur noch ... Minuten Zeit.	**We've only got ... minutes left.**
Lass/Lasst uns ... schnell machen und dann mit ... fortfahren.	**Let's do ... quickly and then go on to ...**
Vielleicht sollten wir ... weglassen/ etwas zu ... sagen.	**Maybe we should leave out ... / say something about ...**
Wir sind fast fertig.	**We've nearly finished.**

Bei einer Präsentation	Giving a talk / presentation
Das Thema meines Vortrags ist ...	**The topic of my talk/presentation is ...**
Ich werde meinen Vortrag in ... Teile gliedern.	**I'm going to divide my talk into ... parts.**
Erstens/Als nächstes/... würde ich gern ...	**First/Next/... I would like to ...**
Zum Schluss werde ich etwas über ... erzählen.	**Finally, I'll tell you something about ...**
Auf der ersten Folie links/rechts könnt ihr sehen ...	**On the first slide on the left/right you can see ...**
Zusammenfassend möchte ich sagen ...	**To sum up I'd like to say ...**
Gibt es/Habt ihr Fragen oder Kommentare dazu?	**Are there any questions or comments?**

What YOUR TEACHER says / Was DEIN/E LEHRER/IN sagt

What YOUR TEACHER says	Was DEIN/E LEHRER/IN sagt
Copy/Fill in the chart/form.	Kopiert/Füllt die Tabelle/das Formular aus.
Correct the mistakes.	Verbessert die Fehler.
Don't forget to check your spelling.	Vergesst nicht die Rechtschreibung zu überprüfen.
Be careful with the word order.	Achtet auf die Satzstellung.
Write it on the board, please.	Schreibe es bitte an die Tafel.
Compare your sentences/answers/... with your partner.	Vergleiche deine Sätze/Antworten/... mit deinem Partner/deiner Partnerin.
Discuss ... in your group.	Diskutiert ... in der Gruppe.
Practise/Act out the dialogues with a partner, please.	Bitte übe/spiele den Dialog mit deinem Partner/deiner Partnerin.
Walk around the class and ask other students.	Geht durch die Klasse und fragt andere Schüler/innen.
Take/Make notes.	Macht euch Notizen.
Imagine you are ...	Stellt euch vor, ihr seid ...
What do you think of ...?	Was haltet ihr von ...?
Have you got any other ideas?	Habt ihr andere/sonstige Ideen?
Give three reasons.	Nenne drei Gründe.
Have you finished?	Seid ihr/Bist du fertig?
Present your talk/poster/... to the class.	Präsentiere dein Referat/Poster/... vor der Klasse.
Do exercise 3 for homework, please.	Macht bitte Übung 3 als Hausaufgabe.